The Adventure Guide
to the
Virgin Islands

The
Adventure
Guide
to the
VIRGIN
ISLANDS

Harry S. Pariser

HUNTER
PUBLISHING INC

Hunter Publishing, Inc.
300 Raritan Center Parkway
Edison NJ 08818
(908) 225 1900 Fax (908) 417 0412

ISBN 1-55650-597-3

© 1994 Hunter Publishing, Inc. (3rd Edition)

ACKNOWLEDGMENTS

Many thanks to my publisher Michael Hunter. Thanks also go out to Betty Sperber, Miles Sperber, and family, the Hurd family, mapmaker Joyce Huber, Ivy O'Neal, Ernestine L. Harrigan, Gar Smith, Catherine Taylor, Frank H. Davis, Jr. (St. Thomas updates), John W. Davis, Ann Eaton, Joyce and Jim Hurd, Don Near, Tom Oat, Peggy Mahoney, Longin Kaczmarsky, Dean Morgan, Mark Ferdschneider, Nadine Battle, Monica Allen, Elizabeth Armstrong, Kenneth Blake, Beverly Nicholson, VINP ranger Chuck Weikert, and a very special thanks to William Cissel of Ft. Christiansvaern for his invaluable historical corrections. Don Wilford of St. Thomas was of great help. Susan Ivy on St. Croix also gave invaluable assistance. A final thank you goes out to my mother who always worries about me.

Other Books by Harry S. Pariser from Hunter Publishing:

Jamaica: A Visitor's Guide 1-55650-253-2 $15.95
Adventure Guide to Barbados 1-55650-277-X $16.95
Adventure Guide to Costa Rica 1-55650-598-1 $15.95
Adventure Guide to Puerto Rico 1-55650-178-1 $14.95
Adventure Guide to Belize 1-55650-557-4 $14.95
Adventure Guide to the Dominican Republic 1-55650-537-X $13.95

Maps by Joyce Huber, PhotoGraphics.
All photographs by author, except as indicated.
Cover: Trunk Bay, St. John

Contents

The British Virgin Islands

Tortola

List of Maps

Note

Rates are given as guidelines only; price fluctuations can and will occur. Mention of a hotel does not necessarily constitute a recommendation. Summer season generally runs 4/15 to 11/15 or to 12/15; check with hotel concerned for specifics. All USVI hotel addresses are completed with United States Virgin Islands (USVI) and then the zip specified. Area code for the Caribbean is 809. All USVI rates listed are low season and do not include the 7.5% accommodation tax, unless specified otherwise. BVI rates normally start with the lowest off-season rate; a 7% tax will be added in most cases. To estimate high season rates, add 20-40%. For current rates contact the hotel in question. All transportation times and carriers are subject to change. Be sure to confirm departures ahead of time.

About the Author

Harry S. Pariser was born in Pittsburgh and grew up in a small town in southwestern Pennsylvania. After graduating from Boston University, Harry hitched and camped his way through Europe, traveled down the Nile by steamer, and by train through Sudan. After visiting Uganda, Rwanda, and Tanzania, he traveled by ship from Mombasa to Bombay, then on through South and Southeast Asia before settling down in Kyoto, Japan, where he studied Japanese and ceramics, while supporting himself by teaching English to everyone from tiny tots to Buddhist priests. Using Japan as a base, he returned to other parts of Asia: trekking to the vicinity of Mt. Everest in Nepal, taking tramp steamers to remote Indonesian islands like Adonara, Timor, Sulawesi, and Ternate, and visiting rural parts of China. He returned to the United States in 1984 via the Caribbean, where he researched two travel guides – *Guide to Jamaica* and *Guide to Puerto Rico and the Virgin Islands* – the first editions of which were published in 1986. Returning to Japan, he lived in the city of Kagoshima at the southern tip of Kyushu, where he taught English and wrote for *The Japan Times*. He currently lives in San Francisco. Besides traveling and writing, his other interests include printmaking, painting, cooking, hiking, photography, reading, and music – especially jazz.

We Love to Get Mail!

Reader's Response Form

The Adventure Guide to the Virgin Islands

I found your book rewarding because:

Your book could be improved by:

The best places I stayed in were (explain why):

I found the best food at:

Some good and bad experiences I had were:

Will you return to the Virgin Islands?   If so, where do you plan to go?

If not, why not?

I purchased this book at:

Please mail completed form to Harry S. Pariser, c/o Hunter Publishing, 300 Raritan Center Parkway, Edison, NJ 08818 USA.

The U. S. Virgin Islands

Introduction

Offering superb beaches, magnificent panoramas, and an almost ideal climate, the U.S. Virgins have been part of the United States for over half a century, yet many Americans have never even heard of them. These islands (pop. 102,000) have a largely black population, yet their society is culturally and ethnically a composite of many influences.

Set in the Caribbean's NE corner right at the end of the Greater Antilles, the USVI comprise some 50 islands and cays. The three main islands–St. Thomas, St. John, and St. Croix–are easily accessible from neighboring Puerto Rico. Each has its distinct personality and resembles the others only in having beautiful white beaches and offlying coral reefs.

Land And Climate

Located 1,500 miles SE of New York and 1,000 miles S of Miami, the United States Virgin Islands are bounded on the N by the Atlantic Ocean and on the S by the Caribbean. Covering 132 sq miles of land area, these islands–of which St. John, St. Croix, and St. Thomas predominate–are volcanic in origin. Well-exposed and only slightly deformed rocks give a nearly complete record of evolution dating back more than 100 million years. Primary growth having vanished long ago, vegetation is largely secondary; there are few streams and water is frequently in short supply. Except on St. John, soils are thin and number among the stoniest in the world. No minerals of any value are found here save salt and blue green stone or blue bitch, an excellent building material. A ridge of high hills runs almost the entire length of St. Thomas. Although its rocks are chiefly sedimentary, limestone reaching up to the peak of Crown Mountain (1,550 ft.) tells a story of cyclical earthquakes, submergence, and upheavals. St. John, terminating in a narrow curving neck enclosing a series of bays, rises abruptly from the sea, with 1,277-ft. Bordeaux Mountain being the highest point. Coral Bay, on the S side of St. John, is the best harbor in the islands. Saint Croix, a fraternal rather than identical triplet, lies 32 miles to the S separated by 1,000-2,400-fathom trenches. Its topography is quite different from the other islands. The N upland contains 1,165-ft. Mt. Eagle, the S side is a broad coastal plain, while the E end is a rough, arid scrubland.

USVI Climate Chart

	Aver. temp °F	Rainfall days
January	77	4.3
February	77	1.9
March	78	2.0
April	79	7.5
May	80	1.3
June	82	2.9
July	84	5.6
August	84	4.1
September	83	6.6
October	83	5.6
November	80	5.4
December	78	3.8

climate: Rarely does it rain on these islands. (Average rainfall is only 40-50 in. per year). When rain does come, it usually lasts only a few minutes. May, Sept., and Oct. are the wettest months. During the day, temperatures range in the 80s, dropping to the 70s in the evening.

hurricanes: Cast in a starring role as the bane of the tropics, hurricanes represent the one outstanding negative in an otherwise impeccably hospitable climate. The Caribbean as a whole ranks third worldwide in the number of hurricanes per year. These low-pressure zones are serious business and should not be taken lightly. Where the majority of structures are held together only by nails and rope, a hurricane is no joke, and property damage from them may run into the hundreds of millions of US dollars. A

hurricane begins as a relatively small tropical storm, known as a cyclone, when its winds reach a velocity of 39 mph. At 74 mph it is upgraded to hurricane status, with winds of up to 200 mph and ranging in size from 60-1,000 miles in diameter. A small hurricane releases energy equivalent to the explosions of six atomic bombs per second. A hurricane may be compared to an enormous hovering engine that uses the moist air and water of the tropics as fuel, carried hither and thither by prevailing air currents–generally eastern trade winds which intensify as they move across warm ocean waters. When cooler, drier air infiltrates as it heads N, the hurricane begins to die, cut off from the life-sustaining ocean currents that have nourished it from infancy. Routes and patterns are unpredictable. As for their frequency: "June–too soon; July–stand by; August–it must; September–remember." So goes the old rhyme. Unfortunately, hurricanes are not confined to July and August. Hurricanes forming in Aug. and Sept. typically last for two weeks while those that form in June, July, Oct., and Nov. (many of which originate in the Caribbean and the Gulf of Mexico) generally last only seven days. Approximately 70 percent of all hurricanes (known as Cabo Verde types) originate as embryonic storms coming from the W. coast of Africa. Fortunately, though, they are comparatively scarce in the area around the Virgin Islands. Hurricane "season" commences on Supplication Day (July 25th) when church services are held to pray against hurricanes) and end Thanksgiving Day (October 25) when services again

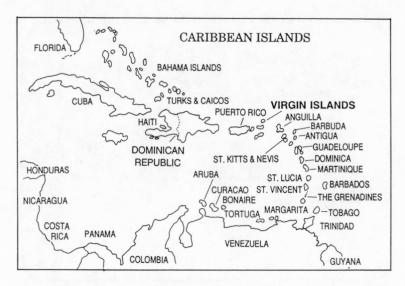

thank the meterological Commander in Chief for not sending a storm. Indeed, the islanders must have a good relationship with the powers that be because a major hurricane did not hit the islands from 1932 until Sept. 1989's Hurricane Hugo.

Plant Life

These islands display an amazing variety of plantlife, from lichen and mosses to fruit trees and orchids. Considering its tiny area, St. John has an extraordinary diversity of tropical foliage. There are 260 different species of plants, vines, shrubs, and trees. A century-old botanical survey of St. Thomas found 1,220 plants in its 32 sq miles. Saint Croix also has a wide diversity of plants: in addition to numerous trees and shrubs, it has 42 varieties of orchids and nearly twice as many types of morning glories.

Trees

Many of these lend a riot of color to the landscape. Native to the VI, the red, yellow, and pink frangipani blooms both in gardens and in the wild. Its elliptical, short-pointed leaves have hairy underparts and large, waxy yellow, orange or white flowers. A native of Madagascar, the orange-red flamboyant flowers during

Hispaniola, Puerto Rico and the Virgin Islands

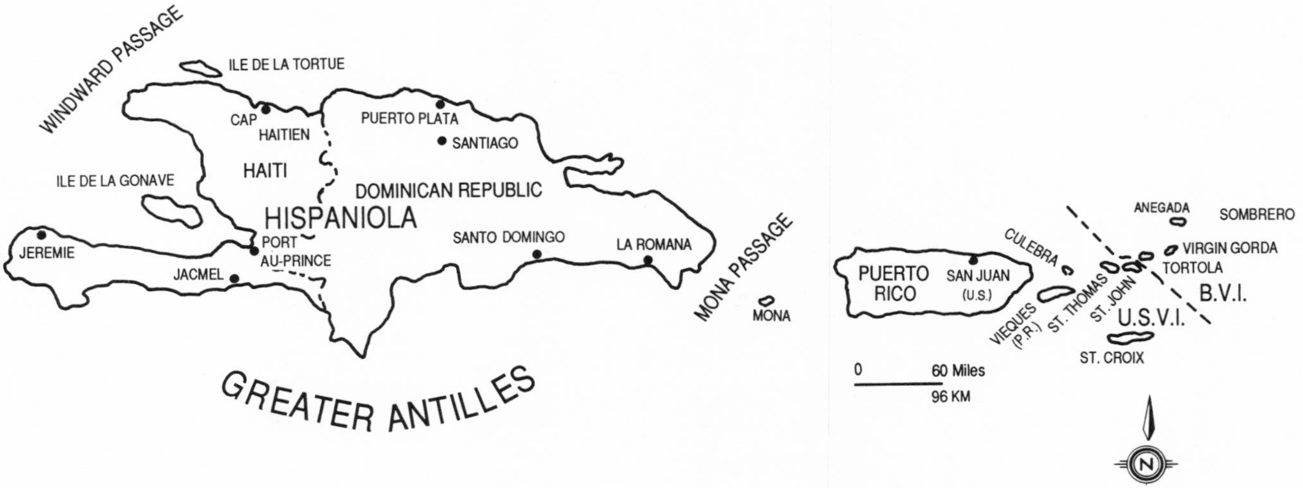

the summer and bears a 20-in. seedpod; its leaf consists of ten or 20 pairs of smaller leaves, which in turn have 20-30 pairs of small, light green leaflets. Also orange-red are the cuplike blossoms of the African tulip tree which catch water and provide watering holes for birds. A petite yellow bloom with a sweet fragrance, the ginger thomas or yellow elder is the territorial flower.

aromatic trees: With an oil traditionally obtained through distillation of its leaves and twigs, the bay rum tree has small, white flowers and gives off a heady, pungent odor when its leaves are crushed or broken. There is little incentive to use the poor quality wood of the wild cinnamon or canella and their spreading branches provide shade. with shiny green leathery leaves. These trees produce small red flowers and inedible red or purple berries. Their smooth gray bark is aromatic and has been used medicinally.

fruit trees: Famous for its yellow fleshy fruit which has a large pit at its center, the mango tree has dark green leathery leaves which are pointed at both ends. With compound leaves that have four nearly stalkless leaflets, the genip bears small green fruits in grape-like clusters. A short (generally under 20 ft.) tropical American native, the sugar apple has 3-5-in. leaves which are double rowed and alternating. Either round or heart shaped, its distinctive fruit may be eaten raw or used to make a drink or sherbert. With sharp leaves pointed at both ends, the soursop has one of the most distinctive fruits around. While unripe soursop may be cooked as a vegetable, the ripe fruit, which may weigh up to five lbs., can be used in sherbert, drinks, and in preserves. A S Pacific native, the breadfruit has deeply lobed leaves which may reach three ft. It is best known for its fruit; a single tree may bear up to 800 per year, and these can be baked, boiled, roasted, fried, consumed raw, or ground into a high-carbohydrate flour.

palms: Known locally as the broom teyer or silver palm, the wild palm is a Puerto Rican/VI native which grows in abundance. Its leaves are pleated, almost circular fans which lack a midrib. When exposed in the wind, the soft, silver underside of its leaves give it one of its names. Generally found along the coast and widespread in the world's tropics, the coconut palm is one of the world's most useful.

uniquely named: Colorfully called a pig turd in the VI owing to its distinctively shaped pods, the *moca blanca* has light grey bark and smells somewhat like cabbage when cut. Native to the area, the West Indies locust produces an edible, bad smelling pod whose pulp can be used to make a drink. Large, symmetrical, strong, and stout, the sandbox tree's name comes from its fruit; the ribbed peel, when de-seeded and flattened, was used to sprinkle sand used for blotting ink on parchment. Monkey pistol, its other name, comes from the noise its seedpods make when they split open. Its acrid, milky sap is a skin irritant. Having yellow green leaves with orange or pink colored stems and small, fragrant white flowers, the fiddlewood bears clusters of reddish brown or blackish berries. One of the most notable tropical trees, the strangler fig begins life as an epiphyte, sending down woody, clasping roots that wind themselves around the trunk as they extend into the earth. As the roots grow in size, they meld into a trunk which surrounds the tree. These "strangler figs" most likely kill the tree–not through strangulation but by robbing it of canopy space. They can grow in the ruins of buildings as well. Strangler figs are often the only trees left in an otherwise cleared tract of forest. A native of India, the painkiller or morinda has 5-11-in. dark green leaves and small white tubular flowers. Its soft and juicy greenish fruit has a cheeselike odor. With alternating leaves colored blue-green or green, the seagrape grows on the shore where it provides shade as well as helps retain sand on the beaches. Resembling grapes in appearance, its fruits may be eaten raw or made into jelly or even wine. Early in the colonial era, the leaves were used as a substitute for paper, and Virgin Gorda's Fischers Cove Hotel uses them for menus today. The fish poison tree produces pink flowers in March and April. Its scalloped pods and bark contain a poison used by fishermen to stun fish. Named because of the odor exuded by its sticky gum, the turpentine tree will repel insects and prevent infection. Because its thick, shiny, reddish-brown bark peels off in scales, it is also known as the "tourist tree."

other trees: The mahogany was introduced in the 18th C and is famous for its use in furniture. In the Caribbean, the shortleaf fig is commonly used for fence posts, wood, and fuel. With alternating leaves which are sharply pointed at their ends, it exudes a white latex when parts are cut or broken. Once believed by slaves to walk at night, the ceiba or silk-cotton tree has a distinctively massive grey or grey-green trunk. Known as kapok (which is the name given the tree in Indonesia), the seed pod is filled with many wooly-haired seeds; it was once a major provider of stuffing for pillows, life preservers and the like. Still others include the umbrella tree, false almond, West Indian ebony, West Indian almond, buttonwood, horseradish tree, boxweed, beach maho, black wattle, sweet lime, tan tan, tamarind, and guava.

mangroves: Mangrove forests are found along the coasts; these water-rooted trees serve as a marine habitat which shelters sponges, corals, oysters, and other members of the marine community around its roots–organisms, which, in turn, attract a variety of other sealife. Some species live out their lives in the shelter of the mangroves, and many fish use these roots as a shelter or feeding ground; lobsters use the mangrove environs as a nursery for their young. Above the water level, the mangroves shelter seabirds and are important nesting sites. Their organic detritus, exported to the reef by the tides, is consumed by its inhabitants, providing the base of an extensive food web. Mangroves also dampen high waves and winds generated by tropical storms. In the Virgin Islands, mangroves function as hurricane shelters for boats. By trapping silt in their roots and catching leaves and other debris which decompose to form soil, the red mangroves act as land builders. Eventually, the red mangroves kill themselves off when they have built up enough soil, and the black and white mangroves take over. Meanwhile, the red mangroves have sent out progeny in the form of floating seedlings–bottom-heavy youngsters that grow on the tree until they reach six inches to a foot in length. If they drop in shallow water, the seeds touch bottom and implant themselves. In deeper water they stay afloat until, crossing a shoal, they lodge. Named after their light-colored bark, the white mangroves are highly salt tolerant If growing in a swampy area, they put out pneumatophores, root system extensions which grow vertically to a height that allows them to stay above the water during flooding or tides and carry on gaseous exchange. Producing a useful wood, the black mangrove also creates pneumatophores. Smaller than the others, the buttonwood is not a true mangrove but is found on the coasts where no other varieties are found.

Other Plants

Plants here have colorful histories, and there may be more to them than first appears. Many plants have had practical uses: while switches for beating slaves were made from the tamarind tree, calabash gourds were perfectly suited for bailing devices, eating utensils, and dishes. Natural herbs and herbal remedies were made from the sandbox, mahoe, and other trees, shrubs, and plants. Guinea grass, which covers many island hillsides and provides feed for livestock, was originally introduced by mistake. Brought over as birdseed for the governor's pet birds, who rejected it, the seeds were tossed out and the grass began to proliferate on its own.

cacti and related plants: The most noticeable of these is the large century plant. It has a rosette of thick spiked leaves at its base which, after 20 years, sends up a 10 to 20 ft. stalk and blooms. Then it dies. Named for its distinctive shape, the pipe organ cactus is generally found in the islands' driest areas. A native of Africa and the Mediterranean, the aloe is a single-stalked succulent reknowned for its healing properties. The barrel-shaped Turk's Cap is topped with red flowers, and the prickly pear is a small, rapidly spreading cactus which has innumerable spines and yellow flowers.

shrubs: The guana tail and the penguin are shrubs frequently used as hedges. The penguin, a type of bromeliad with sharp end spines on its leaves resembles the pineapple. The four o'clock is a small shrub with trumpet-shaped purple blossoms which open at 4 PM each day.

flowers: Brought to the West Indies in the 1700s by the French navigator Bougainville, the bougainvillea can be seen cascading over garden walls. A native of Hawaii, the flowering hibiscus comes with apricot, red, pink, purple, or white blossoms. A vine with yellow flowers which trails along walls and fences, the cup of gold is another frequently seen flower. The oleander has a delicate beauty but is deadly if eaten. A variety of orchids also thrive here as do poinsettias.

forbidden fruit: The machineel, said to be the original apple in the Garden of Eden, secretes an acid which may be deadly. Biting into this innocuous-looking yet highly poisonous fruit will cause your mouth to burn and your tongue to swell up. In fact, all parts of this tree are potentially deadly. Cattle, standing under the tree after a torrential tropical downpour, have been known to lose their hides as drops fall from the leaves. Other tales tell of locals going blind after a leaf touched an eye. Slaves wishing to do away with a particularly despicable master would insert minute quantities of juice into an uncooked potato. Cooked, these small doses were undetectable but always fatal if served to the victim over a long period of time. If you see some of these trees, stay well away!

name game: Many of the imaginatively named species have colorful stories behind their names. The "love "plant" was so named because an aspiring suitor would write his lover's name on the leaf; if it remained for a time, it meant that he could count on acceptance of his proposal. The "catch and keep" sticks to everything it touches, while the "jump up and kiss me" is well endowed with small, seductive blossoms. The trunk of the "monkey-don't-climb tree" bristles with thorns, while the "nothing nut" is so named because that's exactly what it's good for. The pods of the "woman's tongue" tree clatter on and on in the breeze like gossiping housewives. Other unusually named plants include the "jumbi-bread" vine with its knife-shaped miniature red blossoms, the "stinking toe," "bull hoof," "poor man's orchid," "powder puff," "crown of thorns," "lucky nut," "burning love," and the "lady of the night."

Animal Life

Save for the now-extinct agouti, a rodent once considered a delicacy by local Indians, very few land animals existed here before the coming of Europeans. Today, monkeys and wild boars have disappeared, though a few scattered deer still remain. Introduced in legend rather than fact, werewolves were once hunted by slaves who believed in this European folktale. Perhaps the legend was kept alive in order to cover up for the master when he went on a sexual rampage. Unique to St. Croix is the husbandry of Senepol cattle. More than a half century ago, a Cruxian plantation owner named Nelthrop was kicked by a cow. Determined to create a new and improved version, he crossed the African Senegal with the English Red Poll. The result was a new breed that is hairless, shortlegged, requires less water, and is disease resistant. The mongoose, introduced to kill snakes and rats, has just about done in the reptile population as well as many birds instead. Mongooses are diurnal, while rats are nocturnal. The two seldom cross paths.

birds: There are over 200 species of birds, including brightly colored wild parakeets, pelicans, and egrets. Since most of the swamps have been drained, the sea bird population has dwindled. Land birds include hawks, doves, sparrows, thrushes, West Indian crows, wild pigeons, canaries, and several varieties of hummingbirds. The yellow breast is the territorial bird.

reptiles, crustaceans, and insects: Lizards include several varieties of ground and tree lizards. The colorful herbivorous iguana, whose tail has long been considered a culinary delicacy, is on the way out. Although centipedes and scorpions live on these islands, they maintain passive, nonaggressive attitudes towards humans unless they are disturbed. The same goes for the wasps, whose nests are a common feature on St. Croix. The long nosed termite builds the gigantic nests which you'll see on St. Croix. They coexist with a healthy tree. The harmless hairy tarantula hides underground in his nest.

Sealife

Divers and snorkelers will find a dazzling array of coral, fish, and sponges in all colors of the rainbow. Delicate in appearance only, yellow or purple (depending on diet) sea fan, a coral with fanlike branches, is so strong that it will support a man's weight without tearing. Normally the size of a pinhead, the sea jewel (*valonia*) is the largest single-cell animal in existence. Saclike and round in appearance, it reflects the colors of whatever's nearby. A kaleidoscope of fish include the doctorfish, grouper, old wife, one-eye, silver angelfish, sergeant fish, marine jewel, and trunkfish.

sea turtles: Sea turtles are some of the the most interesting creatures found here. Medium-sized with a total length of about a three ft. and weighing some 400 lbs., the large-finned, herbiverous green turtle lays eggs every two to three years, storming the beaches in massive groups termed *barricadas*. It is readily identifiable by its short rounded head. One of the smallest sea turtles, at 35 in. or less, the hawksbill has a spindle shaped shell and weighs around 220 lbs. Because of its tortoise shell–a brown translucent layer of corneous gelatin that peels off the shell when processed–it has been pursued and slaughtered throughout the world. It dines largely on sponges and seaweed. Worldwide demand for its shell, which sells for a fortune in Japan, appears to have condemned it to extinction. With its large head, twice the size of the green turtle's and narrow and bird-jawed, the short-finned loggerhead turtle rarely grows longer than four ft. It dines on sea urchins, jellyfish, starfish, and crabs. The loggerhead is threatened with extinction by coastal development, egg gathering, and from hunting by raccoons. Black with very narrow fins, the leatherback's name comes from the leathery hide which covers its back in lieu of a shell. It grows to six ft. in length and weighs as much as 1,500 lbs. The leatherback's chief predator has always been the poacher.

echinodermata: Combining the Greek words *echinos* (hegehog) and *derma* (skin), this large division of the animal kingdom includes sea urchins, sea cucumbers, and starfish. All share the ability to propel themselves with the help of tube "feet" or spines. Known by the scientific name *Astrospecten*, starfish are five-footed carnivores which use their modified "tube-feet" to burrow into the sand. Sluggish sea cucumbers ingest large quantities of sand, extract the organic matter, and excrete the rest.

Avoid trampling on that armed knight of the underwater sand dunes, the sea urchin. Consisting of a semi-circular calcareous (calcium carbonate-built) shell, the sea urchin is protected by its brown, jointed barbs. It uses its mouth, situated and protected on its underside, to graze by scraping algae from rocks. Surprisingly to those uninitiated in its lore, sea urchins are considered a gastronomic delicacy in many countries. The ancient Greeks believed they had aphrodisiacal and other properties beneficial to health. They are prized by the French and fetch four times the price of oysters in Paris. The Spanish consume them raw, boiled, in gratinés, or in soups. In Barbados they are called "sea eggs," and the Japanese eat their guts raw as sushi. Although a disease in recent years has devastated the sea urchin population, they are making a comeback. If a sea urchin spine breaks off inside your finger or toe, don't try to remove it; you can't. You might try the cure people use in New Guinea. Use a blunt object to mash up the spine inside your skin so that it will be absorbed naturally. They then dip the wound in urine; the ammonia helps to trigger the process of disintegration. It's best to apply triple-antibiotic salve. Preventing contact in the first place is best. Sea urchins often hide underneath corals, and wounds often occur when you lose your footing and scrape against one.

sponges: Found in the ocean depths, reddish or brown sponges are among the simplest forms of multicellular life and have been around for more than a half billion years. They pump large amounts of water through their internal filters to extract plankton.

jellyfish: The jellyfish season is Aug. to Oct. Most jellyfish are harmless. If you should get stung, get out of the water and peel off any tentacles. Avoid rubbing the injured area. Wash the wound with alcohol and apply meat tenderizer for five to ten minutes. The floating Portuguese Man-of-War is actually a colony of marine organisms. Its stinging tentacles can be extended or retracted; wordwide, there have been reports of trailing tentacles reaching 50 feet!

crustaceans: The ghost crab (*Ocypode*) abounds on the beaches, tunneling down beneath the sand and emerging to feed at night. Although it can survive for 48 hrs. without contacting water, it must return to the sea to moisten its gill chambers as well as to lay its eggs, which hatch into planktonic larvae. The hermit crab carries a discarded mollusc shell in order to protect its vulnerable abdomen. As it grows, it must find a larger home, and you may see two struggling over the same shell.

other underwater hazards and cures: Not a true coral, firecoral mimics coral's appearance; it may appear in many forms and has the ability to encrust nearly anything and take its host's form. Generally colored mustard yellow to brown, it often has white finger-like tips. A cut is quite painful. As with coral wounds, you should wash the affected area with soap and fresh water and apply a triple-antibiotic salve. Found on rocky or coral bottoms, spotted scorpionfish are well camouflaged so it's easy to step on them. Although the Caribbean

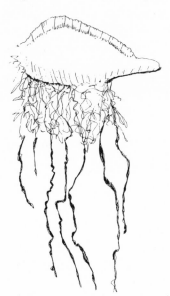

Portuguese Man-of-War

species is non-lethal, their bite can be painful. Another cleverly camouflaged denizen of the deep, the stingray will whip its tail if stepped on–driving the serrated venomous spine into the offender. If this happens, see a doctor. Fuzzy creatures which have painful-when-touched defense mechanisms, bristle worms have glass-like bristles which may break off in the skin and be very painful. Apply tape to the skin and attempt to pull the bristles out; reduce the pain with rubbing alcohol. Tending to bite things thrust at them, moray eels can be difficult to dislodge. Once again, preventing bites is best. Always exercise caution before reaching into a crevice!

The Coral Reef Ecosystem

One of the least appreciated of the world's innumerable wonders is the coral reef. This is partly because little has been known about such reefs until recent decades. One of the greatest opportunities the tropics offer is to explore this wondrous environment, one which in many ways goes beyond the limits of any wild fantasy conjured up in a science fiction novel. It is a delicate environment: the only geological feature fashioned by living creatures. Many of the world's reefs–which took millions of years to build–have already suffered adverse effects from human activity.

Corals produce the calcium carbonate (limestone) responsible for the buildup of most of the island's offlying cays and islets as well as most of the sand on the beaches. Bearing the brunt of waves, they also conserve the shoreline. Although reefs began forming millenia ago, they are in a constant state of flux. Seemingly solid, they actually depend upon a delicate ecological balance to survive. Deforestation, dredging, temperature change, an increase or decrease in salinity, silt, or sewage discharge may kill them. Because temperatures must remain between 68° and 95°F, they are only found in the tropics, and–because they require light to grow–only in shallow water. They are also intolerant of fresh water, and reefs can not survive where rivers empty into the sea.

the coral polyp: While corals are actually animals, botanists view them as being mostly plant, and geologists dub them "honorary" rocks. Acting more like plants than animals, corals survive through photosynthesis: the algae inside the coral polyps do the work while the polyps themselves secrete calcium carbonate and stick together for protection from waves and boring sponges.

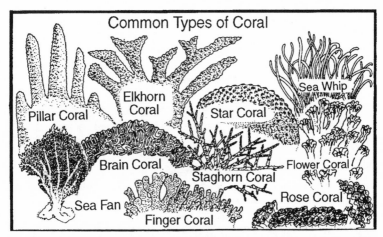

Common Types of Coral

Pillar Coral · Elkhorn Coral · Star Coral · Sea Whip · Brain Coral · Staghorn Coral · Flower Coral · Sea Fan · Finger Coral · Rose Coral

Bearing a close structural resemblance to its relative the anemone, a polyp feeds at night by using the ring or rings of tentacles surrounding its mouth to capture prey (such as plankton) with nematocysts, small stinging darts.

The coral polyps appear able to survive in such packed surroundings through their symbiotic relationship with the algae present in their tissues. Coral polyps exhale carbon dioxide and the algae consume it, producing needed oxygen. Although only half of the world's coral species possess this symbiotic relationship with these single-celled captive species of dinoflagellates (*Gymnodinium microdriaticum*), these species–termed hermatypic corals–are the ones that build the reef. The nutritional benefits gained from their relationship with the algae enable them to grow a larger skeleton and to do so more rapidly than would otherwise be possible. Polyps have the ability to regulate the density of these cells in their tissues and can expel some of them in a spew of mucus should they multiply too quickly. Looking at coral, you can see the brownish colored algal cells showing through transparent tissues. When you see a coral garden through your mask, you are actually viewing a field of captive single-celled algae.

An added and vital, but invisible, component of the reef ecosystem is bacteria, micro-organisms which decompose and recycle all matter on which everything from worms to coral polyps feed. Inhabitants of the reef range from crabs to barnacles, from sea squirts to multicolored tropical fish. Remarkably, the polyps themselves are consumed by only a small percentage of the reef's inabitants. They often contain high levels of toxic substances and are thought to sting fish and other animals that attempt to consume them. Corals also retract their polyps during daylight hours when the fish can see them. Reefs originate as the polyps develop–the calcium secretions form a base as they grow, and a single polyp can have a thousand-year lifespan.

coral types: Corals may be divided into three groups. The hard or stony corals (such as staghorn, brain, star, or rose) secrete a limey skeleton. The horny corals (for example sea plumes, sea whips, sea fans, and gorgonians) have a supporting skeleton-like structure known as a gorgonin (after the head of Medusa). The shapes of these corals result from the fashion in which the polyps and their connecting tissues excrete calcium carbonate; there are over a thousand different patterns–one specific to each species. Each also has its own method of budding. Found in the Caribbean, giant elk-horn corals may contain over a million polyps and live for several hundred years or longer. The last category consists of the soft corals. While these too are colonies of polyps, their skeletons are composed of soft organic material, and their polyps always have eight tentacles instead of the six or multiples of six found in the stony corals. Unlike the hard corals, soft corals disintegrate after death and do not add to the reef's stony structure. Instead of depositing limestone crystals, they excrete a jelly-like matrix which is imbued with spicules (diminutive spikes) of stony material; the jelly-like substance gives these corals their flexibility. Sea fans and sea whips exhibit similar patterns. The precious black coral, prized by jewelers because its branches can be polished to high gloss ebony-black, in its natural state resembles bushes of fine grey-black twigs.

competition: To the snorkeler, the reef appears to be a peaceful haven. The reality is that because the reef is a comparatively benign environment, the fiercest competition has developed here. Although the corals appear static to the onlooker, they are continually competing with each other for space. Some have developed sweeper tentacles which have an especially high concentration of stinging cells. Reaching out to a competing coral, they sting and execute it. Other species dispatch digestive filaments which eat the prey. Soft corals appear to leach out toxic chemicals called terpines which kill nearby organisms. Because predation is such a threat, two-thirds of reef species are toxic. Others hide in stony outcrops or have formed protective relationships with other organisms, as in the classic case of the banded clown fish which live among the sea anemones, protected by their stingers. The cleaner fish protect themselves from larger fish by setting up stations at which they pick parasites off their carnivorous customers. Mimicking its coloration and shape, the sabre-toothed blenny is a false cleaner fish which takes a chunk out of the larger fish and runs off!

coral love affairs: Not prone to celibacy or sexual prudery, coral polyps reproduce sexually and asexually through budding, and a polyp joins together with thou-

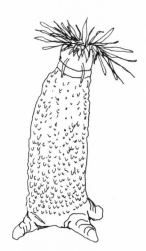

Sea anemone

sands and even millions of its neighbors to form a coral. (In a few cases, only one polyp forms a single coral). During sexual reproduction polyps release millions of their spermatozoa into the water. Many species are dimorphic–with both male and female coral. Some species have internal, others external fertilization. Still others have both male and female polyps. As larvae develop. their "mother" expells them and they float off to found a new coral colony.

exploring reefs: Coral reefs are extremely fragile environments. Much damage has been done to reefs worldwide through the carelessness of humans. Despite their size, reefs grow very slowly, and it can take decades or even hundreds of years to repair the effects of a few moments. Do nothing to provoke moray eels which may retaliate when threateded. Watch out for fire corals–recognizeable by the white tips on their branches–which can inflict stings. In general, "look but don't touch."

Virgin Islands coral reefs: The islands' coral reefs are a priceless treasure comparable to Yosemite's granite peaks and waterfalls or Yellowstone's geysers. The most famous excursion is to the reefs lying off of Buck Island a few mi. away from St. Croix. St. John's reefs include Leinster Bay's Waterlemon Cay, an islet in Leinster Bay, and the reef lying off Trunk Bay–which has suffered greatly

from abuse and overuse by tourists. Others include Steven Cay and Fishbowl at Cruz Bay, Johnson Reef on the N coast, and Horseshoe and South Drop on the S coast.

underwater flora: Most of the plants you see underwater are algae, primitive plants that can survive only underwater because they do not have the mechanisms to prevent themselves from drying out. Lacking roots, algae draw their minerals and water directly from the sea. Another type of algae, calcareous red algae, are very important for reef formation. Resembling rounded stones, they are 95 percent rock and only 5 percent living tissue. Land plants returned to live in the sea, sea grasses are found in relatively shallow water in sandy and muddy bays and flats; they have roots and small flowers. One species, dubbed "turtle grass," provides food for turtles. In addition, sea grasses help to stabilize the sea floor, maintain water clarity by trapping fine sediments from up-land soil erosion, stave off beach erosion, and provide living space for numerous fish, crustaceans, and shellfish.

History

The original inhabitants of the Virgin Islands were members of the Inerí tribe. Little is known about them and few reminders remain save some archaeological sites. Later joined by the Tainos (Arawaks), both tribes were conquered and enslaved by invading Carib Indians. During Columbus' second voyage, the admiral sighted St. Croix. Christening the island Santa Cruz (Holy Cross), his fleet anchored in Salt River Bay. After putting ashore in a small boat, the island's first tourists made the village rounds. On the way back, Columbus' boat, seeking captives, attacked a canoe full of Caribs, who immediately fled at the strange sight of white men, firing arrows to cover their escape. The Caribs fled inland, leaving behind some Taino slaves whom the sailors "liberated." Continuing on his voyage, Columbus and his men passed a great number of islands, cluster after cluster, some verdant, others naked and sterile. The islands, seemingly thousands of them, with their combinations of glistening white and azure rocks were, he supposed, filled with jewels and precious stones. Accordingly, he named the islands Santa Ursula y las Once Mil Virgines (Saint Ursula and the 11,000 Virgins). Prior to sainthood, Ursula was a proper British princess. Engaged to marry a foreign king, she begged a pleasure cruise from her father as a wedding present. This three-year, eleven-ship voyage came to a brutal end when, arriving in Cologne just as it was being sacked by the Huns, Ursula and her comrades were raped and slain.

colonization: After Columbus' visit, not much attention was paid to the islands, except in frequent raids by Spaniards, as they carted off natives to slave in Dominican gold mines. These raids led to the complete extermination of the local population. By 1625 the Dutch and English were settled on St. Croix. Control of St. Croix passed from English to Spanish to French hands. Finally, a second Danish West India Company, organized by a group of court insiders, was chartered on March 11, 1671, and a decision made to settle on St. Thomas. A little more than eight months passed before the Company had two ships on the way. One was forced to turn back; the other, waylaid by inclement weather, managed to limp into the harbor of what was to become Charlotte Amalie more than six months after the date of departure. It had been a horrendous voyage for the *Pharoah*: only six of the 239 who had boarded in Copenhagen survived. Other ships followed, some with clergy to

IMPORTANT DATES IN
UNITED STATES VIRGIN ISLANDS HISTORY

1493: Columbus discovers St. Croix and the other Virgin Islands.

1625: The Dutch and English settle on St. Croix.

1650: The English are driven from St. Croix by Puerto Rican Spaniards. The French take over from the Spanish.

1651: Chevalier de Poincy, Lt. General of the French West Indies, buys St. Croix from the bankrupt French West Indies Company.

1653: Ownership of St. Croix is transferred to the Knights of Malta.

1665: Erik Neilson Smith, a Danish sea captain, is granted a charter from the Danish king to colonize St. Thomas and is named royal commandant and governor. Saint Croix is purchased from the Knights of Malta by the French West Indies Company.

1666: Schmidt takes possession of St. Thomas only to die 6 months later; he is replaced by Lutheran pastor Kjeld Slagelse.

1667: Saint Thomas is captured by the English, who soon abandon it.

1668: Slagelse and most of the island's Danish inhabitants return home.

1671: Danish King Christian V issues a new charter to the West India and Guinea Company.

1672: Danes, under Gov. Iverson, formally take possession of St. Thomas.

1673: The first consignment of African slaves arrives on St. Thomas.

1674: The king of France takes over St. Croix as part of his dominions from the French West Indies Company.

1681: Taphus (Charlotte Amalie) is founded on St. Thomas.

1684: Saint Thomas formally takes possession of St. John.

1685: Saint Thomas is leased to the Brandenburgh Company to carry on commerce for 30 years.

1691: Saint Thomas is leased to George Thormohlen, a Bergen merchant, for 10 years.

1694: Thormohlen's lease ends in a lawsuit.

1696: French settlers abandon St. Croix.

1716: Export and import duty is reduced to 6 percent *ad valoreum.*

1717: Planters from St. Thomas occupy St. John and begin cultivation.

1724: St. Thomas is formally declared a free port.

1726: The first Supplication Day (to pray for "aid against hurricanes") is held.

1730: Taphus is renamed Charlotte Amalie.

1733: Saint Croix is purchased from France by the Danish West Indies Company; slaves on St. John openly rebel.

1734: The St. John insurrection is put down.

1735: Danes formally take possession of St. Croix; Christiansted is established.

1751: The town of Fredericksted is established.

1764: Saint Thomas and St. John again granted free port status.

1792: Denmark outlaws slave trade.

1801-2: Britain again occupies the islands.

1804: Much of Charlotte Amalie is swept by fire.

1806: Two more fires devastate Charlotte Amalie.

1807-15: Britain again occupies the islands.

1825: Yet another fire sweeps through Charlotte Amalie.

1826: Another fire on St. Thomas.

1831: Still another fire on St. Thomas.

1848: Slaves on St. Croix are emancipated by Governor-General Peter von Scholten after demonstrations.

1867: A treaty is signed in Denmark for the sale of St. Thomas and St. John to the U.S. for $7.5 million.

1870: The treaty of sale is rejected by the U.S. Senate.

1872: Charlotte Amalie once again becomes the administrative seat of the islands.

1892: Poor economic conditions, coupled with a lack of stable currency, cause a rebellion on St. Thomas.

1898: The U.S. again attempts to purchase the islands.

1902: A second treaty, granting the islands to the U.S. in exchange for $5 million in gold, is signed; it is rejected by the Danish parliament.

1916: Treaty selling the islands to the U.S. for $25 million is signed.

1917: Treaty of sale is ratified and the islands formally become part of the U.S.	**1954:** Revised Organic Act passed.
1927: U.S. citizenship is granted to most island residents.	**1956:** National Park on St. John approved by U.S. Congress.
1931: Jurisdiction of the islands is transferred from the Navy to the Dept. of the Interior; President Hoover visits the U.S.V.I.	**1959:** The Revised Organic Act is amended.
	1968: Passage of the Virgin Islands Elective Governor Act permits the U.S.V.I. to elect a governor.
1936: The first Organic Act is passed.	**1969:** Dr. Melvin Evans, first native black governor and last appointee, takes office.
1940: Population shows an increase for the first time since 1860.	**1970:** Dr. Melvin Evans elected governor.
1946: First black governor of the islands, William Hastie, is appointed.	**1972:** Hon. Ron de Lugo elected as first Congressional delegate from the Virgin Islands.
1950: Morris De Castro, first native-born governor, is appointed.	**1989:** Hurricane Hugo devastates the islands.

provide spiritual guidance. However, of the first priests sent over, most simply couldn't adapt and one had to be sent home for drunkenness. ("Kill devil," as the local unaged rum was called, was potent stuff indeed!) By 1679 there were 156 whites and 176 slaves on St. Thomas. Tobacco, indigo, cotton, and dyewood were the main exports to Denmark. A series of vile rascals reigned as Danish West India Company presidents. With St. Thomas a haven for privateers, pirates, and all manner of shady operators from every part of the Caribbean, there were visits from Bluebeard, Blackbeard, Captain Kidd, and other such "Brethren of the Coast." The harbor was also renowned for its slave market: buyers would come from as far away as Curacao and the Carolinas. Saint Croix, purchased from France in 1733, was also a base for the "Triangle Trade." New England ships would buy rum, carry it to Africa, use it to buy slaves, and return to sell the slaves and buy more rum. Of a total of 123,000 slaves brought over between 1733-82, about 70,000 were re-exported, while the rest were retained. During the severe drought of 1725-26, a number of planters let their slaves starve to death. On Sept. 5, 1733, Governor Philip Gardelin announced a new mandate. Among the 18 conditions were: that a leader of a runaway slave should be pinched three times with a red hot iron and then hung; that "slaves who steal to the value of four dollars shall be pinched and hung"; that a slave who lifts his hand to strike a white or even threatens him with violence would be pinched and hung; a slave meeting a white should step aside until he passed or risk flogging; and all dances, feasts, and plays among slaves were forbidden. In 1764 Charlotte Amalie was declared a free port for intracolonial trade. Its neutrality attracted privateers of all nations who arrived to sell their booty. In 1815 this trade was extended internationally.

emancipation: Denmark's King Frederick VI appointed Peter von Scholten governor in 1827. An unusual man, versed in Creole and comfortable among slaves, von Scholten lived with Anna Heegard, the granddaughter of a freed slave. Perhaps under her influence, he began urging freedom for all slaves. In 1847 he implemented the policy of "gradualism," whereby slave children born during the succeeding 12 years were to be free at birth. All slaves would then be free at the end of the 12-year period. Resentment by slaves against the system, however, continued to build. Receiving word of a planned slave rebellion, von Scholten emancipated the slaves on July 3, 1848, on his own initiative, from Fort Frederik in Christiansted. The rebellion began in Frederiksted before the news reached there. After the news arrived, however, the violence turned into a jubilant celebration. Brought back to Copenhagen for trial, von Scholten was acquitted. Emancipation led to dire poverty for freed slaves and to labor riots on St. Croix in 1878, during which most of Frederiksted burned.

sale to United States: During the U.S. Civil War, the danger of having an unprotected Atlantic coastline, along with the strategic value of having a Caribbean colony, became clear. Saint Thomas was seen as a Caribbean Gibraltar: a fortress at sea, surrounded by impregnable coral reefs, strategically located, and with harbors eminently suited for naval vessels. Negotiations, opened secretly by Secretary of State Seward in Jan. 1865, were delayed by Lincoln's assassination, but finally culminated in a treaty signed on 24 Oct. 1867, which provided for the sale of St. Thomas and St. John for $7.5 million, or a half million more than Seward had paid for Alaska. As a stipulation of the treaty, a referendum among the local populace was held in 1868; a majority of the 12% of the population who qualified for suffrage voted in favor, and the sale was considered by both nations to have been approved. However, although the treaty passed in the Danish Rigsag or parliament, it failed to pass a U.S. Senate divided and impassioned by President Johnson's impeachment. In the 1890s private American operators, attracted by the possibility of a 10% commission, negotiated with the Danes. Interrupted by the Spanish-American War, negotiations resumed again in 1900, at which time a Standard Oil vice-president joined the group. Boasting that he had 26 senators under his control, he claimed he could deliver a treaty for the price of a Standard depot on St. Thomas. Meanwhile, with the islands an expensive financial liability, the Danes were hoping to swap them with Germany in exchange for the return of North Schleswig. The Treaty of 1902, from which any mention of citizenship was deleted, arranged for the sale of all three islands to the U.S. for a bargain basement $5 million. Although the treaty was passed in the U.S. Senate, it failed by one vote in its Danish counterpart–largely because the U.S. refused to hold a plebiscite. Fresh negotiations dragged on again until the beginning of WWI. Faced with the prospect of the Kaiser's armies marching into Copenhagen, American naval strategists began to fear for the safety of the Panama Canal and the Danes' stretegic islands in the Caribbean. Negotiations began again under President Woodrow Wilson. Seizing advantage of the situation, the clever Danes, reluctant to negotiate at first, pushed the price up five times to $25 million. The U.S. accepted the offer without attempting to bargain, and a treaty was signed on April 14, 1916. At $290 an acre, the islands represent the most expensive U.S. government land purchase in history.

United States takeover: On 31 March 1917, the Stars and Stripes were raised by the U.S. Navy, ending 245 years and six days of Danish rule. Packing up everything moveable–from furniture to the rope belonging to the Government House flagpole–the Danes were happy to leave. At the time of the U.S. takeover conditions were absolutely abominable. A high death rate was coupled with a high rate of infant mortality. Agriculture was confined to small crops of yams and sweet potatoes. Malaria, typhoid, leprosy, diphtheria, and elephantiasis were widespread. There were four miles of roads on St. Thomas, no high school, and only 19 elementary school teachers. The brutality of the slavery system, one of the harshest in the Western Hemisphere, was transformed after emancipation into an almost complete neglect of the poor. As the islands were acquired by the U.S. purely for their strategic value rather than out of any concern for the inhabitants or for economic reasons, the most expedient thing to do was to transfer them to military rule and worry about status, citizenship, human rights, and such other troublesome issues sometime in the future. Under the Navy, all of the authoritarian local laws remained in force. This surprised locals who, having opted against Danish citizenship, assumed they would automatically be granted American citizenship. The Navy found a strange world. White Naval officers, many of them from the South, were astounded to find themselves dealing with high-ranking local blacks. Run-ins between locals and intoxicated Marines frequently resulted in violence. A succession of Southern Caesars as military governors, hard-core white supremacists all, fanned the flames.

civilian administration: The 14 years of Naval control ended on March 18, 1931 as control passed to the U.S. Department of the Interior and Paul Pearson was sworn in as the first civilian governor. President Hoover, visiting eight days later, declared, "Viewed from every point except remote naval contingencies, it was unfortunate we ever acquired these islands." Although the Jones Act had granted citizenship to Puerto Ricans in 1917, Virgin Islanders were denied this because the treaty of purchase spoke of citizenship "in" the U.S. as opposed to citizenship "of" the U.S. Citizenship was finally granted in 1927 to most residents, but not until 1932 was this privilege extended to all. The Basic Organic Act, passed in 1936, gave the vote to all citizens who were able to read and write English, and made the U.S. Constitution operative in the Virgin Islands. In addition, all federal taxes collected were to be held for use by local governments in the Islands. Pearson, known as the "Experimenting Quaker," although unpopular with both the left and right, continued as governor under President Franklin Roosevelt. During the New Deal, the Public Works Administration instituted the Virgin Islands Company (VICO), a public corporation which grew and refined sugarcane, distilled and marketed rum, and controlled water supplies and power production. Rum was produced and sold under the brand name "Government House," bearing a label personally designed by Roosevelt. Unlike its mainland counterparts, VICO (later renamed VICORP) wasn't really such a good idea, as the Virgin Islands are not particularly well suited to sugarcane cultivation.

the governors: President Truman appointed William H. Hastie to be the Islands' first black governor in 1946. He was succeeded by Morris F. Castro in 1950 who, in turn, was replaced by Archie Alexander. Alexander resigned in 1955 under the guise of ill health after allegations of conflict of interest and misuse of government funds had been made against him. In 1954 Congress passed the revised Basic Organic Act which established a unicameral legislature and allowed all federal excise taxes collected from rum sales to be returned to the Islands. A succession of governors ruled until President Kennedy–under pressure from his father, who had been a friend of the rum distilling Paiewonsky family–appointed entrepreneur Ralph M. Paiewonsky governor. A bill providing for the direct election of governors became law on 23 Aug. 1968. Selected by President Nixon, Dr. Melvin H. Evans became the last appointed governor on 1 July 1969. In the first gubernatorial elections, held in Nov. 1970, Cyril King was elected. After the death of his successor Melvin King (no relation) in Jan. 1978, Juan Luis became acting governor and was subsequently elected in Nov. 1978 and re-elected in 1982. In 1986 Democrat and Yale Law School graduate Alexander Farelly defeated State Senator Aldebert Bryant of the Independent Citizen's Movement. Tapping the resentment the lower class feels towards the well-to-do, Bryant (a former St. Croix policeman) waged the first real challenge to the status quo in the islands' electoral history. In Sept. 1989, Hurricane Hugo hit the islands severely. On St. Croix, 70% of the buildings were destroyed or severely damaged, some 150 inmates were freed and went on a crime rampage, and federal troops patrolled the island. The Federal Emergency Management Agency (FEMA) estimated that the USVI suffered at least $400 million worth of damage.

Government

As citizens of the nation and residents of an unincorporated territory under the U.S. flag, at four-year intervals Virgin Islanders elect their own governor, legislature, and a non-voting representative to Congress. The legislature, the backbone of the local government, is a unicameral body of 15 members who are elected to two-year terms. Its main powers and duties derive from the 1954 Revised Organic Act. Although the system may sound ideal, the realities have been different. In the USVI, politics has always been politics. For years the autocratic legislature has been dominated by the Unity Democrats. Party of the Creoles, it has allowed entry into the political process of only a few Continentals and Puerto Ricans, while the vast number of alien residents remain unrepresented. Party politics are confusing and crossing of party lines while voting is common.

constitution: It's been in the works for a while. On Nov. 4, 1981, Virgin Island voters rejected the latest draft of their proposed constitution. This is the fourth constitution rejected since 1964. The first constitution failed to pass Congress; the second (1972) was approved by Congress only by an insubstantial margin; and the third (1979) was also rejected by the voters. The latest constitution defined a "Virgin Islander" as one born on, or with one parent born on, the islands–a designation which would have conferred no special benefits. The original draft contained a specification that the governor must be a native. After residents from the States complained, it was removed. Regarding the modest voter turnout for the election (47%), Judge Henry Feuerzeig–who helped draft and actively campaigned for the constitution–pontificated: "Constitutions aren't sexy. You can't identify with them as you can with a candidate."

Economy

No other Caribbean island or island group has ever undergone such a fast-clipped transformation, ethnic or economic, as did the U.S. Virgin Islands during the 1960s. Although the entire population of the USVI was only 100,000 in the late '70s, the government budget was larger than that of San Juan with its one million people! The islands have the highest per capita income in the Caribbean, about $7,100 per year, but they're also plagued by prices higher than Stateside, without wage levels to match. The presence of continentals, while stimulating to the economy, has served to drive up land values and cause considerable resentment. While the typical native Virgin Islander works for the government, most of the service industry jobs are held by continentals or the down-islanders, disparagingly nicknamed garotes, after the tropical bird that flies from island to island–consuming everything in sight before flying home. These aliens live in housing conditions that are among the worst in the US. Today, only 45% of the islanders are native born. Median income among whites averages around $18,000, while blacks make just $10,000. Overall rates are low, but unemployment among local youth remains high. The average family–with the help of food stamps–is just making it: more than one third live below the poverty level.

government: Surprisingly, the largest employer in the USVI is the territorial government. Its more than 13,000 employees give the islands the highest ratio of bureaucrats to taxpayers of any area of the United States. Although the government employs a full third of the working force and receives more per capita in federal funds than any state or territory save the District of Columbia, it has been ponderously slow to deal with practical concerns such as power plants, desalinization plants, and new roads. Stories of corruption are legendary. The Farrelly Administration has been wrestling with the financial disarray left by his predecessor Juan Luis. Having called the government "a shambles" and proposing to reduce the bureaucracy and turn over certain public services to the private sector, he has as yet done nothing. Despite the hefty taxes and subsidies, the money just disappears, and the government faces a $135 million deficit! Problems include nepotism, corruption, incompetence, and increasing violence in the schools.

industry: None exists on St. Thomas or St. John. Harvey Alumina constructed a $25 million alumina processing plant on St. Croix's S shore, then sold it to Martin Marietta, who worked the plant for 10 years and then closed it! It adjoins the 1,200-acre Hess Refinery, the presence of which does not stop the islands' gas prices from being among the highest in the nation. Completed in 1993, Hess's $1 billion catalytic-cracking unit has increased the refinery's ability to produce high-octane cleaner-burning gasolines that are important in complying with environmental regulations.

tourism: This economic sector is the major income earner. Hotels have increased dramatically over the years as have the number of visitors. St. Thomas alone has some 3,500 hotel rooms. Tourists have been attracted because of the "duty-free" (7% import duty) shopping available, as well as the sense of security offered by islands that are part of the United States.

agriculture: Almost totally neglected. The only fresh milk available on the islands is found on St. Croix; St. Thomian milk is reconstituted. Obstacles to agriculture include aridity and the high cost of land, which finds more remunerative use in tourism. Native Virgin Islanders have a negative view of menial labor in general and agriculture in particular–rooted in the sufferings of the slave era.

Festivals and Events

With 23 official holidays, Virgin Islanders have plenty of time off–perhaps more than anyone anywhere else in the world! Various public holidays are marked by special celebrations and events peculiar to the USVI. **New Year's Day** features a children's parade in Fredericksted. **Three Kings Day**, which follows on Jan. 6, constitutes the finale of St. Croix's Christmas Festival with a colorful parade of costumed children and adults. **Transfer Day**, March 31, celebrates the transfer of the islands to the U.S. in 1917. **Easter** is marked by church services; outdoor sporting events are held on Easter Monday. St Croix holds a **Sportsweek Festival** around the beginning of April. Events range from foot racing to tournament tennis, deep sea fishing, and underwater photography competitions. It's usually followed by the **American Paradise Triathalon** (swimming/ bicycling/running). The **Rolex Regatta** usually comes in mid-April, as does **St. Thomas' Carnival** which takes place during the last eight days of April. Parades and ceremonies are commonplace throughout the islands on **Memorial Day**, and yacht races are featured on St. Croix. A special ceremony marking **Danish West Indies Emancipation Day** takes place in Fredericksted, St. Croix, on July 3, because the proclamation was first read there. All three islands celebrate this day with parades and ceremonies: Cruz Bay, St. John, features a miniature version of St. Thomas' Carnival. Also in July, many residents of these islands attend services marking **Hurricane Supplication Day** to pray that no hurricanes will visit them (it worked for more than half a century). Special festivities are held on all three islands on **Labor Day** just as they are held on the mainland. **Columbus Day** is also known as Puerto Rico/Virgin Islands Friendship Day; a traditional boat trip from St. Croix to the Puerto Rican island of Vieques is made on this day. **Liberty Day**, Nov. 1, commemorates the establishment of the first free press in 1915. The **Virgin Island Charterboat League Show** takes place in mid-November. **Veterans Day**, Nov. 11, features parades and ceremonies.

Music

While the Virgin Islands do have deep musical roots, the islands are deeply indebted to their more populous brothers and sisters such as Jamaica and Trinidad for their music. Today, you can hear rock, calypso, reggae, soul, steel band music, and disco on the islands.

reggae: Originally emanating from the steamy slums of Jamaica, reggae has swept the world and gone international. No one is quite sure exactly from where it appeared, but it appears inseparably linked to the maturation of the Rastafarian movement. Reggae may be defined as the synthesis of electrified African music coupled with the influence of ska, rock steady, and American rhythm and blues. Some give the Wailers credit for transforming reggae

USVI Public Holidays

1 January:	New Year's Day
6 January:	Three Kings Day
15 January:	Martin Luther King's Birthday
February:	Lincoln's Birthday (movable)
31 March:	Transfer Day
March/April:	Holy Thursday, Good Friday, Easter Monday (movable)
May:	Memorial Day (movable)
June:	Organic Act Day (movable)
3 July:	Emancipation Day
4 July:	U.S. Independence Day
July:	Supplication Day (movable)
September:	Labor Day (movable)
October:	Columbus Day, Virgin Islands/Puerto Rico Friendship Day, Hurricane Thanksgiving Day (movable)
1 November:	Liberty Day
11 November:	Veterans Day
November:	U.S. Thanksgiving Day (movable)
25 December:	Christmas Day
26 December:	Second Christmas Day

into its present format. No sooner had the band gained international fame in the early 70s than its members went their own separate ways, with the band's major singer-songwriter Bob Marley changing the name to Bob Marley and the Wailers. By the time of his death from brain cancer at the age of 36 in 1981, Robert Nesta Marley had become an international superstar. His influence remains strong to this day, and no one has yet quite succeeded in filling his shoes. Although reggae is not strongly developed in the Virgins, there are a few bands playing reggae, and the music (particularly the rapid fire "dance hall" deejay style) permeates the island.

steel band music: Of Trinidadian origin, this unique orchestra style has spread all over the Caribbean. Despite its low-life beginnings–when it was a scorned child of the lower classes–it is now the darling of every tourist board. From their humble origins, the orchestras have grown as large as 200 members. Although it is often maintained that the instruments are the progeny of African drums, they have much more in common rhythmically with African marimbas. In truth, they are far removed from either. The pans–as the individual drums are called–are made from large oil drums. First, the head–along with 6-12 inches of the side–is severed. Then, the top is heated and hammered until a series of large indentations emerge. Each of these produces a musical note. Each pan is custom designed. While some produce many notes to carry the melody, the bass pans have only three or four notes. Bands are now divided into three major sections. The "ping pong" (or soprano pans) provide the melody using 26-32 notes; the larger pans ("guitar," "cello," and "bass") supply the harmony; and the cymbals, scratchers, and drums supply the groundbeat. A contemporary steel drum orchestra in Trinidad generally contains 20 or more pans; those found in the Virgin Islands commonly have considerably fewer.

calypso: Perhaps no music is so difficult to pinpoint, and none is quite so undefinable as calypso. Next to reggae, it is the best known music to come out of the English speaking Caribbean. Its rhythm is Afro-Spanish: sometimes the Spanish elements dominate, sometimes the African. Call-and-response is employed frequently. It is strikingly African in the nature and function of its lyrics. While the tunes don't vary a whole lot–there are some 50 or so–the lyrics must be new! And, without exception, they must also pack social bite. Like reggae, calypso is a political music–one which more frequently than not attacks the status quo, lays bare the foibles of corrupt politicians, and exposes empty programs. The songs often function as musical newspapers providing great insight into society. And, as even the briefest listening will reveal, calypso is also a very sexual music. One of the most frequent themes is that of the wrath of a scorned woman focused on an unfaithful male partner. No one can say precisely where or when calypso began. Each island claims it for its own, and certainly all of the islands had music similar in style to calypso. In fact, some of them were also called calypso. These styles were all influenced by Trinidadian calypso, however. Partially because of the popularity of Trinidad's calypso and also partially because the same businessman who had the island's calypsonians under contract owned a group of record stores on the other islands, calypso on the smaller islands came to resemble the Trinidadian style. The famous Trinidadian calypsonian Atilla the Hun (Raymond Quevedo) maintained that the calypso's origins were undoubtedly African. According to Quevedo, the first calypsos were sung during *gayap*– a grouping of organized communal workers which has equivalents in West Africa. These work songs–which can be found in every African community in the Americas–still exist. And, their more ribald counterparts, which served to spread gossip concerning plantation folk, paralleled modern day calypso. However, it is more likely that they were merely an influence. Certainly, there are many African elements present in the music including the use of dynamic repetition, call-and-response patterns, and the rebuking of socially reprehensible behavior–a frequent theme in African traditional songs.

Whatever its roots, calypso seems to have reached its stylistic maturity in the 1870s. It was originally accompanied by rattles, a scraper called a *vira*, drums, and a bottle and spoon used like a West African gong. During the '40s and '50s, calypsonians first began twisting words–executing swift ingenuity–to contrive rhymes that also produced a wide range of rhythmic effects in the vocal line. Lines which vary in length as well as short phrases or cries, juxtaposed between the lines of verses, also serve to enliven and add gaiety to the music's spirit. Calypso music has incorporated elements of jazz, salsa, Venezuelan, East Indian, and R&B music. But–like all great musical forms–it has been strengthened rather than inundated by their influence. As with most contemporary popular music, the singer is at the focus of the music. Like the American and British rock stars, the calypso kings are sexual objects, dashingly and wickedly attractive to swooning women. One qualification is to be unemployed–the image is of the witty indigent–bordering, but not entering, criminality. Like the griot musicians of West Africa, the first calypso singers lived through donations. And flamboyant titles–be it the Mighty Sparrow or Atilla the Hun–have served to reinforce the high-and-mighty image. Crowned in a "tent" (whether the carnival is in St. Thomas or in Trinidad) he becomes the symbol of masculine prowess incarnate.

USVI Practicalities

getting there: It's still possible to visit the Virgin Islands relatively cheaply. And though the only really cheap way to get there is to swim, you can still save money by shopping around. A good travel agent should help you to find the lowest fare; if he or she doesn't, find another agent, or try doing it yourself. Check the phone book–most airlines have toll-free numbers. In these days of airline deregulation, fares change quicker than you can say "No Problem,

Mon" so it's best to check the prices well before departure–and then again before you buy the ticket. APEX (advance purchase excursion) fares, weekday and night flights, and one-way fares are among the options that may save you money. The more flexible you can be about when you wish to depart and return, the easier it will be to find a bargain. Whether dealing with a travel agent or with the airlines themselves make sure that you let them know clearly what it is you want. Don't assume that because you live in Los Angeles, for example, it's cheapest to fly direct from there. It may be better to find an ultrasaver flight to gateway cities like New York or Miami and then change planes; it may also be cheaper to purchase a RT San Juan ticket and find your own way over to the islands. Fares tend to be cheaper on weekdays and during low season (mid-April to mid-December). TWA and American, which has made San Juan its Caribbean hub, also fly. Puerto Rico can be reached by air from everywhere in the Caribbean except Cuba. Even if you don't intend to visit San Juan, it may be necessary to switch planes at San Juan International Airport. From San Juan it's a short hop by small aircraft (such as Sunaire Express) to either St. Thomas or St. Croix. While discount OW fares are not available, shop around for various RT inter-island fares which may be available. These–like everything else–are cheapest off-season. Many of the major airlines have contracts with small carriers that service the islands. For St. John it's best to take a ferry from Red Hook, St. Thomas. **carriers:** One major reliable carrier currently serving the Virgin Islands is Continental. The airline serves more than 200 cities worldwide. Continental flies nonstop from Newark to St. Thomas and St. Croix daily. Connections are available to and from Newark to most US cities; there are also flights from Newark to Paris, London, Madrid, Frankfurt, and to Munich. Free trips can be earned through the OnePass system. Call 1-800-525-0780 for information and reservations. US Air flies from a number of major cities into San Juan. Delta flies direct from Orlando to St. Croix and offers nonstop service from Atlanta to San Juan; connecting service is available via Orlando or Atlanta to San Juan. United flies nonstop from Dulles (Washington DC), to San Juan. American Airlines flies directly to St. Thomas and St. Croix from NYC and Raleigh/Durham. It also flies into San Juan. **from Europe:** In addition to Continental's connecting flights, British Airways, Iberia, BWIA, and Lufthansa all fly to San Juan.

from the Caribbean: British West Indies Airlines services St. Croix and St. Thomas from other Caribbean islands, as does LIAT.

getting around: Local taxis–shared or unshared–are expensive. Be sure to decide the price before entering. Inefficient and limited local bus service is available on St. Thomas. Hitching is easiest on St. John. A must for anyone is the "Official Road Map" of the islands available free of charge at tourist information offices. However, be sure to note that the St. John map is wrong with respect to the roads around Bourdeaux Mountain. The best map sold is the Virgin Islands Map (1:50,000) produced by ITMB (tel. 604-687-3320, fax 604-687-5925) of Vancouver, BC. Contact any good store specializing in travel guides or maps. **renting a car:** On islands this small, it's difficult to get lost. Expect to spend $35-65 pd with unlimited mileage. Weekly rates are available. **driving:** Don't forget that you drive on the left hand side of the road although the vehicles are right-hand drive! There is no "R turn on red," but you can go L on red at an intersection. Left turns at traffic lights are permissible unless marked otherwise. Watch for "no turn" signs because there are plenty of one-way streets in town areas. Expect traffic jams during Charlotte Amalie's early morning and late afternoon rush hours. Keep a look out for cars pulled over in the fast lane: locals frequently stop to pick up and discharge passengers without pulling off the road or even using indicator signals! It is common courtesy here to stop to allow other vehicles to enter from driveways and intersections. It's also the custom to sound your horn when you round a corner. If you see the driver in front of you wagging his or her hand out of the window that means you should slow down or stop. Always expect the unexpected: some drivers may pull L before turning R and vice versa. You should note that, owing to high jury awards, liability insurance and car insurance is nonexistent. **by plane:** With the exception of smaller islands such as St. John and Jost Van Dyke, the Virgins, American and British, are well connected by local air service. The most prominent of the local carriers is Sunaire Express, which is based on St. Croix and flies from there to Tortola and Virgin Gorda in the BVI, to St. Thomas, and to Fajardo, Vieques, and to San Juan in Puerto Rico. They also connect these destinations with each other, generally via St. Thomas. Sunaire is an extremely reliable airline, has very hospitable personnel, and is a pleasure to fly. To contact Sunaire Express write Box 1527, Kingshill, St. Croix 00851-1527; call (809) 778-9200, 800-595-9501 (Puerto Rico), or 800-524-2094 (in the US);

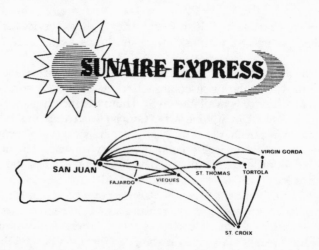

or fax (809) 773-4628. Discount airfares are available if requested in advance. **by ferry:** Those available run between Charlotte Amalie, St. Thomas and Water Island and from Charlotte Amalie, and Red Hook, St. Thomas to St. John. Ferries also run between the USVI and Tortola, Virgin Gorda, and Jost Van Dyke in the British Virgins. **hitchhiking by yacht:** Hitchhiking by boat through the Caribbean can be easy if you have the time and money to wait for a ride and are at the right place in the right season. Best time to head there is about mid-Oct. just before the boat shows and the preparation for the charter season. Along with those at English Harbor on Antigua, the marinas on St. Thomas (at Red Hook and at Charlotte Amalie) have the greatest concentration of boats and the most competition for work of any island in the Caribbean. Many times it's easy to get a ride from one island to another. Just hang around the docks or pubs and ask! As far as working on yachts goes, it's hard work, low wages, and long hours, and you must have a real love for sailing and the sea. Depending upon whether you are working on salary or for piece work, the salary may or may not depend on how many hours are actually involved. Usually you will be engaged in some sort of activity from early morning until late at night. Some boats may be more lax than others, but it generally involves pretty continuous work. Check out *Sail* magazine or *Yachting* for the addresses of charter companies. But it's really unnecessary to write: most people are employed on the spot.

accommodations: These islands make their living from tourists and housing is tight, so the cost of lodging is correspondingly high–from $50 d to $400 or more per night. And the 7 1/2% room tax along with a frequently applied 10% service charge makes the islands even more expensive! It's cheapest to visit these islands off-season (mid-April through mid-December). Camping (bare sites and rented tents) is available only on St. John and (to a more limited extent) on St. Croix. It's a good idea to get the current rates from the tourist board (1-800-USVI-INFO). If they don't list the rates, it's just that the hotels haven't supplied them to the board so use the address or phone number listed to contact them. There are also rental agents on the islands, and they are listed in the text.

weddings and honeymoons: Many resorts offer special packages. Specializing in weddings on all three islands, **Creative Wedding & Honeymoon Experts** (tel. 778-5933) offer a range of wedding ceremonies ranging from Caribbean Morning Glory to Virgin Island Best which has a helicopter flight to a private island or a wedding at sea aboard a luxury yacht. Write Box 2849, St. Thomas 00803-2849 or Box 861 Richmond, St. Croix 00821-0861. **Fantasia Occasions** offers a variety of wedding packages ranging from "tropical fantasy" to "custom fantasy" which take place on a 65-ft. wooden schooner. Call 776-0960, 800-FANTASA, fax 776-0020, or write Ste. 310, 168 Crown Bay, St. Thomas 00802.

food: You will find high prices and a dearth of local cuisine, which has been largely supplanted by hamburgers, hotdogs, and Kentucky Fried Chicken. Most restaurant prices reflect the high cost of importing food. Local establishments tend to be expensive because of the local economy and because the ingredients for local food are also expensive. Native cuisine vaguely resembles that of Louisiana, with peppers, eggplant, tomatoes, and okra numbering among the standard ingredients. Local foods that you should definitely try include **fungi** (a light, steamed cornmeal dumpling mixed with ground okra), **kallaloo** (a stew made with local greens, okra, boned fish, diced pork, and hot pepper), **maubi** (a drink made from tree bark, herbs and a pinch of yeast), **souse** (pig's head, feet, and tail stew with lime juice), **johnny cakes** (unleavened fried bread originally known as journey cakes), **conch salad** (cold salad mixed with pieces of the mollusk) and **patés** (pastries stuffed with spiced beef or saltfish). Traditional bush teas are made from sasparilla flowers and leaves (for head and chest colds), papaya seeds (for diabetes), tan-tan leaves (for colds), marsh mallow leaves (for prickly heat), and thibbet leaves. The street vendors on

St. Thomas sell largely junk food; the ones in Christiansted, St. Croix sell a mixture of junk and nutritious food. Some also sell local food. There are a few bakeries in the main towns where you can buy bread. If you want to eat well here, you'd better plan on parting with a lot of green. Even food in the supermarkets runs 75-200% higher than Stateside on the average so it's better to bring what you can–especially if you plan to camp on St. John..

tips for vegetarians: If you're into salads and the like, it should be easy for you to eat here. In Charlotte Amalie, St. Thomas the best place to eat vegetarian food is at **Rootsie's**. Most restaurants will cater to your preferences and salads are ubiquitous so you should have no real problems eating, even if you are a vegan. Things like nuts and other specialty items are expensive so you should bring a supply. Restaurants serving vegetarian food as well as health food stores are listed in the text.

alcohol: Most major brands of U.S and imported beer are available here and comparable prices prevail. Virgin Islands rum (notably Cruzan Rum) is quite cheap–$2.50-$3 a fifth. Another Cruzan product is Buba Touee, a liquor made of rum, lime, and spices.

Deep-Sea Fishing in the Virgin Islands

Fish	Location	Season
Blue marlin	100 fathom edge	All year; July-Oct. best
White marlin	100 fathom edge	All year. Spring
Sailfish	Offshore	Oct. to April; Dec and Feb. best
Wahoo	Offshore	All year. Sept. to May
Allison tuna	Offshore	All year
Dolphin (fish)	Offshore	Spring, Fall, and Winter; Spring is best
Kingfish	Reef-banks	All year; Spring is best
Tarpon	Inshore	All year; Spring is best

sports: Swimming, snorkeling, scuba, and boating are tops here. It is famous for its beautiful beaches, and all are public by law whether hotels are built on them or not. All of the better-known beaches rent water sports equipment, have locker and shower facilities, and serve food. The water is warm for diving and visibility is good. Deep-sea fishing is excellent for blue marlin as well as for dolphin, sailfish, tuna, wahoo, skipjack, and kingfish. The islands are legendary for boaters because of their sheltered anchorages, fantastic weather, and incomparable beauty. The best spot for surfers is Hull Bay on the N coast of St. Thomas, where the waves are most vicious during the winter months. Windsurfing is also good, with St. Croix being the place for beginners. Specifics on all of the above–from beaches to windsurfing–are detailed under the individual islands in the travel section.

shopping: Shops are open Mon. to Sat. 9 AM-5 PM; they close for official holidays. Hotel shops close at 9 PM. These islands still maintain the minimal Danish import duty of 7%, which has made them into a "duty-free" shopper's paradise. Charlotte Amalie and Christiansted are the two main shopping centers. High overhead and avarice have made these islands less competitive with San Juan and even the mainland, but watches, gold, crystal, and liquor are still relatively good values. There some more unique souvenirs, among them local condiments such as Pineapple Sizzle and Papaya Fire, which are manufactured on St. John, not to mention cheap Cruzan rum, and local artwork and crafts.

American customs: Returning American citizens, under existing customs regulations, can lug back with them up to $1,200 worth of duty-free goods. Items sent by post may be included in this tally, thus allowing shoppers to ship or have shipped goods like glass and china. Over that amount, purchases are dutied at a flat 5% on the next $1,000. Above $2,200, duty applied will vary. Joint declarations are permissible for members of a family traveling together. Thus, a couple traveling with two children will be allowed up to $4,800 in duty free goods. Undeclared gifts (one per day of up to $100 in value) may be sent to as many friends and relatives as you like. Obtain a Customs Form 225 if you've placed a special order. One gallon (or five fifths; six if the sixth is a local product) of liquor may be brought back as well as five cartons of cigarettes and 100 cigars. Pre-1881 antiques, unset gems, and local handicrafts are also duty free. Plants in soil may not be brought to the mainland but most fruits can. For any questions contact the Customs Bureau (tel. 774-2510) or the USDA (tel. 776-2787). **Canadian Customs:** Canadian citizens may make an oral declaration four times per year to claim C$100 worth of exemptions. These may include 200 cigarettes and 40 fl. oz. of alcohol. In order to claim the exemption, Canadians must have been out of the country for at least 48 hours. A Canadian who's been away for at least seven days may make a written declaration once a year and claim C$300 worth of exemptions. After a trip of 48 hours or longer, Canadians receive a special duty rate of 20% on the value of goods up to C$300 in excess of the C$100 or C$300 exemption they claim. This excess cannot be applied to liquor or cigarettes. Goods claimed under the C$300 exemption may follow but merchandise claimed under all other exemptions must be accompanied.

German customs: Residents may bring back 200 cigarettes, 50 cigars, 100 cigarillos, or 250 grams of tobacco; two liters of alcoholic beverages not exceeding 44 proof or one liter of 44 proof-plus alcohol; and two liters of wine; and up to DM300 of other items.

money and measurements: Monetary unit is the US dollar; measurements are the same as those used in the States. The islands operate on Atlantic Standard Time.

broadcasting and media: Local TV, largely consisting of recycled pap from the States, is available for those addicts who positively must watch. Cable, HBO, MTV, and CNN may be available at your hotel on St. Croix or St. Thomas. *The San Juan Star* is available on St. Thomas and St. Croix. Saint Thomas has *The Daily News* (owned by the Gannet Chain), St. John has the weekly *Tradewinds*, while St. Croix has the *Avis*. WIVI (96.1 FM) programs new wave, country music, Grateful Dead, reggae, heavy metal, and classical; it's also available on St. Thomas-St. John cable. Off-island coverage is poor and headlines in the *Daily News* may read "Navarrete soars to top in spelling bee." Mainland newspapers are available but exhorbitant. There are innumerable free publications of various kinds.

visas: All visitors from abroad (except U.S. citizens and Canadians) require a U.S. visa. It's best to obtain a multiple-entry visa and, if possible, do so in your own country, because U.S. embassies and consulates tend to be persnickety about issuing visas to citizens of countries other than the one they're stationed in.

Carnival, Charlotte Amalie

health: Good but expensive medical care is available. But if you have a serious illness, you should fly to Puerto Rico or the mainland. Make sure you have adequate health insurance. Hospitals and clinics are located in or near the island's main towns (see individual sections for listings).

conduct: Many people (especially aliens from the West Indies) do not appreciate having their pictures taken without their permission. There is a great deal of racial tension and animosity (largely found on St. Thomas), so do nothing to make the situation worse. Going shirtless, wearing only a swimsuit, or wearing too short shorts is illegal on streets. Traditional Virgin Islands culture is polite to the extreme, with an emphasis on saving face: to be accused of being "rude" is worse than being called "lazy" or "shiftless," though this has begun to change dramatically in recent years. Inquiries are usually prefaced by a "Good Morning," "Good Afternoon," or "Good Evening." These simple courtesies go a long way. Don't rush an answer either. Locals will answer you at their own pace. On St. Croix remember to respect private property while visiting ruins; be sure to ask permission first. All beaches in the USVI are public by law from the vegetation line down to the water. Expect to be charged ($1-3), however, if you use private facilities like lounge chairs or changing rooms. And remember that you are sharing the beach. Don't litter or make excessive noise.

theft: Saint Thomas and St. Croix have very high crime rates which have been exacerbated by the drug (chiefly crack) problem. Getting mugged on these islands (St. Thomas in particular) is a very real possibility, so exercise caution while walking around the streets at night. It's better to go with someone, especially if you are a woman. Too many cruise ship passengers have caused too much resentment by flashing too much money around. Try to avoid this and keep valuables safely locked up—or, better yet, leave them at home! It isn't that locals are dishonest or try to help criminals. There are a lot of convenient alleyways for thieves to run to; police are insufficient in number and they have a very real fear of recrimination. In fact, it's not unlikely that the thief has a relative on the police force. It would be advisable, if you're going out for dinner on the island of St. Thomas, to travel by cab and make an appointment for the driver to pick you up afterwards. Avoid the waterfront between town and the St. Thomas marina—especially the area around the housing projects. If camping on St. John, don't leave

On the Johnny Horn Trail, St. John

valuables in your tent. Never, never leave anything in an unoccupied vehicle.

environmental conduct: Dispose of plastics properly. Remember that six pack rings, plastic bags, and fishing lines can cause injury or prove fatal to sea turtles, fish, birds, and other marine life. Unable to regurgitate anything they swallow, turtles and other sea creatures may mistake plastic bags for jellyfish or choke on fishing lines. Birds may starve to death after becoming entangled in lines, nets, and plastic rings. And all of these objects take hundreds of years to decompose and can do a lot of damage in the interim. If you should see someone capturing or harming a sea turtle or taking eggs contact the Bureau of Environmental Enforcement (774-3320, St. Thomas; 773-5774, St. Croix) or the National Marine Fisheries Law Enforcement Division (tel. 774-5226). All of these activities are illegal. Remember that the parks and reserves were created to preserve the environment and refrain from carrying off plants, rocks, animals, or other materials. Buying black coral jewelry also serves to support reef destruction and turtle shell items come from an endangered species. On St. John remember not to feed the donkeys or to leave food within their reach. **undersea conduct:** Respect the natural environment. Take nothing and remember that corals are easily broken. Much damage has already been done to the reef through snorkelers either standing on coral or hanging onto outcroppings. As stony corals grow at the rate of less than half an inch per year, it can take decades to repair the desecration caused by a few minutes of carelessness. It's wise to keep well away just for your own protection: many corals will retaliate with stings and the sharp ridges can cause cuts that are slow to heal. In order to control your movement under water, make sure that you are properly weighted prior to your dive. Swim calmly and fluidly through the water and avoid dragging your console and/or octopus (secondary breathing device) behind you. While diving or snorkeling resist the temptation to touch fish. Many fish (such as the porcupine) secrete a mucous coating which protects them from bacterial infection. Touching them removes the coating and may result in infection and death for the fish. Also avoid feeding fish, which can disrupt the natural ecosystem. In short, look, listen, enjoy, but leave only bubbles.

boating conduct: In addition to the behavior patterns detailed above, always exercise caution while anchoring a boat. The single most serious threat to the marine resources of the VI comes from cruise ship anchors. Improperly anchoring in seagrass beds can destroy wide swathes of the grass, which takes a long time to recover. If there's no buoy available, the best place to anchor is a sandy spot, where you will cause relatively little environmental impact. Tying your boat to mangroves can kill the trees, so you should do so only during a storm. In order to help eliminate the unecessary discharge of oil, maintain the engine and keep the bilge clean. If you notice oil in your bilge, use oil-absorbent pads to soak it up. Be careful not to overfill the boat when fueling. Emulsions from petrochemical products stick to fishes' gills and suffocate them, and deposits in sediment impede the development of marine life. Detergents affect plankton and other organisms, which throws off the food chain balance. When you approach seagrass beds, slow down because your propellor could strike a sea turtle. Avoid maneuvering your boat too close to coral reefs. Striking the reef can damage both your boat and the reef. Avoid stirring up sand in shallow coral areas. The sand can be deposited in the coral and cause polyps to suffocate and die. If your boat has a sewage holding tank, empty it only at properly equipped marinas. Avoid using harsh chemicals such as ammonia and bleach while cleaning your boat; they pollute the water and kill marine life. Use environmentally safe cleaning products whenever possible. Boat owners should avoid paint containing lead, copper (which can make molluscs poisonous), mercury (highly toxic to fish and algae), or TBT. Finally, remember that a diver-down flag must be displayed while diving or snorkeling.

Virgin Islands Dos and Don'ts

- Don't condescend to locals. Do treat the local people as you would like to be treated yourself. Allow them the courtesy of answering at their own pace. Do try local food.

- Don't just stay lounging around your hotel. Do get around and explore. Don't overextend yourself and try to do too much.

- Don't dump your garbage at sea or litter in town. Do protect the environment and set a good example for others.

- Don't remove or injure any coral, spear fish, remove tropical fish, or annoy turtles or touch their eggs. Do not feed fish.

getting married: It is a simple matter to marry here. Simply pick up the relevant papers from any USVI Division of Tourism office, mail them around three weeks prior to your trip, and pick up a license from the Territorial Court.

what to take: Bring as little as possible, i.e., bring what you need. It's easy just to wash clothes in the sink and thus save lugging around a week's laundry. Remember, simple is best. Set your priorities according to your needs. If you're planning to do a lot of hiking, for example, hiking boots are a good idea. Otherwise, they're an encumbrance and tennis shoes will suffice. With a light pack or bag, you can breeze through from one hotel to another easily. Confining yourself to carry-on luggage also saves waiting at the airport. See the chart for suggestions and eliminate unnecessary items.

photography: Film isn't particularly cheap here so you might want to bring your own. Kodachrome KR 36, ASA 64, is the best all around slide film. For prints, 100 or 200 ASA is preferred, while 1000 ASA is just the thing underwater. For underwater shots use a polarizing filter to cut down on glare; a flash should be used in deep water. Avoid photographs between 10 and 2 when there are harsh shadows. Photograph landscapes while keeping the sun to your rear. Set your camera a stop or a stop and a half down when photographing beaches in order to prevent overexposure from glare. A sunshade is a useful addition. Keep your camera and film out of the heat. Replace your batteries before a trip or bring a spare set. Finally, remember not to expose your fast speed exposed film to the X-ray machines at the airport. Hand carry them through.

Services and Information

Mail service is not the most reliable in the world. In fact 6,000 advertising circulars, magazines, and packages arrived in Puerto Rico on Nov. 5, 1985 from Jacksonville, Florida via the Commonwealth's shipping line. Trailer Marine Transport, which was supposed to transport them to St. Thomas, forgot completely about them for the next 2 1/2 years. They were finally delivered in March of 1988! Things are improving however.

Zip codes for St. Thomas are: 00802 (Charlotte Amalie street addresses), 00801 (Sugar Estate, Boxes 7001-12440), 00803 (Veteran's Drive, Boxes 1701-5686), and Emancipation Garden Station

(00804, Boxes 0001-1694, 6001-6880). For St. John: Boxes 0001-8310 are 00831, and Cruz Bay street addresses use 00830. For St. Croix: 00821 (Christiansted, Boxes 0001-1786), 00822 (Downtown Station, Christiansted, Boxes 2501-4622), 00823 (Sunny Isle, Christiansted, Boxes 4951-8710), 00824 (Gallows Bay Station, Christiansted, Boxes 24001-16610), 00851 (Kingshill, Boxes 0001-3032), 00841 (Fredericksted, Boxes 0001-3569), 00820 (Christiansted street addresses), 00810 (Frederiksted street addresses), and 00851 (Kingshill street addresses).

phone service: VITELCO, the local phone company, is notorious for its bad service and high basic service charges ($26/month). It costs 25 cents to call any of the three islands via pay phone for five minutes; no warning will sound so keep a check on your watch if you don't want to be cut off in mid-sentence. Area code for the islands–as well as Puerto Rico and the BVI–is 809. As bad as VITELCO is, WAPA (the Water and Power Authority) is worse. For information about local events, be sure to pick up current copies of *St. Thomas This Week* and its St. Croix equivalent. There are a seemingly unlimited number of other publications, most of which are chock to the brim with advertisements.

organizations: If you've been impressed with the natural beauty of places like Salt River and Jacks Bay on St. Croix and wish to keep them that way, you may want to contribute to the **St. Croix Environmental Association**, Box 3839, Christiansted, St. Croix, USVI 00822. Student membership is $10, individual $25, and family $40. Membership ($15 individual, $25 family) in the **Friends of Virgin Islands National Park** offers you a chance to directly participate in the preservation of this fantastic area. Write Box 8317, Cruz Bay, USVI 00831. **The Nature Conservancy**'s program in the USVI aims to protect high quality lands and waters as well as biodiversity and to establish cooperative conservation, stewardship and science programs with federal and territorial governments. For more information and to contribute ($25 for membership) contact Carol Harris Mayes, Program Director, The Nature Conservancy, 14B Norre Gade, Upstairs, Charlotte Amalie USVI 00802. Another worthy organization to support is the **St. John Community Foundation** (Box 1020, St. John 00830) which has put together a 13-month 1994 environmental calendar. **The Virgin Islands Audubon Society** can be reached at Box 67, Cruz Bay, St. John 00830. To become a tax deductible member of the **St. George Village Botanical**

Garden of St. Croix (tel. 772-3872) send $25 to Box 3011, Kingshill, St. Croix 00851-3011. If you're concerned about the state of coral reefs worldwide, contact **Coral Forest** (tel. 415-291-9877), 300 Broadway, Ste. 39, SF, CA 94133. **Earthwatch** (tel. 617-926-8200) sends paying volunteers out to assist researchers working in the field. Costs are tax deductible, except for airfare. Write 680 Mt. Auburn St., Box 430-P, Watertown MA 02272 or call 1-800-776-0188.

activism: Whether you're a visitor or a resident, it is important to make known your concerns on social or environmental issues. Be sure to state your opinion clearly, include examples and key information, and include a return address. Write Governor Alexander Farrelly, Government House, St. Thomas 00801; The Honorable Ron DeLugo, US Representative to Congress, US House of Representatives, Washington, DC 20515. Letters to senators should be sent to The Honorable (name), VI Legislature Building, St. Thomas 00801.

USVI Tourism Offices

In the US, you can call the Tourist Board at 1-800-USVI-INFO. Honeymooners should be sure to ask for the current Honeymoon guide.

Atlanta: 225 Peachtree St., N.E., Suite 760, Atlanta GA 30303, 404-688-0909, Fax 525-1102.

Chicago: 122 S. Michigan Ave., Suite 1270, Chicago IL 60603, 312-461-0180, Fax 461-0765.

Los Angeles: 3460 Wilshire Blvd., Suite 412, Los Angeles CA 90010, 213-739-0138, Fax 739-2005.

Miami: 2655 Le Jeune Rd., Suite 907, Coral Gables FL 33134, 305-442-7200, Fax 445-9044.

New York: 1270 Ave. of the Americas, Suite 2108, New York NY 10020, 212-332-2222, Fax 332-2223.

Washington DC: 900 17th St. N.W., Suite 500, Washington DC 20006, 202-293-3707, Fax 785-2542.

San Juan: 1300 Ashford Ave., Condado, Santurce, Puerto Rico 00907, 809-724-3816, Fax 724-7223.

St. Croix: PO Box 4538, Christiansted, US Virgin Islands 00822, 809-773-0495, Fax 778-9259.

Frederiksted, Custom House Bldg., Strand St., US Virgin Islands 00840, 809-772-0357.

St. John: PO Box 200, Cruz Bay, US Virgin Islands 00830, 809-776-6450.

St. Thomas: PO Box 6400, Charlotte Amalie, US Virgin Islands 00804, 809-774-8784, Fax 774-4390.

Canada: 33 Niagara St., Toronto M5V 1C2, 416-362-8784 or 800-465-8784, Fax 362-9841.

England: 2 Cinnamon Row, Plantation Wharf, York Place, London, SW11 3TW; 071-978-5262, Fax 924-3171.

Germany: Postfach 10 02 44, D-6050, Offenbach; 069-892008, Fax 898892.

Italy: Via Gerardini 2, 20145 Milano; 02-33105841, Fax 33105827.

Japan: Discover America Marketing, Inc., Suite B234B, Hibiya Kokusai Bldg. 2-3, Uchisaiwaicho 2-chome, Chiyodaku, Tokyo 100; 3-3597-9451, Fax 3-3597-0385.

St. Thomas

Most populous and popular of all the United States Virgin Islands, St. Thomas measures three by 13 miles and is the self-styled "American Paradise" (to quote their license plates). It hosts one million tourists a year but only around 49,000 souls are permanent residents. Flanked by the Atlantic to the N and the Caribbean to the S, the land is hilly and rugged. Hills, running up to 1,500 ft., give incredible views. The main town here is Charlotte Amalie (pronounced Ah-MAHL-ya). Although commercialized, the island still retains substantial charm. If at times it seems overbearing, just remember that throughout its history St. Thomas has always been a place where money and property have come before human beings.

topography: This 33-sq-mi. island has been largely denuded; no primary forest remains. The visitor will find steep roads and, in Charlotte Amalie, innumerable staircases.

history: Arriving in 1666, the first Danish settlers found an abandoned island. To guard the harbor, Ft. Christian was constructed in 1674. First known as "Tap Hus," in 1691 the town was renamed Amalienborg (later Charlotte Amalie) after the Danish queen. In 1755, after the dissolution of the Danish West India Company and purchase by the Danish government, the capital was transferred to Christiansted, St. Croix. A series of fires between 1804 and 1832 destroyed two-thirds of the town before a strict building code was enacted. In 1837 a Lutheran Church census discovered at least 140 nationalities on St. Thomas. Most residents spoke two or more languages; church services were given in three languages and newspapers were printed in several. During this period, Charlotte Amalie was the third largest city in the Danish realm. After the emancipation of slaves in 1848, the island was transformed from an agricultural community into a supply depot for blockade runners and privateers from the South, as well as the US men of war that chased them. Capital status was restored to Charlotte Amalie in 1871. During the last quarter of the 19th C, St. Thomas became a coaling depot for European steamship companies. When the US Navy took possession of the island in 1917, they dredged a large channel between St. Thomas and neighboring Hassel I. to allow them an alternate escape route in case of attack. Since the end of WW II, tourism has become the chief "industry" of St. Thomas.

Island-Wide Practicalities

Arrival and Transport

arriving by air: From San Juan a beautiful flight takes you past Icacos, flying directly over Culebra with Vieques in the background. Houses on St. Thomas look like white dots on a patch of green moss. The aircraft main terminal, to the W of Charlotte Amalie, belongs to the cement box school of architecture. A branch of the Chase Manhattan Bank is open Mon. to Thurs. 9-1, Fri. 9-2. The **tourist information kiosk** is open daily 9-7. The Hotel Association also maintains a counter.

From the airport to town, a van will cost you $4.50, or $4 pp if you share, plus 50¢ per bag. For rates to other destinations see the chart later in this chapter. To take the bus, turn R at the gate and wait for the VITRAN (around $1; exact change, check for current rates) operating every 20 min. from 6:07 AM to 8:30 PM It passes through Frenchtown, then through downtown Charlotte Amalie. If proceeding directly to St. John, you can take the ferries from Charlotte Amalie to Cruz Bay or Caneel Bay or take a bus or taxi to Red Hook and then the ferry on to St. John.

St. Thomas Taxi Fares

The first rate shown in each column is for one passenger. In parentheses is the rate per passenger if more than one are travelling to the same destination.

	Town	Airport
Airport Terminal	4.50 (4.00)	
Al Cohen Plaza	2.50 (2.50)	4.50 (4.00)
Amer. Yacht Harbor	9.00 (5.00)	10.00 (5.50)
Anchorage	11.00 (6.50)	12.00 (6.50)
Baci's Restaurant	6.00 (4.50)	7.50 (5.00)
Barnacle Bill's	3.00 (3.00)	3.00 (3.00)
Bavarian Restaurant	4.00 (3.00)	5.00 (4.00)
Blackbeard's Hill	2.50 (2.50)	5.00 (3.50)
Bluebeard's Castle	2.50 (2.50)	5.00 (3.50)
Brewer's Bay	4.00 (3.50)	3.00 (2.50)
Cabrita Point	13.00 (8.50)	14.00 (8.50)
Caribbean Mini Golf	6.50 (3.50)	7.50 (4.50)
Club Z	5.00 (4.00)	4.50 (3.50)
Coral World	7.50 (5.00)	8.50 (6.00)
Coki Beach	7.50 (5.00)	8.50 (6.50)
Compass Point	6.00 (4.50)	7.50 (5.00)
Cowpet Bay Village	11.00 (6.50)	12.00 (6.50)
Crown Bay Dock	3.00 (3.00)	3.00 (3.00)
Drake's Seat	4.50 (3.00)	6.50 (4.00)
Emerald Beach Hotel	4.00 (3.50)	2.00 (2.00)
Eunice's Terrace Restaurant		
Crown Bay	3.00 (3.00)	3.00 (3.00)
Smith Bay	6.50 (3.50)	7.50 (4.50)
Ferrari's Restaurant	7.50 (4.00)	9.00 (5.00)
Fiddle Leaf Restaurant	2.50 (2.50)	2.50 (2.50)
Fort Mylner Shopping	4.50 (3.00)	6.00 (4.00)
Frenchman's Reef	6.00 (4.00)	7.50 (4.50)
Frenchtown	2.00 (2.00)	4.00 (4.00)
Grand Palazzo	11.00 (6.50)	12.00 (6.50)
Havensight Mall	3.50 (2.50)	4.50 (4.00)
Hull Bay Beach	7.50 (4.50)	9.00 (5.00)
Island Beachcomber	4.00 (3.50)	2.00 (2.00)
Island View	5.00 (4.00)	5.00 (4.00)
JP's Restaurant	5.00 (4.00)	4.50 (3.50)
Lagoon Fishing Center	6.00 (4.50)	7.50 (5.00)
Lindbergh Bay	4.00 (3.50)	2.00 (2.00)
Mafolie Hotel	4.50 (3.00)	6.50 (4.00)
Magens Bay	6.50 (4.00)	8.00 (5.00)
Magens Point Resort	6.00 (3.50)	8.00 (5.00)
Mahogany Run	7.00 (4.50)	8.50 (6.00)
Morningstar Beach	6.00 (4.00)	7.50 (4.50)
Mountain Top	7.00 (4.50)	8.00 (5.00)
National Park Dock	9.00 (5.50)	10.00 (6.00)
Nelson Mandela Circle	2.50 (2.50)	4.50 (4.00)

Paradise Point	6.00 (4.00)	7.50 (4.50)
Pavilions and Pools	8.50 (5.50)	10.00 (6.00)
Point Pleasant	7.50 (5.00)	9.00 (6.00)
Ramada Yacht Haven	2.50 (2.50)	4.50 (4.00)
Red Hook	9.00 (5.50)	10.00 (6.00)
Reichhold Center	4.00 (3.50)	3.00 (2.50)
Sapphire Resort	8.50 (5.50)	10.00 (6.00)
Secret Harbour	8.50 (4.50)	10.00 (6.00)
Stouffer Grand Beach Resort	7.50 (5.00)	9.00 (6.00)
Sub Base	3.00 (3.00)	3.00 (3.00)
Sugar Bay Plantation	8.50 (5.50)	10.00 (6.00)
Tillett Galleries	5.50 (4.00)	6.50 (4.50)
University of the VI	4.00 (3.50)	3.00 (2.50)
Vessup Bay	9.00 (5.50)	10.00 (6.00)
Water Isle Dock	3.00 (3.00)	3.00 (3.00)
Watergate Villas	7.00 (4.50)	8.00 (5.00)
West Indian Co. Dock	2.50 (2.50)	4.50 (4.00)
Wheatley Shopping Plaza	2.50 (2.50)	4.50 (4.00)
Windward Hotel	2.50 (2.50)	4.50 (4.00)
Woolworth's	2.50 (2.50)	4.50 (4.00)

arriving on a cruise: There are two cruise ship piers. If your ship arrives while a few others are docked, you may be shuttled in by small boat. If arriving at the West India dock, it's best to take the taxi shuttle into town. From the Crown Bay pier, you'll have to walk along the hot and heavily-trafficked main road so you may wish to take a taxi.

getting around: The only local bus service, VITRAN (tel. 774-5678 or 776-4844, ext. 108) runs to the airport, Red Hook, and Bordeaux (five times daily). The half-hour airport route extends from St. Thomas Hospital down Long Bay Rd. past Nelson Mandela Circle, down Veteran's Drive past Frenchtown, the Nisky Shopping Center, and on to the Airport. Buses leave the Market Place for Red Hook ($3) hourly from 8:15 to 5:15 and return from 7:15 to 5:15. Country Buses ($1) run by VITRAN also travel every half-hour but don't travel anywhere visitors will want to go. Admiral's Inn (tel. 774-1378) rents bicycles for $15/day; deposit required. **ferries:** A harbor shuttle (the *Reefer*, tel. 776-8500, ext. 145) operates between the vicinity of Charlotte Amalie waterfront's Yacht Haven Marina (near the Coast Guard dock) and Frenchman's Reef Hotel. It takes 15 min., the fare is $3, and it runs every half-hour (hourly on Sat.) except Sun., from 8:30 to 5. It also stops each way at Hassel Island. Ferries ($3.50) run to Water Island from Crown Bay Marina (Sub Base) at 7, 8, 11, 12, 2, 4, 5, and 6 from Mon. to Sat.; 8, noon, and 5 on Sun; and additional ferries run at 9 and 10 PM on Tues., Fri., and

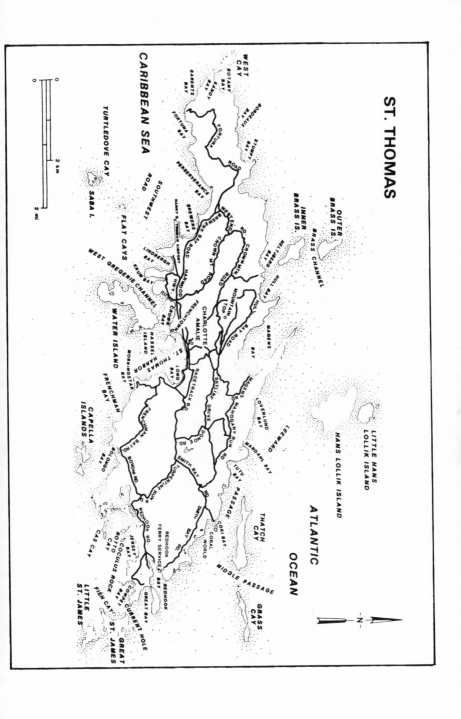

ST. THOMAS

St. Thomas Taxi Services

Antilles Taxis	774-3414
East End	775-6974
Four Winds	775-2800
Independent Taxi	776-1006
Islander Taxi	774-4077
VI Taxi Radio Dispatch	774-7457
VI Taxi Association	774-4550
24-Hour Radio Dispatch Taxi Service	776-0496
Wheatley Taxi Service & Tours	775-1956

Sat. evenings. **taxi service:** Other island destinations are reachable only via expensive shared meterless taxis. (Recent prices are included in chart). Suitcases are 50¢ each; 15¢ is charged per min. of waiting time after the first 10 min.; RT fares are double plus additional for waiting time; between midnight and 6 AM there is an extra charge of $1.50 for out-of-town fares, and a $2 minimum applies in town. For complaints call Mr. Douglas Williams, the Taxi Commission's Director, at 776-8294 from Mon. to Fri, 8-5. Be sure to have the offending taxi's license plate number. **other:** Hitching is possible, but locals are not as accommodating as their St. Johnian neighbors. Numerous guided tours (including helicopter tours) are also available and many are listed later in the text. Taxis offer a two hour sightseeing tour for $30 for two passengers; additional passengers are $12 each. **Atlantis Submarines** (776-5650) offers dives departing from Havensight Mall (see below). **renting a car:** Jeeps, cars ($35-75 per day, unlimited mileage) can be rented on a daily or weekly basis. Agencies include: **ABC** (tel. 776-1222), **Ace** (tel. 776-1628), **Anchorage** (tel. 775-6255), **Antilles** (tel. 773-2411), **Aristocrat** (tel. 776-0026), **Avis** (tel. 800-331-1212, 774-1468, 774-4616), **Budget** (five locations; tel. 800-626-4516, 776-5774, 774-5774), **CM** (tel. 776-7100), **Caribbean AMC Jeep** (tel. 776-7811), **Cowpet** (775-7376), **Dependable** (tel. 774-2523), **Discount** (776-4858), **Dollar** (tel 776-0850), **Econo** (tel. 775-6763), **Fun** (tel. 774-5733), **Hertz** (tel. 800-654-0700, 774-1819, 774-0841, 774-1879, 774-0841), **Holiday Jeep** (tel. 776-2848), **National** (tel. 776-2557), **Paradise** (tel. 776-5335), **Real Deal** (tel. 776-7100), **Sea Breeze Discount** (tel. 774-7200), **Sun Island** (tel. 774-3333), **Think Left** (tel. 774-9652, 776-5569), **Thrifty** (tel. 776-3500, 776-2500), **Tradewinds** (tel. 775-6262), **VI Auto Rental** (tel. 776-3616), and **Zenith** (tel. 776-2095). **driving:** Gasoline runs around $1.50/gal. Park in town in the municipal parking lot to the E of the fort which is 50¢/hr., $4 pd; evenings, weekends, and holidays are free. Illegally parked vehicles can be ticketed ($25). Expect late afternoon traffic jams in town. (St. Thomas could be the first island in the Caribbean to experience gridlock!) Unless otherwise noted, speed limits are 20 mph in town and 30 mph everywhere else. Narrow roads race up and down hillsides; one of the best views to be had is from Rte. 30 just above Havensight.

Hotel 1829 1-800-555

St. Thomas Accommodations *1212*

Sky-high for what you get, especially in season. The demand for rooms is just tremendous so there are no deals! Hotel owners will tell you that their costs (especially water) are so high that "I even charge my relatives." Those on a low budget would be better off avoiding this island and pitching a tent in the campsite at Cinnamon Bay. Guesthouses are the next least expensive alternative. **rental agents: Leisure Enterprises** (tel. 775-9203, 800-843-3566; Box 11192, St. Thomas 00801) offers a variety of luxury accommodations including homes, condos, hotels, and special wedding and honeymoon packages. **Moran Rentals** (tel. 774-0933; Box 936, St. Thomas 00804) offers short- and long-term rentals of cottages, condos, private homes, and hotel rooms. **McLaughlin Anderson Vacations, Ltd.** (tel. 776-635, 800-537-6246, fax 777-4737; 100 Blackbeard's Hill, St. Thomas 00802) is another agency. **note:** All street and route mailing addresses should be completed with 00802.

Charlotte Amalie Accommodations

guest houses and small hotels: An intimate guesthouse is the 13-rm. **Danish Chalet Inn** (tel. 774-5764, 800-635-1531, fax 809-777-4886; Box 4139, St. Thomas, USVI 00803). Most roooms have a/c. Commanding a fantastic view of the harbor from its breezy balcony, the Danish Chalet is an example of a guesthouse whose personality mirrors its owners. Ex-Californians Frank and Mary Davis fell in love with St. Thomas years ago while sailing in the VI. Set in the heart of a St. Thomian neighborhood, it's a short but steep walk from the marketplace and Main St. A complimentary Continental Breakfast (cinnamon flavored coffee, orange juice, and Danish) is served. There's also a $1-for-everything mix-your-own-drink honor bar, an open air Jacuzzi, and a sun deck. Frank and Mary are gracious hosts and will do everything they can to make your stay comfortable. The minimum stay here is only one night (which makes it popular with cruise-ship passengers beginning or ending their trip and with sailors who need a place to overnight before heading on to Tortola). Rates start at $60 s or d and peak at $75-$85 w/bath. Breakfast is included. **Miller Manor** (tel. 774-1535; Box 1570, St. Thomas 00804) is another guest house nearby which features similarly personalized service. Run by transplanted New Yorker/San Franciscan Diane Goh, eight-rm. **Heritage Manor** (tel. 774-3003; 800-828-0507; Box 90) is a restored early 19th-C building which has a pool, sundeck, and honor bar. The a/c rooms (named London, Paris, Rome, and so on) have ceiling fans and brass beds. During the winter season, breakfast is included. Intimate five-room and one-suite **Calico Jack's Courtyard Inne** (tel. 774-7555) is at 5 Garden St. near the PO. It includes a restaurant. Rates are from $65 s or d. A small locally-run establishment, **Midtown Guest House** (tel. 774-6677, 776-9157, 424-9159, fax 776-8253; 1B Commandant Gade) is near Emancipation Gardens. Rooms have TVs and phones. Rates start at $52 s, $61 d. The 15-room **Bunker Hill Hotel** (tel. 774-8056), up the street at 9 Commandant Gade, has pool, TV, phones, and a/c; its rooms run from $59 on up to a high of $90. A full breakfast is included in its rates. Originally built by a French sea captain for his bride, **Hotel 1829** (tel. 776-1829, 800-524-2002, fax 776-4313; Box 1567, St. Thomas 00804) is a National Historic Site. The a/c rooms have bar, phone, and cable TV. A restaurant and bar is open for lunch and dinner, and there's a small pool. Rates start at $50 s and $60 d for the moderate rooms. Superior, deluxe, suite, and penthouse suite accommodations are also available. On Kronsprindsens Gade, **Le Petit Motel** (tel. 775-2310) offers 12 a/c rooms with TV and free parking. Write Box 1701, St. Thomas 00803. Set next to the watchtower of the same name, the 20-rm. **Blackbeard's Castle** (tel. 776-1234, fax 776-4321, 800-344-5771; Box 6041, St. Thomas 00804) has a pool and gourmet restaurant. Rooms have cable TV, ceiling fans, and a/c. Complimentary breakfast as offered at the gourmet restaurant, and there's a large pool. Rates start at $95 s or d for a standard room and rise to $190 for an apartment suite during the winter season. A 10% service charge is added. Set on Blackbeard's Hill, **The Mark St. Thomas** (tel. 774-5511) has a pool and restaurant. Rooms start at $90 off-season.

near town: At 4 Raphune Hill, **Villa Blanca** (tel. 776-9059, fax 779-2661; Box 7505, St. Thomas 00801) has great views from private balconies, TV, kitchenette, a/c and fan, and also a pool. Rates are available upon request. Anna and Hal Borns' **Villa Fairview Hotel** at 8 Catherineberg (tel. 775-4795, fax 774-8010, 800-544-0493) overlooks the town. All three types of rooms (standard, ocean view, and the ocean view suite) have phones, ceiling fan, refrigerator, clock radio, cassette stereo, louvered windows, and high ceilings. A complimentary shuttle to nearby Magens Bay Beach is provided, as is breakfast. There's a garden and pool on the premises. Rooms start from $60 for s or d. Top range is the ocean view suite (great for honeymooners), which rents for $100 during the winter season. **The Kyalami Guest House** (tel. 774-2153), 27 Elizabeth, offers five rooms from around $115 with a continental breakfast. The housekeeper will cook meals upon demand, or you can use the kitchen. Run by Donna and John Slone, serene **Galleon House** (tel. 774-6952; fax 774-6952; 800-524-2052; Box 6577) is centrally located. Breakfast is included and ranges from coconut muffins to waffles and bananas to French toast with sliced peaches. You'll have to stay two weeks for a repeat. Amenities here include pool, sun deck, complimentary snorkeling equipment, entertainment by player piano during the evenings, cable TV/HBO, phones in rooms, and a choice of fans or a/c. Rates run from around $49 s, $59 d during the off season to $10 add'l per room during the peak season. The best rooms are $79 off season as opposed to $119 during the winter months. Located to the N of town in the hills, 15-room **Island View Guest House** (774-4270, 800-524-2023, fax 774-6167; Box 1903, St. Thomas 00803) offers rooms with fans (optional a/c in deluxe rooms), and twin, queen, and king beds. An efficiency and a two-bedroom efficiency is also available. Facilities include TV, fax machine, laundromat, pool, and complimentary breakfast. Room rates (not including 15% service charge) start at $40 s or $45 d with shared bath, $50 s and $55 d for private bath. Set 800 ft. above town, **Mafolie Hotel** (tel. 774-2790, 800-255-7035; Box 1506, St. Thomas 00804) offers complimentary continental breakfast, RT transport to Magens Bay Beach, pool with deck, and a restaurant. Prices range from $56 s, $64 d. Sleeping four, the mini suites ($90) have cable TVs and refrigerators. A 15 min. walk to town, **Admiral's Inn** (tel. 774-1376, 774-8010, 800-544-0493; Box 6162, St. Thomas 00803-6162) offers 16 a/c rooms with color cable TVs and verandas or balconies. There's also a pool, two restaurants (complimentary breakfast is served), and tours. Rates start from $79 s or d.

larger hotels: Right on the waterfront, **Windward Passage** (tel. 774-5200; 800-524-7389; Box 640, St. Thomas 00804) has 139 rooms and 11 suites. Facilities include a/c, cable TVs, balconies, and phones. Multi-beach shuttle service and buffet breakfast are included in the rates. Rates start at $90 s, $100 d for a standard room and increase to $160 s and $180 d. Winter season rates are higher. In Puerto Rico call 800-595-9512. The 170-room **Bluebeard's Castle** (tel. 774-1600, fax 774-5134, 800-524-6599/223-0888; Box 7480, St. Thomas 00801) is set next to a tower constructed in 1679 by Carl Baggart as a lookout to protect the town from attack. Rooms are equipped with refrigerators, cable TVs, and a/c or fans. There are two restaurants with nightly entertainment and dancing, a waterfall-fed pool, tennis, and a fitness center. There's also an executive conference center and banquet facilities. Prices start at $140 s or d for standard rooms. **Ramada Yacht Haven Hotel** (tel. 774-9700, 800-2-RAMADA; Box 7970, St. Thomas 00801) has 151 rooms featuring a/c, radio, cable TV, and VCR; there are two pools, watersports, two restaurants, and complimentary beach shuttle. Rates range from $80 off-season with a winter high of around $160.

Accommodations East of Charlotte Amalie

Marriott Resorts: The island's two Marriott Resorts, **Frenchman's Reef** and **Morningstar Beach** (tel. 776-8500; 800-524-2000, Box 7100, St. Thomas 00801), are interlinked. Facilities include five restaurants and three lounges, tennis, two pools, Jacuzzi, shops, exercise room, unisex salon, and the USVI's largest conference center. All told there are 525 rooms and suites, including 96 at the more expensive Morning Star. All offer a/c, cable TV, phone, and mini-bar. A full range of water sports including scuba and deep-sea fishing are available. The resorts are connected to town by *The Reefer* ferry. Rates vary tremendously depending on the season, whether they are all-inclusive, and the number of people involved. Least expensive ($200 pp) is for three nights in a triple during the off-season for the "Sun, Sand, and Free," program which includes some amenities (such as a sunset cruise) but not meals. Top price is $2,154 for a five-night "No Nonsense All-Inclusive Vacation" at the Morningstar. Wedding (call 800-FOR-LOVE) and honeymoon packages are availabile, as is a "Caribbean Diving Adventures" package.

The Bolongo Beach Resorts (Club Everything): These are three distinct properties (tel. 779-2844, fax 775-3208, 800-524-4746; #50 Estate Bolongo, St. Thomas 00802) with two different types of all-inclusive rates: "club all-inclusive" (which does not include meals and drinks) and "club everything all-inclusive" (which includes meals, drinks, airport transportation, scuba lesson, shuttle service, watersports, half-day snorkel, full-day yacht trip to St. John, and sunset cocktail cruise). Taken together, the three properties offer three beaches, seven restaurants, and a range of nightly entertainment. A ferry runs between the different properties.

Bolongo Bay Beach & Tennis Club & Villas features 150 rooms and villas (the latter with kitchens; up to six persons), two pools, tennis courts, and diving. It has "Kid's Corner," a babysitting center. The island's only all-inclusive resort, the 84-rm., 24-acre **Bolongo Limetree Resort** has pool and Jacuzzi, clubs, and restaurants. At Cowpet Bay, the **Bolongo Elysian**, the newest of the three, has 180 rooms and suites. It offers all-inclusive and semi-inclusive plans.

Rates vary tremendously but range from a low of $135 s or $145 d for the Bolongo Limetree to a high of $692 for a two-bedroom plus loft at the Elysian during the winter season. The least expensive three-night, four-day all-inclusive package costs $1,125. If staying here, you'll probably want to pick your hotel on the basis of what facility(ies) it has that you will be most likely to use. Some facilities are available only at added cost, unless you have an all-inclusive package. Read the fine print carefully: there's plenty of it! For information on planning a wedding, convention, or honeymoon here call 800-343-4079. In Britain contact Unique

Resorts at tel. (0-453) B35801, telex. 43205 UNIHOT, or fax (0453) B35535.

Watergate Villas: Near Bolongo Bay, Watergate Villas (tel. 524-2038, fax 775-4202, 800-524-2038; PMC, Rte. 6, St. Thomas 00802) has pools, beach bar, snorkeling equipment, and diving. Rates start at $116 for a one- or two-person studio; they rise to a high of $370 (1-6 persons) for a three-bedroom unit. A 10% surcharge is added.

East End St. Thomas Accommodations

Formerly known as Harbour House Villas, hilltop and private **Secret Harbourview Villas** (tel. 775-2600, fax 775-5901, 800-874-7897; Box 8529, St. Thomas 00801) has studio, one- , two- , and three-bedroom units. Each has a kitchen, a/c, phone, TV, balcony, and maid service. On the premises are a Jacuzzi, pool, tennis courts, and workout center. These facilities are shared with Secret Harbour Beach Resort which has 20% higher rates. Rates start at $130/studio and range up to $355/two-bedroom during the peak season. **Secret Harbour Beach Resort** (tel. 775-6550, 800-524-2250) offers the same facilities and has a dive shop, watersports, and a/c full suites with private balconies or terraces. Rates start at $169 for a studio suite for two. Write 6280 Estate Nazareth, St. Thomas 00802. Set near Red Hook, 28-rm **Anchorage Beach Villas** (tel. 524-2038, fax 775-4202, 800-524-2038; PMC, Rte. 6, St. Thomas 00802) has a pool, tennis, snorkeling equipment, and diving. Rates start at around $73 for a two-bedroom a/c villa with a two-person limit; they rise to a high of $370 (1-6 persons) for a three-bedroom unit. A 10% surcharge is added. Also nearby and run by St. Thomas Condos, **Cowpet Bay Village** (tel. 775-6220, fax 775-4202, 800-524-2038; PMC, Rte. 6) has from one- to four-bedroom villas. Prices are similar, but there's no 10% surcharge. Done up in Italian Renaissance style, the 150-suite **Grand Palazzo Hotel** (tel. 775-3333, fax 775-4444, 800-283-8666/637-7200) overlooks St. John. Opened in Aug. 1992, it includes the Palm Terrace Restaurant, four tennis courts, fitness center with aerobic workouts, complimentary watersports, private catamaran, and beach bar. In addition to the landscaped gardens, there's a lagoon where you can birdwatch. Rooms have private balconies, digital safe, minibars, radios, cable TVs, room and bath phones, hair dryers in bathrooms, and climate controls. Rates range from $230-$495 off season. In Britain contact

Morris Kevan International Ltd., International House, 47 Chase Side, Enfield, Middlesex. Call 081 367 5175, fax 081 367 9949 or telex 24457. At Nazareth, **Sea Horse Cottages** (tel. 775-9231, Box 2312, St. Thomas 00803) has a pool, beach, and kitchens. Rates run from $60-$100 off season. Within walking distance of the St. John ferry, **Red Hook Mountain Apartments** (tel. 775-6111; Box 9139, St. Thomas 00801) offers ten condos with studios and one- or two-bedrooms. All have private decks facing the ocean and kitchens. Rates are from $80 s or d. Set near the beach of the same name, **Sapphire Village** (tel. 524-2038, fax 775-4202, 800-524-2038; PMC, Rte. 6, St. Thomas 00802) features studios and one- or two-bedroom a/c villas with kitchen, living/dining room, telephone, cable TV, and maid service. It has a beachside restaurant, pool, tennis, snorkeling equipment, and diving. Rates start at around $116 for a studio. Set on Sapphire Beach, **Sapphire Beach Resort & Marina** (tel. 775-6100, fax 775-4024; Box 8088, St. Thomas 00801) offers private suites and villas in a total of four categories. Rooms have private balconies, kitchens, and satellite TVs. Boardsailing, snorkeling, sunfish sailing, cocktail hour, rum bottle, and children's activity program are complimentary. There are also four tennis courts, a quarter-acre pool, and a 67-slip marina. A variety of wedding packages are available. Rates range for $198 for a beachfront suite to a winter season high of $330 for a "Yacht Harbor View" villa. While suites can accommodate four, villas can hold six, and there is a charge of $25 for each additional person. MAP is $50 pp add'l pd. Children under 12 stay and eat free. Call 800-524-2090. Located on Rte. 6 at 6400 Estate Smith Bay (a mi. W of Red Hook and adjacent to Sapphire Bay) the condo complex **Pavilions and Pools** (tel. 775-6110, 800-524-2001; Rte. 6, St. Thomas 00802) offers a daily shuttle into town. A manager's cocktail party is held each Tues., and a restaurant is open nightly for dinner (except Tues. and Fri.) A preview video is available for $9.95, which will be credited when you check out. There are two types of pavilions–the 1,400-sq.-ft. International and the 1,200-sq.-ft. Caribbean. Both feature a private swimming pool, a/c living and dining area, kitchen, and sunken garden shower. Prices start at $175 for the Caribbean Pavilion. On Sapphire Beach, **Crystal Cove Villas** (tel. 524-2038, fax 775-4202, 800-524-2038; PMC, Rte. 6, St. Thomas 00802) has studios and one- and two-bedroom a/c villas with kitchen, living/dining room, telephone, cable TV, and maid service. The premises have a salt water pool, cable TV, beachside restaurant, and watersports. Prices start from around $173 for a two-bedroom.

Pineapple Village Villas offers garden bedrooms and suites which have phones, cable TV, a/c and fans, plus kitchenettes or kitchens. Call 800-TRI-1-SUN in the US and Canada, 800-992-9232 in the US, and 800-891-762 in the UK. Rates run from $100-$150 off season. **Pineapple Rooms and Villas** (tel. 775-0275) nearby run from $100-$150 off season. The only AAA Four-Diamond resort on the island, **Stouffer Grand Beach** (tel. 775-1510, fax 775-2185, 800-HOTELS-1; Box 8267, St. Thomas 00801) has rooms decorated in cool pastels and rattan and each features a private balcony or patio, cable TV, phones, climate control, and refrigerator/bar. Complimentary coffee comes with your wakeup call. A full range of water sports are available, as is tennis and the nearby Mahogany Run golf course. There's also a pool and a choice of restaurants. Also inside this complex is **Blazing Villas** (tel. 776-0760, fax 776-3603, 800-382-2002), a set of luxury units. Another alternative on the grounds of Stouffers, **Jean's Villas** (tel. 775-7078, 800-874-5326) start at $100 pn and also share its facilities. Located at Estate Smith Bay #4, 15-acre **Point Pleasant Resort** (tel. 775-7200, 800-524-2300, fax 776-5694) has 134 villa-type suites. Each has a/c living and dining areas, balcony, kitchen, and daily maid service. There are hammocks and a beach as well as tennis. Rates include complimentary use of rental car (four hrs. daily), shuttle service to Sapphire Beach, 15 acres of gardens and nature trails, water sports, and tennis. MAP, wedding services ($495 and $750) and "Honeymoon Hideaways" are also available. Rates start at $195 for the superior suites and reach a high of $515 for a two-bedroom suite during the winter season. A Holiday Inn Crowne Plaza Resort, the 300-room **Sugar Bay Plantation Resort** (tel. 777-7100, fax 777-7200, 703-342-4531, 800-338-3033) has three interconnected swimming pools with waterfall, seven tennis courts (including a stadium court), health club, spa, restaurant, nightclub, bars, a ballroom and more than a dozen conference rooms. Following the land contours, the rooms and suites nestle into the hillside. Rates start at $185 s including an ample buffet breakfast.

Northern St. Thomas Accommodations

This area has only a few establishments. Private and with great views, the **Sign of the Griffin** (tel. 775-1715; Box 11668, St. Thomas 00801) is a/c and has kitchens. Rates start at $125 off season. Located on Magens Bay Road, secluded and intimate **Magens Point Resort** (tel. 775-5500, 800-524-2031) has a pool and lighted tennis courts. All other sports are nearby. Within walking distance of the beach which it overlooks, its a/c hotel rooms feature phone, TV, and balcony. Junior and full suites also have queen size sofa bed, living room, and kitchenette. Its restaurant offers Italian and seafood dishes. Dining, golf, and honeymoon packages are offered, and rates start at $100 s or $113 d off season, peaking at $300 for a full suite d during the winter season. A $3 pp pn energy surcharge is added. On Rte. 6, **Tree House Villas** (tel. 524-2038, 800-846-1135, fax 775-4202) sleeps from one to four and has great views. Rates start at $79.

Southeastern St. Thomas Accommodations (Near the Airport)

Set on Lindbergh Beach, the **Island Beachcomber Hotel** (tel. 774-5250, 800-982-9898/742-4276, fax 762-3577; Box 2579 VDA, St. Thomas 00803) offers 48 a/c rooms with refrigerator, phone and cable TV. Use of water rafts, snorkeling gear, and chaise lounges is complimentary. The Garden Restaurant is on the premises. Rates start at $90 s and $95 d for standard rooms. A 10% service charge is added. In the US, write Box 540, Wilton, CT 06897-0540 or fax 203-762-3577. Next door, three-level, four-building 90-rm **Emerald Beach Resort** (tel. 777-8800; fax 800-233-4936, 800-595-9509 in Puerto Rico; Box 340, St. Thomas 00801) has a pool, balconies, marble bath, phone, restaurant, water sports, a/c, in-room safe, and tennis. Superior rooms run from $160 on up. Three-night (four-day) packages including tax run from $699 on up. Seven-night (eight-day) packages are also available. Dive packages are offered in conjunction with Sea Trade Ltd. Farther on to the SW at Estate Fortuna, the **Fortuna Mill Estate** (tel./fax 776-1461) is a four-acre mountaintop estate with a fully renovated 18th C sugar mill. It holds up to six and has fans, a pool, TV, and phone. It rents for around $5,000-$7000 pw. **note:** Accommodation on Water Island is listed under that section.

St. Thomas Dining and Food

You won't go hungry here. Food is generally expensive, especially in the gourmet restaurants. There aren't a whole lot of places where you can eat well for less than $8. Generally, a meal in a local restaurant costs this much. For a relatively complete list of current dining, together with opening hours and credit cards accepted, check the "Weekend" section of Friday's *Daily News*. note: In describing restaurant prices in this section, *inexpensive* refers to places where you can dine for $15 and under including a drink, appetizer, and dessert; you may in fact pay more. *Moderate* means $16-$25; *expensive* is $26-$40, and *very expensive* means over $40 a meal.

vegetarian dining: Set at 36 Kronspindsens behind the Windward Passage, **Rootsie's Ital** (tel. 777-5055) is a tasty Rastafarian takeout. Rootsie cooks all his food in clay pots; dishes are tastefully spiced with local herbs. Bowls of vegetables range in price from $4-8. Otherwise, there isn't much in the way of strictly vegetarian dining in Charlotte Amalie, although it's easy enough to order a salad and some restaurants have vegetarian plates.

inexpensive dining: On the waterfront and right in the town center, the **Green House** (tel. 774-7998) serves three meals per day and features entrees such as mango banana chicken. Set behind the Green House, the **Upper Crust** serves breakfast and lunches with subs, sandwiches, soups, quiches, and vegetarian dishes. On the Waterfront, **Bumpa's** serves breakfast and lunch. In the Windward Passage Hotel along the Waterfront, the **Capital City Grill** has a good value buffet lunch. Down A.H. Riise Alley, inexpensive **Café Amici** (tel. 774-3719) is open for lunch and serves Italian/Continental cuisine with pasta dishes and salads accompanied by fresh baked breads. On Back St. inexpensive **Coconuts** serves American dishes and seafood lunches, and inexpensive **Daddy Lou's** offers pizza and Italian specialties as well as deli and sub sandwiches. In Drake's Passage, inexpensive **Drake's Inn** serves internationally-flavored breakfast and lunch. Inexpensive **Palm Passage Restaurant**, Palm Passage, serves Italian lunches. It also serves expressos, cappucinos, and afogados (vanilla ice cream and expresso) drinks.

At 5 Garden St., **Calico Jack's Courtyard Inne** serves lunch and features American, international, and Caribbean cuisine. Run by Texas transplants, **Panchita's** (tel. 776-8425) offers inexpensive to moderate Tex-Mex cuisine and is in Kronprindsen's Market on the waterfront. Also on the waterfront, the local branch of the inexpensive **Hard Rock Cafe** has a menu which includes vegetarian dishes. On Back St., **Rosie O'Grady's** serves pizza and sandwiches. At Bakery Square and offering Middle Eastern fare, **Sinbad's Garden Restaurant** offers inexpensive breakfasts and lunches. At the base of Bluebeard's at #7 Bjerge Gate, **Truck Stop**

& Auntie Em's Fine Food Emporium serves sandwiches, salads, fish and chips, and other dishes. Set above town on Raphune Hill, the **Bavarian Restaurant and Pub** (tel. 775-3615) serves German and American food with beer and live music from Wed. to Sun. An "all-you-can-eat" salad bar is available at lunch for $5. **That Pizza Shoppe** on the same hill sells pizza, salad, and frozen yogurt. **local food:** Set back from Main St., inexpensive **Gladys' Cafe** (tel. 774-6604) serves a varied breakfast and lunch as well as local specialties such as saltfish and dumplings or conch and fungi. **Cuzzin's Caribbean Restaurant and Bar,** Back St, offers dishes such as conch creole and local drinks set in an a/c 200-year old building. Inexpensive **Percy's Bus Stop**, also on the waterfront, serves West Indian food, as does the **Petite Pump Room** next to Tortola Wharf. Other inexpensive places downtown serving West Indian food include **Laurel Sam**, 19 Commandant Gade; **The Squirrel Cage**, 11B Norre Gade; **Red Snapper**, Back Street; **Diamond Barrel**, 18 Norre Gade; **Ricky's Diner**, 3B Kongens Gade; **Tasha's Place** in Market Square; **Crazy Cow**, 33 Raadets Gade, and **Red Snapper**. At Estate Elizabeth, **Sib's Mountain Bar and Restaurant** serves American and Caribbean cuisine including all-you-can-eat chicken and ribs.

more formal in-town dining: One of the most attractive places to dine, the inexpensive/moderate **Parkside** (tel. 774-1405) is in an elegant and tastefully restored old home at #1 Torvet Straede along Roosevelt Park and serves gourmet Continental fare for lunch and dinner. Offerings include stir fry and "papaya, pineapple, orange, and kiwi salad with mango frappe." Seating about 40 and quite popular, **Virgilio's** (tel. 776-4920), Back Street, is colorful with brick walls and Italian gourmet cuisine. Entrees run from $16 to about $39. Set on Back St. across from Bakery Square in the former Daily News Building (now called A Taste of Italy), expensive **Il Cardinale** offers gourmet food. There's also a deli and a coffeeshop, **I Cappucini**, in the same building. Extremely expensive **Hotel 1829** (tel. 776-1829) offers dishes such as roasted rabbit, Anguillan rock lobster, and soufflé for dessert. On Government Hill and open nightly for dinner, the very expensive **Fiddle Leaf** (tel. 775-2810) serves Caribbean cuisine with a contemporary flavor, including dishes such as spinach and smoked salmon salad, West Indian sauteed shrimp, and papaya and Brie quesadilla. Also on Government Hill, **Zorba's** (tel. 776-0444) offers inexpensive to moderate Greek cuisine. With two locations (one at Red Hook, tel.

775-6124, and the other at Mafolie, tel. 774-2790) moderate to expensive **Frigate** serves fish, steaks, and teriyaki dishes. Moderate to expensive **The Mark** (tel. 774-5511), Blackbeard's Hill, serves international cuisine. Also atop Backbeard's Hill, moderate to expensive **Blackbeard's Castle** (tel. 776-1234), recipient of a Practical Gourmet magazine award for best restaurant on St. Thomas in 1990, serves lunch and dinner and features a variety of imaginative dishes. Offering French and Italian dishes in a romantic, candle lit setting overlooking the harbor, expensive to very expensive **Entre Nous** (tel. 776-4050) at Bluebeard's Castle offers seafood specialties (Norwegian salmon, Maine lobster) and some special low-sodium content items. One of its desserts is flaming baked Alaska. Also at Bluebeard's Castle Hotel, moderate to expensive **Sunset View** serves three meals per day including Continental and Caribbean specialties as well as West Indian buffets. Atop Crown Mountain and serving dinner, **The View** (tel. 774-4270) is in the Island View Guest House. In addition to the splendid view, it offers tuna West Indian, coconut fried shrimp served with fried bananas, and pasta entrees. Conch chowder and shrimp de Jong number among the appetizers.

Frenchtown Dining: In Frenchtown's Villa Olga, the moderate **Chart House** specializes in a 45-item salad bar with soup as well as seafood, meat, and fowl entrees. Meals are served on a covered, open-air terrace overlooking the harbor. The moderate to expensive **Café Normandie** (tel. 774-1622) offers 20 different hors d'oeuvres, fish dishes, meat and fowl, as well as desserts such as chocolate fudge pie. Set in the heart of Frenchtown, **Provence** (tel. 776-5797) has an excellent wine selection and a frequently changing S French menu which includes salmon, lamb, and other dishes. West Indian art adorns the walls. Open air and on the dock in Frenchtown, **Hook, Line, and Sinker** (tel. 776-9708) offers burgers and daily specials. Its best known dishes include bouillabaisse and almond crusted yellowtail. In Gregerie East Channel at 17 Crown Bay, the inexpensive to moderate **Sugar Reef Cafe** (tel. 776-4466, 777-4560) offers seafood and international fare and has good specials. Dishes range from Caribbean lobster bisque soup to linguini to grilled scallops with tomato and garlic. It also offers a complete West Indian menu for $21.50, with a choice of appetizers, entrees, and dessert, plus coffee, tea, or expresso. **Wok on the Water** in Frenchtown serves good Vietnamese, Chinese, and Thai food. Popular with residents year 'round, **Alexander's** (tel. 774-4349) serves German dinners at reasonable rates. Reservations are advised. Its Bar and Grill has burgers, steaks, and the like for lunch and offers breakfasts as well. Behind Alexander's, **Epernay** (tel. 774-5348) offers sushi, appetizers, dessert, and other dishes. Ranging in price from inexpensive to moderate, **Gouchos Hardwood Grill** serves SW US and Mexican food.

Sub Base (Crown Bay Marina)/Contant dining: To the W of town, this is a popular area for dining. At Club Z in a former great house on Contant Hill, **Andiamo Ristorante** (tel. 776-4655) features inexpensive to moderate Italian-American food. Drink specials are available, and Club Z is next door for dancing. Situated a half-mi. up Contant Hill along Rte. 33, **JP's Steak House at the Old Mill** (tel. 776-3004) is constructed around a two-century-old sugar mill and offers steak and seafood dishes as well as nightly specials. A sugar plantation exhibit is on the upper floor. Inexpensive **Chester Chicken**, a West Indian restaurant at Contant, serves three inexpensive meals daily. A Sunday brunch is offered. Casual and open daily from 11-11, inexpensive **Barnacle Bill's** (tel. 774-7444)–at the Crown Bay dock on Rte. 304–serves pizza, sandwiches, and seafood plus other special dinner entrees. Bands (Wed. to Sun.) and an amateur night (Mon.) are also featured. Artists like Steve Forbert have played here. Inexpensive **Pinocchio's Lounge and Restaurant** (tel. 776-9459) serves American and West Indian dishes for breakfast and lunch; the **Shining Star** also serves West Indian lunches. Offering American food, **Trickles Restaurant** (tel. 776-1595) is at Dockside Pub in Crown Bay. Inexpensive to moderate **Pilot House** (tel. 776-1595) serves steak and seafood dinners. **Raffles** is at Crown Bay Marina, as is **Dottie's Front Porch**. With no phone number and all home cooking, it relies upon word of mouth and repeat business. Set in an outdoor garden and both informal and intimate, it serves quiches, great baked goods, and soups; jars of Dottie's chutneys, jams, and vinegars are for sale. It's closed Thurs. At the Sub Base on Rte. 34 near the Crown Bay dock, moderate **L'Escargot** (tel. 774-6565), one of the island's oldest eating establishments, serves lunch and dinner and offers French, American, and Caribbean dishes. In addition to meat dishes, lobster thermidor, red snapper creole, and grouper in herb sauce are served. **Victor's New Hideout** serves West Indian lunches and dinners. Inexpensive **Arian's** (tel. 776-1401) serves three West Indian and American meals daily. **The Gourmet Gallery** in Yacht Haven has sandwiches. In the AQ Building along the Moravian

Hwy., **Kum Wah** (tel. 774-5575) offers Chinese lunches and dinners. Near the airport, the **Island Beachcomber** (tel. 774-4250) serves moderate American and West Indian dishes. In the Emerald Beach Resort nearby, **The Palms** (tel. 777-8800, ext. 5300) has three meals a day. An attractive circular bar and restaurant, its lunch and dinner entrees are Mediterranean influenced and include pizzetas (thin crusted pizza) and bouillabaisse, the house specialty.

Long Bay dining (E from Charlotte Amalie): With American and West Indian dishes, inexpensive **Café Havensight** is in Havensight Mall. At Al Cohen's Mall right across from Havensight Mall and the cruise ship dock, **Patty King** (tel. 776-2704) serves Jamaican-influenced Caribbean food including a catch of the day prepared either in brown stew, Oriental steamed, escovitched (marinated), or in jerk fashion. Seasonal fruit drinks are served, as are patties–crusty meat-filled pastries which are a Jamaican staple. At the Ramada Yacht Haven Marina, **Acacía** (tel. 777-5383) offers Catalan/Spanish cuisine including everything from baby eels to paella to special deserts. Also here, **Castaways** serves moderate dishes including sandwiches, seafood and pasta; the inexpensive **Cream and Crumb Shop** serves pizza, soup, sandwiches, ice cream, and yogurt; the **Delly Deck** has American food; inexpensive to moderate **Ocean City** offers Chinese dishes; **Creperie Bretonne** serves crepes and omelettes; and the **Virgin Oar House** has three inexpensive to moderate American-style meals. Boarding at Ramada Yacht Haven, *Tallship Resolution* (tel. 690-7351), a three-masted schooner constructed in 1926, serves cocktails, hors d'oeuvres, and dinner for $85 pp. There are two sailings per evening, and credit cards are not accepted. In Barbel Plaza **Little Bo Peep** serves West Indian breakfasts and lunches. In Vitraco Park, the **Farmer's Bakery and Restaurant** also has West Indian dishes. In Wheatley Shopping center, **Moghul** (tel. 776-3939) offers Indian and Chinse cuisine.

E of Charlotte Amalie: In Frenchman's Reef (776-8500), moderate to expensive **Caesar's** offers Italian dishes. In the Marriott Frenchman's Reef, the **Top of the Reef** (tel. 776-8500) serves a four-course dinner ($38) in conjunction with a "Calypso Carnival" performance. Its **Oriental Terrace** serves Japanese and "Pacific Rim" a la carte cuisine. Light meals are served at the **Raw Bar** here, and the **Lighthouse** sells food (burgers, BBQ, and the like) from 7-3; **Windows on the Harbour** serves breakfast buffets, seafood buffets, and brunches on Fri. and Sun. At Morningstar Beach, the **Tavern on the Beach** has American food; it's the best restaurant there but also the most expensive. Set atop Watergate Villas on Bolongo Bay, inexpensive to moderate **David's** (tel. 777-3650) serves seafood and daily specials in a casual atmosphere. **Mim's Seaside Bistro** (tel. 775-2081), at Watergate, serves lunch and dinner; all-you-can-eat shrimp is on Thurs. At Bolongo Bay, inexpensive **Coconut Henry's Smokehouse** (tel. 775-1800) has BBQ meat and fowl dishes for lunch and dinner daily; moderate **Lord Rumbottoms** is open for dinner and offers prime ribs and a salad bar. At the Bolongo Limetree (Club Everything), the moderate **Caribbean Lobster House** (tel. 776-4770) serves dinner; it features a raw bar and seafood dishes; inexpensive to moderate **Iggies** here has seafood, pasta, burgers, and steaks.

East End/Red Hook dining: In the lagoon, moderate **Rock Fever Cafe and Wine Bar** (tel. 777-7969) serves Continental lunch and dinner. Featuring Italian cuisine with Tuscan specialties, intimate and moderate **Baci's Ristorante** (tel. 775-2822) at Saga Haven Marina (also on the lagoon on Rte. 32), is open evenings. Named after the puzzles and games set out on its bar and tables, **Puzzles** (tel. 775-9671) is a riverboat piano lounge offering a variety of appetizers and desserts; it's tied up at Saga Haven Marina. A beachside restaurant and bar at Scott Beach near Compass Point on the E side off of Rte. 32, inexpensive to moderate **For the Birds** (tel. 775-6431) offers BBQ, Tex-Mex, steaks, seafood, and 48-oz. margaritas. At Compass Point off of Rte. 32, **Windjammer** (tel. 775-6194) offers seafood and German food including wiener schnitzel, chicken a la Bremen, and meatballs with creamy caper sauce. At Compass Point off of Rte. 32, moderate **Raffles** (tel. 775-6004) serves dinners ranging from Maryland soft shell crabs to marinated two-day duck. At Secret Harbour, **Secret Harbour Beach Cafe** (tel. 775-6550, ext. 191) has fish dishes, sandwiches, and salads; it offers breakfast and lunch as well as a Sun. brunch; **Tamarind by the Sea** here serves seafood, pasta, and meat dishes for dinner nightly. At the Bolongo Elysian, moderate **Viola's Calypso Kitchen** offers West Indian food for lunch and dinner, and the moderate **Palm Court** has Danish-influenced cuisine for lunch and dinner. In the American Yacht Harbor, **The Deli** can fix you up with an inexpensive box lunch or serve you breakfast or a salad. In Red Hook, American-style breakfast and lunch are found at **The Three Virgins**. Doubling as a fish retailer, the **Fish Shack** serves three meals daily.

Locals hang out at the **East Coast Bar and Grill**, with both Caribbean and Continental cuisine; it has a Sun. brunch. The **Piccola Marina Café-Bar** (tel. 775-6350) is on the waterfront at Red Hook. It has salads, homemade pasta dishes, and meat dishes. Also at Red Hook, moderate to expensive **Frigate Restaurant** (tel. 775-6124) serves fish, steaks, and teriyaki dishes. In the Independent Boat Yard below the entrance to Compass Point on Red Hook Rd., inexpensive **Bottoms Up** offers three meals daily and features fish and chips and sandwiches. Near the East End Road Park at Red Hook, **Fabian's Landing** (tel. 775-9742) serves American and Caribbean breakfasts and lunches. At the Grand Palazzo, casual **Café Vecchio** (tel. 775-3333) offers three meals daily featuring Italian style cuisine, including pizza, pastas, salads, seafoods, and fowl dishes. On Rte. 38, **Seagrape at Sapphire** (tel. 775-6100/9750) stretches along one of the most attractive beaches and has meat, seafood, and pasta. At the Stouffer Grand Beach Resort, inexpensive to expensive **Bay Winds Restaurant** (tel. 775-1510, reservations requested) serves three Caribbean-American style meals daily. Also here, the **Smugglers Bar and Grill** has steak and seafood dishes and offers a Sun. buffet. Featuring seafood, salad, and pasta and only open for dinner, moderate to expensive **Agavé Terrace** (tel. 775-4142) is at Point Pleasant Resort, Smith Bay Rd. (Rte. 38). It has a good wine list. A steel band plays here Tues. and Thurs. evenings. **The Lookout Lounge** is open inside the restaurant, and the resort's inexpensive **Bayside Cafe** offers up paper plate cuisine such as grilled items as well as fruit drinks. At Smith Bay, inexpensive **Pizza Plus** serves pizza plus chicken and ribs, **Lake's Chicken Fry** also has seafood, **Super Pool Barbeque** offers BBQ chicken and West Indian food, and expensive **Romano's** (tel. 775-0045) has Italian and Continental cuisine. For local food out of town try inexpensive to expensive **Eunice's Terrace** (tel. 775-3975), Smith Bay, which is E of the Coral World turnoff on Rte. 38. Specials here may include fish, conch fritters, lobster, and steak. Dishes are accompanied by sweet potato and your choice of peas and rice or fungi, fried plantain, or green banana. **Akasha Sweet Life Cafe** (tel. 775-2650), in Smith Bay at the turnoff for Coral World, has health food including "vegeburgers" and fish dishes. At Coral World, inexpensive **Tropical Terrace** (tel. 775-1555) serves Caribbean and Continental breakfast and lunch. At Sugar Bay Plantation, the inexpensive to moderate **Mangrove Cafe** (tel. 777-7100, ext. 2232) offers pizza, salads, pasta, and meat dishes for lunch and dinner; the moderate **Manor House** serves seafood and Continental dinners and offers a Sun. brunch; and the **Turtle Rock Bar and Grill** (ext. 2235) serves pasta, meat dishes, pizza, and grilled entrees. At Four Winds, inexpensive **Sisserou Restaurant** has three meals daily and offers daily specials. At Tillett Gardens, inexpensive **El Papagayo** is the place for Mexican food and BBQ, either lunch and dinner.

North Side dining: In the N along Rte. 33, moderate **Berry's Farm Garden Bar & Restaurant** (tel. 774-3020), presents American food and seafood; homegrown veggies are used. Laid back and set on Crown Mountain Rd. on the N, inexpensive to moderate **Ferrari's** (tel. 774-6800, reservations recommended) serves dinner, specializes in Italian dishes (pasta, veal, chicken, and seafood) and has delicious garlic bread and pizza. At Magens Bay Beach, **Magens Bay Cafe and Pizzeria** serves breakfast and lunches. In Magens Point Resort, Italian and expensive **Mona's Place** (tel. 775-5500) offers three meals daily. On Fri. night, jazz singer and owner Donafaye Dominic entertains. In Hull Bay, the **Northside Hideaway** (tel. 774-8955) serves lunch and dinner daily. Also here is moderate **Bryan's Bar and Restaurant**.

bakeries and snacks: There are a large number. **The Daylight Bakery** is at 57 Prindsens Gade and at 10 Norre Gade. **Bachman's Bakery** has a branch at Four Winds Plaza and one at Wheatley Center. **The Farmers Bakery** is in Vitraco Park. **Little Vienna** is in the Kronprindsens Market. S and E Bakery is at 60 Kronprindsens Gade. **The Upper Crust Bakery** is at 23 Dronningens Gade. **Weekes & Weekes Bakery** is at 3 Gamble Gade. **The Cream & Crumbs Shop** is in Havensight as is **Uncle Willie's Caribbean Rum Cakes**.

fast food: The island is saturated! **Arby's Roast Beef, Burger King, Flavor Pit, Subway, Kentucky Fried Chicken** and **Pizza Hut** are conveniently located along the waterfront. A **Taco Bell** is located near Charlotte Amalie High School. Others are scattered across the island at the malls, Sub Base, and at Crown Bay.

markets and supermarkets: There're plenty of these. If shopping in one, check your receipts after purchase: mistakes do happen! Along the harbor, a pickup truck sells fruit and vegetables. Right on the waterfront on the way to Frenchtown and strategically located across from the cemetery, **Health is Wealth** (tel. 774-1810) sells expensive health food items and some cooked food such as baked potatoes and soup. At Long Bay and Sub Base (Crown Bay), the **Natural Food Grocery and Deli** serves vegetarian food as well as meat and cheese. Also at Long Bay, Sugar Estate, Estate Thomas, and at Four Winds Plaza, **Pueblo** is one of the islands' largest chains. Sample prices: sugar two kg./$1.79, red Rome apples $1.49/lb., black plums $2.49/lb., Libby's pineapple juice $1.79/16 fl. oz., Bounty paper towels $1.29/pkg., corn three ears/$1.59, eggplant $1.39/lb., green pepper 2/99¢, and milk $1.19/qt. **National Food Discount** is next to Pueblo at Home Gas Station, Estate Thomas. Another large supermarket is **Grand Union. Quality Plus** is at Four Winds Plaza. **Compass Foods** is at Compass Point. **Gonzi's Seafood and Mini Mart** is at 105 Smith Bay. **Red Hook Market** is at Red Hook Shopping Center. **Super Foods** and **Super Foods Warehouse** are at the Sub Base (Crown Bay Marina).

St. Thomas Entertainment and Events

entertainment: St. Thomas has the greatest variety of nightlife found on any of the Virgins. Unfortunately, because of the crime here, it's recommended that you take a taxi while in transit from location to location. To find out what's going on specifically check the "Weekend" supplement to the Thursday *Daily News*. *The Island Trader* also features a "Creative Loafing" section which is updated weekly. Call up for directions and cover charge. **performances:** The open-to-the stars ampitheater at **Reichold Center for the Arts** (tel. 774-4482) has plays and performances. **Top of the Reef** at Frenchman's Reef puts on a "Calypso Carnival Revue" dinner show on Mon. to Sat., at 8 and 10, $40 admission. Limbo shows are held on Friday night at the **Carib Beach Hotel** and on Friday and Saturday nights at the **Virgin Islands Hotel**. **Berry's Farm** (tel. 774-3020) has performances on Sat. nights. **music/dancing:** The **Hard Rock Cafe** has live rock music from 10 PM nightly except Sunday. Barnacle Bill's (tel. 774-7444) in Frenchtown has live music as well as billiard tables; **The Green House** has DJs nightly except Sun. At Crown Point Marina, the **Indigo Blues Club** offers calypso and reggae. In the Al Cohen Mall, the **New Virgins' Oar House** has live entertainment on Sat. and Sun. They "welcome the Navy" and have a pool room. Live rock venues include **Green House** in town on the waterfront (Veterans Drive), **For the Birds** at Compass Point, **Hillside Club** along Mafolie Road, and **Ralph's By the Sea** at Crown Bay. **Jimmy's Club "Z"** restaurant turns into a disco later on; other discos include **La Terraza Lounge** in the Frenchman's Reef Hotel, **Walters Living Room**, 7B Crystal Gade, on Government Hill, **Sugar's Nite Club** at Old Mill in Contant, and **Blue's** on Raadet's Gade. **Barnacle Bills** at the Sub Base has live entertainment as do **Sparky's Waterfront Saloon, Larry's Lagoon Saloon** in Nadir, and **Sib's Mountain Bar & Restaurant** in Estate Elizabeth. **The Green Parrot** at Magen's Point has daytime jazz on Sundays. **Panchita's** has Mexican guitar on Fri. and Saturday evenings. Up at Hull Bay, **Northside Hideaway** (tel. 774-8955) has live rock on Sun. afternoon along with a beach BBQ. **hotel entertainment:** Many of the hotels have disco and/or live music. **Bluebeard's Castle Hotel** presents steel band music or jazz several times per week. **Blackbeard's Castle** features a jazz vocalist. **Bolongo Bay Beach Hotel** has calypso or steel band music most nights as do **Bolongo Limetree Resort** (Club Everything), **Virgin Island Hotel**, and **Windward Passage Hotel**. The **Grand Palazzo Hotel** has jazz trios, steel band, and calypso performances. **The Mark** offers calypso on weekends. At Magen's Point Resort, **Mona's Place** has piano-accompanied vocalists. **cinema:** The island is monopolized by Four Winds Four Cinemas at Four Winds Plaza and Cinema Three downtown; both are under the same management. **cruises:** The *Amalie Queen* (tel. 774-9652) is a party/dinner boat.

events: Chief among these is **Carnival**. Revived in 1952, it is usually held during the last eight days of April. The parade, which takes place on the last day, features the King and Queen of Carnival, Mocko Jumbie ("imaginary ghosts") mounted on 17-ft.-high stilts, and local contingents of steel and calypso bands, dance troupes, and floats. Local delicacies are served in Market Square, and events are held inside compact Lionel Roberts Stadium (near Bluebeard's Hill). There are two nights of calypso revues featuring the best of the Caribbean's calypso singers (from the Mighty Gabby of Barbados to Swallow from Antigua), a Brass-O-Rama marching band tune competition, a Pan-O-Rama featuring steel band competitions, and the selection of king and queen. At night action centers around the food stalls with a special "food booth day" as a traditional part of the festivities. In 1993 a tumultuous controversy centered around this day when the governor–in response to the deficit–refused to allow government employees to take their traditional day off with full pay so they could sample the food booth goodies. If you're staying over on St. John, you can take special late night ferries back after events. For more information contact the VI Carnival Committee at 776-3112, fax 776-3112. Another major event is the **Hook In and Hold On** (HIHO) board sailing race usually held in late June. Every **St. Patrick's Day** local Irish residents hold a parade. Three times per year the **"Arts Alive"** fair takes place at Tillett Gardens in Tutu and features sales (and even demonstrations) by more than 50 craftspeople and artists. Music, stiltwalking, storytelling, and art and music workshops for children are also featured.

St. Thomas Shopping

Know your Stateside prices before arriving if you intend to save money on duty-free goods. (for limits see "shopping" under introduction.) The island's main shopping areas are in town and at Havensight Mall where the cruise ships dock. Others include resort gift shops, shopping centers, and Mountain Top. The free Shopping Map is a good guide to businesses. But the most fun way to shop is just to go browsing. Things tend to be expensive.

crafts and unique items: Local crafts are uncommon but still can be found. The best place to shop for local art and crafts is the **Art Exchange** (tel. 777-5006), Back St., which is above Parrot Fish Music and is open from 9-5 daily. Saint Thomas' **Crafts Cooperative** on Back St. handles rag dolls manufactured on nearby islands. **Zenaida Plus** on Garden St. has a number of handicrafts from South America. **Down Island Traders** in Bakery Square, has a variety of teas, spices, and unique fruit jellies. Their **Gallery**, above them, sells paintings and folk art. A second store is located on the waterfront. Set three stores back from the waterfront in the Royal Dane Mall, the **Guava Gallery** offers a variety of crafts, giftware, and furniture. **The Mahogany Art Center** has Caribbean crafts and work by Haitian artists. Located at A. H. Riise Alley and at Mountaintop, **MAPes MONDe** offers a fine line of map and print reproductions as well as books.

clothing, shoes, and leather: The former Daily News Building on Back St. has been beautifully restored and now houses the A Taste of Italy complex which includes an Italian boutique. Featuring Swiss brand Bally shoes for over two decades, **Cosmopolitan** sells name brand clothing and is on the waterfront. The **Ralph Lauren Factory Store**, 24 Commandant Gade, offers these name brand goods at a discount. Near the park and across the street, **Zora the**

Aerial view of St. Thomas

Downtown Charlotte Amalie

Sandalmakers, 34 Norre Gade, sells a variety of handmade sandals and bags. One of the most popular shops is **Java Wraps**, 24 Palm Passage, which offers a variety of batik clothing. **Big Planet**, an adventure travel outfitter, is across from it. On Garden St., **Thriving Tots Boutique** sells just what the name implies in sizes infant to 14/16. In Bakery Square, **Lucinda's Dress Shop** offers designer dresses and accessories. **The Shoe Tree** at 37 Dronningens Gade offers European imports. Batiks are sold at **Java Wraps** on Main St.

cameras and electronics: Boolchands has stores at Havensight and on Main St; they also sell linen and lace. With stores at 23 and 33 Main St. and at Havensight, **Royal Caribbean** is one of the largest camera and electronic stores.

jewelers: There are innumerable jewelry shops. Impoverished window shoppers and the well-heeled alike may feast their eyes on the gems and jewelry displayed at **Columbia Emeralds** at Royal Dane Mall; they have a wide variety of gems and watches. **Cartier** is on Main St. Set inside A.H. Riise on Drongens Gade, the **Ilias Lalao Unis** counter offers a variety of handcrafted Greek designs. One of the largest of the island's jewelry shops, **Cardow** has a good selection of diamonds and emeralds. Their two shops on Main St. are right across from each other. **H. Stern Jewelers** has two jewelry (and one watch) store on Main St., and stores in the Frenchman's Reef, Bluebeard's Castle, and at Havensight. There are four **Little Switzerlands** which offer jewelery, watches, crystal, and other luxury items; one faces Emancipation Park between the waterfront and Main St. The other three are on Main St. and in Havensight. **Diamonds International**, on Main St. next to Drake's Passage, offers gold jewelry and a wide selection of loose diamonds, rubies, emeralds, sapphires, topaz, and amethysts which may be matched with the setting of your choice. Offering cultured pearls as well as other goods, **Irmela's Jewel Studio** is in the Grand Hotel at 43-46 Norre Gade. Set on the Waterfront, the **West Indies Ice Company** is the only factory outlet jewelry and watch store. **Aperiton Fine Jewelers** offers high quality 18 and 22 karat gold jewelry crafted in Greece. Many of these are replicas of ancient pieces. Italian jewelry, watches and furs are also carried. Housed in an attractive old building, **A. H. Riise** sells jewelry and other goods including Javanese and Balinese handicrafts. In A.H. Riise Alley, **Ciro** is part of an international jewelry chain which offers a wide selection. Set in Drake's Passage (between Main St. and the waterfront), **Uncle Sam's Jewelry and Gift Emporium** sells just what its name implies. Part of a worldwide chain, **Amsterdam Sauer**, 14 Main St., carries gems especially topaz. Also check out **Blue Carib Gems and Rock Factory** in Bakery Square which polishes many of the stones it sells on the premises.

linens: Boolchands has stores at Havensight, on Main St., and on Dronningens Gade. They feature Battenburg lace and hand embroidered goods. The Linen House is at 37 Dronninggens Gade and at 7 Royal Dane Mall. **Linen House, Inc.** has stores at 7-A Royal Dane Mall, on Main St., and in Palm Passage. At 6 Main St. (and Nye Gade), **Mr. Tablecloth** offers a wide variety of Chinese imported tablecloths, and also sells dresses and bed linens.

records: On Back Street, **Parrot Fish** sells a good variety of cassettes, records and CDs including lots of Caribbean tunes. The **No Attitude Record Store** is on Garden St. Another good record store is **Modern Music** which is in Nisky Center, Havensight, and at the American Yacht Harbor. **International Records & Tapes** is at 3 Store Strade.

alcohol: You can take advantage of liquor-tasting bars to get plastered even if you don't intend to buy any liquor. If you do intend to buy some, shop around for the lowest liquor prices. A large number of stores on and around Main St. sell booze. Set at Lockhart Shopping Center one block up from the cruise ship dock, **Woolworth** has about the lowest alcohol prices. **Joe's Discount Liquor** is at 15 Sub Base.

Havensight Mall: Located alongside the West Indian Company Cruise Ship Dock, the Havensight Shopping Mall has a concentration of more than 40 shops along with a bank and restaurants. You can find nearly everything–clothes, jewelry, watches, leather goods, candies, crystal, luggage–you might want to buy under one roof here. Many of the shops here also have a branch in town. **Outriggers** sells swim and resort fashions.

other stores: Located near the waterfront at the end of Riise's Walkway, the **Lion in the Sun** offers large selection of international clothing as well as original jewelry. Two **Tropicana Perfume** shops are located on Main St. **The Leather Shop** sells suitcases and other leather goods. **Scandinavian Center** sells jewelry, glassware, and other goods. Selling everything from cameras to watches to pearls, **Royal Caribbean** has two Main St. stores. On the waterfront at Raadgets Gade, the **English Shop** sells crystal and china. On Trompeter Gade, **Dilly D'Alley's** sells a variety of fashionable clothing including resortwear and European swimwear; specializing in beachware and accessories, the **Beach House** is upstairs. **Mini Mouse House** sells a variety of imported toys. **Royal Dane Mall** has three shop-filled alleys. **G'Day** sells colorful tropical resort wear, jewelry, and accessories. **The Land of Oz Store** is filled with a variety of imported toys. **Towel'n Sun** offers a large range of towels as well as sunning accessories. **Carson Company Antiques** sells everything from pottery to prints to costume jewelry. At 25 Main St., **Brumney's Gem Shop** carries pearls, gems, and watches. Inside, you can find the **Luisa Boutique** which offers expensive European designed clothing. Set on Garden St., **Local Color** offers tee-shirts, sweatshirts, totes, and beach towels featuring the bold and colorful designs of St. Thomian artist Kerry Topper. In Palm Passage, the **Joanna White Art Gallery** highlights her art as well as carrying pottery, jewelry, pots, and other items. **Janine's Boutique** carries fashions for both men and women. **Universal Liquor and Gifts** is at Market Square and features a variety of jewelery and watches. In the Al Cohen building across from the entrance to Havensight Mall, **Coin D'Oro** imports gold jewelry, necklaces, silver, crystal, and pens.

outlying shopping: On Rte. 38 across from Four Winds Plaza (where you get off if arriving by bus) and set between Point Pleasant and Stouffer's Grand Beach Resort, Tillett's Gardens houses the **Jim Tillett Art Gallery and Craft Studios** which contains a variety of silk screen fabrics, enamelware, stained glass, and pottery–all of which are designed on the premises. Here, **Kilnworks Pottery and Fine Crafts Gallery** sells a variety of work including Peggy Seiwert's Caribbean cloud pastel vases as well as sculptures, enamels, and watercolors; the **Caribbean Enameling Guild** offers handpainted enamels including brooches and earrings; **Okidanokh** offers gold designs as well as silver jewelry; **Ocean's Bounty** has framed seashell and coral specimens. Opened in June 1993, **Tutu Shopping Center** features a K Mart and 20 or so other stores and restaurants. It's next to the **Four Winds Shopping Plaza** (Pueblo, Western Auto, drugstore) and across from **Fort**

Mylner Shopping Plaza which has expanded as Rte. 32 has been altered.

St. Thomas Information and Services

information: *St. Thomas This Week* is the most useful of the free publications; single copies ($2) are available by mail by writing Box 1627, St. Thomas 00804. There are also a near infinite number of other free handouts including the *St. Thomas St. John Vacation Handbook.* Others include *Be Our Guest* and *The US Virgin Islanders Magazine.* Staffed with volunteers, the **Hospitality Lounge** inside the Grand Hotel (facing the same park) dispenses advice and checks luggage ($1). You can pick up a lot of useful information here. Be sure to read *The Daily News* while on the island; the Friday edition has an extremely useful "Weekend" section. The **St. Thomas/St. John Hotel Association** (Box 2300, St. Thomas 00803) can be reached at 774-6835.

services: There are three **post offices**. One is at Emancipation Gardens on Main St. in downtown Charlotte Amalie near the fort. Another is at 100 Veteran's Drive in Frenchtown and is about 20 min. on foot from the town center along the waterfront. The third is at 9630 Estate Thomas. **The Virgin Islands Public Library and Archives**, Main St. between Guttets Gade and Queen's Quarter, are open Mon. to Fri. 9-9; a quiet place to pass the time. **The National Park Service Headquarters** are at Red Hook, as are the offices of the **Island Resources Foundation** (tel. 775-6225, Box 33, St. Thomas 00802). **Banks** are open Mon. to Thurs. 9-2:30, Fri. 9-2, 3:30-5. **Knud Hansen Hospital** is located near downtown. Its emergency room is open 24 hours a day. **Blazing Photos** (three locations) has one hour film processing. **Fax** service is offered by Copy Cat, 24B Norre Gade. For local and international calls (as well as video rentals and fax service), you can also try **The Calling Station** (tel 776-8355), Bakery Square and Nye Gade up from Back St. It's open Mon. to Thurs. 7:30 AM-7:30 PM and Fri. and Sat. 7:30 AM-9:30 PM. A second location is at Al Cohen's Mall in Havensight (tel. 777-8205). Look for the white horse. **Showtime Video** (tel. 775-7756) is at Four Winds is in Nisky Center. **St. Thomas Video and CDs** is in Al Cohens Plaza Bldg. at Havensight. A launderette is located in Solberg Suprette atop Solberg Hill. **Caribbean Laundry Unlimited** (tel. 774-7114), 6 Crystal Gade, offers drop off specials for laundry and pressing. For a workout, try **The**

Downtown Club Fitness Centre (tel. 776-0700) at 80 Kronprind-sens Gade. Rates start at $10 per day, $20 per wk, $60 per mo., and on down. For yoga classes, massage for couples, Thai medical massage, and nutritional/fitness advice, call **Loving Touch** at 776-5685. **OTC Drugs, Inc.** sells herbal remedies. **Joe's Discount Pharmacy** is at Four Winds as well as Pueblo. **Mom's Day Care Center** at 394-325 Anna's Retreat (tel. 495-0526) takes care of kids (two mos. to 12 years) from 6-6 for around $35 weekly including two meals and baths.

bookstores: Hospitality Lounge, inside the Grand Hotel Building, has a selection of books pertaining to the USVI. **Dockside Book-shop** is inside Havensight Mall. **The Island Newsstand** on Norre Gade has a fine selection of magazines and bestsellers. **Modern Music, Modern Books** (tel. 775-3310) is in the American Yacht Harbor Bldg. in Red Hook.

Useful St. Thomas Phone Numbers

Air Angulla	778-9177
Air Center Helicopters	775-7335
Ambulance	922
American Airlines	800-474-4884
American Eagle	776-2560
American Express	774-1855
Antilles Helicopters	776-7880
Caribbean Air	774-7071
Chamber of Commerce	776-0100
Continental Airlines	777-8190
Decompression Chamber	776-2686
Delta Airlines	800-221-1212
Dial-a-Ride (wheelchair taxi)	776-2043
Fire	921
Hospital	776-8311
Hospitality Lounge	776-9493
LIAT	774-2313
National Park	776-6201
Police	915
Sunaire	776-9322
Tourist Information	774-8784
Virgin Air	776-2722

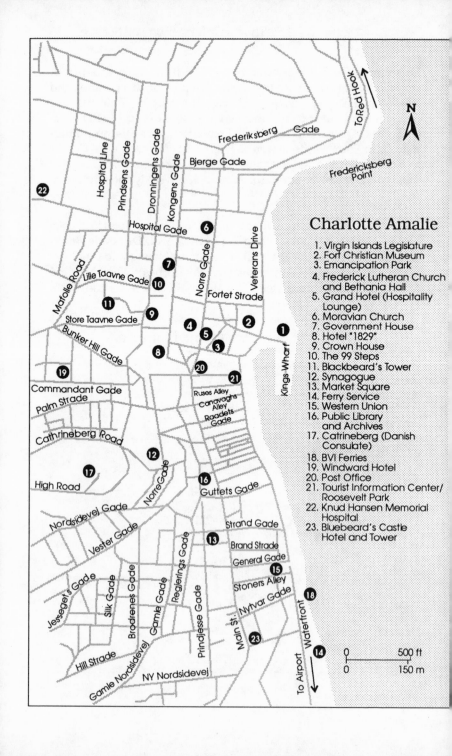

Charlotte Amalie

1. Virgin Islands Legislature
2. Fort Christian Museum
3. Emancipation Park
4. Frederick Lutheran Church and Bethania Hall
5. Grand Hotel (Hospitality Lounge)
6. Moravian Church
7. Government House
8. Hotel "1829"
9. Crown House
10. The 99 Steps
11. Blackbeard's Tower
12. Synagogue
13. Market Square
14. Ferry Service
15. Western Union
16. Public Library and Archives
17. Catrineberg (Danish Consulate)
18. BVI Ferries
19. Windward Hotel
20. Post Office
21. Tourist Information Center/ Roosevelt Park
22. Knud Hansen Memorial Hospital
23. Bluebeard's Castle Hotel and Tower

Charlotte Amalie

Most of the 51,000 St. Thomians live in this small but attractive town. Although cruise ships rather than slavers visit the harbor these days, the smell of history is still in the air. The shops lining the streets running parallel to the harbor were originally pirate warehouses. As a reminder of the colonial past, street signs affixed to corner buildings are in both English and Danish, and cars drive on the left side of the streets. The three main streets are Dronningen's Gade (Main St.), Norre Gade (North St.), and Vimmelskaft's Gade (Back St.). A series of interlocking alleyways (converted into shopping malls) runs from Dronningen's Gade down to Waterfront Drive, a four-lane thoroughfare which parallels the waterfront. By all means, avoid downtown when the cruise ships unleash their passengers and it becomes a struggle just to walk.

Charlotte Amalie Sights

Best way to see this town is on foot when no cruise ships are in the harbor. Among its most charming features are the stone stairways which were constructed because the steep hillsides rising behind the town made road building problematic. While out and about, be sure to keep an eye out for the numerous iguanas among the hibiscus and mango trees. If you can ignore the touristic, sales-minded atmosphere that prevails downtown, there's plenty to see. You're sure to find your own attractions in addition to the ones listed below.

Virgin Islands Legislature: This lime-green building with white shutters, constructed in 1874, served as the Danish police barracks before housing the U.S. Marines. It became a school in 1930 and then the legislature building in 1957. For a unique glimpse of local politics in action, check out the heated, virulent debates which take place inside.

Fort Christian Museum: Enter along Veterans Drive. Built shortly after the arrival of the first colonists, this imposing red landmark, in neoclassic style, is the oldest building on the island. Completed in 1672, the masonry ramparts and bastions were added in the 18th C; the fort was completely renovated in 1871 when Charlotte Amalie regained its status as capital. A building of many uses, the fort has housed the governor, the artisan community, and in times of natural disaster during its early history, the entire population. It has also served as the local branch of the Lutheran Church, as a site for pirate executions, and (in its present function) as a jail. The small museum occupies a few fluorescent-lit cells in the basement. Note the archaeological artifacts, shells, old mahogany furniture, and display of household utensils, including a hollow glass rolling pin which could be filled with water to keep dough from sticking. Open Mon. to Fri. (9:30-5, Sat. and Sun. 12:30-5. Free admission.

Emancipation Park: These small public gardens near the fort mark the spot where Governor von Scholten proclaimed the emancipation of the slaves on July 3, 1848. A bell on the SW corner is a replica of the United States' Liberty Bell, and the statue is of King Christian IX.

Frederick Lutheran Church: One of the most beautiful architectural treasures on St. Thomas, this, the oldest church on the island and the second oldest Lutheran building in the Western Hemisphere, is located uphill from Emancipation Park along Norre Gade. Built in 1793, it was renovated in 1826 and 1973. **Bethania Hall**, which serves as the Parish Hall, is adjacent to the church. A Danish manor, it was built as the private residence of one Jacob S. Lind in 1806. The nearby **Grand Hotel** dates from 1840. Once the headquarters for the social elite, it now houses shops and restaurants. Farther down Norre Gade is the Moravian church which dates from the nicely numbered year of 1888.

Government House: Atop the hill on Kongens Gade. Stand in the small park across the road and view the impressive architecture and the black limos parked outside. Inform the guard at the entrance as to your mission, and he'll escort you around the areas available to the public. Now the official office-residence of the elected governor of the USVI, this elegant brick-and-wood three-story mansion was built in 1867. Inside, large paintings depicting Transfer Day and Salt River, St. Croix adorn the staircase walls, while two paintings by St. Thomas-born Camille Pissarro hang in the ballroom upstairs. Beautiful view of the harbor from the window. (Open daily during working hours.) To view the reception room make an appointment with Mrs. Gresens at 774-0001. Farther up the same street to the W is **Hotel "1829"** which is a good example of 19th C architecture.

Crown House: Climb either of the two step streets along Kongens Gade to reach here. Now privately owned, this 18th C mansion once functioned as the governor's residence. Recently remodeled, it's filled with antique furniture. This mostly stone two-story house has a Dutch gambrel hipped roof. Peter von Scholten lived here when he was governor of St. Thomas in 1827. Inside, note the handsome ceiling, carved woodwork, the 18th C Chinese wall hangings, and the French chandelier which is said to come from Versailles. Admission includes a guide and a hit of rum. Open Mon. to Sat., 10-5.

Seven Arches Museum: A 19th C Danish craftsman's house restored in traditional style by Barbara Demaras and Philbert Fluck, this is the only private home on the island open for viewing. Originally there was a staircase between the first and second floor. Now, however, the second floor is a museum, and the couple live on the first. Nearly all of the furniture is from Barbados. A few pieces are from Haiti, and the bed is from the VI. The Royal Copenhagen porcelain is from Barbara's parents. This is a good place to take a refreshing break from your shopping. From the second floor you can see a nightblooming cactus on a structure which used to be the servants' quarters for the house next door. Watch for the iguanas which have trained Philbert to feed them hibiscus flowers from the lovely small garden below. Be sure to check out the comments in the guest book and add your own. Admission ($7.50) includes a complimentary fruit punch. It's open 9 to 4. Call 774-9295 for information.

99 Steps and Blackbeard's Tower: The step street perpendicular to Blackbeard's Tower is the 99 Steps, most famous of the town's step streets. As you climb, count to see how many there actually are. Note the multicolored bricks: they arrived here as ship's ballast; the yellow ones are from Denmark, the reds come from England, France and Spain.

Synagogue of Beracha Veshalom Vegimulth Hasidim: On Crystal Gade. Take the stairs up to the entrance. Rebuilt in 1833 on the site of previous temples, this building was constructed in a mixture of Gothic Revival styles in 1833. Still in use today, it's the oldest synagogue on the island and the second oldest in the Western Hemisphere. Sand on its floors commemorates the exodus of the Jews from Egypt. It's open Mon. through Fri. from 9-4.

market square: The site of what was once the largest slave market in the Caribbean, located along Kronprindsens Gade near the library. Here, locals sell a vast variety of fruit and vegetables ranging from tannia to okra to cassava. Its roof was imported from Europe.

Paradise Point: Set atop Flag Hill and overlooking town, this shopping area, restaurant, and bar can be reached by road. A tramway is under construction as are historical exhibits and a nature path.

Frenchtown

Town within a town, this small community in the SW part of Charlotte Amalie, is home to one of the smallest but most conspicuous ethnic groups in the Virgin Islands–descendants of the French Huguenots. Also known as Careenage because old sailing boats careened here for repairs, the brightly painted houses have immaculate, packed-dirt yards. Local watering hole is the **Old Normandy Bar**.

history: Centuries ago, Protestant French Huguenots, fleeing religious persecution in Catholic France, were among the earliest settlers in the Caribbean. They arrived on several islands, including miniscule St. Barths (St. Bartolemy). In 1848, two members of the La Place family migrated to the site of Frenchtown and to sleepy Hull Bay along the N coast. Emigration began in force between 1863-1875, when economic conditions on St. Barths worsened and many sought to flee that tiny, rocky wart of an island.

the people: Some 1,500 strong, the "Frenchies" are a tough people renowned for their fishing and fighting abilities. The two French communities speak different dialects of archaic W. Indian French and retain their cultural distinctions; there has been intermarriage and sociability between them. Traditional dress was unique and resembled that found in their native Brittany. Women's heads were adorned with the ealeche, the traditional shoulder-length headdress; men wore black and calico shirts with their denim trousers rolled halfway up their legs and went barefoot. Retaining this style of dress after arrival caused the locals to make fun of them. In return, the vitriolic French spat out "cha cha" which means "go to the devil." Ironically, the locals began to refer to the community as

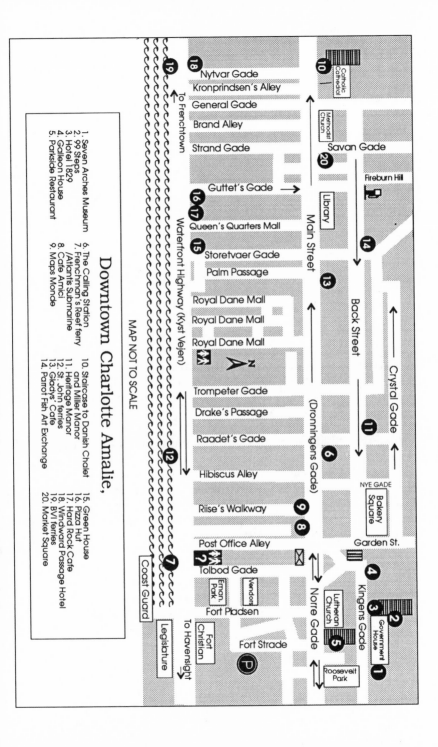

Downtown Charlotte Amalie,

MAP NOT TO SCALE

1. Seven Arches Museum
2. 99 Steps
3. Hotel 1829
4. Galleon House
5. Parkside Restaurant
6. The Calling Station
7. Frenchman's Reef ferry /Atlantis Submarine
8. Cafe Amici
9. Maps Monde
10. Staircase to Danish Chalet and Miller Manor
11. Heritage Manor
12. St. John ferries
13. Gladys' Cafe
14. Parrot Fish Art Exchange
15. Green House
16. Pizza Hut
17. Hard Rock Cafe
18. Windward Passage Hotel
19. BVI ferries
20. Market Square

To Frenchtown

Waterfront Highway (Kyst Vejen)

Coast Guard

Legislature

To Havensight

Nytvar Gade
Kronprindsen's Alley
General Gade
Brand Alley
Strand Gade
Savan Gade
Guttet's Gade
Queen's Quarters Mall
Storetvaer Gade
Palm Passage
Royal Dane Mall
Royal Dane Mall
Royal Dane Mall
Trompeter Gade
Drake's Passage
Raadet's Gade
Hibiscus Alley
Riise's Walkway
Post Office Alley
Tolbod Gade

Main Street
Library
Back Street
(Dronningens Gade)
Crystal Gade
Fireburn Hill

Catholic Cathedral
Methodist Church

NYE GADE
Bakery Square
Garden St.

Nørre Gade
Eman. Park
Vendors
Fort Pladsen
Lutheran Church
Kingens Gade
Government House
Fort Christian
Fort Strade
Roosevelt Park

N

"Cha Cha Town," a name which sticks to this day. There has been no love lost between the French and the local blacks–each side regarding the other with derision. Long the lowest socio-economic class in the USVI, in recent years the French have emigrated in droves to the mainland where they are readily assimilated. **events:** Traditional events such as St. Anne's Day, Bastille Day, and the Christmas Day parade are still observed. Father's Day is a big celebration here.

Hassel Island

This small island guarding Charlotte Amalie harbor is one of the most important historic sites in the USVI. Today, the National Park Service manages 90% of its 135 acres.

getting there: Access is restricted due to a lack of docking facilities, unstable structures, and the potential problem of trespassing on private property. If you wish to spend more than just a short time on the island, get a visitor use permit from Red Hook Headquarters (tel. 775-2050). For ferry ($3) information call 776-9500, ext. 445 or 775-6238. Be sure to see the fortification at Cowell's Point which was restored by the British in 1801 and named after the colonel to whom St. Thomas surrendered.

history: Activities ranging from agricultural to commercial to military have gone on here. Originally a peninsula attached to St. Thomas, it became an island in the 1860s when the Navy cut through and dredged the narrow connecting isthmus in order to allow docking ships easier access to the harbor. During the early 1800s, when steamships stopped at Hassel to transfer cargo and take on fuel, the island had two working marine railways, three coaling docks, and a floating drydock. Fort Willoughby was constructed during the 1801 and 1807 British occupations of the island. A U.S. Naval Station was located on Hassel I. from 1917-31; it was reactivated during WW II but abandoned thereafter. Much of the island was acquired during the 1930s by the Paiewonsky family, chiefly in order to provide water for their rum distilleries. During the 1970s, Ralph Paiewonsky wanted to develop the island but his conservationist brother Isidor opposed the move. Lucrative offers, including one of $3 million from Reverend Sun Myung Moon, were turned down. Finally, the two brothers compromised by selling the land to the Department of the Interior for incorporation

in the USVI National Park. Today, there are a few hiking trails.
They run to all of the sights.

Water Island

Fourth largest of the US Virgins (2.5 mi. by 1.5 mi.), Water Island is
the oldest centerpiece of the Water Island Formation, a geological
configuration consisting of 70 million year old lava flows. Its
highest point is some 300 ft., and there are many irregular bays and
peninsulas. The island today is largely a community of retirees.
Residents have built and maintain the road system and provide for
their own fire protection and garbage collection.

getting there: The ferry runs from Crown Point Marina at 7, 8,
noon, 12, 2, 4, 5 and 6. On Sun., it runs at 8, noon, and at 5:30.
Additional ferries run at 9 and 10 PM on Tues., Friday, and Sat.
nights. Ferries return soon after arrival.

history: Although there is not evidence of any permanent settlement, the island's first visitors were Arawaks. In the Postcolum-
bian era, it became a popular hangout for pirates who would
shelter in its bays to await quarry. The island's name comes from
its fresh water ponds, where windjammers would refill their water
casks. The earliest Danish land title known for the island dates
from 1807, and the British may have granted it to Italian emigrant
Joseph Daniel during their occupation (as part of the War of 1812-
14) as a reward for his services as a shipyard owner. In any event,
it remained in his family's possession until 1905 when, under
coercion, they sold it for $21,000 to the West Indian Co., Ltd. Their
idea was to rent the property to foreign governments to use for
manuevers, but after the US purchase in 1917 this became unfeasi-
ble, and the island remained undeveloped. In 1944, the US government purchased the island for $10,000 and began constructing an
army base. Construction ceased right after the end of WWII, and it
was given over to the Chemical Warfare Division who tested
poison gases on pigeons and goats here. The army leased the
island to the St. Thomas Development Authority. Aspiring retirees
Walter and Floride Phillips, arriving in March 1951, saw the pos-
siblilities for development. The island was transferred to the Dept.
of the Interior in 1952 and a 20-yr. lease signed with Water Island,
Inc. which gave the VI corporation the opportunity to renew automatically after 20 yrs; the extension expired at the end of 1992. It is

now a matter of controversy whether the island's housing sites will be sold to its present inhabitants or what should or will happen.

sights: Partially an artifical creation, Honeymoon Beach is the main attraction here. There's also a small botanical garden.

practicalities: There are currently no stores or restaurants. The only accommodation here is at **Limestone Reef Terraces,** a set of 10 studio apartments; rates start at around $65 s or d. These feature ceiling fans, kitchenettes, and lounge chairs. Another alternative is the fully-furnished **Murray House,** which can hold six or more people; rates start at $110 for two. Use of a car is provided with the latter. For more information call (908) 329-6309, (800) 872-8784, or write Island Vacations, RD 4, Princeton, NJ 08540.

Around St. Thomas

Although Charlotte Amalie is the island's heart, there are a number of other settlements and scattered points of interest. Just on the edge of town atop Denmark Hill sits **Catrineberg**, a mansion built around 1830 in modified Greek Revival and classical Georgian styles. Visible along Skyline Drive is **Luisenhoj**, a giant castle built by publishing tycoon Fairchild (both are closed to the public). Restored **Nisky Moravian Mission**, which dates from 1777, stands along Harwood Highway. The **Orchidarium** is located in the shopping center off Harwood Highway to the W of town. Admission charged for guided tours. **Mountain Top** on the North Side, is a heavily tourist infested viewpoint but–at 1,500 ft. (450 m)–is the island's highest point. It has a/c shopping, a tropical aviary and aquarium, and international stores. The **Jim Tillett Boutique/Art-Gallery** and **Kilnworks Pottery** are in Tutu. Set at 1,200 ft (360 M), **Fairchild Park** offers views of both N and S coasts.

beaches: There are more than 40 beaches on this small island, so there's plenty of territory to explore. Beaches are open to the public because private property begins only above the high tide mark. Remember to take the usual precautions while visiting: Never leave anything of value in your car or unaccompanied on the beach. And be sure to use plenty of suntan oil; the sun is hot! Also, nudity and toplessness are frowned upon. Following is a list of prominent beaches running counter clockwise from Charlotte Amalie. Set to the SE off Rte 30, the very accessible **Morningstar**

Beach is a family beach with beige sand and occasional surf. All of the amenities are found here: snorkel gear, small sailboats, sailboards, tennis courts, etc. It lies behind the luxurious Frenchman's Reef hotel and the Morning Star Beach Resort. You may take the "reefer" Ferry to get there. (See "getting around.") Off of Rte. 30, the **Limetree Hotel Beach** nearby is palm-lined and tranquil. Most of its visitors are staying at the hotel. Ask to see the iguanas. **Bolongo Beach** has a high per capita population of honeymooners. You can generally find a volleyball game in progress. Scuba and snorkel equipment are for rent. **Scott's Beach** is next. Small but attractive, it's for strong swimmers only as the water gets deep a short distance from the shore and the waves are feisty. To get here take Rte 32, turn at Compass Point, and the beach is on the L. Enter through the restaurant. The secret is out about **Secret Harbour Beach**. There's a hotel (Secret Harbour Beach Resort) here, diving and snorkeling rentals, and restaurant/bar; sunsets are magnificent, and palm trees shade the sand. Picknicking is prohibited. It's accessed by Rte. 322. You should turn R just before the St. John ferry dock, follow the road, make a sharp R, and then a sharp L. Circled by Bolongo Elysian Beach Resort, the Cowpet East/West, and The Anchorage condos, **Cowpet Beach** has windsurfer rentals. It has a beachside restaurant at The Anchorage and food and drink and rentals at the Elysian.

Great Bay Beach has high winds but (accordingly) great windsurfing. No equipment rentals available. **Vessup Beach**, reached by rough Rte. 32 (Red Hook Rd.), has picnic tables, grills, and little shade. **Sapphire Beach** is noted for its reef populated with fish and its waves peopled with suntanned windsurfers. On Sun. PM, there's a band and a party-down atmosphere. Sailboards, snorkel gear, small sailing craft, and lounge chairs are for rent. The recently-constructed Sapphire Beach Resort stands here. To get here take Rte. 38 to the signed turnoff and follow the road. Also known as Pineapple, **Stouffers Grand Beach Resort**, one of the island's "see and be seen" beaches, is located in Smith Bay. You must enter through the resort. Pineapple Village Villas and others are here as well. It's accesed via Rte. 38 (Smith Bay Rd.). Small **Coki Beach**, reputed to have the island's best snorkeling, lies next to Coral World at the NE end via Rte. 388. It becomes crowded when cruise ships are in port. There's a great view of Thatch Cay offshore. Lockers are available in Coral World; theft on this beach is rife. Visitors may find **Mandahl Beach** disappointing: sand is scarce, the access road is rough, and there are a large number of sea urchins. Frenchies moor their boats in the lagoon here. The water is perhaps most appropriate for board (not body!) surfing when conditions are right. Stop in at The Inn for a drink. **Magens Bay**, off Magens Rd. (Rte. 35), is on nearly every list of the world's best beaches. Surrounded by the luxurious villas of the wealthy, palm groves are set to the back. This magnificent mile-long horseshoe of sand was given to the local government in 1946 through the beneficence of publishing tycoon Arthur Fairchild. It is the only beach which charges admission, ($1 per vehicle and 50 cents per person, 25 cents for children under 12). Facilities include changing rooms, toilets, and a refreshment and gift center. The arboretum at the rear of the beach is being restored after abandonment by the local Rotary Club. Be sure to visit. From here you can proceed through dry forest filled with lignum vitae, genip, cashew, and other woods to the **Peterborg Peninsula** which encloses the N side of the bay. Once the sight of Larry's Hideaway Campgrounds, **Hull Bay** still has Frenchie fishermen hauling in their catch. Snorkelers and (under appropriate conditions) board and body surfers abound. Imbibe at the Northside Hideaway bar which has the island's sole horseshoe pitch. Follow Rte. 37 to the bottom of the road and make a sharp R onto the beach. One of the less frequently visited beaches, **Stumpy Bay** has plenty of surf and few people. To get here drive a mi. down a road off Rte. 30 W and then walk a half mi. to the beach. Accessible by bus from Charlotte Amalie, mellow **Brewers Beach** lies off Rte. 30 near the University of the Virgin Islands. It has plenty of facilities including a complete watersports center. Snack wagons circle here on weekends. Owing to its W End location, the sunsets are fantastic. For a quick dip after arriving or before departing the island, **Lindbergh Beach**, named after the famous flier who landed here during his world tour in the 1920s, is conveniently located across the street from the airport. Accessed by Airport Rd., it stretches from the Emerald Beach Resort past the Island Beachcomber Hotel and has a smooth, sandy bottom.

Coral World: One of the only underwater observation towers in the Western Hemisphere, this touristic attraction is located near Coki Beach on the island's NE. Along with the Atlantis Submarine, it's a good way for non-divers to view underwater sea life. Daily at about 10 and 11 AM, a diver hand-feeds the fish; sharks are fed at 2. Guided tours are led daily from 3 PM. From the two-level deck, observe life on the sea floor as well as the circling sharks, barracudas, and stingrays above. Marine Garden Aquariums have 21 saltwater tanks featuring zoological curiosities such as purple anemones and fluorescent coral. They also have a glass bottom boat. Open daily 9-5; Thurs., Fri., and Sat. until midnight; $14 adult admission, $9 children. Locals are given a hefty discount. Information: 775-1555.

Drake's Seat: This panoramic viewpoint is on Skyline Drive in the center of the island towards the N shore. Legend has it that Sir Francis Drake sat here and peered through a telescope to watch for Spanish galleons approaching what is now known as Drake's Passage. Off in the distance you can see St. John and the uninhabited Hans Lollik Islands. Thatch Cay and other islets lie directly below. Rendered obsolete by Toyota pickup trucks, the last donkeys–a reminder of the era when they sufficed for the island's automobiles–have been shuttled up here so that tourists may have the privilege of paying to take their pictures. North coast "Frenchies" attend the Our Mother of Perpetual Help Catholic Church nearby.

Estate St. Peter Greathouse and Botanical Gardens: Here you can find some 500 varieties of plants and trees which are identified on a nature trail running through the three landscaped acres. Open Mon. to Sat. from 9-3, it charges $15 for a tour for two.

Stouffer Grand Beach Resort: Free botanical tours and slide orientations are offered here on Fri. at 10; other times are available by special arrangement. There's also a self-guiding trail booklet. Call Ed Sallee at 775-1510.

St. Thomas Tours, Excursions, and Charters

land tours: There are a large number of basic tours around the island. The **Taxi Association** (tel. 774-4550) offers a $14, 2.5-hr. trip along scenic Skyline Drive with stops at St. Peter Greathouse and Botanical Gardens and Mountain Top. This is the most extensive tour for the cheapest price. They also have a "Greathouse and Coral World" tour ($15) which does not include admission fees. **Fun Water Tours** (tel. 775-7245) runs a similar tour as well as a three hr. $15 Island/Magens Bay tour and a St. Thomas Shopping Tour ($18). **Destination VI** (tel. 776-2624) offers an island tour with swimming at Magens Bay. They also have a half-day "Paradise on

Display" tour ($25) which is slightly more extensive as well as a half-day "Eastern Highlights" tour which includes Coral World and an all-day "Grand Island Tour" ($60) which goes everywhere from Magens Bay (swimming) to Coral World to Frenchtown.

St. John tours: Most of these are listed under the St. John section. Also see **Seaborne Seaplane Adventures** below. For package tours to St. John call **Tropic Tours** (tel. 774-1855) whose Island Safari Running departs at 9, Mon. through Sat.. To hike the Reef Bay Trail (see St. John section) with the Park Service (tel. 776-6201), take a 9 AM ferry from Red Hook; the bus departs at 9:45 on Mon. and Wed.

specialty and other tours: Walking tours of Charlotte Amalie are offered by **St. Thomas Tour Specialist** (tel. 776-7900, $25) and **Destination VI** (tel. 776-2824, $10). **for the disabled:** You are welcome aboard the Kon Tiki Raft (tel. 775-5055, $29), and Destination VI (tel. 776-2424) and Tropic Tours (tel. 774-1855) both can arrange tours for those in wheelchairs.

helicopter/air tours: A daily gambling-excursion flight departs for the Sands Hotel in San Juan. Call 1-791-0914. There are several other alternatives. **Antilles Helicopters** (tel. 775-7335) offers 10-min. ($50 pp) and half hour ($110) tours as well as half day excursions for couples to uninhabited Hans Lollik. **The Air Center** (tel. 775-7335) offers tours for $110/pp on up. **Seabourne Seaplane Adventures** (tel. 777-4491) offers a 45 min. air tour ($169) that combines with a St. John island tour, beach buffet, and a motorboat return to St. Thomas.

St. Thomas Water Sports and Excursions

dive sites and snorkeling: There are 34 or so dive sites here within twenty min. by boat from the shore. Most sites are 25-85 ft. deep. One of the most popular sites, the West Indian Transport Shoal was sunk intentionally in 1984. It houses corals, nurse sharks, stingrays, and a colorful menagerie of fish. Expect to spend around $40 for a one-tank dive and $55 and up for a two-tank dive. Visibility often reaches 150 ft. in the vicinity of Sail Rock, nine miles from St. Thomas harbor. Farther still is Saba Island with three different dive sites. Grain Wreck, the unmarked site of a 450-ton cargo ship sunk in the 1960s as an exercise for the Underwater Demolition Team, is restricted to experienced divers. At 70-110 ft., you can find rays, turtles, and sharks here. Apparently sunk during WWII, the Barges lie in 40 ft. and house nurse sharks and other fish. The wreck of the *Warrick* (1816) rests on Packet Rock while *Cartanser Senior*, a small packet ship, is nearby. French Cap Cay is a rocky underwater promontory surrounded by a myriad variety of sealife. In addition to a beautiful pinnacle, it features fire and pillar corals. Farther offshore than most, it is less frequently dived. Tunnels, reefs and huge boulders comprise Cow and Calf, the top dive spot on the island and well suited to novice divers and snorkelers. Depths here range from 5-25 ft. Several dive spots on the N coast are near Thatch Cay–where a series of underwater tunnels allow divers to swim–and near the wreck of *General Rodgers*. Another good spot is Carvel Rock. Dive courses are frequently held at Coki Beach. Experienced divers frequent Congo Caye which has huge boulders and lava archways 30 ft. (9 m) undersea. Situated SE of St. Thomas, St. Thomas's Buck Island has the ruins of the now coral-encrusted *Cartanser*, a WWI cargo vessel. Snorkelers can also see it. A shallow dive, Little St. James has majestic pillar corals and ledges housing schools of goatfish and grunts. Set on the S side of Grass Cay, The Mounds are a collection of around 20 pinnacles with star and pillar corals as well as the occasional eel and turtle. At Hans Lollick, The Pinnacle is 40 ft. in diameter and 65 ft. in height. You can find tarpon and rays here. Coki Beach is a great night dive area; you can see octopus, oval squid, and moray eels. **instruction:** The **Coki Beach Dive Club** (tel. 775-5620) provides introductory diving lessons for $25. Offering trips to the Rhone in the BVI as well as other small-group excursions, the **Chris Sawyer Diving Center** (tel. 775-7320) is also of note. They run four-hour morning and two-hour afternoon dives to the *Cartenser Sr.* **Aqua Action** at Secret Harbour (tel. 775-6285) also runs dives to this wreck. In its third decade of operation, the **Joe Vogel Diving Company** (tel. 775-7610) offers individualized instruction and night dives. In Crown Bay Marina, **Sea Horse** (tel. 776-1987) offers a variety of dives including lobster dives and night dives. At the Grand Palazzo, the *"Chaucito,"* a 25-ft. Seahawk offers a customized experience. Call 775-3356. The **VI Diving School** (tel. 774-8687) offers group instruction. At Coki Beach, the **Coki Beach Dive Club** (tel. 775-4220) specializes in beginners and offers tours, rentals, and night dives for those certified; four-day PADI and NAUI certification courses are available. There are a number of others.

the Atlantis Submarine: One of the most unusual activities available on the island is an underwater voyage on the Atlantis Submarine. Brainchild of Canadian Dennis Hurd, this US$3 million recreational sub is one of a small fleet deployed at tourist concentrations throughout the world; the others are at Kona and Honolulu (Hawaii), Catalina Island (near Los Angeles), Grand Cayman, Barbados, and at Guam. Before you depart, a videotape supplies orientation. After your voyage, you return to the center where a dive certificate is awarded. It's located in Havensight Mall, Bldg. VI, Bay L. To book, call 776-0288 (info), 776-5650 (reservations) or 1-800-535-6564 (Caribbean Appetizers) stateside. It costs $68 for adults, $34 for teens, and $25 for children; night dives are additional.

semi-submersibles: A 56-ft. a/c semi-submersible boat, the *Reef Explorer* (tel. 771-1492) has windows which allow you to view the reef during a one-hour ($20, $12 for under 12) and three-hour ($38, $20 for children under 12) adventure; it leaves from Sugar Bay Plantation daily. Another alternative is **Seaworld Explorer Tours** out of Coral World at Coki Beach which offers a 20 ($12) and 40 ($28) min. trip in a similarly designed submersible.

sea excursions: Most trips average around $30 for a sunset sail, $50 for a half-day sail, and $65 for a full-day sail. These include the *Independence* (tel. 775-1405), a 44-ft. ketch; the *Naked Turtle Too* (tel. 774-9873), a 53-ft. catamaran which offers both a sunset and a moonlight cruise; the *Ann-Marie II* (tel. 771-1858, 776-6922), a 40-ft yacht accommodating a maximum of four; the *Spirit of St. Christopher* (tel. 774-7169), a 70-ft. catamaran. The *"Mu Mu Sunset"* (tel. 774-5862) sails to St. John for snorkeling. At Red Hook, the *Spirit* (tel. 775-1629) is a 76-ft. catamaran which offers half- and full-day sails to Buck Island and St. John as well as sunset and cocktail sails. A 41 ft. yacht, the *Triumph* (tel. 774-1350) offers half- and full-day sails. *True Love* (tel. 775-6547/6374), is a 54-ft. schooner which sails from Sapphire Beach Marina to St. John for snorkeling and/or the beach. Drinks and a champagne buffet lunch are included. The *"Troubador"* (tel. 774-5630, fax 774-3074) offers Hassel Island trek/harbor tour and other harbor cruises out of Yacht Haven. *Coconuts* (tel. 775-5959), a 51-ft. trimaran, departs from Stouffer Grand Beach Resort and visits St. John and surrounding islands; it also offers sunset sails. The *Stargazer* (tel. 776-5506/8282/5630, 800-334-4760) offers half and full-day sails as well as sunset sails with snorkeling instruction. The *Daydreamer* (tel. 775-2584), a 43-ft. trimaran, has day sails to St. John as well as a sunset cruise and a sail to Jost Van Dyke ($90); dinner cruises are also available. At Sapphire Marina, *Halycon Days* (tel. 775-7211) has day and sunset sails with snorkeling. The *Limnos II* (tel. 775-3203) is a 46-ft. twin engine catamaran which offers a 70-mi. day cruise to visit The Caves at Norman Island, passing by Salt I. and Ginger I. on the way to Virgin Gorda, then returning to St. Thomas. A continental breakfast, picnic lunch, and open bar are included. The *New Horizons* (tel. 775-1171), a 60-ft. custom ketch, offers full-day sails and sunset sails, and *The Alexander Hamilton* (tel. 775-6500), a 65-ft. schooner, has full-day sails with banquet lunch. The *My Way* (tel. 776-7751) sails to uninhabited Hans Lollick Island. The 50-ft. yawl *Nightwind* (tel. 775-4110/6666) runs from Red Hook to St. John. Others include the *Independence* (tel. 775-1408/6547), a 44-ft. ketch (six passengers maximum); *Stormy Petrol* (tel. 775-7990); *Jelly Moon* (tel. 776-6239); and *Your Way* (tel. 775-6285). **rentals:** Rent a 21- , 25- , or 27-ft. motorboat from **Nauti Nymph** (tel. 775-5066); a 21-ft. one from **Rich & Famous** (tel. 777-7500) in Red Hook; a 22-ft. from **Virgin Voyages** (tel. 775-7891) in Sapphire Beach, Calypso (tel. 775-2628), or See An Ski (tel. 775-6265). Operating out of Red Hook at 82 Red Hook Center, **Rafting Adventures** (tel. 779-2032) explores the BVI and St. John on speedy 27-ft. deep-V inflatables; half- or full-day trips are available. They also have week-long camping trips. The **Kon Tiki Raft** is a harbor tour which departs daily between 1 and 2 PM; there's a glass bottom, a beach stop, calypso music, limbo, rum punch, and unlimited soft drinks. For Virgin Gorda trips contact **Transportation Services, Inc.** at 776-6282 (Sun. and Thurs.) or **Native Son** (tel. 774-8685, Sun. and Wed.). The latter also runs to Tortola.

sailing schools: There are two: the **Captain Course Houston** (tel. 776-2278; Yacht Haven Hotel, St. Thomas 00801) and the **International School of Sailing** (CYOA, tel. 774-3677; Yacht Haven Marina, St. Thomas 00801).

deep-sea fishing: Boats here include the *Prowler* (tel. 779-2515) and *The Naked Turtle* (tel. 776-5506), a 33-ft. Bertram cabin cruiser stationed at the Ramada Yacht Haven which is available both for charter and fishing. At Piccola Marina on Red Hook Rd., **St. Thomas Sport Fishing** (tel. 775-7990;) offersfishing charters. *The Fish Hawk* (tel. 775-9058; 54 Frydenhoj, St. Thomas 00802) is at Fish

Hawk Marina at East End Lagoon. The *Ocean Quest* (tel. 776-5176) offers inshore light tackle fishing. At 181 Dominica Building in Sapphire Village, *Bluefin II* (tel. 775-6691) has a 44-ft. custom-built sportsfisherman. The *Phoenix*, a 46-ft. classic Rubovich (tel. 775-6100; Box 8088, St. Thomas 00801) is geared towards guests at the Sapphire Resort. Headquartered at Sapphire Bay, the **Charterfishing Fleet** (tel. 775-3690) offers a variety of charters in 36- to 46-ft. boats. At Red Hook, these include the *Abigail* (tel. 775-3690; Box 72, St. Thomas 00802) which is a 43-ft. Custom, and *El Zorro 11*, a 31 ft. Innovator. Also at Red Hook, the **Boobie Hatch** (tel. 775-6683; Box 79, St. Thomas 00802) has a 45-ft. a/c Trojan with a marlin tower. The *Tara* II (tel. 775-6683; Box 72, St. Thomas 00802) is a 45-ft. Hatteras running out of Red Hook. Another company is **Arawak Marine and Island Holiday** (tel. 775-6500; Box 7362, St. Thomas 00801). The *Easy Living* and the *Cruzan Gold* (tel. 775-6235; Ste. 37, St. Thomas 00802) are at Red Hook Plaza. Capt. Clarence Clark at the American Yacht Harbor (tel. 775-6454) also has charter boats. Also contact John Holmberg (tel. 775-4738; Box 11516, St. Thomas 00801).

boating and sailing: The island's boating center is at Red Hook. For fishing boats see above. For chartering bareboats or yachts, try the **VI Charter Yacht League** (774-3944; 800-524-2061) in Red Hook's Yacht Haven Marina which rents boats from a day on up. Located at Yacht Haven Marina, **Captains and Crew**, a service which places crew with captains and vice versa, charges $15 per year along with a portion of the first pay check.

surfing: The only spot is at Hull Bay which gets rough during the winter months.

windsurfing: The best windsurfing is found at the E end (in locations such as Sapphire and Virgin Grand beaches) during the middle of the day when winds are high. While Morningstar to the S offers the gentlest winds, Hull Bay on the N is the roughest. **instruction:** Schools are located at Pt. Pleasant and at Sapphire Beach resorts.

parasailing: Call **Caribbean Parasailing** (tel. 771-3938) if riding on a sail 500 ft. in the air is your cup of tea. Another alternative is **Blue Dolphin Watersports** (tel. 771-1138, 777-4226).

St. Thomas Sports

golf: The only 18-hole course is at **Mahogany Run** ($60 pp, including cart rental; rates come down after 2). Challenging and naturally lush, the course tests control as opposed to power. Its course record is 66 strokes, it's rated at 70.1, the total yardage is 6,022, the longest hole is 564 yds., and the shortest is 153 yds. The **University of the Virgin Islands'** 9-hole course charges $3 pp. At Smith Bay, 18-hole **Caribbean Mini Golf** ($6 adults, $3 children) is open Mon. to Fri. from 11:30 to 10 and Sat. and Sun. from 10 to 10. It has a course designed to resemble the three islands complete with sugar mill ruins.

tennis: Six **public courts** are free of charge: two each at Crown Bay (Sub Base), Bordeaux, and at Long Bay. Those at the Sub Base are open until 8 on a first-come, first-served basis. The major hotels also have private courts with private lessons available. **Blue-beard's Castle** (tel. 774-1600, ext. 196), has two lighted courts open to 11. Non-guests pay $3/pp per court. The **Bolongo Bay Beach and Tennis Club** (tel. 775-1800, ext. 468) has four lighted courts open to 10, but it is open to non-guests and members for lessons ($15/30 min.) only. **Limetree Tennis Center** (tel. 774-8990) has two courts which are lighted until 9. Lessons are $16/30 min., and non-guests pay $6/hr. per court. **Sapphire Beach Resort** (tel. 775-6100, guest services) has four courts; lessons are $16/30 min., and court rentals are $10/hr. per court. **Marriott's Frenchman's Reef** (tel. 776-8500, ext. 444) offers four lighted courts which are open until 9; non-guests are charged $10/hr. The **Mahogany Run Tennis Club** (tel. 775-5000) has two lighted courts open until 10. Charges are $8/hr. per court until 6 and $10 thereafter. The **Stouffer Grand Beach Resort** (tel. 775-1510) has six courts lit until 10 PM. Non-hotel guests pay $10 ph. **The Grand Palazzo** (tel. 775-3333) offers a day membership which enables you to use its courts. The **Sugar Bay Beach and Racquet Club** (tel. 777-7100, ext. 2007) has seven courts including a stadium court (holds up to 250); all are lit until 11 PM, and there's a pro shop and non-hotel guests pay $9 ph.

horseback riding: Rosendahl Riding Ring (tel. 775-2636) offers ring and group rides for adults and children as well as customized excursions. **Pony Express** (tel. 776-6494) is over on St. John. They offer rides from $40 for one hour on up to $100 for moonlight beach rides which are custom tailored.

From St. Thomas

for St. John: Ferries run on the hour (6:30, 7:30 AM, 8 AM to midnight) between Red Hook, St. Thomas, and Cruz Bay, St. John ($3 OW, 20 min.), and between Charlotte Amalie, St. Thomas, and Cruz Bay, St. John ($7 OW, 45 min.). In addition, ferries ($12, 45 min.) run from Charlotte Amalie and the National Park Pier at Red Hook to Caneel Bay, St. John. Call 776-6111 ext. 220 for times. To get to the ferry from Red Hook, you can either take a local bus, taxi, or a shuttle bus. Get off when you see the 7-11 convenience store. Water taxis (tel. 775-6501, 775-6972) run to St. John by appointment.

for St. Croix: Sunaire (tel. 778-9300) flies daily (25 min) as does American Eagle.

for Tortola: Sunaire (tel. 778-9300) flies daily (20 min.). Four Star Aviation (tel. 777-9900) also flies daily. Ferry times listed below are accurate at time of publication. For current information about schedules call the ferry lines or see the schedule in *St. Thomas This Week*. **from Charlotte Amalie:** For the West End and Road Town, Smiths Ferry Services (tel. 775-7292, $32 RT, 45 min. to West End, 1.15-1.5 hrs. to Roadtown) depart from Mon. to Fri. at 8:30, 12:30, and 4:30; on Sat. at 8:30, noon, and 4:30, and on Sun. at 8, 11, and 3. Inter-Island Boat Services (tel. 495-4166 on Tortola) runs from Cruz Bay to West End from Mon. to Sat. at 8:30, 11:30, and 3:30, with an additional trip on Fri. at 5; and on Sun. at 8:30, 11:30, and 4:30. **from Red Hook:** Native Son, Inc. (tel. 774-8685; $31RT, 30 min.) heads to West End, Tortola daily at 11:30, 3:20, and at 5:30. St. John Transportation Services runs a ferry (tel. 776-6282, $30 RT) to Virgin Gorda on Thurs. and Sat. at 3 PM.

for Jost van Dyke: Ferries ply via Cruz Bay. The *Mona Queen* (tel. 776-6597/6282; $31 Rt, 45 min.) departs Fri., Sat., and Sun. from Red Hook at 8 and 2 and on Fri. and Sun. at 5:15 PM as well.

for San Juan, Puerto Rico: Sunaire (tel. 778-9300) and American Eagle fly daily. **from St. Croix:** American Eagle flies nonstop 10 times daily; Sunaire flies via St. Thomas.

for Vieques: Sunaire (tel. 778-9300) flies daily.

for Fajardo: Sunaire (tel. 778-9300) and Vieques Air Link (tel. 777-4055) fly daily.

for San Juan: Sunaire (tel. 778-9300) and American Eagle fly daily.

for Virgin Gorda: Sunaire (tel. 778-9300) flies daily. Virgin Air (tel. 776-2722) flies for around $90 RT. Four Star Aviation (tel. 777-9900) also flies daily ($99 RT including lunch, tour, visit to the Baths). The Bitter End Yacht Club (800-872-2392) runs charter flights each Sat. AM to Tortola which meet the North Sound Express at a cost of $50 pp RT.

for St. Barths: Virgin Air (tel. 776-2722) flies for around $180 RT.

for Fajardo: Sunaire (tel. 778-9300) flies daily. Virgin Air (tel. 776-2722) flies for around $130 RT.

cruises: One original experience is with the *Sir Francis Drake* (tel. 800-662-0090, 303-341-0335, fax 303-341-0412), a three-masted schooner. Summer cruises depart from St. Thomas, journey through the BVI, and end up in St. Maarten, returning along the same route. Three- , four- , and seven-day cruises are available; these begin and/or end in St. John or St. Thomas. Accommodation is in single or double berth a/c cabins with private showers. Rates start at around $450 for a three-day cruise and include use of sunfish, windsurfers, and snorkeling gear. Write Tall Ship Adventures, 1010 South Joliet St., Ste. 200, Aurora, CO 80012. The 100-passenger *M/V Nantucket Clipper* offers eight-day RT cruises between St. Thomas and the BVI, visiting Norman Island, Virgin Gorda, Jost Van Dyke/Tortola, Norman Island, and St. John enroute. Meals, lectures, snorkeling gear, and other facilities are included. Fares range from $1,600 to $2,700, depending upon the accommodation. Contact Clipper at 7711 Bonhomme Ave., St. Louis, MO 63105-1956, or call 314-727-2929 or 800-325-0010.

St. Thomas Itinerary

If you have 3 days:
Spend one day in Charlotte Amalie (shopping and sights), a day seeing the island, and a day visiting St. John or on a sea excursion.

If you have 5 days:
Spend one day in Charlotte Amalie (shopping and sights), a day seeing the island, two days at the beach or on sea excursions, and a day on St. John (hiking and beaches).

If you have one week:
Spend one day in Charlotte Amalie (shopping and sights), one day touring St. Thomas, three days at the beach or on excursions, and two days on St. John (hiking and beaches).

St. John

Although it's only a 20-min. ferry ride away from Red Hook on the E tip of St. Thomas, St. John seems worlds removed from its neighbor. More than any other Virgin, St. John is someplace special. Seasoned Caribbean travelers call it the most beautiful island in the Caribbean. No one who visits can fail to be romanced by the loveliness of its scenic charms and the friendliness of its inhabitants (currently numbering about 3,000). This small (19-sq-mile, pop. 3,400) island has numerous near-deserted beaches with wonderful snorkeling, spectacular and sedate hiking trails, and coral reefs teeming with life. Set amidst a pristine sea, the island is contoured like a maple leaf. More than half of the island's area has been placed under the aegis of the National Park Service. Though the smallest of the "natural area" National Parks of the United States, St. John nevertheless brings together within its 9,500 acres of land and 5,650 acres of surrounding water a natural ecosystem which is amazingly varied and spectacularly beautiful. Its inabitants range from New Age folks heavily into hugs, affirmations, and $4.95 milkshakes to retired millionaire CEOs to a tight community of locals who are mostly all related to each other. A community of (largely) illegal aliens from the Dominican Republic are the most recent arrivals on the scene. **note:** ASAP after arrival here you should visit the National Park Visitor's Center (two locations: in Cruz Bay and in Red Hook on St. Thomas) and take advantage of their brochures, tours, and other information.

topography: Geologically complex, St. John is comprised of multi-million-year-old rock formations which have been rearranged via erosion, changes in the water level, and faulting. Rising steeply and quickly from the shore, St. John's ridges climax in three peaks: 1,193-ft. Camelberg, 1,147-ft. Mamey, and the 1,277-ft. Bordeaux. Its terrain ranges from moist subtropical forests on the NW slopes to the arid wasteland and salt ponds found on the E end.

flora and fauna: There are over 800 species of plants. Mangrove communities are found at Leinster Bay, Hurricane Hole (on the N side of Coral Bay), and at Lameshur Bay on the island's S coast. More than 160 species have been recorded in and around the park and, of these, over 25 nest on the island. Species include the Zenaida dove, gray kingbird, green-throated carib, bananaquit, pearl-eyed thrasher (trushee on St. John), American oystercatcher, Antillean crested hummingbird, and the sandpiper. Used for local transportation until the 1950s, some 400 feral donkeys now freely roam the hills. They have caused extensive ecological damage, resulting in the near extinction of certain species of trees. Other mammals include the mongoose, deer, pigs, and a variety of bats, the only mammals which are indigenous to the islands–ranging from fruit-eating bats to the fish-eating bats found near the harbors.

History

Arawak Indians, existing in frugal harmony with the island's resources, inhabited St. John for 1,000 years before being displaced by arriving Caribs. The latter had already departed by the time the first Europeans arrived. Given by the Spanish, the island's name refers to St. John the Apostle rather than St. John the Baptist after whom San Juan was named. Before the Danish West India and Guinea Company acted to take control of St. John in 1694, the island had only been visited infrequently. It was not until 1717 that the first company-operated plantation was established at Estate Carolina in Coral Bay. Settlers hoped that this area, with its fine harbor, would soon rival Charlotte Amalie in importance. At first, their optimism appeared justified; St. John became one of the most productive spots in the whole region. By 1733, 15 years after taking possession, 101 plantations were under cultivation. Seven-year tax exemptions had attracted 208 whites, who controlled 1,087 black slaves. Danes were overwhelmingly outnumbered by Dutch.

slave rebellions: St. John was used as a training ground where slaves were "broken in" before being shipped to the more sophisticated plantations of St. Thomas. A large number of the slaves were members of the Amina tribe; to these proud tribesmen, tilling the land was women's work and considered degrading. Akamboos, many of whom had been sold to Coral Bay planters, were equally rebellious. In 1733, Philip Gardelin, the new governor of St. Thomas and St. John, issued an 18-point manifesto. Under its terms, punishment ranging from amputation, to beatings, and pinching the skin with a hot iron were prescribed for all types of infractions. Slaves were forbidden all dances, feasts, and plays; any slave caught in town after curfew faced being beaten and locked in the fort. That very same year the island was beset by a hurricane, a long drought, a plague of insects, and a fall storm. Refused rations by their owners owing to scarcity, the half-starved slaves struck decisively for freedom. At dawn on Sun. Nov. 13, 1733, slaves entered Fort Berg carrying the customary load of wood. Whipping out cane knives concealed in the wood pile, they sliced open all of the soldiers save one who had scurried under a bed. They then fired two cannon shots that were the pre-arranged signal to hundreds of slaves to rise up in revolt. All across the island, marching bands of slaves ransacked great houses and burned cane fields. Whole families of settlers were wiped out. Within a few hours, the slaves controlled the entire island.

short-lived freedom: By late Dec., the rebels had been forced into waging a guerilla war in the hills. The British sent 70 men from Tortola, but they withdrew after being ambushed, as did a similar force dispatched from St. Kitts in February. Worried about their holdings in St. Croix to the S, the French sent two warships from Martinique which arrived in April. Finding themselves hopelessly outnumbered in mid-May, the rebels held one last feast in a ravine near Annaberg, then–according to the story, at least–committed ritual suicide en masse. Forming a circle, each shot the one next to him until the last one shot himself. When the planters arrived, they found seven guns–all broken to pieces save one–a symbol that the struggle would continue until freedom had been won. While the ruined settlers chose to relocate, others soon arrived, and St. John became a prosperous colony once again. This lasted until the Napoleonic Wars, when British troops occupied the island in 1801 and again from 1807-13. This second occupation served to depress the economy. The perfection of the sugar beet and the 1848 emancipation resulted in falling profits. Many planters were already facing ruin when a new variety of sugarcane was introduced from Java at the end of the 19th century. After another short-lived burst of enthusiastic activity, the sugar balloon burst again, and the island wandered off in a somnolent stagger, which the transfer to American ownership in 1917 left unchanged.

Islandwide Practicalities

getting there and getting around: Catch the hourly ferry from Red Hook, St. Thomas ($3 OW), or from Charlotte Amalie ($7 OW). See "From St. Thomas" for schedules. The island is also accessible by ferry from Tortola and Virgin Gorda. The ferry dock is located right in the center of town. (The Caneel Dock is at Caneel Bay). It's easy to walk anywhere in town. To visit other parts of the island, take local transport (which can be expensive), hitch, or rent a car or jeep. A few collective taxis ($2-3 pp) run to places like Caneel and Cinnamon. If hitching, stand on the outskirts of town and use your forefinger to point in the direction you want to go. (St. Johnians consider using your thumb to be rude, and you won't get a ride that way). Also, don't try to hitch if there are more than two of your standing together. **tours:** Island tours (two hrs., $30 for two; $12 each for three or more) are available by taxi. Sea excursions including snorkeling are listed in the appropriate sections below.

St. John Taxi Fares

Official rates from Cruz Bay. Round-trip fares are double the one-way fare plus 15¢ per minute waiting charges after the first 10 minutes. Two-hour island tours are $30 for 1 or 2 passengers; for 3 or more, $12 per person.

	1 person	2 people	3 or more (each)
Annaberg	10.00	12.50	5.00
Caneel Bay	2.50	5.00	2.50
Chocolate Hole	4.00	7.00	3.00
Cinnamon Bay	5.50	8.00	3.50
Coral Bay	10.00	12.50	5.00
Gallows Point	2.00	4.00	2.00
Maho Bay	10.00	12.50	5.00
Reef Bay Trail	6.00	9.00	5.00
Trunk Bay	5.00	7.50	3.00
Hyatt Regency	2.50	5.00	2.50

St. John Island-Wide Accommodation

Because of the small land area and the island's extreme popularity, St. John is an expensive place to visit although not necessarily more expensive than the other islands. If planning an extended stay on the island, remember that housing is expensive and difficult to find. If you want to buy a house here, count on shelling out $250,000! **note:** All street addresses should end with St. John 00830, and all PO Boxes with St. John 00831. All phone numbers are in area code 809 unless otherwise specified.

Cruz Bay accommodation: One of the island's best accommodation values is **The Inn at Tamarind Court** (tel. 776-6378, 800-221-1637; Box 350, St. John 00831) which once went by the seemingly unlikely name of Huldah Sewer's Guest House. It has been completely redone by the accommodating and helpful management and is conveniently located in town around three blocks from the ferry pier. Breakfast (superb coffee and croissants) is included. There are 17 comfortable rooms with fans and one with a/c. The bar/restaurant (good local food by Etta) is set in a courtyard and is a local hangout. Rates start at $38 economy (shared bath) s or d, $63 standard s or d. A more expensive family suite (holds up to four) and an apartment (kitchen) are also available. Featuring continental breakfast and a sunset bar, **Cruz Inn** (tel. 776-7688, 800-666-7688; Box 566, Cruz Bay 00831) offers a variety of rooms. Set two blocks from the ferry pier, it is comfortable and has friendly management. Its 14 guest rooms with shared bath start at $45 d; housekeeping units charge $60 and up. Also in town, the attractive **Raintree Inn** (tel. 776-7688, fax 776-7449, 800-666-7688; Box 566, St. John 00831) has eight rooms as well as three efficiencies which rent for $70-$95 with an $8 energy surcharge.

ultra-luxury resorts: Billing itself as "the smaller friendlier hotel," **Gallows Point Suite Resort** (tel. 776-6434, 800-323-7229, fax 776-6520; Box 58, St. John 00831) offers oceanview and harborview loft and garden suites set on a secluded peninsula just five min. on foot from Cruz Bay. Each comfortably-equipped suite has a kitchen, living room, and a private porch area. The large tiled bath has a shower in a garden-like area. Although furnished according to each owner's peculiar tastes, assets generally include TV, stereo, blender, microwave, dishwasher, pots and pans, and a wall safe. There's also a small pool by the sea with good snorkeling off the rocky beach. Service lives up to the hype, and you get a briefing when you check in. Early risers can score a photocopy of faxed news from *The New York Times*. Rates start at $125 for a garden loft and run up to $295 for an oceanview loft. Rates include transport to and from pier, welcome cocktail party (Sat. from 4-6), complimentary continental breakfast, and cocktails at Ellington's Restaurant. Land/sail, honeymoon, and dive packages are also available. Children under five are not welcome here. Located relatively near town at Great Cruz Bay, the **Hyatt Regency St. John** offers tennis, complimentary water sports, pool, an exercise studio, and restaurants. There are 34 acres of gardens overlooking a 1,200-ft. white sand beach. It has 285 luxuriously appointed guest rooms, suites, townhouses, and 48 villas. Rates run from $175 off-season and $305-$495 during the winter. Call 693-8000, 800-233-1234, fax 779-4985, or write Box 8310, Great Cruz Bay, St. John 00831. Its main competitor in terms of exclusivity, Caneel Bay, is described under a separate section later on in this chapter.

camping: "Camping" is available at Cinnamon and Maho Bays (see "accommodations" under respective sections and camping chart), but only Cinnamon Bay has bare sites where you can pitch your own tent. In depth reviews of these are provided in the appropriate sections.

hosteling: While there is no official youth hostel, the **St. John Hostel** (tel. 693-5544) offers the cheapest accommodation on the island at $20 pn for a bunk bed. It's well out of town on Centerline Rd. at the junction with Bordeaux Mountain Rd. You would probably want to have your own wheels if staying here.

rental services: Virgin Islands Bed and Breakfast Homestays (tel. 779-4094, 776-7836) arranges accommodations in private homes. For villa rentals contact **Star Villas** (tel. 776-6704, fax 776-6183; Box 599, Cruz Bay 00831) which offers one- and two-bedroom villas in or near Cruz Bay or Johnson Bay. Rates start at $65 and go up to $225 during the winter. Another alternative is **Catered To** (tel. 776-6641, fax 779-6191; Box 704, Cruz Bay 00831), offering a variety of private homes which may have pools. **Resort Villas** (tel. 779-4723, 800-845-5275; Box 8349, St. John 00831) has a variety of two- to four-bedroom grand suites with pools, gardens, and views. **Caribbean Villas & Resorts** (tel. 776-6152, Box 458) has a wide selection of villas on St Thomas and St. John. Yet another option is

Destination St. John (tel. 776-6969, 800-562-1901; Box 8306). For more information call (800) 338-0987 or fax 779-4044 or 703-378-3039. **St. John Properties** (tel. 776-7223, Box 700) has 20 or so private homes and apartments. **Vacation Homes** (tel. 776-6094) has one of the best selections of house rentals ranging in price from $1,000 to $5,000 pw. For others check the latest issue of the *Tradewinds*.

houses and villa rentals: There are too many of these to describe them all. A private two-bedroom vacation home at Great Cruz Bay, **Grand View** incorporates modern West Indian design. Call (508) 758-9223, fax (508) 758-9762, or write Amy Brownell, Box 819, Mattapoisett, MA 02379. Offering 10 units in two buildings with twin bed in the bedroom, living room with twin studio beds, and kitchen, **Serendip Vacation Apartments** (tel. 776-6646; Box 273, St. John 00830) offers great views of Cruz Bay. Rates start at $60 s, $80 d with weekly rates available. Run by potter Donald Schnell and his wife Deborah, **Villa Bougainvillea** ($145 and up) and **Gift Hill Villa** ($165 and up) are three-bedroom luxury houses which are tastefully furnished and offer great views. Call 776-6420 (day), 776-6856 (eve.), fax 776-6920, call (800) 253-7107, or write Box 349, St. John 00803. **Sea Cay Villa** (tel. 776-6094; Box 272, St. John 00831) is a three-bedroom home with sundeck and private pool overlooking the S shore. Renting for around $138-$195, **Battery Hill** (tel. 776-6152, 800-524-2095; Box 458) is a set of eight two-bedroom villas near a beach and with a pool, kitchen, and A/C. **Edie's Eden** (tel. 776-6061; Box 1) has a fan, kitchen, and TV. It rents from $100-$115. **Intimate Inn** (tel. 776-6133; Box 432) has a pool and kitchen. Rates are available upon request. A set of one- and two-bedroom condos located near Cruz Bay, **Lavender Hill Estates** (tel. 776-6969; Box 8306, St. John 00830) have a pool, kitchen, and TV; some units have a/c. Rates run around $210 for a one-bedroom and $260 for a two-bedroom. Near the Virgin Grand Resort, guests at the **Virgin Grand Villas** (tel. 524-2038, fax 775-4202, 800-524-2038; PMC, Rte. 6, St. Thomas 00802) are permitted use of the former's facilities. It features studios and one- and two-bedroom a/c villas with private pool and Jacuzzi, kitchen, living/dining, telephone, cable TV, and maid service. Rates start at $186 for a one- to four-person terrace studio; they rise to a high of $850 (2-8 persons) for a three-bedroom pool villa. A 10% surcharge is added. Featuring two one-bedroom apartments and a one bedroom home with fans and a TV, **Casa Mariposa** (tel. 776-6639;14 F Enighed, St.

Cruz Bay

Cinnamon Bay

(809)

John 00830) is near the Texaco station and rents for $70 d on up; weekly rates are available. A set of one-bedroom luxury condos with cable TV and a/c, **Cruz Bay Villas** (tel. 776-6146; Box 656) rents for around $135-$175 d. A set of ten a/c villas with kitchens surrounding a large pool, **Pastory Estates** (tel. 776-6152; 800-338-0987; Box 458, St. John 00831) rents for around $150. Three one-bedroom a/c units, **Samuel Cottages** (tel. 776-6643, Box 123; St. John 00831) has kitchens and decks and are near town. They rent for about $70 pn, $450 pw. **Sunset Ridge Villas** (tel. 776-6152, 800-338-0987; Box 458; St. John 00831) has a pool, kitchen, a/c. **Alta-Vista** (tel. 776-7105, Box 184) offers three large houses with six gardens. Rates run from $800 pw up to $1,300 during the winter. **Caribe Havens** (tel. 776-6152, Box 458, St. John 00831) offers eight homes from $750 pw. At Hurricane Hole, (tel. 776-6321) is a set of four one- and two-bedroom houses with gardens and private beach. They rent for $1,000 pw on up. **The Lost Chord** (776-7105, 201-837-6859; Box 37, St. John 00831) is a secluded villa holding from two to eight, charging around $138 pd and $945 pw. A set of seven homes, **Star Villa** (tel. 776-6704, Box 599; St. John 00831) rents for $65 pn summer and $100 pn winter and up. **Vacation Homes** (tel. 776-6094, Box 272; St. John 00831) comprises some 13 villas, homes, and cottages. Eight villas, some of which have pools, **Vacation Vistas** (tel. 776-6462, Box 476; St. John 00831) rents for $560 pw summer and $672 pw winter on up. A set of one- to five-bedroom homes with great views, **Windspree, Inc.** (tel. 776-7423, fax 776-7423; 6-2-1A Estate Carolina, St. John 00830) rent from $130 summer and $145 winter. Renting for $1,200 pw summer and $1,950 pw winter, **The Villa Capiz** (tel. 776-6918, 124 Gift Hill; St. John 00830) is a group of villas with decktop spa which offer great views. Two cottages designed with lovers in mind, **Odessa** (tel. 776-7105, Box 184; St. John 00831) rent for around $900 pw summer and $1,200 pw winter. **The Six Palms Guest House** (tel. 776-7836, Box 191, St. John 00831) rents for $975 pw. Renting out six luxury homes and 18 condos, **Island ReTreats** (tel. 774-3843, 800-562-1901, fax 774-3843; Box 37; St. John 00831) charges from around $560 pw and up.

St. John Food, Dining, and Entertainment

note: In referring to restaurant prices in this section, *inexpensive* means you can dine for $15 and under including a drink, appetizer, and dessert; you may in fact pay more. *Moderate* is $16-$25; *expensive* is $26-$40; and *very expensive* means over $40 a meal.

food: Because so little is grown here and things must be imported via St. Thomas, food is expensive. Right at the pier, the **Dockside Pub** has reasonable prices including breakfast specials. At Meada's Shopping Plaza near the pier, **JJ's Texas Coast Cafe** features moderate Tex-Mex dishes; catfish is served on Fri. nights. **Chicken B-B-Q** stands opposite the PO. **The Back Yard** usually has a luncheon special. **Cafe Roma** (tel. 776-6524) has good pizza as well as seafood, veal parmigiana, and baked pastas. **The Rock Lobster Bar and Restaurant** offers entrees such as coconut prawns ($15), fettuccini ($14), and a half lobster ($20-28). Upstairs from the Convenience Store, **Gumpy's** is one of the most reasonably priced restaurants; it has $5.50 lunch specials and their Sunday Brunch offers all you can eat for $8. Local food spots include **Miss Maeda's** (near The Back Yard), **Fred's**, and **Etta's** ($6 lunches) which is inside the Inn at Tamarind Court. For really good and reasonable local food ($7-8 for a large plate) try **Hercules**, a modest establishment down the road towards the harbor from the Tamarind Inn. They have a $12 buffet on Fridays. **Cap's Place** has conch fritters for $1 as well as other reasonable food. At Wharfside Village, **Wendy's** provides low-cost eating with good chili, a salad bar, and tables right on the waterfront. Located behind the gas station and across from the Cruz Inn, **Paradise Pizza** offers subs, David's Crazy Bread, and falaccio. **The Old Gallery** serves moderate American and Caribbean dishes and features buffet nights. Conspicuously located below The Gallery, **Café Cool** has cappucinos ($1.50), beer, and baked goods. One of the best of the town's restaurants, the **Lime Inn** (tel. 776-6425) has all-you-can-eat shrimp dinners. Across from Chase, **Hitchcocks' Bar & Grill** (tel. 779-4625) offers three meals with a wide variety of dishes and Sun. brunch. The **Barracuda Bistro** at Wharfside Village is a combo bakery. deli, and restaurant. which serves three meals per day. **Pussers**, a cousin of the one found on Tortola, has expensive gourmet terrace dining; the **Crow's Nest** upstairs has expensive snacks ($7 for nachos) and burgers. Also upstairs is the **Paradise Cafe** which serves light food. The **Fishtrap** next to the Raintree Inn offers daily fish specials. Offering counter service, open air **Beni Iguana's** serves stir fry and pricey sushi. It also has expresso ($2!), conch fritters, egg rolls, mozzarella sticks, and other goodies. Named after mystery writer Duke Ellington and his wife Kay who operated an inn here from

1948-1978, **Ellington's at Gallow's Point** offers amazingly diverse continental breakfasts ($6) and other specials. Dishes here include blackened shrimp, swordfish scampi, and linguini with pesto. Offering "positive vibes and hugs," **Luscious Licks and Divine Desserts** has gourmet ice cream (Ben & Jerry's) and sweets. In addition to telling you about its pricey vegetarian dishes ($6 veggie burger and sandwiches), its menu offers useful information about the planet's dietary situation and a "free psychiatric corner" which asserts that "all you really have is the moment" so "be here now." It's down the road along North Shore Rd. along the way to Mongoose Junction. On the road to Mongoose from town, **Morgan's Mango** (tel. 693-8141) offers Caribbean cuisine. One alternative to the restaurants is to load up on bread, cheese, and other such digestible commodities at **Marcelino's Bakery** inside Mongoose Junction; they also sell pizza slices. **Mongoose Restaurant** offers appetizers such as escargot and Greek salad as well as entrees including catch of the day and lobster tail. Tues. is Mexican night here. **The Paradiso** (tel. 776-8806) is upstairs and serves a good selection of N Italian and Continental cuisine. All you can eat pasta nights are on Tues. Out at the Hyatt, **Chow Bella** offers a mixture of Chinese and Italian dishes. Out on Centerline Rd. (Rte. 10) and the junction with Bordeaux Rd. (Rte. 108), **Le Chateau de Bordeaux** is set by a beautiful overlook. Modest but expensive, it offers gourmet cuisine such as saffron pasta, West Indian seafood chowder, and yellowtail tuna. Other restaurants of note are out at Caneel Bay and near Coral Bay (see travel section).

market shopping: Very expensive, so try to bring what you can with you. If you're planning on cooking your own food at the campground and staying a while, it may be worth going over to St. Thomas to shop (as many of the locals do) because the few local stores have a minimum selection of goods at maximum prices. In any event, when buying canned or bottled goods be sure to check the expiration date. Keep an eye out for the fruit and vegetable boat at the harbor which arrives regularly from Puerto Rico. **The Rolling Pin** is next to Elite Dry Cleaners and has an excellent selection of bread and pastries, as does the aforementioned Marcellino's Bakery in Mongoose Junction. For fresh produce (imported, of course) there's a fruit and vegetable stand near the commercial pier and **Lilian Smith's Grocery** is on Centerline Road. **Convenience Market** is in Wharfside Village, and **Swans Deli** is just down the street from Fred's. Set in Boulon Center, **Big**

Al's Supernatural Foods offers a wide variety of basic as well as gourmet food. Sample prices: Tamari $6.95/20 oz., Buena Vista Chardonnay $14.25/liter, blue corn chips $3.95/10 oz., Cherry Garcia $3.85/pint, Arrrowhead Mills peanut butter $6.95/18 oz., and coconut milk $1.95/14 oz. **The Boulon Center Deli** is also here. On Southshore Rd. next to Paradise Laundry, the **Marina Market** offers a wide selection of items. Sample prices: Eden Soymilk $ 4.19 liter, milk $2.95/gallon, eggs $1.79 dozen, large wheat tortillas $1.99/pkg. of eight, Tropicana orange juice $4.19/half gallon, onions $1.29/lb., Budweiser $5.50/six pack, and Pepperidge Farms bread $2.99/lb. At 6M Enighed on the way to the Hyatt, Captain John's Mini Mart & Deli offers giant sandwiches for $5. Next door Pine Peace Liquors has an excellent selection of liquors and gifts. A well-stocked Mini-Mart is in Pine Peace.

entertainment: For its size, Cruz Bay has amazingly vibrant night-life. With a plethora of local guys around, tourist gals won't be lonely long. To find out what's happening where, check local tree trunks and utility poles, as well as the bulletin board across from the bank. Bands (mixing reggae, calypso and other rhythms) play regularly at **Fred's** (tel. 776-6363) as well as at the **Rock Lobster Bar** (tel. 776-6908) in Maeda's Mall. **Ellington's** sometimes offers steel pan music to accompany the view from their Sunset Lounge. **The Lime Inn** across the way is the place to sit and take in the music if you don't feel like dancing. Rock bands play at **Cool Breeze. The Inn at Tamarind Court** has live music on weekends as well as occasional dinner theater ($20). **Cruz Inn** also has entertainment. **Larry's Landing**, a popular hangout, has a pool table, video games, and dart board. Upstairs at Wharfside Village, **Redbeard's** offers cable TV, pool, snooker, shuffleboard, chess, backgammon, and cribbage in an elegant atmosphere. "Club attire" is requested. An Afro Caribe Ancient Drum Revival is held on Sun. at the Hyatt Regency's **Splash Bar**. For the religiously minded, there's tambor-ine rattlin' and heavy prayin' a'plenty in the Church of the **Apostles' Doctrine** incongruously located above Joe's Discount Liquors. **outlying:** There is entertainment in **Spotlight** at Coral Bay and **Shipwreck Landing** (tel. 693-5640), to the S of Cruz Bay, sometimes has jazz on Sundays. **The Still** (tel. 776-6866) in Coral Bay also has live music. Finally, don't miss the nightly audio-visual display put on by the moon, stars, and crashing surf.

Events, Shopping, Information, and Services

events: **St. John's Carnival**, now integrated with the U.S. Independence Day celebrations, commemorates the emancipation of slaves on July 3, 1848. Not as large as the one on St. Thomas but equally intense in atmosphere, the Carnival begins in the first days of July, climaxing on July 4 or 5. Constructed along the waterfront, Carnival Village has handicrafts, food and drink stalls as well as games and pony rides for children. Calypso and reggae bands from all over the Caribbean ride through town on the back of trucks. Celebrating begins in earnest at 4:30 AM on July 4 when St. Johnians depart their homes attired in diapers, pajamas, and other outlandish clothes for the "j'ouvert" (French for "opening" or "break of day") festivities. The parade is the highlight of the festival, and *its* highlight is the moko jumbee dancers who hop, skip, and do acrobatics on stilts. They are followed by the Carnival Queen and various floats. Evening fireworks climax the celebration. The biweekly **St. John Festival of the Arts**, a relatively new phenomenon, also takes place during the summer. Events are held in Cruz Bay's Park, Caneel's Patio, and Maho's Recreation Center. Past performers have ranged from folksinger Oscar Brand to the ultra-eclectic Joan Miller Dance Players. (Detailed information about the festival is available from Maho Bay's New York City office, 17 E. 73rd St., New York, NY 10021). A yearly celebration, commemorating the slave uprising of 1733, takes place around Thanksgiving; it includes a candlelight procession and symposiums.

shopping: The island's mellowness extends into its stores. About the only time these shopkeepers get upset is when they find that a customer has shoplifted an item. While the selection found on St. Thomas isn't available, neither does the "buy, buy, buy" atmosphere prevail. The bulk of the shops are run largely by transplanted continentals and offer attractive, moderately priced goods. Original designers include Janis Rutnik (at **At The Plum Tree**) and Lisa Etre (at **The Pink Papaya**); also **Rudy and Irene Patton** who design silver and gold jewelry. **Laurie's Frame Studio** has island art. **Caribbean Casting** sells (you guessed it). If you forgot or have run out of your art supplies, the extension of the Convenience Store has them at high prices. Back towards town from Mongoose,

Monkeyfist Studios & Gallery carries fine art and is a boutique. Nearby, the **Shirt Shack** has around 300 different tee shirts (including XX sizes) available; many have been designed by local artists. Across from Social Welfare in the town center, **Batik Caribe** carries a line of designs from St. Vincent. **Stitches**, nearby, sells tee shirts, shorts, shirts, and cotton dresses from India. In the Lemon Tree Mall you'll find **Pink Papaya** which stocks Haitian painted tinware and other handicrafts and colorful household items. Located next to the Dockside Pub right at the pier, **The Dock** offers tee shirts and other items. **Shell Seekers**, nearby, sells a variety of books and periodicals among other items. Right next to the Chase Bank and completed late in 1993, **Solomon's Plaza** is the latest shopping mall. The main shopping outside of town is found at the **Virgin Grand**. The **Caneel Bay Gift Shop** carries a line of clothes at high prices.

Wharfside Village shopping: To the R of the ferry dock along the road, this attractive complex contains some 30 stores. **Pussers** has upscale clothing, gift items, and some books. On the second floor, **Cruz Bay Gift Emporium** sells local and continental newspapers as well as magazines, books, and other goods. **Let's Go Bananas** features beachware. **Stitches II** offers tee shirts, shells, and other items. Other shops here include **Blue Carib Gems**, **Colombian Emeralds**, **Simply Cotton**, **Cruz Bay Clothing**, **Baja Beach Club**, **Virgin Canvas**, **Coral Bay Jewelers**, **Freebird Creations**, **Wharfside Garden Center**, and **Athlete's Foot**. Other shops are on the waterfront nearby, including **Sparky's**, which offers free delivery of alcohol to the airport.

Mongoose Junction: This is the island's foremost shopping complex. Inaugaurated in 1987, it continues to expand. Its distinctive masonry design incorporates stone and coral, drawing inspiration from the island's 18th-century plantations. The first building you see coming from town houses **Big Planet** (adventure gear), **Little Planet** (kid's adventure gear), **Seasons** (a boutique for everybody), and the **Paradiso** restaurant. **Mongoose Trading** (home furnishing and clothing), **I-Catchers Sportswear** (handpainted designs), and **Bodywear** (handcrafted jewelery). The next building houses **Columbian Emeralds** (jewelry, perfume, imports), and **Bamboula** (Caribbean folk art, antiques, and clothing). Behind this is **Saja** which is one of the most innovative boutiques on the islands–if not in the entire Caribbean–with clothing made of fabric from all over the globe. In another building, the **Donald Schnell Studio** displays pottery and handblown glass. Among its more unusual features are custom designed signs, fountains, and lighting. **Batik Kibab** offers a variety of examples of this Indonesian dying technique. Near Marcelino's, the **Clothing Studio** has handpainted designs on resort ware and tee-shirts. **Wicker, Wood, and Shells** presents an international selection of hancrafted items and jewelry as well as a good selection of books and art. The **Fabric Mill** offers an international selection of cloth including rolls of batik. In the next building, is the **Canvas Factory** (bags and luggage) as well as **St. John Water Sports** which has scuba rentals ($6/day), beachware, tee shirts, and a good selection of books. Also located in Mongoose, **MAPes MONDe** offers a fine line of map and print reproductions as well as books.

beaches: From Cruz Bay going around the island to the E lie Honeymoon Beach, Caneel Bay, Hawknest Bay, Trunk Bay, Cinnamon Bay, Little Maho Bay, and Francis Bay. Classic and lined by coconut palms, **Honeymoon Bay** is popular with snorkeling boats. You must walk here from Caneel or from town (30 min. via the Lind Point trail). On the way, you'll hit **Solomon Bay**, a small "nudist" beach where the anti-nudist forces have been active of late. Rangers have been coming by to hassle naturists so ask around before you skinny dip. Keep in mind that the locals, a modest people, are offended by nudism. **Caneel Bay** has the resort of the same name. The best snorkeling is found around the point to the R from the main beach. There are also a number of less accessible beaches. **Hawksnest Bay** offers covered picnic tables and pit toilets: don't fall in! Unfrequented on weekdays, it's packed on weekends. **Jumbie Beach** is nearby and down a trail. The most famous beach, **Trunk Bay** has an underwater snorkeling trail and a full range of facilities. It's always packed. Another beautiful beach is **Cinnamon**. Snorkel off the rocks to the R. **Maho Bay** has calm water but not the best snorkeling. Sea turtles may be spotted here. While Little Maho has the campground, Big Maho has no facilities save shade. Neighboring **Francis Bay** is also known for its calm water and sea turtles; birdwatch at the small salt pond behind the beach. Unless graced by a breeze, bugs invade to search for fresh blood in the afternoons. More remote and requiring your own transportation and/or a hike, there are a number of other beaches. **Leinster Bay** is 3/4 mi. past the Annaberg ruins and has superior snorkeling. A visit here may be combined with hiking. Set on the N side and sometimes confusing to find, **Haulover Bay** has good snorkeling off of the reefs to the L. **Salt Pond Bay** provides good snorkeling around the point, and you can hike to Ram Head.

information: The **tourist office** is near downtown next to the new post office. No one would accuse the staff of being overenthusiastic. Be sure to obtain *The St John Guidebook* and the accompanying map. Both are useful for shopping and dining. A copy of the local newspaper, *Tradewinds*, is indispensable, and it also makes a wonderful souvenir. To subscribe send $30 for one year or $55 for two years to Box 1500, Cruz Bay, St. John USVI 00831. Open daily from 8-4:30, the **National Park Service** office (tel. 776-6201), next to the ferry pier, is perhaps the best source of information on the island. Don't procrastinate—make this your first stop. Folders, maps, and an excellent selection of books are available. Ask for information about any of an incredible number of activities including nature hikes, history walks, and snorkel trips. They also present films and talks at Cinnamon Bay campground. Information can be obtained in advance by writing directly to National Park Service, Box 710, St. John, USVI 00830.

services: **Telephones** are located at the dock near the park and across from the **post office**, which, in turn is near the tourist information office. Chase has opened a small branch **bank** near the Lutheran church. The beautiful, carpeted two-story **Elaine Ione Sprauve Library**, a reconstruction of the Enighed Estate great house, is on the same road as the Inn at Tamarind Court. Special cultural programs are often held here. **Inn Town Laundromat** is located next to the Rain Tree Inn. Set on Southshore Road are **Paradise Laundromat** and **Paradise Laundry Service**. **Virgin Islands Communications** (Connections) (tel. 776-6692) offers a variety of services including typing/word processing, laminating, laundry drop off, answering service, mailing service, photocopies, and outgoing phone calls at direct dial rates (in air conditioned privacy). Video ($3/tape; good selection of foreign films) and VCR rentals are available at **Love City Videos** in Bouldon Center.

rentals: It isn't necessary to rent a car if you're willing to do some walking, as local transport (and charter taxis) run all along the North Shore Rd. and head past and/or into Caneel, Trunk, Cinnamon, and Maho. Where a car does come in handy is when visiting areas such as the East End and Lameshur Bay which are more remote. However, a one-day rental should be sufficient unless you are staying well out of town. **Cruz Bay Scooter Rental** (tel. 776-6493) rents motorcycles, scooters, snorkel gear, and underwater cameras. Car rentals include: **Budget** (tel. 776-7575), **Conrad Sutton** (tel. 776-6479), **Delbert Hills** (tel. 776-6637/7947, 800-537-6238), **Cool Breeze Car Rental** (tel. 776-6588), **Hertz/Varlack** (tel. 776-6695), **Spencer's Jeep Rentals** (tel. 776-7784/6628, fax 776-7118), **St. John Car Rental** (tel. 776-6103), and **O' Conner Car Rental** (tel. 776-6343). Gas runs about $1.50/gal. The only gas stations are in Cruz Bay and out of town at Pine Peace so be sure to fill up regularly.

health care: In case of emergency, a doctor can be reached 24 hours a day by calling the **Dept. of Public Safety** (tel. 776-6262). At 3B Sussanaberg, the **St. John Community Health Clinic** (tel. 776-6400, fax 779-6400) can be reached at 922 during an emergency. **Dr. James P. Clayton** (tel. 776-7862) offers emergency medicine and family practice on a 24 hr. basis. Also contact **Dr. Robert C. McMullen** (tel. 776-7903) who has his office near the Inn at Tamarind Court. For dental care contact **St. John Dental** (tel. 776-8688). **St. John Drug** (tel. 776-6353) is across from the Texaco Station. Set in the Inn at Tamarind Court, **Massage Therapy** (776-6080) offers Swedish reflexology, deep tissue massage, and relaxation therapy.

St. John Watersports, Excursions, and Tennis

watersports: Call **Low Key Watersports** (tel. 776-7048, 800-835-7718) at Wharfside Village for parasailing or sea kayaking as well as diving (four different wreck dives $75-130, night dives, and certification courses) and snorkeling. Featuring a wide variety of diving excursions **Cruz Bay Watersports** (tel. 776-6234, fax 776-8303, 800-835-7730) has a free snorkeling map. Also try **St. John Watersports** at Mongoose Junction. Various rentals are available at Cinnamon Bay and Maho Camps. Sunfishes are also at Maho. The **Coral Bay Sailing School** (tel. 776-6922/6665) has a variety of rentals and offers glass bottom boat tours; tickets for the latter may be purchased at Connections. Another valuable connection is **Coral Bay Watersports** (tel. 776-6850, day, 776-7989, eve.) at Estate Carolina, which offers everything from diving to sea kayaking, surfing to mountain biking. **sea kayaking:** Although a number of operations offer sea kayaking, the main company with trips is **Arawak Expeditions** (tel. 693-8312; 800-238-8687). They run introductory half-day trips ($30) as well as full-day trips which visit remote parts of St. John and head over to surrounding islands. Five-day (around $750) and seven-day (around $925) trips are also available. An adventurous five-day trip explores the BVI heading towards the Barths, then along islands such as Salt Island and Dead Chest before crossing the Sir Francis Drake Channel to the West End of Tortola and heading N to Jost Van Dyke before returning. Accommodation is camping. There is also an abbreviated five-day version of this trip. Trips leave from Big Planet (tel. 776-6638) in Mongoose Junction.

boat excursions: Most of these are in the $70 range for a day sail. **Connections** (tel. 776-6922) arranges sailing trips and trips to Jost Van Dyke. The *Jolly Mon* (tel. 776-6239), a 60-ft catamaran, sails around the East End and South Shore. Lunch is provided, and a Champagne Sunday Brunch is offered. The *Cam 'Rita* (tel. 776-6922) offers a day sail on a 50-ft. ketch which includes champagne, lunch, drinks, and snorkel gear and instruction. A classic Morgan 41-ft. custom sloop, the *Shimmer* (tel. 776-6922) leaves from town or the Hyatt and offers full-day, half-day, and sunset sails. *Restless* offers the usual sails as well; call 776-6922, eves. and Suns. 779-4514. *Ocean Diver* (tel. 776-6234, 779-4351) has a variety of snorkeling trips for $25 (3 hrs.) and $40 (6 hrs.). *Sunset Sue* (tel. 776-6922) has a day sail out of Coral Bay which includes champagne, lunch, drinks, and snorkel gear and instruction. *Gypsy Spirit* (tel. 771-1364), a Coronado-27, offers sunset sails, full moon sails, and Sun. three-hour sails.

snorkeling spots, dive spots, and coral reefs: Most dive excursions head for points off the N coast as well as to the E end of St. Thomas. They can take you to the West Indian Transport Shoal (see St. Thomas), and the *RMS Rhone* (see "Rhone National Marine Park" in the BVI travel section). Carvel Rock and the dropoff by Congo Cay are two popular sites. A lovely coral grotto housing nurse sharks and stingrays, Eagle Shoal has numerous crevices. Offshore at Cruz Bay, Steven Cay features sea fans, mountain and star corals, and large numbers of triggerfish and angelfish. Others include Fishbowl at Cruz Bay, Johnson Reef on the N coast, and Horseshoe and South Drop (a fairly narrow ridge of seafloor cracks and fissures which is a good place to spot large fish) on the S coast. A well developed reef structure between Grassy and Mingo cays, Grassco Junction offers seven towers around which turtles, octupi, and stingrays gather. Off of Caneel Bay, you can see spotted eagle rays; avoid feeding them. Owing to the rougher water, the S coast is seldom snorkeled or dived. St. John's reefs include Leinster Bay's Waterlemon Cay (an islet) and the reef (and underwater trail) offshore from Trunk Bay which has suffered greatly from abuse and overuse by tourists. **snorkeling trips:** Offered by the Park Service (tel. 776-6330; check times and reserve), a six-hr. three-stop round-island snorkeling trip ($40) runs Tues. and Friday. There's also a two-stop, three-hr. snorkel tour (Mon. and Wed., 9 AM) and a night snorkel tour (Thurs., 5:30 PM). One snorkel safari (Tues., 2 PM, advanced) meets at the Cinnamon Bay lifeguard station; another meets (Sat., 2 PM, beginners) at Trunk Bay. **scuba rentals/trips:** In town, **Cruz Bay Water Sports** (tel. 776-6234; Box 252, St. John 00830), out at Cinnamon Bay, **St. John Water Sports** (tel. 776-6256; Box 252, St. John 00830), and in Coral Bay, **Coral Bay Water Sports** (tel. 776-6587; Box 569, St. John 00830) rent scuba and snorkeling gear. Another is **Jim Travers Caneel Bay Diving** (tel. 776-6111; Box 550, St. John 00830) which has two diving boats.

boating charters: Contact **Connections** (tel. 776-6922) for information concerning boat charters. **Ocean Runner** (tel. 776-7864) rents 20- , 22- , or 25-ft. hydrasport powerboats.

others: To try **Snuba**, a type of snorkeling using an air source contained on a flotation raft that follows your every move underwater, call 693-8063 or page 776-2052. Trips explore Trunk Bay, and you can also check in at the Gift Shop there. For horseback riding, **Pony Express** (tel. 776-6922, 776-6494) offers trail rides and excursions from $40 for one hour on up to $100 for moonlight beach rides which are custom tailored.

fishing: There is no deep-sea fishing allowed in National Park waters. However, rod-and-reel fishing is allowed from the beaches, but not in buoyed swimming areas. Red Hook (see "St. Thomas") is a center for sport fishing. *Gone Ketchin'* (tel. 776-7709; 1-B Catherineberg 00830) is a 25-ft. cabin boat which offers beginning to advanced sport fishing. **World Class Anglers** (tel. 779-4281; Box 8327, Cruz Bay 00831) offers half- and full-day trips; ask for Capt. Loren Nickbarg.

tennis: In Cruz Bay, two courts are near the fire station and lighted until 10. The **Hyatt Regency** (tel. 776-7171, ext. 1740) offers six lighted courts which are open until 11; non-guests are charged $10/hr. **Caneel Bay** (tel. 776-6111, ext. 234) has 11 courts; lessons ($25/30 min.) are offered to non-guests.

The Virgin Islands National Park

Practically synonymous with the island itself, the Virgin Islands National Park is the island's most valuable resource. Remember that this is a trust held in perpetuity and one which visitors years hence will wish to find in the same shape it is today. Act accordingly.

the making of a national park: In 1939, a National Park Service study compiled by Harold Hubler recommended that a park be established on St. John; the plan was forgotten after the onset of WW II. Cruising around the Caribbean for six years after the war, multimillionaire philanthropist Laurence Rockefeller determined

---

SAINT JOHN HIKING TRAILS

1. Brown Bay Trail (1.2 miles, 2 hours)
2. Johnny Horn Trail (1.5 miles, 2 hours)
3. Leinster Bay Trail (0.8 miles, 30 min.)
4. Francis Bay Trail (0.3 miles, 15 min.)
5. Reef Bay Trail (2.5 miles, 2 hours)
6. Cinnamon Bay Trail (1.2 miles, 1 hour)
7. Cinnamon Bay Self-Guiding Trail (1 mile, 1 hour)
8. Peace Hill (Christ of Caribbean)
9. Water Catchment Trail (0.8 miles, 30 min.)
10. Turtle Point Trail (0.5 miles, 30 min.)
11. Caneel Hill Trail (2.1 miles, 2 hours)
12. Lind Point Trail (1.5 miles, 1 hour)
13. Caneel Hill Spur Trail (0.9 miles, 40 min.)
14. Petroglyph Trail (0.3 miles, 15 min.)
15. Lameshur Bay Trail (1.8 miles, 1 1/4 hours)
16. Bordeaux Mountain Trail (1.2 miles, 1 1/2 hours)
17. Yawazi Point Trail (0.3 miles, 20 min.)
18. Salt Pond Bay Trail (0.2 miles, 15 min.)
19. Drunk Bay Trail (0.3 miles, 20 min.)
20. Ram Head Trail (0.9 miles, 1 hour)

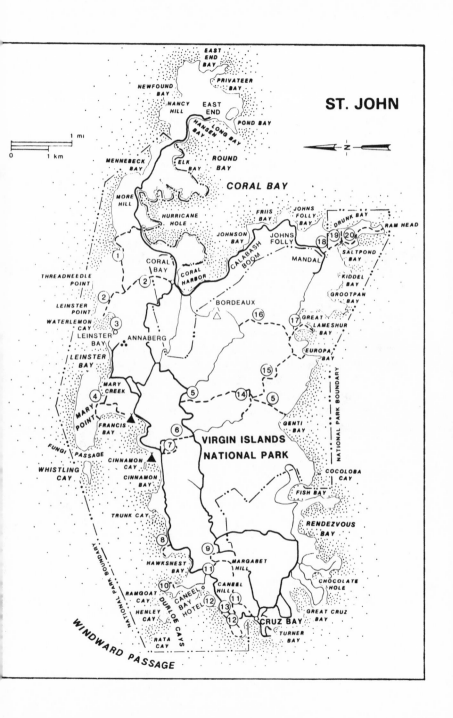

that the island had "the most superb beaches and view" of any place he had ever seen, and that St. John was "the most beautiful island in the Caribbean." He quickly bought up nearly half the island during the early 1950s and established an exclusive resort at Caneel Bay on the grounds of a ruined sugar plantation. Discovering Hubler's report, Rocky transferred the property into his Jackson Hole Preserve Corporation, a nonprofit tax writeoff. Jackson Hole then offered to donate over 5,000 acres, provided they retained franchise rights to the park area. Legislation signed into law by President Eisenhower on Aug. 2, 1956, authorized the federal government to accept donation of up to 9,500 acres. No local opinion was sought before a government bill was introduced in Congress in 1962 which would have authorized $1.25 million to acquire another 3,300 acres of St. John by condemnation–whether the owners acquiesced or not! This sum was contingent upon a Rockefeller offer to provide matching funds. Even the government administrator for the island first heard of the plan over the radio, and he, like other islanders, was outraged. The bill passed (without the condemnation clause) and Rocky withdrew his offer of matching funds. In 1976 the park was included in the initial network of biosphere reserves designated by the United Nations, and a Virgin Islands Biosphere Research Center was completed in 1986. The park's popularity has grown dramatically over the decades: it now receives some 1.2 million visitors per year.

boating: Park waters are subject to regulations designed to help preserve the environment. The N and S offshore areas were added to the park in 1962. Altogether, there are 26 anchorages around the island. Overnight stays in park waters are limited to 14 days per year, and boats are not to be left unattended for more than 24 hours. Charts and maps, along with a complete list of park regulations, are available at the Cruz Bay Ranger Station and at the Visitor's Center in Red Hook. For excursions and charters see "Islandwide Practicalities" earlier in this chapter.

hiking: A total of 21 trails–from brief walks to two-hour jaunts–are probably the most under-utilized of all St. John's resources. Because most are steep and rocky, they give maximum exercise for the time involved. In just a short time, you climb from 700 to 1,200 ft. above sea level, where you get a very different view of the island! Trees creak in the wind and shy feral donkeys scatter when approached. Although NPS tours are available (see "Islandwide

Practicalities"), the best way to go is on your own. If you do go with the park service, be sure to book trips well in advance if possible.

Cruz Bay

Cruz Bay, with its relaxed, ecologically-minded feeling, is like a miniature version of Berkeley, California transplanted to the Caribbean. So small that there are no street signs, its slow pace of life is intoxicating and contagious. Aside from the ultramodern but aesthetically pleasing Mongoose Junction shopping center, there are a few shops, a small park, and a ranger station for the park. **Note:** For accommodations, food, and services in Cruz Bay see "Islandwide Practicalities" earlier in this chapter.

sights: St. John's Administration Building, known as **the Battery**, was built on the foundation of an 18th C fortification. Explore the small museum, which has everything from seashells to antique maps within the narrow confines of old prison cells (open Mon. to Fri. 10-2, free admission). Near the pier stands the **Nazareth Lutheran Church**. **Gallow's Point**, directly across from the harbor and now the sight of numerous developments, served a gruesome purpose in its time. The museum portion of the **Elaine Sprauve Library and Museum** is open Mon. to Fri. 9-5. Farther out of town, along Centerline Rd. (formerly known as "Konge Vej"), stands the **Bethania Moravian Church**. Note the renovated 18th C Parish Hall, the vaulted cistern behind it, and the two Dutch ovens inside the small house to the rear. Near a large green water tank, a short road to the L leads to the ruins of **Estate Catherineberg**. One of the earliest plantations on St. John, it was restored in 1986. Here you'll find a beautifully rebuilt windmill which is one of the most impressive ruined structures in the Caribbean. It is only one of two sugar mill ruins featuring barrelled vaulting; the other is in Smithfield, St. Croix. If it hasn't been already, the road running here is slated to be paved in order to expedite transportation between Cinnamon Bay and the beaches. Back in town, the bandstand in the park was built in 1992 under the auspices of the St. John Community Foundation. The date palm in front of the tourist bureau was transplanted from in front of Oscar's Convenience Store in March 1993. In another direction, the now gunless **Lind Battery**, allegedly constructed in a single night by the English during either their 1801 or 1807 assaults, can be reached by the Lind Point Trail (see "hikes" below).

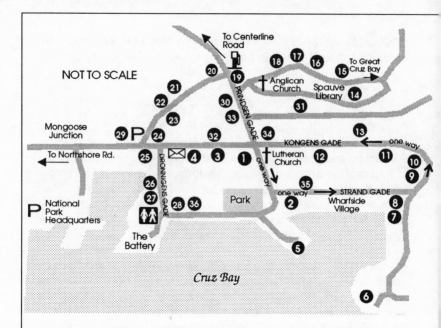

Cruz Bay

1. Connections
2. The Dock Shop
3. Rock Lobster Bay
4. Maeda's Shopping Mall
5. Ferry to Red Hook and Charlotte Amalie
6. Gallows Point Resort/ Ellington's Restaurant
7. Low Key Watersports
8. Beni Iguana's
9. Inn Town Laundromat
10. Raintree Inn/ Fish Trap Restaurant
11. Sutton Car Rental
12. Oscar's Convenience Market/Grumpy's
13. Pink Papaya, Lime Inn
14. Cruz Inn
15. Marina Market
16. Budget Rent-A-Car
17. Inn at Tamarind Court/ Etta's
18. The Rolling Pin
19. O'Conner Jeep Rental
20. St. John Drug Center
21. Big Al's Supernatural Food
22. Cruz Bay Watersports
23. Spencer's Jeep Rental
24. Cool Breeze Jeep Rental
25. St. John Car Rental
26. Virgin Gorda/Tortola Ferry
27. U.S. Customs and Immigration
28. Tourist Information
29. Luscious Licks and Divine Desserts/Morgan's Mango
30. Cafe Cool
31. Hitchcock's
32. Cafe Roma
33. Hitchcock's
34. Chase Manhattan/ Solomon's Plaza
35. Delbert Hill's Jeep Rental
36. De Castro Clinic

hikes around Cruz Bay: The **Lind Point Trail** (1.5 miles, one hour) connects the NPS Visitor Center with Caneel Bay Plantation. Just before the descent to Caneel Bay, the trail reaches an overlook at Lind Point. You enter the trail right in back of the ranger station where an open trail traverses pillar cacti, night blooming cacti, and tan tan, to reach a beautiful overlook facing Cruz Bay harbor; a great place to come for the sunset but bring a flashlight. Solomon Beach is next and then you can get to Honeymoon right next door by heading around in back of the NPS-owned house and following the road on. At Honeymoon, you'll find all sizes and shapes of frog people who have disembarked from yachts and boats and are working on their snorkeling skills. The **Caneel Hill Trail** (2.1 miles, two hours) joins Cruz Bay with the Northshore Rd. entrance to Caneel Bay via Caneel and Margaret Hills. These two trails are interconnected by the **Caneel Hill Spur Trail** (0.9 miles, 40 min.) which crosses Northshore Rd. at an overlook of Cruz and Caneel Bays. Be sure to stop and see Caneel Bay and its beach; the size of the place is incredible. At the main beach, you might find very tame egrets and pelicans at the far end. From here you can proceed to beautiful **Hawksnest Beach** by a curving road. A gem of a small beach, **Jumbie Beach** is nearby and down a trail. Interlocking Centerline and Northshore roads and joining the Caneel Hill trail over a portion of its route, the **Water Catchment Trail** (0.8 miles, 30 min.) has a deep-forest feeling to it. About three miles from town along Centerline Rd. is the shortest hike on the island; it takes 10 min. to get to the island's strangest sight, the **Christ of the Caribbean**. Set amidst the ruins of the Denis Bay Plantation with its sugar mill tower, this armless but enormous concrete statue was donated to the Virgin Islands National Park in 1975. It was built in the 1950s on the orders of a certain Col. Wadsworth, a transplanted mainlander, who dubbed the area "Peace Hill" and dedicated the statue to "inner and outer peace." If you didn't know what it was, you might assume it was some kind of Minoan deity. Jesus appears to be standing on stilts like carnival participant. The breathtaking 360° views and the ruined sugar mill with its exposed colony of bees make this site a must!

Caneel Bay

Here's where good American politicians are sent on holiday. Located about two miles down the road from Cruz Bay, this elite resort–the name comes from *kaneel*, the Dutch word for cinnamon–

is a place at which a select few of the well-connected and well-heeled can relax. Insulated from the plebeians by the surrounding parkland, this 171-room oasis of Florida-style architecture is set on 170 acres including gardens, tennis courts, and seven beaches. The only luxury missing is golf. Although much of its original posh status has been lost to Little Dix, another Rockresort in the neighboring British Virgins, it continues to attract prominent guests, including former President Richard Nixon. Because of the nature of its clientele, it is said that Caneel Bay is for "the newly wed or the nearly dead." Worthy of note on the grounds is the ruins of the Durloe Plantation, which has been ripped apart for transformation into a bar and gift shop.

practicalities: Rooms run from $200 up to a high of $645 during the winter. Room rates include guest room, use of sunfish, windsurfers, snorkeling gear, unlimited use of the ferry to St. Thomas, airport transfers, as well as special weekly activities. The Sugar Mill serves meals, including a Sun. brunch. Rates for visitors arriving for meals include RT fares on a private boat from Red Hook or regular transport from Charlotte Amalie. For more information call 776-6111, 800-223-7637; fax 776-2030; or write Box 720, St. John 00831.

from Caneel Bay: An elite-priced ferry ($12) runs to Charlotte Amalie, St Thomas. Call 776-6111 ext. 220 to check times. The **Lind Point Trail** (1.5 miles, one hour) goes back to Cruz Bay. **Turtle Point Trail** (0.5 miles, 30 min.) begins at the N end of Caneel Bay. (Register at the front desk at the main entrance before using this trail.) Farther down the main road to the E is Hawknest Bay and Peace Hill.

Trunk Bay

Most popular and famous of all the island's beaches, Trunk Bay is named after the "trunkback" or leatherback turtle (which may reach eight ft. and weigh up to 1,000 pounds)–though it's rarely seen around here these days. Another large creature, the cruise ship tourist, has moved in instead. Hundreds of cruise ship passengers may arrive at once. An hour in the water and they're on their way. Trunk Bay is not the place to come for solitude and seclusion. As many as 1,500 people (!) may visit here on a single day including up to a total of 100 power boats, which not infrequently damage the coral with their anchors. Definitely avoid this beach between 10 and 2, the hours of greatest congestion. The parking lot is a circus during this time period. Lockers and snorkeling equipment are available for rent here. A small snack bar (burgers, seafood salad, beers, and ice tea) is also present along with BBQ pits. **snorkeling trail:** Identified by orange markers, it's no longer quite the mecca for snorkelers that it used to be. The coral has been damaged by boat anchors, souvenir hunters, and careless swimmers. Friendly fish still greet you underwater, however, and tiny "ghost crabs" still spook the beach. Watch out for sea urchins.

Cinnamon Bay

This small but pretty beach has an outlying coral reef with lots of fish, a campground, and rewarding walks in the vicinity. Despite the name, no cinnamon grows here; the Danish mistook the smell of the bay rum trees for cinnamon. To get here take either one of the large taxi-buses ($3) from town, hitch, or walk.

accommodations: There are 10 bare sites, 40 erected tents, and 40 cottages available. Up to six people in two tents may occupy the bare sites (around $14 per night for two; add'l persons $4). Picnic table and charcoal grill are provided. Canvas tents (10 by 14 ft. with concrete floor) with camp cots, two-burner propane gas stove, and utensils, are $40 d during the low season; $10 extra third person). Cottages ($53 d during the low season; $10 extra third person) measure 15 by 15 ft., have concrete walls and floors, two screened walls, four twin beds, picnic table and grill, ice chest, propane gas stove, water container, cooking and eating utensils. Linen is changed weekly and a $20 deposit is required. Make reservations well in advance by writing Cinnamon Bay Campground, Box 720, Cruz Bay, St. John, USVI 00830, or Rockresorts Reservations, Box 5025, Boca Raton, FL. Or tel. (809) 776-6330, (800) 223-7637, (800) 442-8198 in New York State, (212) 586-4459 in New York City.

food: Best to bring as much of your own as possible. The commissary only has a limited and expensive supply of goods so it's better to shop in St. Thomas beforehand or even to bring food from the mainland. The snack bar and the **Tree Lizards Restaurant** serve food. Local music is featured on some nights. Cookouts on Sun.

nights provide a good opportunity to socialize with fellow camp-ers.

services and practicalities: Upon check-in (2-8 PM daily), you will be provided with a map of the campground. If arriving before that time, you may use camp facilities. Site assignments will be posted for those arriving after 8 PM. Check-out is 11; luggage may be left in the office. There are four bath houses; water should be con-served. Pay telephone service is available near the registration desk. Campground office numbers are 776-6330/6458, and 776-6111, ext. 260. The bus schedule is posted near the registration desk. Films are shown Sun. nights after the cookouts. Snorkel sets, scuba tanks and underwater cameras may be rented. Bring plenty of insect repellent to combat mosquitos, the most ferocious animals on the island. If you should see any donkeys do not feed them or place any food within their reach. Do not pet them (they can kick and bite without warning) and keep your children well away from them.

hiking: This is a good place to base yourself for hiking on the island. The **Cinnamon Bay Self-Guiding Trail** (one mile, one hour) passes by native tropical trees and the ruins of a sugar factory. The trailhead is a few yards E of the entrance road to the campground. A hundred yards E of the entrance road, **Cinnamon Bay Trail** (1.2 miles, one hour) goes past a stone cistern with guava trees in front to Cinnamon Bay ruins atop the hill. To the R is the estate house and to the L, buried in the bush, are the remains of the sugar factory. Built during the mid 19th C, the original estate house was destroyed by a hurricane during the early 1900s. A quarter mile farther atop a steep incline is a round platform which is the remains of one of a number of charcoal pits found in this part of the island. Still farther, along a path hemmed in by hogplum trees, is the old Danish cemetery. Tombstones here were sized according to the deceased's station in life. Look for thrashers, anis, quail doves, golden orb spiders, and the low-flying zebra butterflies. Also along this trail you may see "starvation fruit," which resem-bles a mushy white potato and Teyer palms, St. John's only indige-nous palm species, which is readily recognizable by its fan-shaped fronds–formerly used to make fish traps, brooms, fans, and build-ing roofs.

Maho Bay

This was the second campground on the island, opened in 1974. Designed with ecological conservation in mind, a series of tent cottages built on wooden boardwalks preserve the natural ground cover to prevent erosion; insecticides are not used here, and taps and communal toilet facilities are specially constructed to conserve water. Seeming more like tree houses than tents, all 105 of these three-room 16 by 16 ft. canvas cottages have completely equipped dining and cooking areas. Propane stove, ice cooler, and electric range are supplied. The living room readily converts to a second bedroom. The bedrooms have reading lamps and can be completely sealed off. Although farther from shore, the hillside tents are cooler during the daytime and have fewer bugs. Everything you need is supplied, and there's a small but complete commissary. Prices are high. Breakfast and dinner are also served. The "Help Yourself Center" has toys, books, and groceries left by departing guests. New Age groups hold occasional seminars here. Snorkeling equipment is available for rent. Estate Concordia, a nearby housing development, is a Maho Bay offshoot project. Rates are $55 per day d ($67 d , Dec. 15 to May 1), plus $10 per extra person. Write to Maho Bay Camps, Box 310, Cruz Bay, St. John, USVI 00830 (tel. 776-6240) or to Maho Bay Camps, 17-A E 73rd St., New York, NY 10021 (tel. 800-392-9004, 212-472-9453).

hiking: At the W end of the Mary Creek paved road, the **Francis Bay Trail** (0.3 miles, 15 min.) passes through a dry scrub forest, and past the Francis Bay Estate House to the beach. Several hundred slaves are said to have leaped to their deaths from Mary's Point during the 1733 slave revolt rather than face recapture. Local legend maintains that the water here turns red each May. At Francis Bay you can see and even swim with sea turtles. At Mary's Point, the rocky and precipitous hammer-headed peninsula set near the trail's beginning, you can see the nesting brown pelicans, an endangered species.

Annaberg Ruins

The attractive ruins of this sugar plantation sit atop a point overlooking Leinster Bay. The structures have been spruced up rather than restored, and a self-guiding tour takes you through what was once one of the 25 active sugar-producing factories on St. John. Imagine yourself back in the 18th C, when the entire surrounding area was covered in sugarcane. Comprising 510 acres and dating back to 1780, the estate was run by overseers, which is why no great house was ever built. Walk through the former slave quarters, the ruins of the village, the remains of the windmill, horsemill, boiling bench, and oven. Drawings of schooners and a street scene, which may date back to Dutch times, decorate the small dungeon. Fruit trees on the property were planted by Carl Francis, a cattle farmer, who lived here during the early 1900s.

vicinity of Annaberg: From here it's a nice–albeit very long–walk, via two interconnecting paths, to Coral Bay. First follow the **Leinster Bay Trail** (0.8 miles, 30 min.), actually the remains of an old Danish road, along the shoreline of Leinster (Waterlemon) Bay to the pebbled beach with its crystal-clear water. Waterlemon Cay (excellent snorkeling with coral reefs) is off in the distance. At Leinster Bay, you'll find a mangrove preserve. Herons nest in the buttonwood trees here, and bitterns, gallinules, lesser and greater yellowlegs, and black-necked stilts can be sighted as well. Next follow the ruins at the other end of the bay to the beginning of the historic **Johnny Horn Trail** (1.5 miles, two hours). The trail climbs a ridge framed by cactus and yellow spaghetti vine. The latter covers trees and bushes and looks as if someone had scattered gallons of spaghetti with tomato sauce. The trail follows the ridges S to the paved road running past the Emmaus Moravian Church in Coral Bay. The unmaintained **Brown Bay Trail** (1.2 miles, two hours) starts from the ridge saddle 0.6 miles along the Johnny Horn Trail. Branching to the E, it descends through a hot and open valley covered with dry thorn scrub before running along Brown Bay, then ascends across the ridge above Hurricane Hole before terminating at the East End Rd., 1.3 miles E of Emmaus Moravian Church.

Coral Bay

Quiet streets and a relaxed atmosphere mark the site of the best harbor in the U.S. Virgin Islands and a burgeoning boating center. More than two centuries ago Admiral Nelson claimed it was large enough to hold most of the navies of Europe. (It is still sufficient for a modern fleet.) Although it was the site of the first Danish settlement on the island, it never grew to the size or prominence hoped for. Originally named Crawl Bay, after the cattle enclosures found here, it was changed to Coral Bay later on by some person with an esthetic sense. Small though it may be, Coral Bay has its problems, as shown by the fact that Guy H. Benjamin School declares itself to be a "Drug Free School Zone."

sights: First to greet the visitor is the **Emmaus Moravian Church**. Constructed during the late 1700s on the site of the Caroline Estate, this large yellow building stands at the edge of town. Judge Sodtmann and his 12-year-old daughter were murdered on this spot during the 1733-34 slave revolt; local legend maintains that a jumbie (spirit) appears as a ram each and every full moon to haunt the premises. The windmill nearby is another relic of the vanished estate. Further to the N past the Moravian cemetery is the beginning of the path to the top of **Fort Berg Hill** which sticks out into the harbor. At the top are the ruins of Fort Berg, which slaves captured and held during the 1733-34 revolt (see "History"). The English Battery, at the foot of the fort, was built during the British occupation of 1807-14; a few rusty cannon are still lying about. (Ask permission from the owners of the Flamboyant Restaurant before exploring these ruins.)

practicalities: Billing itself as "A Pretty OK Place," **Skinny Legs Grill** serves food (burgers, dogs, and sandwiches) and is the local hangout bar; it has live music. **Mickey's Pizza** offers pizza ($1.75/slice) and other fare. Outside town towards the S, **Shipwreck Landing** has a good selection of food, and **Miss Lucy's** (2.7 mi. S) has good local food. Other restaurants include **The Still** and **Sea Breeze** both of which have Sun. brunches. The **Sputnik Bar & Grocery** has a variety of goods. **Joe's Discount** is at Estate Carolina to the S. **shopping: Out A Hand** sells pottery. Right by Shipwreck Landing, **Coral Bay Cabana** offers a variety of goods as does **Tall Ship Trading Co.** and the **Sugar Apple** which sells polished ammonite fossils, tee shirts, shell pillboxes, and unusual prints. **services: Connections** here (tel. 776-6922) offers long distance and local calls, copies, and fax service. **The Still** rents bicycles.

From Coral Bay

to the east: A dramatic road, surrounded by cactus-covered bluffs, leads to Round Bay at the E end of the island. There is an excellent view of Tortola to the L before reaching **Hurricane Hole** to the R where ships still shelter during hurricanes. This area is comparatively undeveloped and relatively few people live at this end of the island. There's no public transport, so drive yourself, hitch or walk. You can eat at **Vies Snack Shack** (conch fritters and other delicacies) or the **End of the Road Stand**.

to the south: From the junction before Coral Bay, take the road (concrete with bits of imbedded shell) along the mangrove-lined coast, which smells strongly of brine. The next town is **Calabash Boom** where there's a health clinic. The **Salt Pond Bay Trail** (0.2 miles, 15 min.) begins 3.6 miles S of Coral Bay and leads to Salt Pond Beach. (Don't leave valuables in your car). From the S of the beach, turn to the E and follow the **Drunk Bay Trail** (0.3 miles, 20 min.) along the N of the salt pond to Drunk Bay Beach (dangerous swimming). Most of the year this bleak and rocky beach ("drunk" means "drowned" in Dutch creole) is swept by 30-mph trade winds. The seaside lavender bay pea vines, which cover the sandy soil, prevent sea erosion. At the far end of Drunk Bay, Ram Head, the oldest rock on the island (dating from the Lower Cretaceous Period over 90 million years ago), overlooks a 200-ft. precipice. Follow **Ram Head Trail** (0.9 miles, one hour) to a blue cobble beach and on to the top. Wild goats and feral donkeys may be sighted in this area. Back on the main road, sandwiched on a peninsula between Great Lameshur and Little Lameshur Bays, is **Yawzi Point Trail** (0.3 miles, 20 min.). Years ago people afflicted with yaws (a contagious tropical skin disease resembling syphillis) were forced to live here in order to avoid spreading the disease. The **Lameshur Bay Trail** (1.8 miles, 1.25 hours) connects Lameshur Bay with Reef Bay trail through open forest. A rock side trail, 1.4 miles before the Reef Bay junction, leads to dramatically silent, pea-soup-colored **Europa Pool** (watch your footing). Look out for the Reef Bay Great House which has been recently restored. **Little Lameshur** features a few boats and snorkelers; donkeys and mongoose can be seen nearby. From Little Lameshur Bay, the sunny **Bordeaux Mountain Trail** (1.2 miles, 1.5 hours) climbs 1,000 feet right up to the top of 1,250-ft.-high Bordeaux Mountain, highest point on the island. Gently sloping and beautiful, it has stone seats by the side of the trails whick overlook Europa and Lameshur Bays. You generally share this blissfully serene trail only with the birds and breeze. There are magnificent views of the British Virgins from here. This trail dates from the time when donkeys laden with bay leaves would descend to the still at Lameshur Bay below. The oil was extracted by boiling in seawater, and then shipped to St. Thomas where it was used to produce St. John's Bay Rum, a famous cologne. From the top, the dirt road connects with Centerline Road and another (much rougher and steeper) runs to Coral Bay, but you'll probably want to come back down again rather than follow it on. **note:** The road down to Lameshur via Rte. 107 is extremely steep, although navigable, and you may wish to think twice before taking the plunge.

Reef Bay Trail

The most popular hiking trail on the island, the Reef Bay trail begins five miles E of Cruz Bay and takes two hours to negotiate. Formerly a wagon road, it was still the best road on the island as late as 1950. An incredible abundance of nature, much of it annotated by the National Park Service, grows along the sides of the trail. Descending through both wet and dry forests, the trail passes the remains of no less than five sugar estates, their stubbles of masonry foundation nearly consumed by strangler figs and wild orchids. Built of red and yellow imported brick, basalt rock, and brain coral, this attractive mosaic is still held together by local mortar of lime made from seashells, sand, molasses, and goat hairs. Stone rocks, laid over the road, act as culverts which divert the torrential rainfall. Along the path, you may see wild pigs, donkeys, or even a hermit crab clatter across the road. The laundry pool along the gutter of the trail was formerly a meeting and gossiping place for housewives. About 100 ft. away from a mango tree on the trail stand the remains of the wattle-and-daub Old Marsh House which was swept away in the Oct. 1970 floods.

Estate Par Force: These ruins are right on the trail. Built before 1780, it was remodeled in 1844. All that remains of the estate are the corral, sugar factory, and horsemill. In lieu of an expensive windmill, horses circumnavigating the 80-ft. grinding stone supplied power to grind the cane.

Petroglyph Trail: Beginning 1.7 miles down the Reef Bay Trail, it takes 15 min. to reach this quiet, peaceful, and secluded pool which teems with life, including wild shrimp. Situated below a small waterfall, chiseled petroglyphs were originally thought to have been the work of indigenous Indians. In 1971, a Ghanaian ambassador visiting the site, noted the resemblance of one of the symbols to an Ashanti one meaning "accept God." More recently, the double spirals have been found to be identical with those on Libyan tombstones dating from 200 A.D. Symbols of purification, these were decoded by Dr. Barry Fell, the world's leading epigrapher; the symbols mean "plunge in to cleanse and dissolve away impurity and trouble; this is water for ritual ablution before devotions."

Reef Bay Estate House and Sugar Plantation: Last stop on the trail. Made of local stone, the great house was originally stuccoed and painted. Its hilltop location enabled it to take full advantage of sea breezes. It has been restored during 1993, so check out the results. Reef Bay Sugar Factory is about 3/4 mile beyond the great house on the main trail. The steam-operated flywheel, standing along the S wall of the boiling platform, operated until 1916.

from Reef Bay: Either climb back up to Centerline Rd. or retrace your steps and take the Lameshur Bay and Yawzi Point trails to reach the main road leading back to Coral Bay.

From St. John

note: Times may shift so be sure to reconfirm before your departure date.

for St. Thomas: A ferry ($3, 20 min.) runs on the hour to Red Hook from 6 AM-10 PM daily; an additional ferry is at 11:15. Discount books of 10 tickets are also available. Beer is served on board. A ferry to Charlotte Amalie ($7, 45 min.) runs at 7:15, 9:15, 11:15, 1:15, 3:45, and 5:15. For Caneel Bay ferry times ($9 and $12) call 776-6111. Water taxis (tel. 775-6501, 775-6972) are available by appointment.

for St. Croix: You must take a ferry to St. Thomas and then fly with Sunaire or another carrier.

for Tortola: West End-bound ferries ($16 OW, $28 RT, 30 min.) leave daily at 8:30 and 11:30; from Mon. to Sat at 3:30; Fri. at 5 PM as well; and Sun. at 4:30 PM as well. Call 776-6597/6282 to check schedule. It's not necessary to have a RT ticket. The ferry leaves from the pier directly in back of the customs building. Follow it along to the L and then around. The best seats are topside on this beautiful, panoramic ride. Sea gulls glide in the wind; cacti arc from the sides of cliffs. On the way you pass by cays covered with tropical forest, much as the whole area was before the coming of Europeans.

for Virgin Gorda: Transportation Services of St. John (tel. 776-6282/6597) operates a ferry on Thurs. and Sun. mornings at 8 with a 3 PM return. RT (1.75 hrs. each way) is $30. The location is the same as that for Tortola above.

for Jost Van Dyke: Transportation Services of St. John (tel. 776-6282/6597) operates a ferry (originating in Red Hook) on Fri. and Sun. at 8:30, 2:20 and 5:40 and on Sat. at 8 and 2 with returns at 10, 4, and 9 .

St. John Itinerary

If you have 3 days:
Spend one day in Charlotte Amalie (shopping and sights), and two days on St. John.

If you have 5 days:
Spend one day in Charlotte Amalie (shopping and sights), and three days on St. John (hiking and beaches).

If you have one week:
Spend one day in Charlotte Amalie (shopping and sights), one day touring St. Thomas, five days on St. John (hiking and beaches). Or take an excursion to St. Croix, Tortola, or Virgin Gorda.

St. Croix

Separated from the other two Virgins by distance, St. Croix (pronounced "Croy") differs in other ways as well. It strikes a comfortable balance between the commercialism of St. Thomas and the tranquility of St. John. Currently it has 55,000 residents, only a few thousand more than St. Thomas, and is comparatively spacious and less developed. Although it was the last island to become Danish, it retains the strongest Danish feeling of the three. There's a real sense of living history here. The island's two towns, Fredericksted and Christiansted, retain old architecture and

streets, and ruined sugar estates dot the countryside. The large
Puerto Rican population adds a Latin element. But the main way
in which the island differs from St. Thomas and St. Croix is in the
diversity of its economic base. While the other two American
Virgins are basically tourist destinations, St. Croix has a modern
West Indian society which you can participate in and experience as
the locals do.

The island offers a wealth of scenic beauty, including a small
rainforest in the W end of the island. Towards the end of the 18th
C, there were 114 cane-crushing windmills and 14 oxen mills. Today, you see their remains wherever you drive, and the island retains the Danish land survey which accords the plots the names
given by a planter or plantation owner from the days of yore.
Fountain River, a 4,085-acre estate formerly owned by the Rocke-
fellers, covers a tenth of the island's land area and includes Davis
Bay Beach and tax-exempt Carambola Golf Course. Covering another 1,600 acres on the S coast in the center of the island, the locally unpopular Amerada Hess Corporation runs one of the
world's largest oil refineries; it produces 700,000 barrels per day.
The largest of the island's few remaining Senepol cattle ranches,
Fritz Lawaetz's Annaly Farms spreads across 5,000 acres near the
island's NW corner.

The Land and Its History

Largest and most fertile of all the US Virgin Islands, St. Croix is 29
miles long by seven miles wide. Its 84 sq miles (more than twice
the size of St. Thomas) are still subdivided into large sugar plots
with names like "Barren Spot," "Wheel of Fortune," "Lower Love,"
"Hard Labor," "Little Profit," "Work and Rest," and "Humbug."
These plantation boundaries were delineated by the Danish West
India and Guinea Company in the 18th C and remain virtually
unchanged to this day. The comparatively flat and spacious island
is blessed with an abundance of vegetation. While the tropical
forests of the W adjoin the arid scrublands of the E, the hills of the
N contrast sharply with the long, even plateaus of the S, which
feature arid scrubland, salt pond, and coastal mangroves. Although water has always been in short supply, the flat S plain is
well suited to sugarcane (unlike the other, almost entirely mountainous islands). The N is frequently lush and verdant, though the
S may be brown and desolate during the drier seasons. The E end
is a virtual desert.

history: Viewed by the superpowers of the time as a small pearl to be fought over, ownership of the island was disputed among English, French, and Dutch settlers. It is said to have borne the flags of seven nations, but there have actually been more owners than that. Between the time Columbus and his men were attacked by Indians at Salt River in November 1493 and the time the island was first settled in 1625, the original inhabitants had disappeared, presumably conscripted to work in the gold mines of Santo Domingo. The Indians had called the island "Ay Ay," and Columbus called it Santa Cruz–the name which stuck. When the dust of disputation settled in 1650, France had control; ownership was transferred the next year to De Poincy, a leading Knight of Malta. In 1653 he deeded his title to the Knights of Malta. The island was then sold to the French West Indies Company in 1665. Twelve years later, the French monarchy took possession of the island from the bankrupt Company, and in 1695, Louis XIV ordered it abandoned. The island was left to unofficial squatters until 1733, when it was sold to the Danish West Indies and Guinea Company which, in turn, sold the island to the Danish government after it too nearly went bankrupt.

Danes and English: Arriving Danish settlers found that large tracts of land had already been cleared by the French, who had set fire to the entire island. For a time thereafter, St. Croix became the richest sugar island in the Caribbean. Within 20 years, there were 1,000 people and 375 plantations. Arriving from neighboring islands, English planters soon outnumbered the Danes five to one. This one-crop prosperity lasted for 65 years, during which cane production swelled from 1.5 million pounds in 1755 to 46 million in 1812. By 1796, more than half of the island was planted in sugarcane. In 1802 there were 30,000 slaves, but the slave trade was abolished the next year. Briefly captured by the British in 1801, the island was held by them again from 1807-15 during the Napoleonic Wars. Already in a slump due to the price drop following the introduction of the sugar beet, the island's prosperity collapsed with abolition of the slave trade and the US foreign sugar tariff of 1826. Further setbacks followed. Part of Christiansted burned in 1866, an earthquake and tidal wave hit the island in 1867, the capital was moved back to Charlotte Amalie in 1871, another severe hurricane struck in 1876, and labor riots occurred in 1878 and 1892. It was almost as though someone had it out for the island, which continued its decline after the U.S. purchase in 1917. The island's fortunes were only reversed following the post-WW II growth in tourism. Devastation again struck the island with Hurricane Hugo on Sept. 17, 1989 when 90% of the buildings were damaged or destroyed and 22,500 people were left homeless. In the rioting that followed, the army had to be sent in to restore order. Recovery is still underway.

Practicalities

arriving by air: Alexander Hamilton Airport, named after the famous American stateman who once lived here, is seven miles from Christiansted on the S coast. Pick up information at the tourist office counter. Shared taxis to Christiansted cost $5 pp plus 50 cents per piece of luggage.

island orientation: Elongated St. Croix is traversed by a number of main roads, with smaller ones branching off. Locations are chiefly identified by their old estate names. The airport is in the island's SW, the small town of Frederiksted lies to the W of it, and Christiansted faces a bay to the NE near the middle of the island. Owing to the lack of water, among other factors, the area to its E, which is narrower and drier than the W, is sparsely populated. The lushest area is the Rain Forest in the NW.

getting around: It's both pleasant and easy to walk around either town. Shared taxi vans ($1.50 to any point; $2 after dark) run

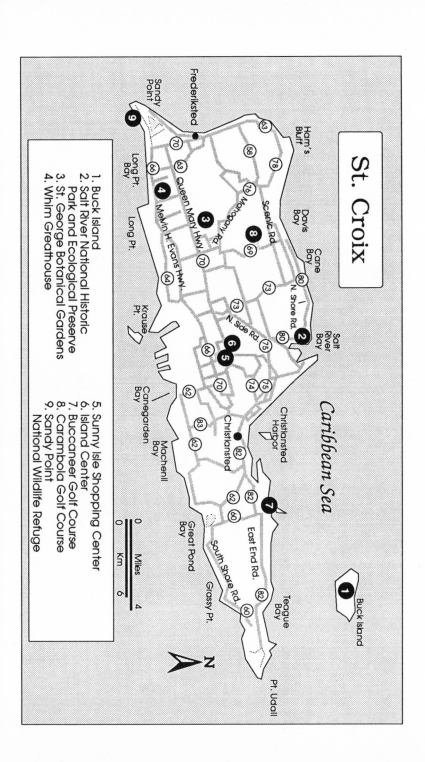

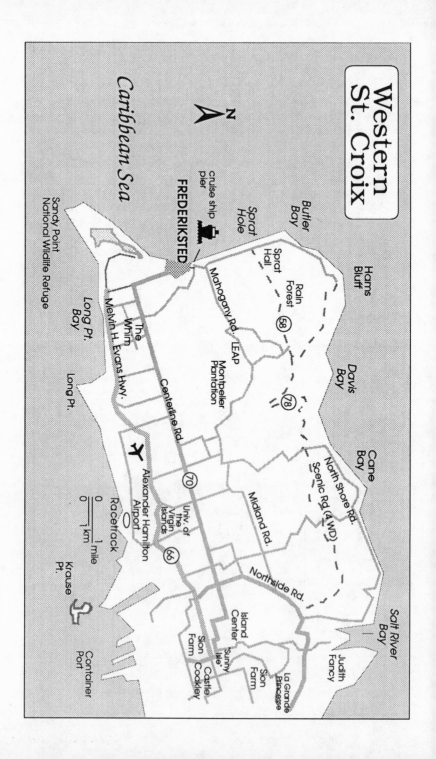

Buck Island, St. Croix

Whim Great House

regularly along Centerline between Christiansted and Fredericksted. Expensive shared taxis are available for other destinations; make sure you get the correct price–not the one reserved for gullible tourists. (Rates are fixed by the local government, are posted in the taxis, and are available from the tourist bureau and the police department). Keep in mind that rates are set for a two-person minimum and that a double fare will apply for just one passenger. A 50¢ charge applies for suitcases and liquor boxes, 40¢ for trunks and boxes. A waiting charge of 10¢ per min. is added and roundtrip fares are double single fares plus waiting charges. **car rentals:** Expect to spend about $40 pd in summer, with unlimited mileage, and in winter $40-50. Gas is additional. Rental companies include **Judy of Croix** (tel. 773-2123), **Atlas** (tel. 773-2886, 800-426-6009), **Olympic** (tel. 800-344-5776, 773-2208, 773-9588, 772-1617, fax 778-7868; Bassin Triangle), **Midwest** (772-0438), **Hertz** (800-654-0700, 778-1402), **Avis** (tel. 800-331-1212, 778-9355, 778-9365), **Burton** (773-1516), **St. Croix Jeep & Honda Rentals** (773-0161, 773-8370), **Budget** (tel. 800-654-3131, 773-2285, 778-9636), **Calypso/Thrifty** (tel. 773-7200), **Go Around** (tel. 778-8881), **Green Cay** (tel. 773-7227), **Midwest** (tel. 772-0438), and **Caribbean** (773-4399, 778-1000). Parking in Christiansted is found near Fort Christiansvaern by King's Wharf; paid parking is available on the W side of town at Strand St.. The island's only two-way divided highway, the Melvin H. Evans (named after the former governor), runs from Sunny Isle Shopping Center west to one mi. before Frederiksted. The Centerline Highway (Queen Mary Highway) runs from Christiansted to Frederiksted. The speed limits are 35-55 mph. Limits on other roads are 35 mph, with 20 mph applying in towns. To tour the E end of the island, drive E on Rte. 82 to Point Udall and then return via Rte. 60. Most fun of all is to explore the roads in the NW portion of the island using a four wheel drive vehicle. **land tours:** Taxis will give you a tour. For information contact the **St. Croix Taxi Association** (tel. 778-1088, 773-9799). **St. Croix Safari Tours** (tel. 773-6700/9561) runs tours (daily from 10 to 2 from King St.) in a 25-passenger open-air bus to most of the major attractions. A similar operation is run by **The Travellers Tours** (tel. 778-1636) and leaves from the Old Customs House in Christiansted. **hiking:** The St. Croix Environmental Association (tel. 773-1989) has hikes; see "information."

water sports and excursions: Parasailing, windsurfing, and kayaking are offered at the **Hotel on the Cay** (tel. 773-7060; Box 4230,

Steeple Building, Christiansted

St. Croix Taxi Fares

Taxis are not metered, so determine your far in advance. Fares listed first in each column are for 1 or 2 passengers; in parentheses is the extra charge for each additional person going to the same destination. Airport vans carry up to 8 passengers with each paying the fare in parentheses.

	From Airport	**To C'sted**	**To F'sted**
Airport		10.00 (5.00)	8.00 (4.00)
Anchor Inn	10.00 (5.00)		20.00 (7.00)
Bay Gardens	10.00 (5.00)	4.00 (2.00)	20.00 (7.00)
Buccaneer Hotel	12.00 (6.00)	6.00 (3.00)	24.00 (12.00)
Candle Reef	12.00 (6.00)	8.00 (4.00)	24.00 (12.00)
Cane Bay Reef Club	13.00 (6.50)	16.00 (8.00)	20.00 (7.00)
Carambola Beach Rsrt	16.00 (8.00)	25.00 (10.00)	21.00 (7.00)
Caravelle Hotel	10.00 (5.00)		20.00 (7.00)
Caribbean View Apts	10.00 (5.00)	5.50 (3.00)	20.00 (7.00)
Chenay Bay Beach Rsrt	13.00 (6.50)	8.00 (4.00)	24.00 (12.00)
Christiansted Town	10.00 (5.00)		20.00 (7.00)
Club Comanche Hotel	10.00 (5.00)		20.00 (7.00)
Club St. Croix	10.00 (5.00)	4.00 (2.00)	20.00 (7.00)
Coakley Bay Condos	13.00 (6.50)	10.00 (5.00)	21.00 (7.00)
Colony Cove Condos	10.00 (5.00)	4.00 (2.00)	20.00 (7.00)
Coral Princess Condos	10.00 (5.00)	5.50 (3.00)	20.00 (7.00)
Cormorant Beach Club	10.00 (5.00)	5.50 (3.00)	20.00 (7.00)
Cottages by the Sea	8.00 (4.00)	20.00 (7.00)	3.50 (2.00)
Cruzan Princess Condo	10.00 (5.00)	5.50 (3.00)	20.00 (7.00)
Danish Manor Hotel	10.00 (5.00)		20.00 (7.00)
Devil's Hole	13.00 (6.50)	8.00 (4.00)	21.00 (10.00)
Eastate Carlton	8.00 (4.00)	14.00 (7.00)	5.00 (2.50)
Frederiksted Town/Pier	8.00 (4.00)	20.00 (7.00)	
Gallows Bay Dock	10.50 (5.25)	4.00 (2.00)	20.00 (7.00)
Golden Rock Shpng Ctr	10.00 (5.00)	4.00) (2.00)	20.00 (7.00)
Green Cay Marina	12.00 (6.00)	8.00 (4.00)	24.00 (12.00)
Hotel on the Cay	10.00 (5.00)		20.00 (7.00)
Island Center	8.00 (4.00)	8.00 (4.00)	15.00 (7.50)
King Christan Hotel	10.00 (5.00)		20.00 (7.00)
King Frederik Hotel	8.00 (4.00)	20.00 (7.00)	3.50 (2.00)
King's Alley Hotel	10.00 (5.00)		20.00 (7.00)
La Grange	10.00 (5.00)	20.00 (7.00)	5.00 (2.50)
Long Reef Condos	10.00 (5.00)	4.00 (2.00)	20.00 (7.00)
Mill Harbour Condos	10.00 (5.00)	4.00 (2.00)	20.00 (7.00)
Moonraker Hotel	10.00 (5.00)		20.00 (7.00)
Paradise Sunset	13.00 (6.50)	25.00 (10.00)	6.50 (3.50)
Penny's Fancy	10.00 (5.00)	4.00 (2.00)	20.00 (7.00)
Pink Fancy Hotel	10.00 (5.00)		20.00 (7.00)
Prince St. Inn	8.00 (4.00)	20.00 (7.00)	
Questa Verde	10.00 (5.00)	5.00 (2.50)	20.00 (7.00)
Reef Condos	16.00 (8.00)	11.00 (5.50)	24.00 (12.00)
Royal Dane Hotel	8.00 (4.00)	20.00 (7.00)	

St. Croix by the Sea	10.00 (5.00)	7.00 (3.00)	20.00 (7.00)
St. Croix Yacht Club	16.00 (8.00)	14.00 (7.00)	24.00 (12.00)
Salt River Marina	12.00 (6.00)	16.00 (8.00)	20.00 (10.00)
Schooner Bay Resort	10.50 (5.25)	4.00 (2.00)	20.00 (7.00)
South Gate Condos	12.00 (6.00)	8.50 (4.50)	24.00 (12.00)
St. Geo Botanical Gdns	8.00 (4.00)	15.00 (7.75)	6.50 (3.50)
Sprat Hall	10.00 (5.00)	21.00 (10.50)	6.00 (3.00)
Sunny Isle Shpng Ctr	8.00 (4.00)	8.00 (4.00)	15.00 (7.50)
United Shopping Plaza	8.50 (4.50)	8.00 (4.00)	15.00 (7.50)
Ville La Reine Shpg Ctr	8.00 (4.00)	8.50 (4.50)	13.00 (6.50
Villa Madeleine	16.00 (8.00)	11.00 (5.50)	24.00 (12.00)
Waves at Cane Bay	13.00 (6.50)	16.00 (8.00)	20.00 (7.00)
Whim Plantation	8.00 (4.00)	20.50 (10.50)	4.00 (2.00)

Taxi Service

Airport	St. Croix Taxi Assoc.	778-1088
Christiansted	Antilles Taxi Service	773-7907
	Caribbean Taxi & Tours	773-9799
	Cruzan Taxi Assoc.	773-6388
Frederiksted	Combine Taxi & Tours	772-2828
	Frederiksted Taxi Service	772-4775

Taxi stands in Christiansted are on King St. opposite Little Switzerland and in Frederksted by Fort Frederik. You may stop by and make arrangements to be picked up later in the day. Complaints, questions? Call the Taxi Commission at 773-8294.

Christiansted 00822). **Mile Mark Watersports** (tel. 524-2012, 773-2628/2285, fax 773-9411, 800-524-2012), located next to the King Christian Hotel's lobby and on the waterfront, offers excursions including the trip to Buck Island (see "Buck Island") as well as fishing charters. Business partners of Mile Mark, **Dive St. Croix** (tel. 773-3434/2285, fax 773-941, 800-523-DIVE) can take you out diving at Buck Island. Windsurfing lessons and board rentals are available from the **Mistral School** (tel. 773-4810/8195, 800-548-4457). Offering all-inclusive trips for up to three nights on the 48-ft. Soverel ketch *Cavu*, **Carefree Charters** can be contacted at 773-7171 and 800-422-4663. **Big Beard's Adventure Tours** (tel. 773-4482) has trips to Buck Island as well as a full day beach BBQ. They also have a tour booking agency near their shop in Pan Am Pavilion.

beaches: The island is blessed with wonderful beaches, but you should take care to leave nothing of value in your car while visiting them. Near Christiansted heading E are the **Buccaneer Beach** at Reef Bay (at the Buccaneer Hotel; you may use the shower facilities). Blessed with a steady breeze, this beach's chairs and towels are reserved for guests. Others are **Shoys Beach**, **Reef Beach**

(windsurfing; Duggan's Reef, Teague Bay off Rte. 82), and **Cramer Park Beach**. Nearer to town, **Hotel on the Cay's beach** is open to public use, but you must take a ferry to get there. Round the E point is **Isaac Bay**, a difficult-access nudist beach. Farther on are secluded **Grapetree Beach** (a thousand-foot stretch of sand off South Shore Road/Rte. 60 at the island's E tip) and **Jack's Bay Beach**. To the W of Christiansted are **Hibiscus Beach** (good snorkeling), **Pelican Cove** (snorkeling at the reef and the home of the Cormorant Beach Club), **Judith's Fancy**, **Salt River**, and **Cane Bay** (excellent snorkeling and diving as well as sea turtles). **Davis Bay Beach** (bodysurfing, no changing facilities) is the home of the Carambola Beach Resort which was reopened in 1993 under the Radisson Resort chain. There's only limited parking available here, and you may have to walk a bit. From Frederiksted, **La Grange Beach and Tennis Club's beach** and **West End Beach** (great snorkeling) are just outside town. The Sundowner Beach Bar is a short walk N from the fort and the pier. **Rainbow Beach** (calm waters and good snorkeling; Rte. 63), **Sprat Hall Beach** (and accompanying renovated great house-restaurant-hotel combination; Rte. 63), and **Monk's Bath Beach** (Veteran's Road) lie farther to the north. The island's most beautiful beach, **Sandy Point Beach** lies to the S of Frederiksted. There's also a beautiful beach on Buck Island off the N coast.

dive sites: Although the island is almost entirely circled by coral reefs, the most accessible stretches with the largest variety of lifeforms are those off Christiansted coast. Good diving is found off of Cane Bay, Northstar, and Davis Bay. Set at the mouth of the river of the same name, Salt River Drop-off actually consists of two sites which are the E and W sides of an underwater canyon. While the E wall is more sloping and hosts schools of fish, the W wall begins at 30 ft. (9 m) and swiftly drops to 90 ft. (18 m), after which it plummets to 1,000 ft. (300 m). Its caves and crevices house black coral forests, tube sponges, and a variety of coral as well as sting rays and other fish. Highlighting a coral pinnacle, Jimmy's Surprise boasts tube sponges, moray eels, and queen angelfish. Cup corals and pillar corals are found at Little Cozumel. Butler Bay has three shipwrecks: *Rosaomaira*, a 177-ft. steel-hulled freighter; *Suffolk Maid*, a 140-ft. trawler; and the *Northwind*, a 75-ft. tugboat sunk in 50 ft. of water. Intentionally sunk in order to attract fish, The Barge is on a reef just outside Christiansted. Lang Bank is a full day trip but is a virgin reef. Dolphins and wahoo can be found here.

You can also dive off of Buck Island, but it won't challenge experienced divers.

fishing and boating: You can fish from shore at Hams Bay. The best sport fishing is found off of the N coast at Lang Bank. Wahoo, dolphin (the fish), and kingfish are the biggest catches. **Annapolis Sailing School** (tel. 773-4709) operates here. **charters:** These include *Afternoon Delight* (tel. 772-3701; 312 Strand St., Frederiksted 00840), *Lisa Anne*, the *Wild, Wild, West*, and the *Catch* 22 (tel. 773-1453; Green Cay Marina, 5000 South Gate, Christiansted 00820). The *Ruffian* (tel. 773-0289; Box 24370, Gallows Bay 00824) is a 41-ft. Hatteras. The *Shenanigan* (Mile Mark Charters, 59 Kings Wharf, Christiansted 00820) is a 42-ft. Ocean Supersport.

tennis: Four free and lighted public courts are located in Canegata Park in Christiansted and two are in Fredericksted across from the fort. In Frederiksted **La Grange Beach and Tennis Club** has the most reasonable price on the island: $2.50 pp, ph. (plus $2.50 daily membership). The **Buccaneer Hotel** has eight courts, two of which are lighted. Call 773-21000, ext. 736 to reserve. Other locations (around $5 ph) include **The Hotel on the Cay, Club St. Croix** (tel. 773-4800), **The Reef Club** (tel. 773-8844), **Chenay Bay Resort** (tel. 773-1965), **Villa Madeleine** (tel. 773-8141), **Sugar Beach** (tel. 773-5345), **Mill Harbour** (tel.773-3840), and **St. Croix By the Sea's St. Croix Tennis** (tel. 778-8600).

golf: The Reef (tel. 773-8844) charges $12 for nine holes plus $12 for a cart or, for 18 holes, $18 and $20 for a cart. Spacious and challenging, this 3,100-yd. course is set in a valley below Reef Villas in Teague Bay. **The Buccaneer Hotel** (tel. 773-2100, ext. 738) charges $30 pp for non-guests, $12 per cart pp for its 18-hole course. Hilly and attractively landscaped, it is rated at 65, its record is also 65, it has a total yardage of 6,116, its longest hole is 587 yds., and its shortest is 152 yds. Designed by Robert Trent Jones, the **Carambola's** course (tel. 778-5638, pro shop) is ranked among the world's ten best resort courses and charges non guests $62.50 with cart for 18 holes and $38 with cart for nine holes. (These rates can change with the season). Situated in a valley with streams and ponds, it is rated at 72.7 and has a record of 66 strokes; its longest hole is 593 yds., and its shortest hole is 139 yds.

horseback riding: The pick of the lot is clearly **Paul and Jill's Equestrian Stables** (tel. 772-2880/2627, $50 for two hrs). just outside Frederiksted. Jill, the daughter of the Sprat Hall Hurds, takes you on a nature tour of the rainforest, matching you with a horse of your choice. Unlike most horse rides where you climb up on sagging Old Blue who seems to have one foot in the pot at the glue factory, Jill's horses have character, spirit, and personality. Moreover, you have the opportunity to trot and canter as well as walk. (Don't worry if you're a beginner; Jill is very patient. But don't overestimate your riding skills either.) A variety of trails take you through the rainforest, pass the island's only dam, and up to plantation ruins for a view. On the way, Jill points out colorfully named natural features (like the "monkey no climb tree") and wildlife. For the ride wear long pants or slacks, and shoes (for protection). Saddlebags for cameras are provided. Unless you're staying in Frederiksted, it's best to come here on the day that you rent a car as the RT taxi fare for two may be comparable anyway. Advance reservations (for the morning or afternoon ride) are required. Write Box 3251, Frederiksted, St. Croix 00841-3251.

plantations and ruins: This may be the island's most attractive feature. Certainly, if you get bored with the beach (or get burnt), exploring these is an alternative. More than 150 windmills whirled over the island for more than 100 years. They were replaced in turn by the steam mills, which died in turn with the sugar industry. **Judith's Fancy**, NW of Christiansted and near St. Croix by the Sea, is the most picturesque ruin on the island. **Sprat Hall**, a French plantation on the W coast above Fredericksted, has been transformed into an inn.

birding: There are more than two dozen excellent sites around the island including Salt River on the N coast; Great Pond and Long Point on the S coast; and Southgate Pond, Coakely Bay Pond, and Altona Lagoon–all to the E of Christiansted. Birds that nest on St. Croix include the egret, common ground-dove, Wilson's plover, smooth-billed ani, the green-backed heron, the common moorhen, and the pied-billed grebe.

Christiansted

Larger of the two towns on the island, Christiansted is by far the most fascinating town in the U.S. Virgin Islands. Founded in 1734 as a planned community by the Danish West India and Guinea Company, it was made the Danish colonial capital in 1755. A discriminatory building code, instituted in 1747, had the incidental effect of preserving the town's old houses for posterity. Christiansted is so well preserved that parts were designated a national historical site in 1952. There are blocks of pastel pink, yellow, and brown colonnaded buildings with high-peaked roofs. The town strikes a balance between Charlotte Amalie's rabid commercialism and Cruz Bay's laid back atmosphere. (Only the shallowness of the town's harbor has saved it from the cruise ships and a St. Thomian fate). Yachts crowd Kings Wharf with its concessionaires selling tickets to Buck Island. Out on the way to Gallows Bay, an atmosphere of pleasant lassitude prevails, with chickens clacking amidst tamarind trees, the smell and crackle of fish frying coming from open windows, and boats careened with peeling paint next to the side of houses. It's as if rural Maine had been transplanted to arid Arizona. Farther on, it's been developed as a business area with shops, delis, coffee houses, and small businesses.

orientation: The Boardwalk faces the water and runs along to the intersection with King St. (Kongens Gade). The Wharf area (along with the ferry to Protestant Cay) are behind the Old Scalehouse at the end of this street. The Old Custom House, Post Office, and Government House are back away from the water along this street, and the Fort is behind the Old Custom House and across from the Steeple Building. Company St. (Companiets Gade) and Queen St. (Dronningens Gade) run parallel to King St. as does Strand St. (Strand Gade) which runs behind King St. and intersects with some major shopping areas: Caravelle Arcade, the Pan Am Pavilion, Comanche Walk, and Kings Alley. From the Fort and the Steeple Building, Hospital St. (Hospital Gade) leads to Lobster St which runs into Anchor Way which leads to the Gallows Bay PO and on to the Rogues Gallery Restaurant., Fort. St., at the intersection of Lobster and Anchor Way, leads to Chandlers Wharf (shopping) and Gallows Bay Market Place.

Sights

This is a lovely town to walk around in. Try to pick a time to explore when no cruise ship passengers have been bused in. Allow a morning for this walking tour.

Scalehouse: Built in 1855-1856, scales stand in the entryway. Imports and exports were weighed in and inspected in this building, and troops were also quartered here. It now houses the tourist information center.

Danish Customs House: Begun in 1751 and completed in 1830, this elegant building now houses the National Park Service scheduled art exhibits on the first floor and administrative offices on the second.

Fort Christiansvaern: One of the best-preserved 18th C forts in the Caribbean, this fortification, painted yellow ochre, has been restored to its 1840 appearance. Standing at the edge of the harbor, there are no outerworks. Enter through the wooden gate flanked by masonry columns. Pick up the self-guiding pamphlet at the Visitor's Center. Built from Danish bricks brought as ballast in sailing ships, the fort was constructed from 1738 to 1749; the walled stable yard to the E of the citadel was added in 1840. It remained the military hub of the island until it was converted into the police headquarters in 1878. Enjoy the great views from the water battery. Open daily, 8-4; $2 admission (ages 16-62).

Steeple Building: Completed by 1753, it was called The Church of Our Lord of Sabaoth. It was the first Lutheran church on the island. The steeple was added in 1794. Since 1831, when it was taken over by the government, it has been used as a military bakery, hospital, and school. Completely renovated in 1964, it now contains a museum whose historical exhibits include architecture, urban black history, maps, photos, and relics. The Indian artifacts displayed (stone, coral, clay, shell, and bone) were chosen from a total of 16,000 artifacts collected on the island by the late Folmer Andersen, a Danish immigrant and a self-trained archaeologist. Open Mon. to Fri, 9-4; Sat. 9 to noon. Free admission.

Danish West Indies and Guinea Company Warehouse: Completed in 1749, it was used to house the slave auction yard, offices, and personnel for the Danish slave trading company. After 1833 it became a military depot and then the telegraph office. It is currently used as the Post Office and US Customs Office.

Government House: Faces King St. at the corner of Queen Cross St. Once housing both the governor and the administrative offices,

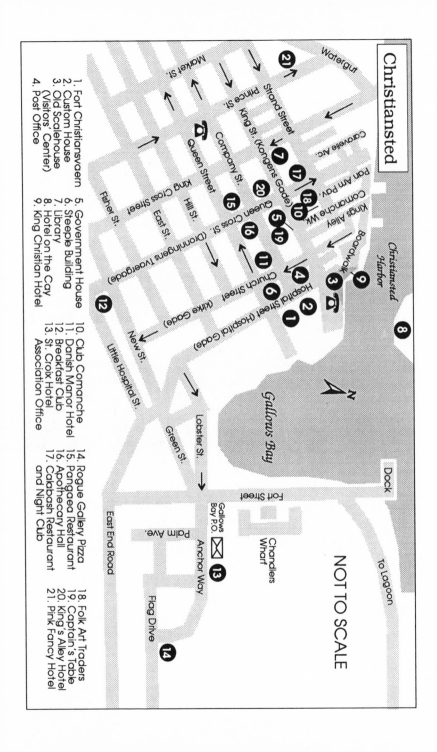

Christiansted

NOT TO SCALE

1. Fort Christiansvaern
2. Custom House
3. Old Scalehouse (Visitors' Center)
4. Post Office
5. Government House
6. Steeple Building
7. Library
8. Hotel on the Cay
9. King Christian Hotel
10. Club Comanche
11. Danish Manor Hotel
12. Breakfast Club
13. St. Croix Hotel Association Office
14. Rogue Gallery Pizza
15. Pangaea Restaurant
16. Apothecary Hall
17. Calabash Restaurant and Night Club
18. Folk Art Traders
19. Captain's Table
20. King's Alley Hotel
21. Pink Fancy Hotel

Watergut
Market St.
Prince St.
King St. (Kongens Gade)
Strand Street
Caravelle Arc.
Pan Am Pav.
Kings Alley
Comanche Wk.
Boardwalk
Company St.
Queen Street
King Cross Street
Queen Cross St. (Dronningens Tvaergade)
Church Street (Kirke Gade)
Hospital Street (Hospital Gade)
Fisher St.
Hill St.
East St.
New St.
Little Hospital St.
Green St.
Lobster St.
Fort Street
Gallows Bay P.O.
Chandlers Wharf
Anchor Way
Palm Ave.
East End Road
Flag Drive
Dock
To Lagoon
Gallows Bay
Christiansted Harbor
N

it is the landmark public building on the island. At its core is a two-story townhouse. Built in 1747, it was acquired in 1771 for use as the governor's residence. In 1828, the neighboring home of a merchant-planter was acquired by Governor-General Peter von Scholten. A link was built between the two dwellings a few years later. The flanking wings were added about 1800 and a third story in 1862. Walk through the iron gates to the second-story reception hall where there's an attractive iron staircase. Although the departing Danes had left nothing in the ballroom save the pitch pine floor, in 1966 the Danish government donated the furniture found there now. The four antique chairs in the antechamber were donated by Queen Margarethe of Denmark during her 1976 visit. Visitors are permitted to enter when there are no events underway.

The Lutheran church: Built in the early 1740s as the Dutch Reformed church and acquired by the Lutherans after they vacated the Steeple Building in 1831. The tower over the front porch was added in 1834.

Protestant Cay: Out across the harbor and popularly known as "The Cay," it is the home of the Hotel on the Cay and the blue-green St. Croix Ground Lizard, exterminated by the mongoose and found now only here and on Green Cay. Its name derives from the French times during the late 1600s when non-Catholics, refused burial on the main island, were interred here. A ferry runs every 10 min ($3 OW).

others: Constructed from limestone blocks, the St. John's Anglican Church on King St. dates from 1842; it was first established in 1760. A few years younger (1852) and a bit farther down the road stands the Fredensthal Moravian Church. Just outside the town are a number of ruins including the Estate Richmond (near Bassin Triangle), the old Danish Prison, Estate Orange Grove, and Estate Hermon Hill (at Questa Verde and Hermon Hill Road). Jacobsberg Ridge (within walking distance nearby) commands an excellent view.

Useful St. Croix Phone Numbers

Ambulance	922
American Airlines	800-474-4884
American Eagle	776-6450

American Express	773-9500
Antilles Helicopters	776-7880
Caribbean Air	774-7071
Chamber of Commerce	773-1435
Continental Airlines	777-8190
Delta Airlines	800-221-1212
Fire	921
Hospital	778-6311
Island Center	778-5272
LIAT	774-2313
Police	915
Sunaire	776-9322
Tourist Information	773-0495

Christiansted Accommodationss

Except for Hotel on the Cay (which has a small beach), none of the hotels here have a beach. Managed by St. Croix Hotel Association President Betty Sperber, the 39-rm. **King Christian Hotel** (tel. 773-2285, fax 773-9411, 800-524-2012; 59 King's Wharf 00822) has a pool. It's conveniently located by the watefront at 59 King's Wharf. The hotel's "superior" rooms feature two double beds, a/c, color cable TV, telephone, refrigerator, room safe, bathroom w/shower, separated dressing area, and balcony. The "minimum" rooms feature private bath, a/c, telephone and one double or two single beds. Ask about their dive packages. Rates start at $75 s and $80 d. At 58A King St., the 31-room **Anchor Inn** (tel. 773-4000, fax 773-4408, 800-595-9500, 800-468-0023 in Canada) is downtown and features a pool, watersports, a/c, porch, radio, cable TV, phone, refrigerator, and restaurant and bar. In Germany call 49-89-555339. At 18 Queen Cross St., the **Breakfast Club** (tel. 773-7383) is a bed-and breakfast which offers five tastefully-decorated rooms with kitchenettes, mahogany beds, and fans. A full breakfast is included as is use of the Jacuzzi and lounge, which has a bookrack. Rates start at $45 s, $55 d, and weekly rates are available. At 44A Queen Cross St., the pink with blue trim two-storey European-style **Caravelle** (tel. 773-0687, fax 778-7004, 800-524-0410) has 43 attractive a/c rms. with phone and cable TV with HBO. Other amenities include pool, restaurant, and watersports. It has the highest occupancy rate on the island. Off-season rates start from $68 s and $78 d. In the alley of the same name, **King's Alley** (tel. 773-0103, fax 773-4431, cable KINGAL; 800-843-3574) has a large

oval-shaped pool. A/c and fan-equipped rooms have balconies
(on upstairs rooms), phones, and cable TV. All rooms have king or
twin beds. Refrigerators are available upon request. Rates start at
$63 s or $76 d. **The Danish Manor** (tel. 773-1377, 800-524-2069) is
at 2 Company St.; its 35 a/c rooms feature refrigerator, phone,
color cable TV with free HBO, and a pool. Rates run from $59 to
$89 s or d during the winter season; summer rates run from
$59-$89. A 10% service charge is added, and weekly and monthly
rates are available. At #1 Strand St., **Club Comanche** (tel. 773-0210)
has a pool and kitchen. No two of its rooms are alike. Now a Best
Western and overlooking the harbor, the **Holger Danske** (tel. 773-
3600, fax 773-8828, 800-528-1234), King Cross St., offers rooms from
$64 s and $74 d. Rooms have a/c, balcony or patio, and phones;
some have efficiencies. At 27 Prince St., **Pink Fancy** (tel. 773-8460,
800-524-2045), a white-and-pink colored historic inn part of which
dates from 1780 and lovingly restored a century later, has a pool
and is near a beach. Amenities in its 13 large rooms include kitchenettes, breakfast, a/c and fans, cable TV, radio, and phone. The
bar is complimentary as is the buffet breakfast served by the pool.
Rooms start at $75. At 17 Prince St., **Prince St. Inn** (tel. 772-9550,
800-524-2026) offers six rooms with kitchen facilities in most of
them and fans. Set on an island just offshore, **Hotel on the Cay** (tel.
773-2035, fax 773-7046, 800-524-2035; Box 4020, Christiansted
00820) offers a pool, tennis courts, and water sports. Honeymoon,
convention, dive, and group packages are available as are an
innumerable number of activities ranging from a scavenger hunt
to sand volleyball. Rooms begin at $95 s and $105 d; tax, a 7.5%
service charge, and a $2 pp energy charge are added to this. It is
also a timeshare. The disadvantage of staying here is that the ferry
ceases running between 1 and 6 AM. One last budget spot is the
Hotel Colibri (tel. 773-6610), 17 Company St., which has a/c rooms
for $35 s and $45 d. At #43A King Cross St, the former Moonraker
Hotel is no longer a hotel property.

Accommodations near Christiansted

heading W: Set 1.5 mi. from Christiansted at 2 Hermon Hill, **Hilty
House Inn** (tel./fax 773-2594; Box 26077, Gallows Bay 00824) is a
five-bedroom 30-year-old house built on sugar plantation ruins
and now converted into a modern bed and breakfast. Run by Hugh
and Jacquie Hoare-Ward, it is one of the most distinctive places to
stay on the island and features a large library/living dining area
with TV; a large pool is just out on the veranda. Each room has its

unique decor with matching tiles. Breakfast features squeezed juice, fruit salads, whole fresh fruits, and muffins, banana pancakes, or bread. Be sure to check out the guest book. Rates start at $60 s and $80 d. The self-catering cottages are more expensive, and breakfast with these is $2.50 pp additional. At 3245 Estate Golden Rock, **Sugar Beach Condominium** (tel. 773-5345, fax 773-1359, 800-524-2049) offers 46 units bordering a 500-ft. stretch of beach. Each one-, two-, or three-bedroom a/c and fan equipped suite has a private balcony with great views and a breeze. Its pool lies by a ruined sugar mill tower. Watersports are available. Rates run from $100 studio, up to $250 three-bedroom during the summer and from $180 studio up to $350 three-bedroom during the winter. Set one mi. W of Christiansted at 3280 Golden Rock, **Club St. Croix Beach and Tennis Club** (tel. 773-4800, fax 773-4085, 800-635-1533) is a 54-condo beachfront resort whose rooms include kitchens, a/c, cable TV, and phone. Facilities include poolside restaurant and bar, three tennis courts, and car rental. A sunset sail, diving introduction, island tour, and cocktail party are all included in its rates. Off-season rates start at $139/unit. At 4118 La Grande Princesse, three mi. from Christiansted and seven mi. from the airport, **Caribbean View Studio Apartments** (tel. 773-3335, fax 773-1596, 800-524-5002, in Puerto Rico 800-595-9515) has 19 one-bedroom apartments with a/c and fan, cable TV/VCR, radio, and maid service. A beach is a half mi. away. Other facilities include a pool, poolside barbeque, gardens, water sports, and nearby golf and tennis. Rates start from $75 s or d. Packages are also available. Fronting a palm-lined beach, the 38-rm. **Hibiscus Beach Hotel** (tel. 773-4042, fax 778-9218, 800-442-0121), 4126 La Grange, has a restaurant, bar, and pool. Rooms feature phone, in-room safe, a/c and fans, balcony or patio, and TV. Off-season rates start at $100/rm. Golf and dive packages are offered. At 4126 La Grande Princesse, **Cormorant Beach Club** (tel. 778-8920, fax 778-9218, 800-548-4460) has a restaurant, bar, pool, tennis, snorkeling, and nearby golf. The 34 deluxe rooms and four suites have a/c, fans, and balcony or patio. Rates start at $135/rm. off season. Dive golf, and honeymoon packages are available. Next door at 4127, **Cormorant Cove** is under the same management as Cormorant Beach Club. It features two- and three-bedroom condos with a/c, cable TV, dishwasher, microwave, and washer/dryers. Tennis and a pool are available. Dine at the Cormorant Beach Club. Rates start at $200/one-bedroom off season.

Northshore Vacation Rentals at Mill Harbour (tel.773-3840, fax 773-1579; Estate Golden Rock) are a collection of one- , two- , and three-bedroom condos with kitchen and cable TV. There are eight restaurants, and there's a pool and tennis courts. Rates are from $65 s, $130 d, $160 quad. Next door at 3221 Golden Rock, **Colony Cove** (tel. 773-1965, fax 773-5397, 800-828-0746) a luxury all-suite, 60-unit beachfront resort, faces a palm-lined beach. Attractive two-bedroom, two-bath suites have kitchen, dining and living room, a/c, phone, cable TV with free HBO, and private balcony. Facilities include pool, tennis, windsurfing, snorkeling, and scuba. One of the resort's best features is its gardens, with a variety of local plants and herbs. Tours are complimentary and a valuable addition to your visit. There's also a weekly manager's poolside punch party as well as a free introduction to snorkel and scuba class. Although the beach is not impressive, the snorkeling is. Be sure to swim out to the tires, which attract a wide range of fish. Prices are $150 s or d off season, $225 in season. Daily housekeeping is 10% of room rate; a midweek cleaning is complimentary. A variety of packages including golf at Carambola, honeymoon, diving, and an "eco-week" are also available. The latter offers a choice of courses in sea ecology, shore ecology, island ecology, and a special children's course. All earn a certificate in Ecology from the University of St. Croix. **Antilles Resorts** at Colony Cove is another marketing unit of the same resort at the same address with identical prices. Set at Cane Bay Beach, the intimate and informal **Cane Bay Reef Club** (tel. 778-2966; 800-253-8534, Box1407, Kingshill) has a large pool and nine two-rm. suites with fully-equipped kitchens and overhanging balconies. The Carambola golf course is nearby. Off-season rates begin at $70 s or d. Set next to Cane Bay Reef Club, **Waves at Cane Bay** (tel./fax 778-1805, 800-545-0603, Box 1749, Kingshill 00851-1749) features 11 studios and one villa; all are equipped with kitchen, ocean-view balconies, radio, fan, and cable TV. Most have a/c. Facilities include a natural grotto pool and a PADI dive center. Rates start at $70/unit. Fronting Davis Bay Beach, the **Carambola Beach Resort's** 26 six-rm. buildings resemble small villas. Each of the rooms includes a/c and fan, bath, radio and there is a pool and beach. There are also four restaurants and two bars. This resort–closed since Hurricane Hugo–reopened in 1993 under the Radison Resort banner. Check with your travel agent or call 800-333-3333 for reservations worldwide. Set on the island's NW at 15 North Side Ham Bluff, **Paradise Sunset Beach Hotel** (tel. 772-2499, fax 772-0001, Box

1788, Frederiksted 00841) offers rooms and studios with a/c and cable TV. Recently restored, it has been built amidst ruins dating back to the 1600s. You can still see the Maltese crest here that reflects its previous ownership as well as a sugar mill and great house. It has a salt water pool, live entertainment on weekends, and a Great House Ballroom which can accommodate up to 300 for weddings, parties, or receptions. Three meals are served daily. Shuttle service to the airport is provided. A beach is within walking distance and rates are from $55 s and $60 d with the most expensive rooms ($120 and up) being efficiency apartments. Special honeymoon packages are available, and tropical weddings can be arranged amidst the ruins.

heading E: Set in Gallows Bay on 240 acres with three beaches, **The Buccaneer** (tel. 773-2100, fax 778-8215, 800-223-1108, fax 914-763-5362, Box 25200, Gallows Bay, Christiansted 00824) has a pool, watersports, 18-hole golf course, 8 tournament tennis courts (two lighted), health spa, and a shopping arcade in a country club setting. There's also an 18-station, two-mi. jogging/parcourse track. Dating from 1948, it is one of the few Caribbean resorts that are still in the hands of the Armstrongs, the original owners. The property has been an estate since 1653, and the ruins of a sugar mill can be seen. A variety of plans are available including "Elope to Paradise". A wide variety of accommodations–from standard to ficus suite–are available. You're taken around the grounds in a van, and a shuttle to town also runs. Rates start at $140 s or $160 d for standard rooms off season (including full breakfast). In the UK call 0-45383-5801 or fax 0-45383-5525. Near Green Cay Marina and providing the privacy of "gardenview" and "oceanview" cottages scattered through 30 acres, **Chenay Bay Beach Resort** (tel. 548-4457, tel./fax 773-2918, 773-2918; Box 24600, Christiansted 00824) offers packages from $480 (five days/four nights). It offers a set of 50 attractive efficiency cottages with kitchen, a/c, and fan. Facilities include a pool, restaurant, windsurfing school, tennis, kayaks, floating mats, complimentary use of snorkeling equipment, grocery shuttle, and entertainment twice pw. Off-season rates start at $120/unit. A week's stay brings use of a rental car. Family, "dine-around," and honeymoon plans are offered. There's a small beach here, but the water remains shallow for a considerable distance from shore. Set 3.5 mi. E of Christiansted, **Estate Tipperary** (tel. 773-0143, fax 778-7408; 5013 Tipperary #10 on Southgate Rd.) is a three-bedroom, two-bath private home which has a Jacuzzi, pool, and housecleaning service. Rentals start at $1,000/wk for 1-4. Write Mrs. Beverly Bell Collins, Salt Box Farm, 1 Wright Lane, Westford, MA 01886. Housekeeping units with patios, **The Reef Condominium** (tel. 773-9040, fax 773-9056; Teague Bay) charges around $750 pw summer and $1,200 pw winter. At 19 Teague Bay near Jacks Bay and above The Reef, **Villa Madeleine** (tel. 773-8141, fax 773-7518, 800-548-4461; Box 24190, Gallows Bay 00824) offers a variety of elegantly attractive one- and two-bedroom villas equipped with kitchen, four-poster beds, a/c, TV/VCR, daily maid service. Set on a hillside, each has its own pool. Facilities include restaurant, bar, library, gardens, and billiard room. Rates start at $300 for a one-bedroom.

camping: The island has three campsites. All are E of Christiansted and would require your own wheels to be practical. **Cramer Park**, on the East end, has free camping. There is a catch, two of them in fact: there's no fresh water and the flush toilets may not be functioning. Built amidst the ruins of Estate Great Pond due SE from Christiansted, **Camp Arawak** rents inexpensive baresites. There are pit toilets and fresh water as well as canoe and diving equipment rentals. For more information write: Camp Arawak, Arawak Program Inc., Box 129, Christiansted, USVI 00820 (tel. 809-773-3944). Amidst the ruins of Estate Fareham, in the Greatpond area, stands the **Boy Scout Camp** which has tent rentals. Compared to the other two, it's a bastion of convenience with showers, restrooms, refrigerators, electrical outlets, and boat rentals. Baresite camping is $10 pp, pd. Tent and mattress are additional. For more information write: Boy Scouts, Box 1353, Frederiksted, USVI 00840 (tel. 809-773-1733).

Christiansted Dining and Food

If you have money to spend and like to dine well, Christiansted (as well as the island as a whole) is an excellent place to be. There are also a number of lower priced places for those who can afford only around $10 a meal or so. **note:** In describing restaurant prices in this chapter, *inexpensive* refers to places where you can dine for $15 and under, including a drink, appetizer, and dessert; you may in fact pay more. *Moderate* means $16-$25, *expensive* means $26-$40, and *very expensive* means over $40 a meal.

light dining: Takeout is available at **Mr. J's "Discount" Sand-wiches** on Company St. and from vendors near the wharf and by the marketplace. Next door to the Chart House on King's Wharf, **the Taste Place** offers breakfasts, as well as packed picnic lunch sandwiches, chips, fruit, ice cream and yogurt. **Pizza Mare**, 2-3 Strand St. has the best pizza (slices available) in town in the classiest environment; it has a second branch at Sunny Isle. **Pizza Hut** is at 27 Church St. **The Alley Galley**, 1100 Strand (under the Comanche) serves sandwiches and salads as well as $2 pina co-ladas. It also opens for pastries and coffee at 7:30 AM (6 on Sun.). On Strand St., **the Berlin Wall**, run by German expat Ingrid Bielack, offers sandwiches, homemade German coffee cake, and other fare. Across from the market, the **Ships Galley Ice Cream Parlor**, 1100 Strand St., sells sandwiches. **Baskin Robbins**, 8AB Company St., has cones ($1.75) and the usual fare. Tucked away on Company St. across from Market Square, **Expressotugo** has great coffee as well as hot chocolate, herbal teas, ice cream and baked goods. One inexpensive to moderate restaurant serving West In-dian and Continental cuisine is **Harvey's** (tel. 773-3433) at 11B Company St. It has a vegetarian plate for $5. At 45 King St., **Kim's Restaurant** is both unpretentious and popular. Up the street, **Cru-cian Creole**, 32 King St. across from St. John Church Rectory, offers local food. Inexpensive **Hondo's Backyard**, 53 King St., serves dishes ranging from Tex Mex to sandwiches to pizza. Inexpensive **Brady's**, 18B Hill St., also serves West Indian food three meals daily. For reasonably priced Mexican-American food, try the inex-pensive **Luncheria** inside Apothecary Hall at 6 Company St. At 54 Company St. and serving food daily until 3 or 4 AM, **Company Street Pub** (tel. 773-6880) offers potato skins, fried mushrooms, taco salad, and hot pastrami. For fish and chips, fried shrimp, and onion rings, try the **Wreck Bar & Grill**, 5AB Hospital St., which is inexpensive. **formal dining:** Try and get hold of the St. Croix Restaurant Association's booklet *Dining in St. Croix* if it's available. Expect to spend around $20-30 pp or more for dinner including tip. Only open during the high season, the inexpensive to expensive **Top Hat** (tel. 773-2346), 52 Company St., features fine Danish and Continental cuisine. At Danish Manor, 2 Company St., moderate **Tutto Bene** (tel. 773-5229) specializes in Italian cuisine. Its name means "everything good," and the menu changes daily. At 2203 Queen Cross St., **Pangaea** has vegetarian dishes as well as chicken and seafood. They cook with fresh island vegetables and herbs and offer everything from W African peanut soup to baked swordfish and spiced red snapper. At 53B Company St., inexpensive **Camille's** (tel. 773-2985) serves breakfasts (banana, strawberry, or banana pancakes), soups/salads, sandwiches (lobster salad, tuna melt, veggie), and fresh fish or steak specials. Dinner specials are $12.95. Set at 54-55 Company St. just up from the PO, the expensive **Captain's Table** (tel. 773-2026) offers a variety of seafood appetizers and entrees ranging from oysters Rockefeller to Virgin Wahoo. On Friday night, it's the legislators' hangout, and you might see the Lt. Governor here. At 52 Company St., inexpensive to moderate **Anabelle's** (tel. 773-3990) is a "tea room" which also serves breakfast and Spanish/Cuban lunches and dinners. At the Anchor Inn Hotel at 58 A King St., inexpensive to moderate **Antoine's** (tel. 773-0263) has a terrace which overlooks the harbor. Three meals a day are served, and the dinner menu has Swiss/Austrian entrees as well as local food such as kallaloo and fish chowder. **The Aqua-Lounge Club** is also at the same hotel and offers weekly sushi night, Monday night buffet, and Sat. all you can eat shrimp dinners. Set in the Caravelle Hotel Arcade bordering the waterfront, the inexpensive to moderate **Banana Bay Club** (tel. 778-9110) is open daily for three meals and offers burgers, platters, stir fries, and a seafood platter. It serves everything from onion loaf to a Bajan Flying Fish sandwich.

Open for lunch and dinner, the inexpensive to moderate **Bombay Club** (tel. 773-1838, reservation suggested), 5A King St., has pasta, quiche, sandwiches, and seafood. At Apothecary Hall Courtyard, inexpensive to moderate **Tommy and Susan's Taverna** (tel. 773-8666) offers Greek (on Mon. night) and international fare. **Harborside Cafe & Cabaret**, 1 King Cross St., serves seafood, meat, pasta, and vegetarian dishes. Wed. is all you can eat shrimp night. A popular restaurant open only for dinner, expensive "Nouvelle American" **Kendrick's** (tel. 773-9199), 52 King St., serves pasta and a variety of meat, seafood, and fowl dishes ranging from sauteed veal to grilled shrimp with spicy gaspacho butter sauce. At 28 King Cross St., the inexpensive to moderate **Golden China Inn** (tel. 773-8181) serves up Cantonese, Szechuan, Mandarin and Hunan specialties including lychee duck, shrimp with peanuts in hot sauce, and vegetable and tofu dishes. **Pentheny's**, 46 King St., serves "international cuisine with an Austrian/German touch." Inexpensive to expensive, **The Chart House**, whose dinners feature steaks and a salad bar, is at 55 King's Wharf near the King Christian Hotel. Set in the courtyard of the Moonraker on 43A Queen Cross St, **the Cultured Pelican** (tel. 773-3333) offers

Chinese, fish, chicken, and steak dishes including items such as baked clams, Caribbean Cobb salad, quesadillas, coconut shrimp, "obscenely stuffed lobster," and vegetarian pasta. Another good restaurant is **Dino's** (tel. 778-8005), 4C Hospital St; a block from the fort, it serves a variety of Italian food ranging from fettucini, shrimps, scallops, and pesto to eggplant ravioli or pan seared scallops. At 625 Strand St., **Café du Soleil** (tel. 772-5400) serves up seafood (panache of seafood, filet of salmon), salads, and meat and fowl dishes. Offering West Indian and Continental cuisine, the moderate **Calabash Supper Club** (tel. 776-0001) is on Queen Cross St. At 39-40 Queen Cross St., **La Guitarra** (tel. 773-8448) serves West Indian cuisine and has daily specials such as saltfish/eggplant on Thurs. Set in the Pan Am Pavilion at 39 Strand St., the informal **Stixx Bar and Restaurant** (tel. 773-5157), a popular and informal, inexpensive to expensively priced watering hole, serves three meals daily and features a special entree nightly. At 39 Strand St., the inexpensive to moderate **Tivoli Gardens** (tel. 773-6782) serves pasta, seafood, and Hungarian goulash as well as vegetable stir fry and snapper Marrakech. There's also an all-day raw bar, salads, lunch specials, and dinner entrees ranging from fried jumbo shrimp to the Admiral's Platter. On Strand St., the moderate to expensive **Comanche Restaurant** (tel. 773-2665) serves seafood, pasta, and curries. George Bush once ate here. At 5A King St., inexpensive to moderate **The Bombay Club** (tel. 773-1838) offers salads–from guacamole to Mandarin, as well as pizza, veggie sandwiches, quiche du jour, and stuffed crabs. The **Amalie Terrace** (crab races at 5 PM on Fri.) and the **Harbormaster Beach Club** (tel. 773-7060) are both at Hotel on the Cay, as is the upscale **The Palms**, which offers steak and lobster. While the Amalie has a Sunday Brunch, seafood, and seafood buffet on Fri., and other fare, The Harbormaster offers a Tues. night beach BBQ with entertainment.

With Thai and Vietnamese cuisine, **Royal Garden**, 10A Hospital St., offers a variety of dishes ranging from green curry shrimp to spring rolls with salad and mint, or shrimp soup with mushrooms and lemon grass. Offering Cantonese-style food, inexpensive to moderate **Golden China Inn** (tel. 773-8181), 28 King Cross St., serves dishes like moo shu shrimp, eggplant in garlic sauce, jumbo shrimp, and black bean sauce with shrimp. The inexpensive to moderate **Anchorage** (tel. 773-4787) at Chandler's Wharf in Gallows Bay serves food ranging from fajita platters to lobster and cajun sausage from noon to midnight. Karaoke is featured on

Wed. and Sat. nights. Also out in Gallows Bay, inexpensive to moderate **Rogues Gallery Pizza** (tel. 773-3813) has a wide variety including veggie combos. They also serve burgers, sandwiches, soups, and salads as well as daily specials. **Cheeseburgers in Paradise** is on the way to Duggan's Reef on the E End. Another inexpensive place to eat is the **Venus Bar & Restaurant** which is at 100 Estate Richmond outside town along the road towards Pueblo. Also cheap, **Martha's Deli** is nearby at 105-106 Richmond.

central west dining: Around the island, a number of roadside vendors sell fresh fruit drinks, sorrel, mauby, and sea moss. Off of Rte. 70 at marker 1.5 in Estate Whim, inexpensive to moderate **Villa Morales** (tel. 772-0556) offers a range of fish and meat entrees served in traditional Spanish and West Indian style. Weekly lunch specials (stew goat, roast pork) are served, as is paella. **Mid-Land Restaurant** in Kingshill serves three meals featuring Continental and native cuisine. At Sion Farm Shopping Center, inexpensive to moderate **China Jade Restaurant** (tel. 778-1996) serves Chinese food including all-you-can-eat buffets on Sat. On Hess Rd. at 114 Castle Coakley, moderate **Gertrude's** (tel. 778-8362) offers Caribbean lobster, broiled snapper with papaya salsa, and other delicacies. Three meals are served as well as Sun. brunch. At Ville La Reine, **Los Chicos Place** serves West Indian and American food and is open for three meals a day. **Junie's Restaurant** (West Indian and seafood) is at 132 Peter's Rest. Inexpensive **Marie's Place** (West Indian cuisine) is at Hannah's Rest. **Bill's Texas Pit BBQ** is at Sunny Isle Shopping Center.

heading W: Due W of town, the inexpensive to moderate **Clubhouse** (tel. 773-7077) at Club St. Croix in Golden Rock has a variety of sandwiches, salads, stir fries, fajitas, and other specialties. Wed. and Fri. nights features local food and entertainment. They serve breakfast, lunch, and dinner daily. At **Five Corners Deli**, 2B-2D La Grande Princesse, Margarita cooks Mexican dishes like flautas, chimichanga and enchilada dinners, and chiles rellenos as well as other dishes. Burritos ($3.75) can be made vegetarian on request; avocado is substituted for the meat. At 17 La Grande Princesse on North Shore Rd., inexpensive **2 Plus 2** (tel. 773-3710) offers shrimp, chicken, and meat dishes; there's also entertainment with DJs. On La Grande Princesse, the **Backyard Inn** (tel. 773-8193) offers inexpensive Continental-style lunches and dinners. In Princesse Plaza, inexpensive to moderate **Di Mitri's** (tel. 773-1100) serves up New

York-style pizza (slices available) with all the toppings as well as pasta dishes. Fronting the beach, the moderate to expensive **Cormorant Beach Club** (tel. 778-8920) at Pelican Beach has dancing under the stars, Sunday brunch, and a Caribbean Grille night on Thursday. In the hotel of the same name, which is next to the Cormorant, the **Hibiscus Beach Restaurant** (tel. 773-4042) serves snacks, fish and light meals. Breakfasts here include a "health conscious" plate. Lunch features a vegetarian salad as well as burgers and dogs. Dinner includes seafood stir fry, and meat and fowl dishes. There's also a Sun. brunch (10:30-2:30). Set at Mill Harbour and Colony Cove to the W, the inexpensive to moderate **Serendipity Inn Beach Restaurant** (tel. 773-5762) serves lunch and dinner (fresh catch of the day; $10 Fri. night BBQ) daily as well as dishes like Cruzan pancakes or coconut shrimp. In St. Croix by the Sea Hotel, **Windows on the Sea** (tel. 778-8600) lives up to its name and serves seafood (coconut prawns, lobster, and other dishes) as well as meat entrees. Located in the upper level of St. Croix by the Sea's Condominium Complex on Judith Fancy Road, **Top of the Sea** serves seafood and steak dishes. Set one mi. E of Cane Bay Beach at the intersection of Rte. 80 and 73, the moderate to expensive **Picnic in Paradise** (tel. 778-1212) offers outdoor dining in a rural atmosphere. Dishes include exotic pasta entrees, fisherman's pan stew, and appetizers such as "pumpkin ravioli with a curry cream sauce and raisins." A West Indian buffet accompanied by live music is on Wed evenings. **Oskar's Bar & Restaurant** (tel. 773-4060), at 4A La Grande Princesse, along North Shore Road, serves sandwiches, hot platters, and steaks, and beef rouade bratwurst. The Cane Bay Reef Club houses the **No Name Bar and Grille**, which offers fresh fish, burgers and dining under the stars, with dishes such as Hungarian goulash and Cornish game hen.

heading E: The Buccaneer has **The Terrace Restaurant** (informal), **the Brass Parrot** (elegant), and the beachside **Mermaid**. Inexpensive to expensive, **Duggan's At the Reef** (tel. 773-9800) Teague Bay, serves seafood, curries, meat, chicken, and pastas. Dishes range from conch tempura to seafood diavolo to Cajun-style blackened fish. **Elena's**, at Coakley Bay Condos, East End Road, offers international cuisine matched with classical music and a view of Buck Island. Featuring waterfront dining with a wide variety of dishes, **The Galleon** (tel. 773-9949), Green Cay Marina at Estate Southgate, offers seafood (fresh island fish and lobster), pasta, steak, lamb, and other dishes for dinner. Black bean soup, salads, and pastas are

also served. Inexpensive **The Deep End**, offering cocktails and light snacks as well as vegetarian dishes, is also here. **Chenay Bay Beach Bar and Grill** (tel. 773-2918) here is very casual and features American/Caribbean cuisine for lunch and dinner, with steaks and seafood; it has a nightly BBQ. Set at Teague Bay in a converted great house, the elegant inexpensive to expensive **Café Madeleine** (tel. 778-7377) serves Italian regional cuisine ranging from pasta and pizza to strudel with fresh lobster.

fast food: Burger King (also downtown), and **Wendy's** are at the Sunny Isle Shopping Center, as is **Kentucky Fried**, which has an additional branch at Golden Rock as well as in Frederiksted. **McDonalds** is at Golden Rock, 11 Orange Grove, and at Ville la Reine. Wendy's is also in Frederiksted, and Burger King is also in Christiansted. **Pizza Hut** is in downtown Christiansted and at Ville La Reine.

food and market shopping: Very little food is found in the town's open air market except on Saturdays. **Stop N' Go Super** stands at the intersection leading to Gallows Bay. **Gallows Bay Foods** is in Gallows Bay itself. A **fish market** is at Gallows Bay; mornings are the best time to catch it, especially Wed. and Sat. around 9 AM. **Pueblo**, the VI's major supermarket chain has one at Golden Rock Shopping Center just outside town at the beginning of Rte. 75 (Northside Road). Sample prices here are 10 lbs. of potatoes/$3.39, apples $1.49/lb., corn $2.99/pkg., mushrooms $1.69/8 oz., one pineapple $2.99, cooked shrimp $7.99/lb., yellowtail $5.99/lb., large eggs $1.37/doz., 1/2 gallon of orange juice $2.79, 1/2 gallon of milk $2.29, Food Club mild cheddar $4.14/lb., generic bagels $2.69/six, and peanut butter $3.39/18 oz. Other locations are at Ville La Reine and at Orange Grove. Offering lower prices and smaller lines, the **Sunshine Supermarket** is at 941-946 Williams Delight. **H & O Food Warehouse** is at Alexander Hamilton Airport. **Concordia Grocery** is at Concordia on Rte. 75. One of the largest supermarkets, **Grand Union** is at Sunny Isle Shopping Center, which also has **Woolworths**, sporting goods stores, bookstores, a drugstore, a bank, and fast food. **Peter's Cellar** which sells imported cheese, international ingredients, and health foods, is also here.

bakeries: Thomas Bakery at 33 King St., with good wholewheat rolls and loaves as well as pastries; they also sell juicy Trinidadian gossip rags such as *The Bomb* and the *Daily Express*. Another stands next to the Golden Cow at Basin Triangle. **The Good Samaritan** is in Sion Farm Shopping Center off Rte. 81. **The Centerline Bakery** is outside of Frederiksted.

Christiansted Nightlife, Events, and Shopping

entertainment: The town's nightlife is neither bland nor extraordinarily exciting. Many restaurants and hotels have an assortment of tourist-oriented nightlife ranging from steel bands to country music to limbo dancing. Check *This Week in St. Croix*, the *Avis*, and Thursday's "Weekend" section in the *Daily News* for details. At night the tourist area echoes with the reverberating sounds of leaking air conditioners and the twangy refrains of "King of the Road," wafting down from a folk guitarist performing in **Moonraker's Bar**. Back up on Company St., latin music battles the pulsating sounds of reggae pouring from competing bars as vehicles and pedestrians cast long shadows on the pavement. Located next to Moonraker and one of the best places to go, **Calabash** has reggae, and calypso after 10 PM, Thurs. through Sat. Dinners are also accompanied by music. **Cocktails** on Company St. has rock music. **The Wreck Bar**, 5-AB Hospital St., has folk music including the local legend, Bean, who returns to Canada during the summer months. **Hotel on the Cay** also has live guitar music as does **Tivoli Garden**, and **Hondo's Backyard**, a disco on King St. which caters to a slacker crowd. At King Street's **Bombay Club**, there's jazz on Fridays. On King St. the **Cilia Grand Nite Club** is one of the island's two strip joints. **outlying entertainment:** Frederiksted's entertainment is listed under that town's section. Outside of town, there's plenty of live music going on during the weekend. **Two Plus Two** (tel. 773-3710), at 17 La Grand Princesse on Northside Rd just 3/4 mi. past the intersection with Rte. 74, offers calypso and reggae on the weekends and disco weeknights. Also outside of town in Kingshill, **Mid-Land** (tel. 778-0979) has a reggae scene on weekends with plenty of friendly locals. It's a great place to go for the adventurous. **Cormorant Beach Club** at Pelican Bay has steel band or Latin dance music on weekends and folk guitar on Wednesday. **Villa Morales** (near Whim Plantation) has a steel band on Friday nights. **Serendipity Inn** at Mill Harbour Condominiums has calypso and steel bands and live jazz on Sunday afternoons. The Buccaneer Hotel's **Brass Parrot** has piano music nightly while its **The Terrace** features jazz on Mon. and Sat., with limbo contests on Sunday evening. **Gertrude's** at Estate Coakley (Hess Rd. at 114 Castle Coakley) has a dance band Sat. evenings.

movies: Films are shown at the **Diamond Twin Cinemas** and **Wometco Theaters** at Sunny Isle and at the **Theatre La Reine** at La Reine Center.

other diversions: Horse races are held once a month at the track near the airport. A real fashion show, it's well worth your time to check one of these out. Cockfights are also held regularly all over; ask around. Blood and flying feathers galore!

hip weekend itinerary: Friday night have cocktails, sashimi, and dinner at the Blue Moon where you catch a jazz performance. Later, returning to Christiansted, head for the Calabash. On Saturday, go to Buck Island, then have dinner at Dino's, Kendricks, or Villa Morales. That evening check out the jazz at the Blue Moon again, and head for Hondo's (if you're under 25). You might also return to the Calabash or head out to the Mid-Lands. On Sunday, go to the beach, then have lunch at King Fredrick, and go to the West End Beach Club (tel. 772-0002) to the N of Christiansted for reggae in the evening; it's popularly known as the Sand Bar.

performances: Out in Gallows Bay, the **Rogues Gallery Pizza Theater** (tel. 773-3813) presents comedies, musicals, and musical reviews for $10 pp. Try to catch a performance by the **Caribbean Community Theater** (tel. 773-2100) which performs at the Buccaneer. Cultural programs are also offered at the Estate Whim

Greathouse by the **Landmarks Society** (tel. 772-0598). Also check to see if anyone is performing at **Island Center** (tel. 778-5272).

events: Starting before Christmas Day, the **Crucian Christmas Festival** culminates on Three Kings Day, Jan. 6. Festivities include calypso contests and other entertainment, the crowning of kings and queens, horse racing, and children's and adult parades. The **St. Patrick's Day Parade** is held in March. The **Sports Week Festival** is held during the beginning of April with the American Paradise Triathalon following. It starts with a 1.24-mi. swim in the harbor, followed by a 34.1-mi. bike ride, and a 7.4-mi. run. (For information on the event write Box 3210, Christiansted 00822, call 773-8222, or fax 773-8249). The three-day **Mumm's Cup Regatta** is held in mid-October. The **Jazz and Caribbean Music and Art Festival** is held during the last two weekends of October. Venues include the Paul E. Joseph Stadium in Frederiksted and bandstands in both Christiansted and Frederiksted. Artists who have appeared include the likes of Tito Puente, Airto and Flora Purim. The **Conchshell Regatta** is held in November.

shopping: Not nearly as big a commercial center as St. Thomas, St. Croix nevertheless has a wide selection of duty-free goods including famous Cruzan Rum. King St. and Camagniets Gade (Company St.) are the main shopping areas. On Strand St. under the Club Comanche Bridge, the **American West India Company** sells locally-manufactured gourmet foods, furniture, coffee and teas, stationary, sea island cotton, and other items made or grown in the West Indies. **The Caribbean Clothing Company**, Company St., specializes in men's clothing and has an excellent selection available. On Strand St., **Simply Cotton** offers colorful women's and children's cotton clothing. Set for nearly three decades at the foot of Company St. across from the Steeple Bldg., **Sony** sells hand wrought jewelry including the original island hook bracelet. On King St., **Down Island** offers a variety of attractive clothing. Also on King St., **1870 Town House Shoppes** has wares ranging from clothing to jewelry. In the Quin House at King Cross and Company Sts., **Russell Waterhouse Gallery** (tel. 773-5999) offers mahogany furniture and fine art. **King's Ransom Gifts** in King's Alley also sells decorative jewelry. **Small Wonder**, 4 Company St., sells hand painted St. Croix sweatshirts. In Hamilton House on King St., **Little Switzerland** sells crystal, china, watches, jewelry, and perfume. One of the town's most popular shops, the local branch of

Java Wraps, which sells Indonesian batik cloth fashioned into reasonably priced clothing, is at Strand and King Sts. A good place to go for tee shirts and books is the **St. Croix Environmental Association**, just to the L of the Apothecary Court entrance at 6 Company St. It is fighting to preserve the mangrove swamps and against excessive development being pushed on the island by outside entrepreneurs. Judith King and Trudi Gillam share the **Gillam King Gallery**, 2111 Company St. Trudi makes copper and brass metal structures while Judith produces colorful island batik art on rice paper and pen and ink watercolors. Her art portrays local life. At 38 Strand St., the **Violette Boutique** (800-544-5912 for brochure/orders) sells a variety of duty-free luxury items. On King St., **Island Botanica** has a wide selection of magic sprays and candles.

jewelry and perfume: On King's Wharf, **Ay Ay Gold** offers gold and gemstone jewelery. **The Gold Shop** is in the Pan Am Pavilion. At 3 Company St., **the Goldworker** offers a wide variety of hand-made and custom designed gold and silver jewelry as well as gold and silver sculptures and crystal. Featuring diamonds and gems, **Pegasus**, 58 Company St., is one of the finer jewelry shops. **Crucian Gold**, 57A Company St., sells original jewelry. At the corner of King and Queen Cross Sts., **St. Croix Perfume Center** offers duty-free fragrances, jewelry, hats and other souvenirs. At 53A-B Company St. at Market Square, **St. Croix Shoppes** sell a wide variety of perfumes, colognes, and cosmetics at duty free prices. At 38 Strand St., the **Violette Boutique** sells Bijan and other perfumes. **Colombian Emeralds International**, Queen Cross St., sells precious stones, gold jewelry, and watches.

bookstores and records: The major bookstore in town (and on the island) is the **Writer's Block**, which has a fine selection. Others include **Jeltrup's Books** on King Cross St., with an excellent selection of local titles as well as used books; **The Bookie** at 3 Strand St.; and **Tropical Paperback Exchange** (used books only) at 15 Church St. Outside of town the largest bookstore is religious **Bethany Book and Gift Shop** at Sunny Isle Shopping Center. **Parrot Fish Music**, 48 King Cross St., sells a variety of CDs, cassettes, and discs, including ones by local artists. **The Pikis Shop**, which specializes in Latin American Music, is at 9-A La Grande Princesse in Princesse Plaza.

alcohol: Cruzan Rum tends to be cheaper here than on the other islands. A liqueur, Buba Touree is locally manufactured and combines rum, lime juice, and spices. At Sunny Isle Center, **Woolworth** has the lowest alcohol prices. However, you can also find an extensive selection in any shopping center, and stores in the towns offer a good selection, so it's not necessary to go out of your way. **Pan Am Liquors**, 12 Pan Am Pavilion, is the town's major liquor store. With two locations (at Gallows Bay and at 59 King's Wharf, **Grog & Spirits** offers a full selection of alcohol as well as snack foods. **Jaime Liquors** is at 18 Company St. **The Spigot** is at King's Wharf.

Pan Am Pavilion shopping: Many Hands has original art including prints, watercolors, ceramics, hand painted note cards, baskets, and Christmas ornaments. **Skirt Tails** sells leisure clothing, straw hats, and bags. **Camp Paradise** offers swim and casual clothing for all ages and sexes. The **VI Divers' Adventure Room** sells dive accessories, gear, body boards, as well as leisure clothing. **Leather Or Not** sells custom made sandals and other leather goods. **Steele's Smokes & Sweets** sells chocolates including handmade fudge as well as everything a smoker could need or want. Opposite the Pavilion on Strand St. is **Folk Art Traders**, one of the finest folk craft galleries in the Caribbean. Here you can find iron sculpture, textiles, carnival masks, jewelry, and fine art as well as books, old maps, gourmet foods, and antiques. **Design Works** is also across from the Pan Am Pavilion.

Caravelle Arcade shopping: The **Royal Poinciana** sells exotic perfumes, local condiments, and cosmetics. The **Jewelry Factory** specializes in handcrafted stone and coral jewelry. **Island Temptations** has expensive home furnishings and art items. **Ritsu's** sells gems, jewelry, and art objects. Set in the Hotel Caravelle on Queen Cross St., the **House of Vizia** offers handcrafted gold and silver jewelry. **Crystal Adventures** sells crystal jewelry, dishes, figurines, and other items. **Courtship and Seduction** sells jewelry, cotton and silk lingerie, and cards and games. **King's Wharf shopping: Mile-Mark Boutique** sells novelty items, swimsuits, and tee shirts. **Dive St. Croix** offers dive items, tee shirts, as well as rental and repairs for scuba equipment. **Chandler's Wharf:** This small plaza is out at Gallow's Bay; a few shops are located here. **Out of the Blue** sells handpainted clothing and accessories. **Fly By Night** is a boutique offering women's fashions and accessories. **Karavan**

West Indies has a wide range of gifts and collectibles ranging from woodcarvings to ceramics and works by local artists.

Christiansted Information, Services, Health, and Diving

information: A tourist information service (tel. 773-7117) is located inside the Scalehouse. **The National Park Service** gives out information inside the Old Danish Customs House. The local **Chamber of Commerce** (tel. 773-1435) is in the Sion Farm Shopping Center on Queen Mary Hwy. They can answer your questions regarding investment, government, business, trade, and trends. The **St. Croix Hotel and Tourism Association** (tel. 773-7117, 800-524-2026) can give you information on accommodation and activities. They're located at Ste. 7, Gallows Bay PO Bldg. In the Pan Am Pavilion, **Island Attractions** (tel. 773-7977) can arrange trips. The **St. Croix Environmental Association** (tel. 773-1989, Box 3839, 00822) has its office next to the Apothecary Hall Courtyard, Company St. It offers boat trips, hikes, runs, and takes visitors in season to see the leatherbacks at Sandy Point. One regular trip ($15 adults, $10 children under 12) leaves every Wed. at 8 AM from Cramer Park. It is led by long-term residents Bill and Betsy Gladfelter. The trip lasts 3-4 hrs. and covers 4-5 mi. It's recommended for those in good physical condition. **Take-A-Hike** (tel. 778-6997 for reservations) offers walking tours of town daily at 10 AM; other walks are available. The office is open Mon. to Thurs. 9 to 2, and Fri. from 10 to 2.

health care: Emergency service (24 hours) is available at the **St. Croix Hospital** (tel. 778-6311, emergency 922, fax 778-5500), 4007 Estate Diamond, on Peppertree Rd. (Rte. 79). It's inferior to the hospital on St. Thomas. **The People's Drugstore** is at 1-1A King St.

services: The **Florence Williams Public Library**, King St., was devastated by Hugo and has a temporary branch on the same street. The **Post Office** is located inside the Danish West Indies and Guinea Company Warehouse at 100 Church St. (corner of Company). A second PO is out at Gallows Bay. Islandwide, others are located at Estate Richmond (near Christiansted on Rte. 75), Kingshill, at Estate Richmond, in Sunny Isle, and in Frederiksted. There are a number of **banks** in town including Barclay's, the Bank of Nova Scotia, Banco Popular, Chase Manhattan, First Federal Savings Bank, and First Pennsylvania. An **American Express** office is located at Southerland Tours in King's Alley. **VI Photo Supply**, 3 Queen Cross St., sells USGS topographic maps. One hour photo developing is offered by **Fast Foto**, 52 King St., and **VI Photo Express**, 2 A-B Strand St. **The Uncommon Market**, 55 Company St., offers one day developing and rents underwater cameras. For video rentals, try the **Green Banana Video** (tel. 773-3868) in Gallows Bay and the **Block Buster Video** (tel. 778-0800) at Ville La Reine. Equipped with a pool and sauna, the **Caribbean Health and Racquet Club** (tel. 778-4144), Golden Rock Shopping Plaza, offers short-term memberships. **Under the Palms** (tel. 778-8018) on Comanche Walk offers theraputic massage, as does **"In Touch"** (tel. 773-0999) in Apothecary Courtyard. **The Caribbean Dance School** (tel. 778-8824), 5 Church St., holds classes in gymnastics, self defense, yoga, jazz, ballet, etc.

media: The most useful of the local free publications is *St. Croix This Week* which is easy to find. (Single copies may be ordered for $2 from Box 4477, Christiansted 00822-4477). Another useful publication is the *Prestige Guide*. Although it's not much in terms of hard news, the *St. Croix Avis* offers a good deal of information on events, as does the *Daily News*. Reggae lovers should check out Kenny Cool J who programs reggae (95.5 FM) from 9 to midnight on Sun. through Thurs.

rental agents: Bidelspacher Rentals, 3 North Grapetree Bay, Christiansted (tel. 773-9250, 773-9040) represents "The Reef" condos (one and two bedrooms) on Teague Bay and two- and three-bedroom homes on the East End. **Island Villas**, 14A Caravelle Arcade (tel. 773-8821, fax 773-8821, 800-626-4521), Christiansted, offers studios on up to five-bedroom residences. Rates for one to six bedrooms range from $500-$7,000/pw. **Tropic Retreats in Paradise**, (tel. 778-7550, 800-233-7944, Box 5219) has deluxe, fully equipped condos and villas.

diving: Offering a complete range of aquatic sport activities including boat, pier, and beach dives from $40 and up, **Cruzan Divers** (772-3701, 800-247-8186), 12 Strand St., rents snorkeling equipment, diving instruction, and sportfishing. A weekly calendar of events is posted at the wharf. Located at Club Comanche, **Dive Experience** (tel. 773-3307, 800-235-9047) is a PADI five star IDC facility. In addition to dive packages, CPR and Medic First Aid courses are also offered. Another PADI five star facility, **VI Divers, Ltd.** (tel. 773-6045, 800-544-5911) has introductory dives, certification courses, equipment rental, and daily dive tours. They're in the Pan Am Pavilion. On the boardwalk at 59 Kings Wharf, **Dive St. Croix** (tel. 773-3434, 800-523-DIVE) is the only dive company authorized to dive off of Buck Island and offers a variety of diving and certification courses as well as rental and repairs for scuba equipment. They also have a branch at Colony Cove's beach shack.

Buck Island Reef National Monument

Comprising 780 acres in total, Buck Island Reef is the only underwater National Monument in the U.S. Its center, 180-acre Buck Island, lies two miles off the N shore of St. Croix. An incredible 30,000 people visit this seductive nymphet of an island every year. Proclaimed a national monument in 1961, the island has been inhabited from the 1750s. The story of its name is a convoluted tale which has been frequently misrepresented. The earliest evidence is a French map dating from 1667 which shows the island called Ile Vert ("Green Island"); the Dutch settlers called it Pocken-Eyland because of the Pokholtz (Lignum vitae) trees, which gave it its greenery. An island to the W, now known as Green Cay, was called Ile a Cabritz (Goat Island). In the Danish period during the early 1700s, the names for the caye and the island were transposed in a mapmaking error. Thus, Buck Island should really be known as Green Cay and vice versa! Today, visitors are permitted onshore only from 8 to 5 daily. Dramatically reforested since the goats' departure, the island today is as close to nature now as it's ever been. Even though the spectacular stuff is really underwater, it's worth a visit just for the island itself. More than 40 species of birds flutter around the 62 species of trees. The island is a rookery for frigate birds and pelicans. A nature trail (takes one hour) runs along the top of the mile-long island; follow the trail to the top of the island for a spectacular view of St. Croix. The beaches here (on the SW and W coasts) are superior to any on St. Croix. Watch out for the machineel trees on the W coast and the touch-me-not which has yellow needles hidden under its green leaves.

downstairs: Originally a simple fringing reef, a magnificent barrier reef stretches 2,000 yards along the eastern half of the island. Its effect is one of sheer fantasy. Swim past the elkhorn coral that marks the entrance to the reef and follow the markers on the bottom to find your way along the 30-min. underwater trail. While underwater, check out the rainbow gathering of fish including the queen angelfish, the foureye butterflyfish, the smooth trunkfish, and the French and blue angelfish. Others include the yellowtail, spadefish, red snapper, tilefish, trumpetfish, and several varieties of parrotfish. Fish here are so naive and trusting that they'll eat right out of your hand. While you're investigating the downstairs branch of this living natural history museum, note the primitive multicellular animals. Most primitive of all are the sponges, which come in all shapes and sizes. A dinosaurian prototype of the starfish, the flexible, multi-armed crinoid anchors itself to crevices with its central, white, root-like pedestal. One of many reef organisms capable of producing sounds underwater, the spotted drum (*Equetus punctatus*) produces a continuous discordant and eerie symphony of snaps, pops, grunts and scraping noises.

getting there: Access is limited to private and chartered boats. Concessioners are licensed by the NPS and must meet strict standards. Expect to pay at least $25 for the 5 1/2-mile sail. A variety of all shapes and sizes of boats (including catamarans, yachts, native sloops, trimarans and glass-bottomed boats) leave from Christiansted's King's Wharf. One of the best operators is **Mile-Mark Charters** (tel. 773-BOAT; 800-524-2012) which has both sail and motorboat trips from $25-$40. Don't worry if you have never snorkeled before or even if you can't swim. They've handled people from Nebraska who've never even seen the sea before! If you're unsure of your abililties just wear a flotation cushion and hold on to the life preserver towed by the guide. A popular boat is Capt. Heinz's *Teroro II* (tel. 773-3161/4041), a 42-ft. trimaran. **Big Beard** (tel. 793-4482) is also well-equipped. **note:** When planning your trip, consider your priorities. For example, do you wish to sail or motor, do you want a glass bottomed boat or not, and how long do you want to spend on the island? All tours stop at the underwater nature trail for around 45 min. The differences between the trips lie in other particulars. You should ask if the boat will dock at Buck Island or merely anchor offshore. If you want to hike the nature trail, allow for an hour ashore.

practicalities: If you plan on snorkeling, hiking, fishing or picnicking, pack appropriately. Although there is a well-equipped picnic area, no food is available on the island, so bring your own. Beware of sunburn, cuts from coral, spiny sea urchins, jellyfish, fire coral.

Never reach into a dark hole, lest you be savaged by a moray eel. White floats are placed around the trail area in case you need to rest. Maneuver your boat slowly through park waters. For further information contact Superintendent, Christiansted National Historic Site, Box 160, Christiansted, St. Croix, USVI 00820 (tel. (809) 773-1460).

Buck Island Concessioners

All addresses are in Christiansted, St. Croix.

Name/location/tel.	Boats/trips
Milemark, Inc., King ChristianHotel, King's Wharf, 773-22856-35	Sail or motor, half-day or full day, glass bottomed boat available.
Clyde, Inc. Box 25690, Gallow's Bay 00824 773-8520	One 6-passenger sail vessel w/ motor available half day or full day.
"Diva" Box 3384 Christiansted 00820 778-4675	One 6 passenger sail vessel w/motor, half-day or full day available.
"Charis" Box 2908 Christiansted 00820, 773-9027	One 6 passengersail vessel half day or full day available
Big Beard Adventures 25-35 Pan Am Building Box 4534, Christiansted 00834 773-4482	Sail or motor, half day or full day, beach BBQ offered
"Teroro II" Green Cay Marina Llewellyn's Charter 773-4041, 773-9027	One 42-ft trimaransail w/motor, 36-ft. trimaran, half day or full day.

Heading East From Christiansted

The farther east you go, the fewer people you find and the drier the vegetation becomes. Take Hospital St. (Rte. 82) E out of Christiansted. Once the island's main industrial port during the 1960s, Gallows Bay is now becoming part of the town's tourist area. The

Carrot Bay, Tortola

Long Bay Tortola

Sir Francis Drake Channel

Century plant, Tortola

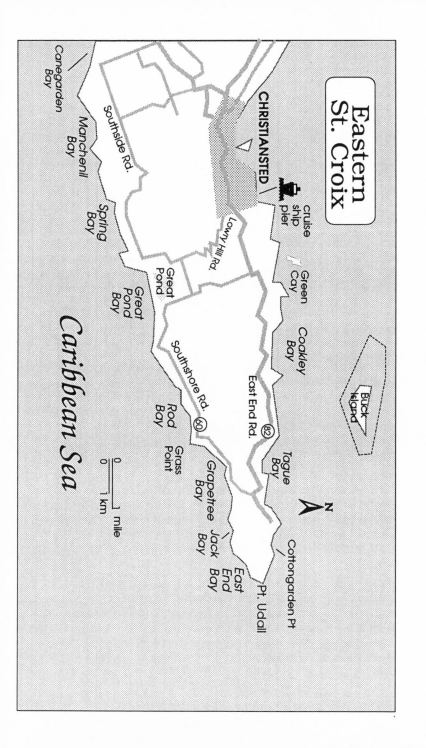

last gas stations are here. **Buccaneer Hotel** ($3 pp for use of beach facilities) lies to the E past Altona Lagoon. Beaches in this area have been given names by the hotel like "Mermaid," "Whistle," and "Grotto." Farther on is **Shoy's Beach** or **Punnett's Bay** where leatherback sea turtles nest. The turnoff for Green Cay Marina is just ahead of this. The 20-acre **Green Cay**–a National Wildlife Refuge for the St. Croix ground lizard (otherwise eradicated by the mongoose) and a rookery for herons and pelicans–lies just offshore. **Green Cay Marina** (tel. 7773-1453, fax 773-9651) at Estate Southgate is a full service yacht harbor Next site on down the main drag (East End Road) is **Hotel Chenay Bay Colony** and its white sand beach. Miss Bea Road leads to normally deserted **Prune Beach**. **Hog Bay's beach** lies near Coakley Bay condominium. Solitude Valley Road leads to **Solitude Country Store** near the ruins of Estate Solitude. The secluded coves of Coakley, Solitude, and Yellowcliff are along this stretch. **Duggan's Reef**, a restaurant and beach area, lies just past Teague Bay. **Villa Madeleine**, one of the island's most elegant restaurants, overlooks the condos here which resemble nothing so much as a set of gigantic personal computers in search of a corporate office. **Smuggler's Cove** has a white sand beach and picnic area. Next is **Cramer Park** which has a campground (no fresh water and the flush toilets are frequently out of order), and a coral sand beach. The only shade here is provided by seagrape trees. The remainder of the island's eastern portion–extending from here 1.5 mi. to Point Udall–has been set aside as the **Farleigh Dickinson Territorial Park**. A path heading E traverses hilly terrain covered with cacti–some of them reaching the height of trees. You may also ascend to the top of 672-ft. **Sugar Loaf Hill**, but permission from the property owner is required. You can follow other paths to white sand beaches whose waters provide good snorkeling. **Boiler Bay** (named for the large algae covered rocks lying offshore) is next. The other beaches in this area (like beautiful East End Bay, Issacs Bay, and Jacks Bay) are best reached on foot. **Point Udall** is said to be the easternmost point in the United States. (It's not; that distinction belongs to Wake I. in the South Pacific.) Its true claim to fame is as the part of the Virgin Islands first sighted by Columbus on Nov. 14, 1493 during his second voyage. The reason to come to this 226-ft. point is the view. You can see as far way as Saba–90 mi. to the E–on a clear day. From here, hike down to the sea along the paths. Exercise care on this path. To reach the S coast, it's necessary to reconnoiter to Rte. 60 (Southshore or Southside Road). Set less than a mi. from Point

Udall, the 82-ft., 260-ton **space dish antenna** (tel. 773-4448) is used to explore quasars, pulsars, radio galaxies, molecular clouds, galactic nuclei, black holes, and other unexplored spots in the cosmos. Funded by the National Science Foundation, construction cost $5 million. Call about possible tours. At **Grapetree Bay** stands the remains of the Hugo-devastated Grapetree Bay Hotel and what appears to be a fine white sand beach. In fact the sand was dredged from Turner Hole to the west. Despite the construction of an expensive barrier, currents periodically sweep the beach naked of sand–revealing the beach's true nature! A trail from near the hotel leads to **Jack Bay** and its white sand beach. Climb Pentheney, the hill behind Grapetree, for the view. On a spit extending into the ocean, **Grass Point** has one of the island's most scenic views. Surf pounds onto the rocks where you may see the rusting wreck of a car. Straight ahead to the W, **Rod (or Red) Bay** has good snorkeling but no beach. Amidst the ruins of Estate Great Pond stands **Camp Arawak**, a campsite (see "camping" under "accommodations") and a grassy beach. **Great Pond Bay** itself has fantastic birdwatching and a nature trail. To return to Christiansted from this point, you can take Rte. 60 N and Rte. 82 (East End Rd.) across or you can continue along Rte. 624 and then take Rte. 62 N which merges with Rte. 624. Further along Rte. 62, Estate Fareham's ruins contains the Boy Scout Camp (see "camping" under "accommodations"); the entrance to the Great Pond nature trail is nearby. **Machenil Bay**, along the S coast heading W, has a fine white sand beach. From Batiste (or Fisherman's) Point nearby one can hike along to Halfpenny Bay, Spring Bay, and Fareham Bay. Southside Road terminates to the W at **Cane Garden Bay**, an interesting hiking and birdwatching area with salt ponds and salt flats. Heading along the S coast, you may see reddish-brown grazing Senepol cattle and dairy cattle.

Along The Northwest Coast

Palm fringed **Little Princess Beach** is off Rte. 75 past Golden Rock. Further on are the ruins of **Estate la Grande Princesse** with Pelican Cove's white sand beach (where the Cormorant Beach Club, one of the island's premier properties, is located). Rte. 751 passes Estate St. John on to the so called "French Ruins" or "Maltese Ruins" of **Estate Judith's Fancy** which are now part of a private home. The road ends at **Salt River Bay** (good surfing and snorkeling). Offshore lies the wreck of the freighter *Cumulus*, which went aground on the reef in October 1977–with its cargo of stolen cars bound for down-island. Back on Rte. 80 lies **Sugar Bay**, with its mangroves.and swamp ferns.

Salt River National Historical Park and Ecological Preserve

Just after Sugar Bay stands the principal sight on this coast. It is thought (judging from the descriptions in the log entries) that Columbus landed here. The Cape of the Arrows here was supposedly named by him after crew members attacked the locals, who retaliated. The area was the administrative center during the French rule in the 1650s. In 1965, the five-acre landing site was purchased by the VI Government and placed in the National Register. In 1978 it was designated a "Significant Natural Area" and an "Area of Preservation and Restoration" under the VI Coastal Zone Management Act. In 1979, a 690-acre site including the entire shoreline, excluding the Cape of the Arrows, was made a National Landmark; this area included the major mangrove stands in Sugar and Triton Bays. Made a National Historic Park and Ecological Preserve in 1993, Salt River may also become a World Heritage Site and a National Marine Sanctuary. At present a 288-room luxury hotel, 300 condos, and a 157-boat marina are slated for construction here. Although the permit was renewed in 1993, construction has yet to begin. **sights:** The parking area's asphalt covers the island's premiere archaeological site, which dates from 350 AD– one of the few Indian ball courts found in the Caribbean. The petroglyph-incised stones have been carted off to a Copenhagen museum. Just keep in mind when you get out of your car that you are standing on sacred ground. Hike W along the beach to find a tidal pool. Set on the estuary's SE end at Triton Bay, Salt River's 12-acre mangrove reserve is under the control of the Nature Conservancy. It is one of the few remaining lagoons. (Krause Lagoon on the S coast was filled in with sand). Including 45 acres of white and black mangroves fringed by red mangroves, this area supports the highest diversity of birdlife known in the VI. These mangrove forests provide a critical habitat for North American land birds who migrate and winter here. Of the 108 bird species, 17 are locally endangered and three (the brown pelican, roseate tern, and peregrine falcon) are federally endangered. There are also seagrass beds offshore, a giant wild fern garden is along the coast, and the endangered least tern nests on a peninsula off the bay's E shore.

Salt River Dropoff is an excellent dive site, and the Salt River Marina, on the bay's W side, is the home of **Anchor** (tel. 778-1522), a dive operator who also offers marine excursions into the mangroves.

from Salt River to the W: Leading off from Estate Clairmont Road just off from its junction with North Shore Road (Rte. 80), **Michael's Hill** commands an impressive view. **Estate Clairmont** itself has been taken over and transformed into a park by the St. Croix Historical Society. There's a self-guiding trail. Rte. 73 leads S to the ruins of Estate Belvedere, Estate Libanon, Estate Little Fountain, Estate Mon Bijou, and (on Rte. 707) the ruins of Estate Slob and Estate Fredensborg. **Cane Bay** (with Cane Bay Plantation Hotel built amidst the estate ruins) is one of the island's top dive sites. From here hike (watch for wasp's nests!) to the sugar factory featuring three extant sugar boiling pots and the remains of cane grinding mills. Heading W from the junction of Rte. 80 with Rte. 69, a road leads on to **Davis Beach**. Davis is small but attractive. Closed for years after Hugo, the former Rockresort of **Carambola** has reopened under the Radisson Resort banner. A rough hike leads to **Annaly Bay** with its tidepools. Rte. 78, Scenic Road West, continues on along a rough road to the lighthouse at **Ham's Bluff**. A steep, overgrown path leads along Furnel Ridge to the N shore. A 360-degree panorama of the island can be had from a hill NW of secluded **Bodkins Mill**, accessible on foot from Scenic Road. Rte. 78 terminates in Hams Bay. S of the junction of Rte. 78 with Rte. 58 lies the **"Rain Forest"** (see below) which is really a secondary tropical forest. Routes 765, 763, and 75 traverse it. Rte. 58 leads to US Navy-constructed concrete Creque Dam. The **Mt. Victory** ruins are on the way to it. Along Rte. 63 heading N lie **Sprat Hall** and then **Butler Bay** with its small beach and inland (sometimes waterless) waterfall. It's a nature reserve and an excellent birding spot. A bit further on lies the so-called **Monks Baths** or Malta Baths whose construction local legend attributes to the Knights of Malta during their occupation (1653-1665) of the island. It is more likely that they are of natural origin. Near Fredensfield and near Creque Dam Road are the ruins of **Morning Star Plantation**.

Enroute To Frederiksted

Centerline Road extends the whole way from Christiansted. Comparatively inexpensive shared taxis run this route. To catch one you should stand by the corner at Chase Manahattan.

Island Center: Aptly located in the center of the island off Centerline Rd. a half mile N of Sunny Isle Shopping Center, this ten-acre complex contains a 1,100-seat amphitheater (600 seats under a canopy and 500 in the open) which showcases cultural events. You might be able to see the Caribbean Dance Company, the African-American Dance Ensemble, or the Michigan Banjos here. Call 778-5272 for information.

St. George Botanical Garden: Located off Centerline Rd. about four miles W of Fredericksted. Originally a 16-acre estate during the 18th-19th C, this garden (tel. 772-3874) contains the ruins of a great house, rum factory, lime kiln, baker's and saddlemaker's shops, and a stone dam. Beginning as the clean up project of a local garden club in 1972, it was also discovered to be the site of the island's largest Arawak village (inhabited from 100-900 AD) in 1976. Currently privately funded and managed by volunteers, the16-acre garden complex has a library (open on Thurs. or by special request) and a variety of ongoing projects, including collecting samples of the plants that Spanish explorer Gonzalo Fernández de Oviedo presented to Queen Isabella in 1536. Note the garden with its pre-Columbian crops (maize, cassava and sweet potatoes) and the old cemetery. Enter through the stone gates along a road flanked on either side by rows of royal palms, the trees grown by Hebraic kings in the Garden of Babylon. The flowers and foliage here are truly wonderful. Note the opuntia and the aloe on which kids have carved their names. In late afternoon, it must be one of the most peaceful tourist spots in the Caribbean. Concerts are occasionally held here on Sundays. The annual Quadrille Ball is also held here. Open daily from 9 to 4; $2 admission; $1 for children.

Whim Greathouse: Located two miles off Centerline Rd. near Fredericksted, this large sugar estate complex (tel. 772-0598) was originally known as St. John's Rest. Restored by the St. Croix Landmarks Society, it was owned by an eccentric Dane named Christopher MacEvoy, Jr. Oval-shaped, the comparatively small one-story estate house has a large number of windows. Built around 1794, its yard-thick walls are made of cut stone and coral held together with lime-and-molasses mortar. A moat surrounds the building. Antiques (both Cruzan and imported) fill the insides. To the rear, the cook house and attached museum contain displays of sugar production artifacts, a pot-still for making rum, engravings, weapons, and the tombstone of Anna Heegard, the famous mistress of Governor-General von Scholten. Reconstructed with numbered blocks brought from Nevis, the windmill fairly represents the ones in use during the island's sugar heyday. The recreated Apothecary Shop (1832) has finishing touches right down to the rocking chair and the fine collection of original bottles and vials on the shelves. Other displays include the ruins of the sugar processing factory, the Scottish steam engine, and the watchhouse. There's also a gift shop which has a good selection of books, prints, watercolors, and crafts. Hours are changeable, but it's generally open Tues. to Sat. from 10-4; $5 admission with guided tour; $1 for children.

others from west to east: The mill and ruins of **Estate Beeston Hill**, located at the junction of Centerline Rd. and Rte. 70, have been incorporated into a private residence. The **USDA Experimental Forest** (mahogany and teak) lies off Rte. 708 to the N of Centerline. **Estate Grange great house,** just past the junction of Rte. 708 with Centerline, contains a monument (placed here 80 years ago by a biographer) to Rachel Faucett Levine, Alexander Hamilton's mother. Hamilton himself lived here from age 10 to 18, over 200 years ago. His mother's bones lie at some unknown spot on the estate. The other monument here is to Dutch sailors who died during a yellow fever epidemic in 1886 when the great house had the unenviable function of serving as an isolation ward. Nearby is an antique Danish bell. (The great house itself is private property and off limits). Nearby stands the **Grange Hill Nursery** and the ruins of **Estate Anna's Hope. Sunny Isle Shopping Center**, at the junction with Rte. 66, is an island mainstay. Note the strange looking sausage trees which flower during the summer. **United Shopping Plaza** is on Centerline about a mile to the east. The cleared ruins of **Estate Spanish Town** lie inside the grounds of the VIALCO aluminum refinery. **Ville La Reine Shopping Center** (and Kingshill Post Office) are on Rte. 75 heading N near its junction with Centerline. A sheltered workshop (open Mon. to Fri., 10-3) sells handicrafts by the handicapped. It's in an old Danish schoolhouse in the Kingshill Barracks near the pink Justice Complex (or Territorial Court). **Fredensborg Pond**, the island's largest freshwater marsh, stands near the old water mill of Estate Fredensborg, off Rte. 707 and near the Bethlehem Old Works. On Centerline Road near the College of the Virgin Islands, **The V.I Government Agricultural Station** (open Mon. to Fri., 8-5) has experimental hybrid crops like mangoes, bananas, etc. The annual Agricultural and Food Fair takes place here in mid-February. Near the station lie the ruins of **Estate Lower Love**. Near Alexander Hamilton Airport stand a miniature mill and stone house of contemporary construction. **The Cruzan Rum Distillery** (tel. 772-0280), located S off of Rte. 64 (West Airport Rd.) and constructed amidst the ruins of Estate Diamond, offers tours of its facilities (8:30-11:15 and 1-4:15) by reservation. Approximately 95% of its product is shipped to New York, where it is bottled. Dating from the last century, the ruins of **Estate Hogensborg** stand to the N of Centerline Road, about a mile before Whim Greathouse. **West End Saltpond** (great birdwatching) and **Sandy Point National Wildlife Refuge**, a fine three-mile stretch of sand, lie along a bumpy road off Rte. 661 to the S. Although there's little in the way of snorkeling, visibility is superb, and the beach is unfrequented. If you want to explore, birdwatch, and get away from the crowds, this is definitely the place. Here is the most important location in the US for regular nesting of the leatherback sea turtle, which–measuring over six feet long and sometimes weighing over 1,000 pounds–is the largest living turtle species. In 1984, the US Fish and Wildlife Service purchased the 398 acres in order to protect the sea turtles. The beach has been continually monitored since 1981, and nesting females are logged and tagged. Poachers are being deterred, and nests facing natural beach erosion are being relocated. Although it is geared for the education of locals, visitors may join tours here. For information call 773-4554. Nesting turtles clamber ashore (Feb. through July) in the dead of night. Each mother digs a large pit and deposits a cache of 80 golf-ball-sized eggs, which she then buries. If you go to see these turtles, don't disturb them before they've settled or they'll haul themselves right back into the sea again. (Green and hawksbill turtles also nest here). Earthwatch runs expeditions to this beach. Keeping the turtles company, least terns also nest here, and brown pelicans, Caribbean martins, American oystercatchers, and white-tailed tropicbirds can also be seen. At West End Saltpond, you can also see everything from black-necked stilts to herons, bananquits to black-faced grassquits and white-crowned pigeons. Brown pelicans, terns, and white-cheeked pintails also nest here. The beach plays host to a tall orchid (in hues of brown, lavender, and ochre) known locally as the Sandy Point orchid, although it is indigenous to the entire Caribbean. The reserve closes at 7 PM, and visitors are urged to leave nothing of value in their locked cars. As they may puncture eggs, items such as beach umbrellas and volleyball nets are prohibited on the beach. Fires are also forbidden.

Frederiksted

Located on the W coast of the island, this town has great views and an impressive colonial legacy. Its tree-lined streets still exhibit a wide variety of colonial architecture. Frederiksted is so quiet and peaceful that it's difficult to believe this town ever burned during riots (in 1878). Cruise ship passengers see most of this town only in their peripheral vision as they are being speedily bused to Christiansted.

history: Established on October 19, 1751 and named for King Frederick V, the town grew slowly. There were exactly two houses in 1755 and still only 314 residents by 1766. Many of the original buildings in town were destroyed by the 1867 tidal wave or the fire (caused by labor riots) of Oct. 1-2, 1878, in which most of the town burned to a crisp. The majority of the remarkable restorations and reconstructions date from then, a period when the Victorian gingerbread style prevailed.

Frederiksted Sights

Fort Frederik: Originally built to discourage smuggling and completed in 1760, this quiet but imposing structure has played an important role in the island's history. From here, the flag of the new American republic was saluted for the first time by a foreign power in 1776. According to local legend, an American brigantine was in port here when independence was declared. When a homemade Stars and Stripes was hoisted, the fort, ignoring the rules of neutrality, returned the cannon fire. This was the first salute to an American ship. Here also, on July 3, 1848, Governor-General von Scholten read the proclamation emancipating the slaves. Restored in 1976, the fort houses a museum (open Mon. to Fri. 8-5). The exterior leads to replicas of living quarters. **the Customs House:** Located S of the fort, this late 18th C structure was badly damaged by 1989's Hurricane Hugo and is now under repair. After completion, it will contain the Tourist Office (tel. 772-0357) as well as Customs and Immigration.

Victoria House: Located a block or two S of the Customs House, this private home, most of which was consumed in the flames of 1878 and rebuilt thereafter, is a local landmark. It's an excellent example of Victorian architecture and has elaborate gingerbread trim.

Bell House (Old Frederiksted Public Library): This stands two blocks farther at Queen Cross St. Once owned by a man named Bell who, appropriately enough, decorated the stairs with those charming chiming objects. The Dorsch Cultural Center here, an open theater (with an attached arts and crafts center), is used for local cultural events. A steel drum band practices here during the school year.

old Danish school: This is about 1 1/2 blocks away on Prince St. Designed in 1835 by Hingelberg, a famous Danish architect in his time, it now houses government agencies. **St. Patrick's Cathedral:** Across Market St., this buiding is a mid-19th C reconstruction of the original 18th C cathedral. **Mt. Victory School:** Located outside of town along Creque Dam Road, Mt. Victory is one of eight schools built around 1840 in accordance with von Scholten's edict proclaiming compulsory education for all children.

St. Croix Aquarium: If you just poked your nose into this small one-room aquarium, you might never expect it to have such alluring fascination. Its attraction rests on resident biologist Longin Kaczmarsky, who gives each visitor or group of visitors a personalized tour. All of the fish are from Crucian waters. Longin returns them to the sea after they have served a short penal sentence. But their involuntary penance is your gain because you are given a very thorough and intelligent rundown on the fish, crustaceans, and other creatures boarding here. Watch the yellow snapping shrimp clicking and clacking as it defends its territory, the spaghetti worm resting inside a broken beer bottle, the dancing sea horses checking out the sand dollar, and the queen angelfish, a typical night forager, hanging out under a rock. You'll be disgusted

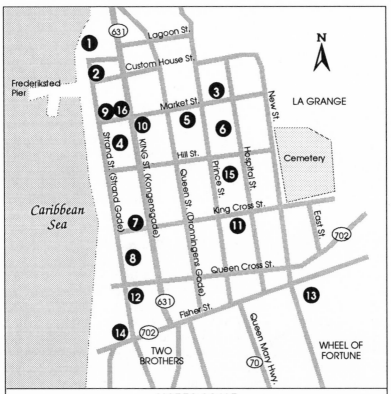

NOT TO SCALE

Frederiksted

1. Fort Frederik
2. Customs House/
   Visitors Bureau
3. St. Patrick's Cathedral
4. Victoria House
5. Market
6. Old Danish School
7. Frederiksted Hotel
8. Hospital
9. Aquarium
10. Tradewinds Bar
    and Deli

11. St. Paul's Episcopal
    Church
12. Old Library
    (Bell House)
13. Post Office/
    Old Danish Customs
    House
14. Cafe du Soleil
15. Prince St. Inn
16. Le St. Tropez

by the rarely sighted frog fish, the most loathesome (though strangely cute) creature here. The blue head wrasse keeps an eye on his harem. After his death, one of the wives–a protagenic hermaphrodite–will change sex and take over. Lorraine the lobster shares a tank with Susan the shark. There's also a poisonous pufferfish which blends right in with coral, the venemous scorpionfish, the butterfly fish, the filefish, and the doctor fish (named after the sharp spine at the base of its tail). Longin is magic with children; watch their eyes light up. Longin can also take you out snorkeling (limited to four). Plans are to double the aquarium's size (perhaps by the time you visit) and a touch pond for children is also projected. Admission is by $2 donation ($1 for children). It's open on Fri., Sat. and Sun. from 10-6. For more information call 772-1345 or write Box 5134, Sunny Isle, St. Croix 00823.

the Mt. Pelier Domino Club: A short ride from town up Rte. 76 from LEAP, this bar is one of the W side's foremost attractions. It features a team of beer swilling pigs: Miss Piggy and Tony and their two rapidly growing youngsters. Although they love their Old Milwaukees, the owners have switched them over to Sharp's, a nonalcoholic brew. The switch was made after Miss Piggy's kids came out of the womb and started shaking with DTs, and, in any event, they don't pass out as quickly so the bar can do more business. To try it out, pick up a brew and offer it to any pig that pokes his head out of the pen. The pig will chomp down on it, and beer will run down his or her face as the can is chomped and swilled. The monument nearby is to Buster, the original beer drinking pig, who died after he was fed poisoned sponges by a malevolent youth. Fried fish and johnny cakes are also on sale, as are $15 tee shirts.

others: Largely deserted, the **open air marketplace** dates from 1751. On Market St. between Prince and Hospital stands **St. Patrick's Church** which dates from 1844. The monument inside the gate to the right memorializes sailors killed when a tidal wave tossed the *USS Monongahela* into Strand St. in 1867. The cemetery of the **Lutheran Church** (on the hill between Hospital and New Sts.) exudes a simple charm amidst panoramic surroundings. There are wooden grave markers and tombs topped with artificial flowers. Because the Atlantic Fleet Weapons Facility is just to the N near Sprat Hall, submarines often can be seen at **Fredericksted dock**. With its plume worms, sponges, and large numbers of miniscule red, yellow, and orange sea horses, this dock is frequently called the most interesting "pier dive" in the Caribbean. So that cruise ships could dock, the pier was rebuilt during 1993, so the undersea life may no longer be up to par when you visit.

Frederiksted Accommodations

accomodations: The Prince St. Inn (tel. 772-9550, 800-524-2026), 402 Prince St. (corner of Hill St.) provides six efficiencies with kitchens starting at $42 s, $65 d. Located at 20 Strand St. near the cruise ship dock, the **Frederiksted Hotel** (tel. 773-9150, 800-524-2025) has a pool and restaurant. Room amenities include a/c, phone, cable TV, and radio. There's good snorkeling offshore. Rates start at $75 s and $85 d and rise to $105 for the best rooms during the winter. Set a half-mi. from Frederiksted, the 17-rm. **King Frederik on the Beach** (tel. 772-1205, fax 772-1757, 800-524-2018; Box 1908, Frederiksted 00841) faces directly onto the beach and has a TV/library room, pool, Jacuzzi, patio, restaurant and bar. Some rooms have kitchens. Rates begin at $50 s or d. It has a largely gay clientele. Set a bit farther S from Frederiksted on the beach, **Cottages by the Sea** (tel./fax 772-0495; 800-323-7252; Box 1697, Frederiksted 00841-1697) has 20 cottages with cable TV, fans and a/c, private patios, and kitchens. There are also three beachside patios with grill areas. Rates start at $65/unit. Triples are also available. Set 1.5 mi. outside of town along the road (Rte. 63) to the rain forest and the N coast, lies **Sprat Hall Plantation** (tel. 772-0305, 800-843-3585; cable: SPRAT HALL, Box 695, Frederiksted 00841), the most unusual accommodation on the island. The great house (circa 1650) is the only remaining French plantation house and is the oldest great house in the Caribbean. Judith Hurd Young, the proprietor, is a 12th generation Cruzan; her mother Joyce started the hotel in 1948 with her New England husband Jim when the ancestral home was for sale. Judith was born in the great house, had always dreamed of operating it as a child, and finally her dream came true. She and her husband have now semi-retired and operate the beachside restaurant. The old home has a number of rooms upstairs. (Downstairs is the TV-equipped living room and the attractive dining room, its tables immaculately set with hurricane lamps during the evening meals.) Mrs. Hurd was born on the horsehair mattress in Room No. 5. Since a writer mentioned it in a guide, this room (not especially superior to the others) has become so popular that the Hurds are considering changing all of the room numbers to 5! The less expensive Arawak Cottages (A/C, cable TV) are also on the grounds. Rates start at $70 s or $80 d. Farther N is the **Paradise Sunset Beach** which is covered under "heading W" in the section on "Accommodation Near Christiansted." On the road between Frederiksted and Christiansted at 82C Whim, **Villa Morales** (tel. 772-0556) is reasonably priced. A 15 min. walk from the main road between Frederiksted and Christiansted at 12 Constitution Hill, **Ackie's Guesthouse** (tel. 773-3759) charges around $50 d.

Frederiksted Dining and Food

food: Me Dundo's Place, Strand St. on the waterfront, serves ice cream with exotic local favors like soursop and guava. **Brow Beverages**, on King St. near market, serves unusual sodas with names like "Kola Champagne" and "American Ice Cream." **Belardo's Restaurant**, 39 King St., serves West Indian and Spanish cuisine. At 24 King St., **Porky's** offers Arubian/Cruzan seafood, pork chops, steak, and spare ribs. **Drake's Paradise Cafe**, 10 Strand St., has steak and seafood dishes. The **P & M Bar & Restaurant**, 21 King St., serves West Indian food, as does the inexpensive **Motown Bar & Restaurant** at 19 AB Strand St. At 16 A King St., inexpensive **Vel's Bar and Restaurant** has West Indian and Spanish lunches and dinners. In addition to a deli, bakery, and liquor store, inexpensive **Tradewinds** offers courtyard dining and an all-you-can-eat buffet on Thurs. evenings, which is accompanied by "Team Trivial Pursuit." It's at 10 King St. in Tradewinds Square. Set to the N of town, the inexpensive **West End Beach Club** (tel. 772-0902), 1A Prosperity, serves West Indian and American dishes for lunch and dinner. **upscale dining:** Featuring quiches, crepes, brochettes, and the like, the 19th C atmospheric, moderate to expensive **Le St. Tropez** (tel. 772-3000), 67 King St., is open for lunch and dinner and is one of the island's nicest restaurants. Entrees range from poisson du marché to scampi pescatori. Housed in a historical building, the eclectic and bohemian King Frederik's moderate **Sunburst Bistro** (tel. 772-5566, 772-1205—ext. 203) offers gourmet Italian and Mediterranean dishes ranging from hot potato and leek soup to tortellini in tomato basil sauce. At 17 Strand St., the Blue Moon's **Rick's American Cafe** (tel. 772-2222) offers dishes ranging from shrimp gaspacho to salmon Wellington. Jazz is featured on Fri. and Sat. nights. On the waterfront, **The Frederiksted** (tel. 772-0500) has a poolside breakfast daily and dinner Thurs. to Sun. **Café du Soleil**

(tel. 772-5400), Prince Passage at 625 Strand St., offers Continental cuisine at lunch, dinner, and Sunday brunch as well as great sunsets. Famous for its Sunday brunch, the **Paradise Sunset Beach** serves fish or chicken dinner specials. The **Brandy Snifter**, 326 King St., has continental cuisine, steak, and seafood (with $9.50 special vegetarian entrees), as does the Royal Dane Hotel's **Le Crocodile**, 13 Strand St., and the **Swashbuckler**, 37 Strand St. Popular **La Grange Beach and Tennis Club** (tel. 772-0100), at 72 La Grange near the pier, serves lunch (Tues. to Sat), "moonlight dinner" (Thurs. and Sat.), and Sunday brunch. Among the nightly specials are "peel & all you can eat shrimp." La Grange has "fine dinng and spectacular sunsets" as well as daily specials. The island's most uniquely memorable dining experience can be found at **Sprat Hall** (772-0305 for reservations) to the N. Mrs Hurd sets a wonderful table (see "accommodations" for description). You might hear a local–who dines here frequently–complimenting her: "It's always so easy to sit at your table." Expect to pay about $20 pp all inclusive for dinner. Usually, you'll have your choice of three entrees and two desserts. Lunch is served at their **Sprat Hall Beach Restaurant** (11:30-2:30) which is wheelchair accessible. Try the handmade ice cream which often comes with mango.

market shopping: As is the case with its Christiansted cousin, the **outdoor market** (dating from 1751), located on the appropriately named Market St. at Queen, doesn't have a great deal to offer. Several other small stores are in town. **The Midas Touch**, inside Geaden's Court, sells wholewheat bread. A **fish market**, located at the junction of Strand St. and Rte. 702, is most active on Wed. and Sat. mornings around 9.

entertainment: Pretty dead at night. **The Sundowner** has live music on Sundays. Attracting a crowd in their 20s and 30s, the **West End Beach Club** (tel. 772-0002) at Rainbow Beach to the N of town, has a West Indian BBQ on the beach with reggae, a beer drinking contest, and volleyball on Sun. afternoons. Across from the Frederiksted Ball Park, the **Sand Bar** is closer to town and provides similar entertainment. On Sun. at 6, the **Domino Club** at 48 Montpelier (see "sights" above) offers a one-man calypso band.

services and information: A Division of Tourism office (tel. 772-0357) is located inside the Port Authority Building in the harbor; it is scheduled to move to the Old Customs House upon completion of renovation. **Take-A-Hike** (tel. 778-6997 for reservations) offers daily walking tours of town from 10 AM. **Paul and Jill's Equestrian Stables** (see "horseback riding") offers rides. **The Caribbean Dance School** (tel. 778-8824), 11 Strand St, offers classes in gymnastics, self defense, yoga, jazz, and ballet.

events: New Year's Day features a children's parade. A special ceremony takes place in town on July 3, **Danish West Indies Emancipation Day**.

shopping: The most interesting stop in town is actually outside it and to the N on Rte. 76. **LEAP Woodworking** produces an assortment of cutting boards, clocks, and other items. All are reasonably priced considering that they're crafted from the island's native wood. Mahogany, thibet, and saman are used. On the way you'll pass three gigantic statues carved from wood (by David Boyd and Jeffrey Barber), reminiscent of the guardians found in in front of Japanese temples. Inside the enormous workshop pavilion, "Cheech" Willie Thomas, wearing a pair of blue noise retarding phones around his ears and a dust mask, will show you around. Also out of town, one mi. N, is **Estate Mt. Washington Plantation** (tel. 772-1026), which offers mahogany reproductions, fabrics, and antiques. It's open Sat. from 10-4 and weekdays by appointment. Back in town, things are still recovering to pre-Hugo levels. Improving the pier should help matters, and things should have picked up by the time of your arrival. **Me Dundo's Place** on Strand St. sells local crafts, as does **Cariso Arts & Crafts** nearby. **Lucan Gift Shop**, 1 Strand St., sells fine china, jewelry, crystal, and figurines. **Shops at The Mall**, on King St. (between Custom and Market) sell liquor, tee shirts, jewelery, shoes, and athletic ware. **Olde Towne**, at Strand and Market, is a restored courtyard of old Danish buildings with shops including **Colombian Emeralds International**. **Royal Frederick Gift Shop**, Strand and Custom Sts., features a pan-Caribbean selection of gift items and handicrafts. **I Am Inn Designs**, inside Geaden's Court which spans King Cross St. and Strand St. next to the Frederiksted Hotel, sells local handmade ethnic ware. **Sylvia's Dress Shop**, on Custom St. between Queen and King Sts., sells dresses made to order and available in just a few hours. In Tradewind Square at 302 King St., **La Femme Amor** offers a wide selection of French perfumes as well as jewelry, leather bags, watches, and other items. **Gone Tropical**, Church St., has nice decorator items.

excursions: One of the best experiences around is to take a snorkeling trip with **Longin Kaczmarsky** (tel. 772-1345; Box 5134, Sunny Isle, St. Croix 00823), a very informative marine biologist. Groups are limited to four. Junie Bomba's **Sunset/Cocktail Cruises** (tel. 772-2482) are sunset sails limited to six guests.

Vicinity of Frederiksted

The Rain Forest: Situated N of Frederiksted, the island's NW corner–lushly covered with tropical vegetation–is called a rainforest but is actually a tropical dry secondary forest. It receives only 40 in. of rain while a true rainforest receives upwards of 80. The best road for exploring is Mahogany Rd. (Rtes. 76, 763, 765), named after its stands of majestic mahogany trees over two centuries old. Along this road you can also find gumbo limbo, samaan (rain tree), and silk cotton trees. While strap and swamp ferns grow along gullies and guts, a variety of fruit trees–ranging from mammee apple to mango and breadfruit–can be seen near the remains of former estates such as Estate Prosperity. More remote areas (four-wheel-drive recommended) are accessed by the narrow, unpaved, and winding Scenic Rd. (Rte. 78), Western Scenic Rd. (63/78), and the Creque Dam Rd. (Rtes. 58/78). A number of unmarked footpaths lead off the roads..

St. Croix Itinerary

If you have 3 days:
Spend one day in and around Christiansted (shopping and sights), one day on Buck Island, and one day touring the island (beaches and sights).

If you have 5 days:
Spend one day in and around Christiansted (shopping and sights), one day on Buck Island, one day on the east of the island, and two days around the island (beaches and sights).

If you have one week:
Spend one day in and around Christiansted (shopping and sights), one day on Buck Island, one day on the east of the island, and four days around the island (beaches and sights). Or take a day excursion to St. Thomas or Virgin Gorda.

The Scenic Rd. heads E via pink-and-white cedar forested hills which have steep, sometimes hard-to-follow paths leading up its sides. It continues E to Eagle Ridge, from where you can ascend flat-topped Mt. Eagle (1,165 ft., 334 m) and the antennae-and-radio-dish-topped Blue Mtn. (1,096 ft., 334 m), the highest points on St. Croix. A more direct approach to this area is from the E end of Scenic Rd. between Canaan Rd. (Rte. 73) and River Rd. (Rte. 69).

Beginning at Hams Bay on the NW, the Western Scenic Rd. is described in "Along the Northwest Coast," above. From the W coast, Creque Dam Rd. intersects the Sprat Hall Estate before reaching the lush Creque Dam and Forest, where you can find mahogany, turpentine, white cedar, and silk cotton trees.

From St. Croix

for St. Thomas: St. Croix based Sunaire (tel. 778-9300; Box 1527, Kingshill 00851-1527) is the major carrier flying to St. Thomas. Check in a half-hour before your flight or you risk losing it. If you have no checked baggage, go directly to the gate; the entrance is just behind and to the R of the check in counter. When your flight is called, you gather outside the gate door in the open and then walk together to board the 20-seat plane. The best places for photos are in the back, where your view is unobstructed by the wings. Island Attractions (tel. 773-7977) arranges trips to St. Thomas. **for St. John:** You must fly to St. Thomas or one of the British Virgins and take a ferry. **for Tortola:** Sunaire flies via St. Thomas. **for Virgin Gorda:** Sunaire flies via St. Thomas. BIA (tel. 778-9177) offers charter flights to Virgin Gorda, $125 RT with four-person minimum. Lunch at Fischer's Cove, an island tour (including a visit to the Baths), and taxi fares are all included. **for Vieques:** Sunaire and Vieques Air Link fly. **for Fajardo:** Sunaire flies via St. Thomas. **for San Juan:** Sunaire flies via St. Thomas. **for Anguilla:** American Airlines flies direct.

for the Southern Caribbean: LIAT flies to Antigua, Barbados, Dominica, and Point a Pitre (Guadeloupe). LIAT and Coastal Air Transport fly to Nevis. LIAT flies to St. Kitts and St. Maarten. LIAT and BWIA fly to St. Lucia.

The British Virgin Islands

Quiet and peaceful, the British Virgin Islands offer solace to the traveler weary of the commercialism and despoiled atmosphere of the Caribbean's larger islands. Incredible scenery lies both above and below the water. These islands are the premier yachting destination in the Caribbean, and their beautiful beaches and hiking trails are attractive to landlubbers as well. **note:** Many aspects of the USVI Introduction (flora and fauna, etc.) also apply here. If you are only visiting the BVI, be sure to read this section as well.

The Land

Comprising the eastern portion of the Virgin Islands archipelago, these islands, like their neighboring American cousins, are primarily volcanic in origin. (A notable exception is Anegada, which is a limestone and coral atoll.) Grouped for the most part around the Sir Francis Drake Channel, and lying 60 mi. E of Puerto Rico, these 50 or so islands, cays, and rocks date from eruptions that took place 25 million years ago. Altogether, the islands comprise 59 sq miles of land area, with Tortola, the largest and most rugged, taking up 21 of these. Most are uninhabited; the largest inhabited islands are Tortola and Virgin Gorda. Rivers are nonexistent and, owing to the aridity of the climate, water is in short supply. The only notable mineral deposit is the salt on Salt Island.

climate: Really fine! Set within the tradewind belt, temperature on these islands rarely drops below 70 degrees F at night; daytime temperatures range between 80-90 degrees F throughout the year. Rain, and water in general, is scarce.

History

Columbus sailed by the British Virgin Islands on his second voyage in 1493. In the early 1500s the Spaniards settled for a while on Virgin Gorda to mine copper and, stopping in on Tortola, gave it its name (meaning "turtle dove"). At first, few migrants were attracted by Tortola's steep hills. Unsettled and unclaimed, it remained the province of buccaneers who utilized its hidden caves as hideouts. The first actual settlement on Tortola was by pirates at Soper's Hole, West End. The Dutch began the first permanent settlement on Tortola in 1648. A mixed band of pirates drove out the Dutch in 1666 and, in turn, invited the English to come in. Soon after, however, the French took the island, but the British recaptured it in 1672. A migration of Anguillans followed.

With the exception of the islands already taken by Denmark, the British gradually began to occupy all of the unclaimed islands remaining in the Virgin Islands group. Before the end of the 17th C, the planter class had achieved a degree of prosperity. (Planters here, however, never made the fortunes their counterparts did on the flatter, wetter islands such as St. Croix and Barbados). Crisis followed crisis in the 18th C as the European nations brought their chess game to the Caribbean.

By 1720, the population was 1,122 whites and over 1,500 blacks. The Virgins (including Anguilla) were given their own lieutenant governor under the British-regulated Leeward Islands government. Along with Anguilla, St. Kitts and Nevis, the Virgins were incorporated into the separate Leeward Islands Colony in 1816. More than half the white residents fled in 1831 after discovery of a slave plot which, had it succeeded, would have resulted in the murder of them all. In 1853 a revolt began in Road Town and spread all over Tortola and nearby islands. Tortola was reclaimed by the bush and remained largely wild for decades.

In 1872, the islands were placed by Britain under the Leeward Islands Administration and admitted as a crown colony. Severe hurricanes in 1916 and 1924 caused extensive damage. The Legislative Council was abolished in 1902, and the governor-in-council became the sole legislative authority. A presidential legislature for the islands was established in 1950 with elected and appointed members. The 1967 constitution granted the islands a ministerial government, and a few years later, after the de-federation of the Leewards Island Colony, the Virgins were set up as a separate colony. On Dec. 31, 1959, the Office of the Governor of the Leewards was abolished; the administrator on Tortola became the Queen's Representative. The British Virgin Islands had obtained its present territorial status.

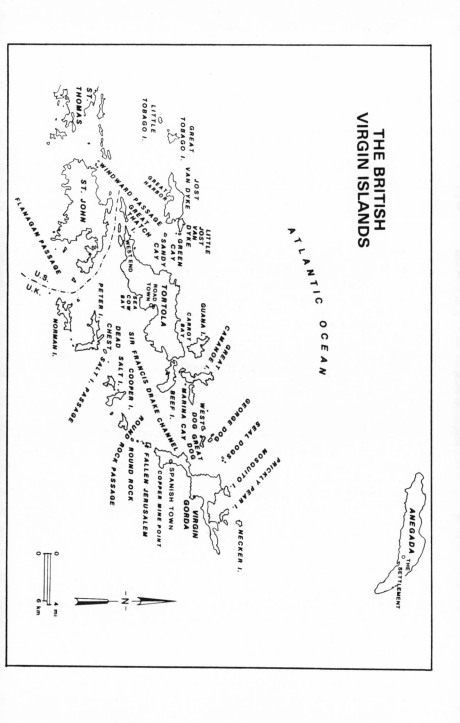

THE BRITISH
VIRGIN ISLANDS

ATLANTIC OCEAN

ST. THOMAS

LITTLE TOBAGO I.
GREAT TOBAGO I.

JOST VAN DYKE

GREAT HARBOR

LITTLE JOST VAN DYKE

WINDWARD PASSAGE
GREAT THATCH I.

GREEN CAY

SANDY CAY

WEST END

ST. JOHN

FLANAGAN PASSAGE

U.S.
U.K.

ROAD TOWN

TORTOLA

SEA COW BAY

CARROT BAY

GUANA I.

CAMANOE

GREAT CAMANOE

WEST DOG
GREAT DOG
MARINA CAY

GEORGE DOG

SEAL DOGS

NECKER I.

PRICKLY PEAR I.

MOSQUITO I.

PETER I.

DEAD CHEST I.

SIR FRANCIS DRAKE CHANNEL

BEEF I.

SALT I.

SALT I. PASSAGE

NORMAN I.

COOPER I.

ROUND ROCK

ROUND ROCK PASSAGE

FALLEN JERUSALEM

COPPER MINE POINT

SPANISH TOWN

VIRGIN GORDA

ANEGADA

THE SETTLEMENT

N

0   4 mi
0   6 km

Important Dates in BVI History

1493: Columbus sails by the British Virgins. Some of present-day Virgins included in grant to Earl of Carlyle.

1648: Dutch buccaneers settle Tortola.

1668: English buccaneers expel Dutch.

1680: Planters from Anguilla begin to settle Tortola and Virgin Gorda; deputy governor and council selected.

1685: English settlements on Tortola and Virgin Gorda raided by Spaniards.

1718: Spanish attack Tortola and attempt settlement.

1774: British House of Assembly commences meeting in Road Town, Tortola.

1802: Road Harbour (present-day Road Town) becomes a free port.

1803: Last public slave auction held on Tortola.

1808: Slave trade abolished by Britain.

1816: Along with Anguilla, St. Kitts, and Nevis, the Virgins are incorporated into the separate Leeward Islands Colony.

1834: Slavery abolished on British islands.

1853: Revolt begins in Road Town and spreads all over Tortola and nearby islands; cholera outbreak reduces population by approximately 14%.

1872: Islands placed under Leewards Island Administration and admitted as a separate colony.

1905: Government Savings Bank established.

1922: First hospital opened.

1943: First secondary school opened.

1949: Demonstrations held throughout the islands demand representative government and closer association with the U.S. Virgin Islands.

1956: Leeward Islands Federation dissolved; commissioner of B.V.I. becomes administrator.

1959: First issue of first newspaper (*Tortola Times*) published.

1966: Queen Elizabeth II and Duke of Edinburgh visit.

1967: New constitution granted.

Government

One of the most stable in the Caribbean, the B.V.I. are a self-governing Dependent Territory (read: colony) with a governor appointed by the British queen. The current governor is J.M.A. Herdman. The island's chief minister is elected by the locals. Residents seem unconcerned with independence and at present content with the status quo. These islands were once seen as being the least important place in the British Empire. When asked where the British Virgin Islands were, Sir Winston Churchill is said to have replied that he had no idea, but he should think that they were as far as possible from the Isle of Man. As the British Empire continues to contract, the symbolic importance of these islands has grown. Queen Elizabeth II has seen fit to arrive here by royal yacht twice during a ten-year period.

Economy

Until very recently the British Virgin Islands have known nothing but poverty. Tourism–responsible for more than half of the $20 million GNP–has brought a measure of prosperity. The tourism boom began in the mid-60s, with the construction of the Rockresort at Little Dix Bay on Virgin Gorda, and today the islands are the yachting capital of the Caribbean, with 13 yacht marinas, 300 bareboats and around 100 charters. More than 200,000 visitors arrive annually, and some 67% of these stay on these "floating hotels." The islands have a standard of living second in the Caribbean only to the US Virgin Islands. And they have gained the benefits of financial shoulder-rubbing with their wealthier neighbor, without contracting its serious problems. Since the 1940s, thousands have migrated to the USVI, relieving population pressures and transferring savings back home. After the collapse of the plantation system in the 19th C, the planters left and either sold the land cheaply or gave it to their former slaves. As a consequence–in contrast to other Caribbean islands where a small elite control the land–the common people of the BVI own their own turf. And because there are few land deeds or titles as such, locals are not able to sell and prefer to rent rather than deed land. Most goods are imported. There is no industry to speak of, and agriculture is largely confined to garden plots. One big business these days is the result of the International Business Company legislation passed in 1984 which gives locally-registered companies tax incentives. Some 16,000 businesses have signed up.

Festivals and Events

Regattas, regattas, and regattas. For current information on major yachting, angling, and rugby events in the BVI, write to the **BVI Yacht Club** (tel. 494-3286), PO Box 200, Road Town, Tortola, BVI. Also, be sure to obtain an annual calendar of events from the Tourist Board. The **West Indies Windsurfing Games** are held in

Jan. The BVI Yacht Club also holds the **Polar Bear Sailing Race** this month. On Valentine's Day, the **Sweetheart's of the Caribbean Schooner Race** (West End Yacht Club, tel. 495-4353/4559) and the **Classic Yacht Regatta** (the following day) are held at the West End. The BVI Yacht Club also holds the **Hearts and Flowers Sailing Race** on Feb. 14th. The BVI Botanic Society holds an annual **Horicultural Society Show** each March. Also in March, the **Six Four Mile Legs Race** zig zags down the Sir Francis Drake Channel. The BVI Yacht Club holds the **"Tides" of March Sailing Race**, and at the end of March, the Moorings (tel. 800-535-7289) holds the **One-Design Charter Race Week**. Now into its second decade, the **BVI Spring Regatta**, third leg of CORT (Caribbean Ocean Racing Triangle involving Puerto Rico and St. Thomas), usually takes place in mid-April. It is preceded by Puerto Rico's Copa Velasco Regatta and followed by St. Thomas's Rolex Cup Regatta, and many racers compete in all three. Festivities take place at the Regatta Village which is generally on Nanny Cay. An **Easter Monday Fishing Tournament** is also in April. Sponsored by the Cedar School, a big **Mother's Day Music Festival** is held at Thee Wedding (tel. 495-4022) every Mother's Day in Cane Garden Bay. In addition to a BBQ, there are raffle prizes, and children's games are held on the beach. Reggae, scratch, and guitar ballads are featured. The BVI Yacht Club sponsors a **May Pole Sailing Race** in mid-May as well as a **Ladies' Fishing Tournament**. In June, the **Peter Stuyvesant Travel Blue Marlin Surf Tour** attracts both amateur and professional windsurfers. One course leads racers from North Sound on Virgin Gorda past the Dogs, Ginger, Scrub, and Beef islands, to a finish at Marina Cay. Also in June, The BVI Yacht Club sponsors the **Pursuit Sailing Race**. Generally held from late July through early Aug., the **Hook-In-Hold-On Windsurfing Challenge**, with 12 point-to-point windsurfing and sailboat races, is sponsored by The Moorings (tel. 800-535-7289). A **Bacardi Rum Beach Party** is held at Cane Garden Bay (tel. 495-4639) in conjunction with Territory Day on July 1. On July 4th, fireworks explode above Long Bay Beach Resort. In mid-month, the **Match Racing Championships** are sponsored by the BVI Yacht Club. Held from late in the month before, the **BVI August Festival** features traditional steel band, calypso, soca, and fungi music. It commemorates the emancipation of the islanders from slavery on Aug. 1, 1834. August Monday, August Tuesday, and August Wednesday are official holidays, but the entire festivities consume two weeks. Boldly decorated booths are erected at the Festival Village in Road

Town, and traditional food and drink as well as carnival rides are available. Nightly entertainment takes place on a central stage. On August Monday, a grand parade with marching bands and floats moves down the waterfront road. The Miss BVI "Queen Contest" is also held. The BVI Yacht Club sponsors the **BVI Gamefish Tournament** in August as well as the **Anegada Sailing Race**. **Foxy's Wooden Boat Regatta** (tel. 495-9258) takes place in Sept. Airline companies compete in the **Interline Regatta**, a nine-day sailing event held annually in October; it's sponsored by The Moorings (tel. 800-535-7289). The same month finds the **Captain's Fishing Tournament** and the **Virgin's Cup/***William Thorton***,** sponsored by the BVI Yacht Club. The **Charter Yacht Show** (tel. 494-6017) is held in November as is the **Round Tortola Sailing Race**, sponsored by the BVI Yacht Club. The Bitter End Yacht Club (tel. 800-872-2392) sponsors the **Fast Track Sailing Festival** and the **Pro-Am Regatta**. December finds the **Gustave Wilmerding Race** (sponsored by the West End Yacht Club (tel. 495-4353/4559) and the **Commodore's Sailing Race** sponsored by the BVI Yacht Club. **Women's Sailing Week** is sponsored by the Bitter End Yacht Club.

Public Holidays

1 Jan.:	New Year's Day
March:	Commonwealth Day (movable)
April:	Good Friday (movable)
	Easter Monday (movable)
May-June:	Whit Monday
June:	Sovereign's Birthday (movable)
1 July:	Territory Day (movable)
Aug.:	Festival Monday, Tues., Wed.
21 Oct.:	St. Ursula's Day (movable)
14 Nov.:	Birthday of Heir to the Throne
26 Dec.:	Boxing Day

Practicalities

getting there: The BVIs are a bit difficult of access, which is what gives them a good portion of their charm. The easiest–but most expensive–way is to fly from San Juan or St. Thomas to Tortola or Virgin Gorda. (If you're flying from the US or Canada, you'll have no choice but to change planes in one of these two places). Most flights arrive at Beef Island International Airport, linked to Tortola by a narrow bridge. This airport's runway is being lengthened, and direct jet flights may be arriving by the time you read this. Another alternative is to fly to Virgin Gorda, or take ferries from St. Thomas and St. John to Jost Van Dyke, Virgin Gorda, and Tortola. Or you can fly to Tortola and then take a ferry to Virgin Gorda. No discount air fares from Puerto Rico or the VI are generally available, but you may get a discounted ticket by making an advance purchase or buying a RT ticket. From Puerto Rico, Sunaire Express, American Eagle, and LIAT all fly. From St. Thomas, Sunaire and Air Anguilla also fly. Sunaire flies to Tortola and Virgin Gorda via St. Thomas. As carriers have changed frequently in the past, be sure to check with your travel agent. **from Great Britain:** British Airways flies to Antigua and Air Anguilla flies from there to Beef Island. Another possibiliity is to fly to the US and enter via the USVI.

by sea: From St. Thomas ferries run to Tortola, Virgin Gorda, and Jost Van Dyke. Boats from St. John leave for West End, Tortola, and occasional daytrips for Virgin Gorda are available. Round trips are discounted but limit your travel options as you must return with the same line. Tall Ship Adventures (described under "St. Thomas") sails from St. Thomas to islands such as Jost Van Dyke and Virgin Gorda. A new cruise ship pier was built in 1993 and larger ships are now calling at Tortola.

getting around: There is no local transport other than expensive shared taxi service available on Tortola and Virgin Gorda; rates are fixed by the local government. Settle the price before you get in. A beautiful but strenuous way to see the islands is on foot. Slopes are incredibly steep, but views are magnificent. Other alternatives include renting a car or using your thumb. Hitching is easy: both locals and visitors are usually happy to get riders, but don't try it after dark. **car rentals:** Rates are around $30-60 per day plus gas ($1.60/gal.) with unlimited mileage; off-season rates are lower. It doesn't take long to drive around any of these islands so, if you want to economize, it might be better to rent a car for just a day and see the sights. A BVI license ($10 for temporary permit) is needed; it may be obtained, upon presentation of a valid foreign driver's license, from either the police headquarters or the rental companies. **note:** most of the rental companies are listed under the appropriate part of the travel sections. Other rentals are also noted. **driving:** The maximum speed limit is 30 mph which decreases to

10-15 in residential areas. Driving is on the L hand side and roads are narrow and winding.

Sailing and Yacht Charters

If you're a typical visitor, this will be one reason you're coming here. Be prepared for a few discomforts: hand-held showers situated right next to the toilets are standard fare. Plan your itinerary at least six months in advance if you're interested in peak times like February, March, Easter, Thanksgiving, and Christmas. The poorest conditions for sailing run from the end of August through the middle of October. Bring dramamine for the unlikely possibility that you will get seasick. The most useful book for yachting is *Yachtsman's Guide to the Virgin Islands and Puerto Rico*, published by Tropic Island Publishers (PO Box 611141, North Miami, FL 33161), which gives you in-depth sailing information. You can expect to spend $1,000-$2,000 pp for an eight day/seven night cruise with all meals, alcohol, and use of sports equipment included.

qualifications: Because most boats are heavy displacement vessels with a lot of momentum, you should have adequate experience skippering this type of boat as well as a good basic understanding of inboard engines. Although requirements vary in their specifics, aspiring captains of smaller boats should have experience in regularly skippering at least a 25-ft. sail boat. Applicants customarily fill out an application which includes a resume of sailing experience. Generally, you must agree that the charter company retains the right to place an instructor/guide on your boat at your expense should it prove necessary after a trial run. Another alternative is to pre-book a skipper for all or part of your holiday. **chartering:** There are a large number of charter operations. Most offer day sails as well, and skippers are generally available for bareboats. Based in Road Town, **Virgin Island Sailing Ltd.** (tel. 494-3658, 800-233-7936; Box 11156, St. Thomas 00801) offers sailing courses, scuba/sail packages and crewed charters. At Road Reef Marina, **Tortola Marine Mgt. Ltd.** (tel. 494-2751; Box 3042, Road Town) rents 30- to 51-ft. sailboats, a 37-ft. trawler, and 39-ft. catamarans. At Maya Cove, **Tropic Island Yacht Mgt.** (tel. 494-2450, 800-356-8938; Box 532, Maya Cove) rents 30- to 51-ft. bareboats, 50- to 212-ft. crewed sailboats, and catamarans. Accommodating 6-10, **Yacht Promenade** (tel. 494-3853, 494-5577; Box 3100, Road Town) rents a 65-ft. crewed trimaran which offers diving, skiing, and watersports. In the Inner Harbour Marina, **BVI Bareboats** (tel. 494-4289, 800-648-7240; Box 3018, Road Town) rents 32-ft. to 50-ft. bareboats with skippers available. Set at the Mariner Inn at Wickham Cay II on the E side of Road Town, **the Moorings** (tel. 494-2331, Box 139, Tortola) offers 39- to 51-ft. sloops as well as a variety of sloops and ketches. In the US, contact 1305 US 19 South #402, Clearwater, FL 33546, tel. 813-530-5651. From Fort Burt Marina, **Conch Charters, Ltd.** (tel. 494-4868, fax 494-5793; Box 920, Road Town) offers a number of 30- to 51-ft. fully equipped bareboat sailing yachts. At Treasure Isle Jetty, the *New Hope* (tel. 494-4092; Box 68, Road Town), a 42-ft ketch, has mini cruises and gives sailing instruction. Based in the Treasure Isle and with branches in Florida, Cape Cod, and St. Lucia, the **Offshore Sailing School** offers introductory sailing courses. Call 800-221-4326, 813-454-1700, or write 16731-110 McGregor, Ft. Meyers, FL 33908. Operating out of Nanny Cay, the *Foxy Lady* (tel. 494-3540, Box 710, Road Town), a 24-ft. Seabird, and the *Patsy Lady* a 43-ft. motorcruiser, are available for daily or weekly charter. **Johnny's Maritime Services** (tel. 494-3661/2330; Nanny Cay) here rents 37-ft. and 43-ft. trawlers; both bareboats and crewed charters are available. Also at Nanny Cay, **North South Yacht Vacations** (tel. 494-0096, 800-387-4964; Box 281, Road Town) offers 34-ft. and 45-ft. sail and power boats. Both crewed and bareboat charters are available, and they operate a sailing school. Also here, the **Offshore Sail and Motor** (tel. 494-4726, 800-582-0175; Box 281, Road Town) has a number or boats and offers crewed and bare boat charters. They will teach you to sail. Another Nanny Cay resident, **Paradise Yacht Charters** (tel. 494-0333, fax 494-0334; Box 11156, St. Thomas 00801) operates Thomas Sailing, a sailing school, and has 40- and 50-ft. yachts with bareboat or crewed charters. At Fat Hogs Bay, **Seabreeze Yacht Charters** (tel. 495-1560, fax 495-1561) rents both sail boats (30 to 54 ft. with five to ten berths in two to six cabins) and motor boats (35-42 ft. with three to five cabins). Contact them at Box 528, East End, Tortola. **Sunsail** (tel. 495-4740, fax 495-4301; Box 609, West End) rents 32-ft. to 51-ft. Brenterus; day sails, bareboats, and a skipper are available. **note:** Boats offering day sails are listed under Tortola or Virgin Gorda in the travel section. Caribbean Sailing Yachts (CSY) has gone bankrupt.

Charter Yacht Society charters: For more information on the following yachts, contact the Charter Yacht Society (tel. 494-6017) at Box 3069, Road Town, Tortola or the address/phone given below.

Employing a crew of six, the *Wanderlust* is a 65-ft. trimaran ketch which can accommodate up to 16. The 46-ft. sloop *Gypsy Wind* specializes in luxury cruises for two, notably honeymooners. A 51-ft. luxury ketch, *Camelot* (tel. 494-3623; Box 3018, Road Town) provides two double staterooms, crew quarters, and two heads. Snorkeling, scuba, sunfish, and windsurfing are available. Bread is baked on board.

Renting a 105-ft. sailing catamaran fully staffed and equipped for diving, the **Trimarine Boat Co., Ltd.** (tel. 494-2490, fax 494-5774; Box 362, Road Town) operates two trimarans. Claimed to be the world's largest trimaran, the 105-ft. *Cuan Law* can accommodate up to 20 in staterooms with private baths. There's also a large salon as well as a lecture and video theater. Its sister, the *Lammer Law*, is smaller yet similar; it is currently in the Galapagos. A 52-ft. trimaran operating out of either Road Town, West End, or Trellis Bay, the *Encore* (tel. 800-648-3393; Box 3069, Road Town) has four guest cabins, windsurfing boards, scuba, and snorkel gear. Accommodating up to two couples and featuring all-teak and leather interiors, the *Spice* is a 51-ft. sloop. With a comfortable double cabin with private bath and two bunks, the *Vanguard*, a 42-ft. ketch, can hold either a couple or a family of four. One of the BVI's plushest trimaran schooners, the 65-ft. *Promenade* can hold up to five couples. Water sports offered include scuba. A 71-ft. custom built oak and teak 60-ft. sailing ketch, the *Tamoure* has a spacious deck as well as a raised salon; it can accommodate six. Continental cuisine is featured. With four staterooms and private baths, the *Endless Summer II* (tel. 494-3656; Box 823, Road Town) is another luxurious yacht. A 72-ft custom ketch, it offers four a/c cabins TV/VCR, CD-equipped stereo, and watersports. A 53-ft. sloop, the *Footloose* has two a/c queen-sized cabins, icemaker, washer/dryer, cellular phone, and a windsurfer. Running out of the West End, the *Golden Skye* (tel. 496-0236; Box 3069, Road Town) is a 63-ft. custom aluminum ketch with three cabins (sleeps six) and two large baths; it offers scuba, waterskiing, snorkeling, and windsurfing. With one stateroom, the yacht *Jaguar*, a John Alden-designed Cheoy Lee Offshore 50-ft. ketch, offers waterskiing, snorkeling, and windsurfing. A Mason 63-ft. ketch specially designed for tropical chartering, the *Zinja* carries two couples. Featuring an on-board scuba compressor, the *Windwalker* offers guitar sing alongs at night. A 54-ft. ketch, it accommodates four. With four double cabins, the 60-ft. *Whakatane* is a high tech schooner. Providing accommodations for up to six in three staterooms, the *Footloose of Canada*, a 60-ft. ketch, has windsurfing, fishing, and snorkeling. A 52-ft. Irwin ketch designed for comfortable sailing, the *Obsession* offers spacious and private accommodation in three double staterooms with bathtub/showers. A TV/VCR and cassette stereo grace the main salon, and water skiing and snorkeling are featured. Carrying six guests in two king size staterooms and one double cabin, the 43-ft. catamaran *Spendidum* even has a freezer and microwave. With four staterooms, the 65-ft. schooner *Windchild* offers waterskiing, use of a sunfish, and snorkeling. A customized 51-ft. Beneteau sloop designed with tropical chartering in mind, *Effects* offers three double staterooms and a salon with library and music center. It accommodates six in three a/c staterooms with private baths. Windsurfing is featured, as is an evening showing of the day's videotaped goings on. Offering two private cabins, the *Shalimar*, a 50-ft. motor yacht, has diving (all levels catered to), windsurfing, waterskiing, and island hiking. A 71-ft. Trumpy motor yacht holding up to eight, the *Capricorn Lady* (tel. 494-3174; Box 638 Road Town) comes equipped with a 20-ft. speedboat, water skis, windsurfer, VCR, phone and a/c.

BVI Popular Anchorages

Soper's Hole: At the W end of Tortola. Deep and sheltered, it has complete facilites.

Road Town: There are a number of marinas here. You can also anchor at Brandywine Bay and Maya Cove just past Road Harbour.

Deadman's Bay: On the E tip of Peter Island and a short sail from Road Town. Anchor in the extreme SE corner and watch for swells (especially in the winter). Marina available.

Beef Island: Anchorages at Trellis Bay and out at Marina Cay. Marinas available.

Salt Island: Moorings at Lee Bay (near the wreck of the Rhone) and at Salt Pond Bay. Both are rough and recommended for day use only.

Cooper Island: Moorings at Lee Bay and Salt Pond Bay. Restaurant and other facilities available.

Virgin Gorda: Moorings at The Baths, North Sound, and other locations. Marinas available at North Sound and in The Valley.

The Dogs: On good days the best anchorages are on the bay to the W of Kitchen Point (George Dog) and off the S side of Great Dog.

Jost Van Dyke: Anchorages at Little Harbour, Great Harbour, and White Bay. While Little and Great are easy to enter, you must enter White Bay through a channel in the reef's center. It is subject to winter swells.

Sandy Cay: Moorings offshore of this uninhabited island set to the E of Jost Van Dyke. Watch for swells.

Norman Island: Moorings near the entrance to The Caves and at The Bight.

Pelican Island and The Indians: Near The Bight off of Norman Island. Moorings offshore.

---

moorings: One important aspect of nautical travel around the BVI that visitors should be aware of is the system of moorings. Begun by the Virgin Islands Dive Operators Association, with funding from the Canadian government and with the full support of appropriate BVI governmental agencies, the number of moorings has grown to over 120 with a total of 250 permanent moorings projected. Each mooring consists of a stainless steel pin which is cemented into the bed rock; its eyehook is attached to a polypropylene rope which is about 10 ft. longer than the water's depth. A half-pound lead weight is attacted to the top of the cord; this keeps the extra cord from floating to the surface during slack periods at low tide. A plastic-filled mooring buoy is attached to this. It has a 15 ft. polypropylene rope with an eye splice at its end. This ingenious rig was invented by Dr. John Halas of Florida's Key Largo National Marine Sanctuary. Buoys are color coded as follows: red buoys denote non-diving day use; yellow are restricted to commercial dive boats; and white are for dive use only on a first come, first served basis. There is a 90 min. limit on the white buoys. No vessels over 55 ft. or 35 tons may use the buoys. You must attach to the pennant eye and make sure that there is no chafing with your boat. If the configuration provided proves incompatible, it is your responsibility to attach an extension line to the pennant eye. All buoys are used at your risk, and neither the government nor the National Parks Trust bears any responsibility for losses or injuries. All users of moorings must have legally met BVI Customs and Immigrations requirements and hold a valid National Parks Mooring Permit. If you are impressed by the buoy system and wish to support it, you may contribute to the Friends of the National Park Trust (see "organizations").

Other Practicalities

accommodations: Although these islands have intentionally geared themselves towards tourism for the wealthy and the super rich, some good values include campsites on Tortola, Anegada, and Jost Van Dyke. The only reasonably priced hotel accommodations are on Tortola (see "accommodations" and chart under "Tortola"). A 7% hotel tax applies to all accommodations save campsites, and a 10-15% service charge frequently is applied. (Tipping may be expected on top of this). The BVI Tourist Board in New York City (tel. 212-696-0400, 800-835-8530) offers a free fast and reliable reservation service which represents major properties in the BVI. (For details see "How to Make Reservations" in the current version of the annual *Tourism Directory*). One firm that arranges accommodations (including hotels, vacation apartments, and villas) is **Best Vacations Imaginable** (tel. 494-6186, fax 494-2000), Box 306, Road Town.

food: High prices prevail. In the restaurants, if you're from New York City, you'll pay the equivalent of home. Ask to see the menu before you sit down. Locals get by with small vegetable gardens and food sent over from St. Thomas by boat from relatives. Small stores sell groceries on the islands. If camping, it's best to bring over everything you can, save the ridiculously cheap demon rum.

shopping: Other than the duty-free alcohol (one liter) allowed by U.S. customs, there's not much to buy here besides some souvenirs in shops; most are imported from the other Caribbean islands. Some alternative souvenirs include the postage stamps and sets of mint coins offered by the General Post Office in Road Town on Tortola, and Sunny Caribbee's line of Caribbean seasonings and artwork.

money: The US dollar reigns supreme here. Because of the physical proximity and economic ties with the USVI, the dollar was made the official currency back in 1962. While allowed at many tourist-oriented places, credit cards are not as universally accepted as they are in the US Virgins. Measurements are the same as in the United States. Time here is permanently Eastern Daylight Time (EDT).

Tortola sunset (Cane Garden Bay)

Road Town

Cane Garden Bay, Tortola

Coral Bay, St. John

broadcasting and media: Cable TV brings over a number of stations from the mainland, the USVI (PBS only) and Puerto Rico. The only AM station is 10,000-watt ZBVI (780 AM) which broadcasts weather reports every half-hour from 7:30-6:30. The FM stations are ZROD (103.7), Z Bold (91.7), and The Heat (94.3). The only newspapers are the twice weekly *Island Sun* and the weekly *Beacon*. A free guide, *Limin' Times* highlights TV and entertainment. Pick one up at Bobby's Supermarket in Road Town, which also has a wide variety of imported newspapers.

visas: Visitors may stay for up to six months, provided they have return or onward tickets, sufficient funds (as judged by the customs official), and pre-arranged accommodations. (In practice, the last two are seldom required for shorter stays). Although a passport is required for entry, birth certificates or voter registration cards are sufficient for US or Canadian citizens. Cruising permits are required for all charter boats.

health: In Road Town is 50-bed **Peebles Hospital** (tel. 494-3497), eight doctors, two dentists, and two visiting eye specialists. There is only one doctor on Virgin Gorda. There's no decompression chamber (for divers) in the islands.

conduct: People here are among the most friendly and hospitable in the whole Caribbean. Keep in mind, however, that the local culture is still highly conservative, so be sure to dress conservatively (e.g., confine your bathing suit to beach areas) and adopt a suitable demeanor. There's less theft here than in the USVI, and theft was the last thing on anyone's mind a few years ago. These days, however, crime is on the increase and reasonable caution is advised.

services and information: For information about the area, either the superbly informative and free bimonthly magazine *The Welcome* or the annual *Tourism Directory* is a must. Obtain a copy before arrival by calling the tourist company at (800) 835-8530. But if you're going soon, let them know. **Banks** are open Mon. to Fri., 9-2 and also on Fri., 4:30-5:30. **telephone services:** Although all seven digits are provided in the text, you only need to dial the last five digits while in the BVI. The provider is Cable and Wireless, whose main office is on Main Street in Road Town. International phone calls may be made from inside. To dial the islands from the US, dial

809 (the area code) + 49 (BVI code) + the remaining five digits. A recent development is the phone card (available in a number of denominations), which simplifies dialing. Coins are not accepted in these phones. In the remaining pay phones, which also offer digital readouts, local calls are 25 cents and only quarters are accepted. Information is 119. **postal services:** Road Town's GPO, on Main Street, is open Mon. to Fri. 9-4, Sat. 9-noon. Post offices are found on Tortola at East End, West End, Cane Garden Bay, Carrot Bay; on Virgin Gorda at The Valley and North Sound; and on Jost Van Dyke and Anegada. Rates on letters (per 1/2 oz.) are 35¢ for US/Canada, 40¢ for UK/Ireland, 60¢ for Europe, and 65¢ for Asia, Africa, and Australia. Postcards are 20¢ for US/Canada, 25¢ for UK/Ireland, 30¢ for Europe, and 35¢ for Asia, Africa, and Australia. **getting married:** For information, contact the Registrar's Office (tel. 494-3701, ext. 303/304, 494-3492), Box 418, Road Town.

Useful British Virgin Island Phone Numbers

Air Anguilla	495-1616
American Eagle	494-2357
Atlantic Air BVI	495-2000
Bobby's Cinemax	494-2098
British Airways	494-2215
BVI Hotel and Commerce Assoc.	494-3514/2947
BVI Taxi Association	494-2332
Directory Assistance	119
Gorda Aero Service	495-2271/2197
Liat	495-1187/8/9
Peebles Hospital	494-3497
Police	494-3822
Sunaire Express	495-2480/5635

organizations: The offices of the **National Park Trust** (tel. 494-3904) are on Fishlock Rd. It is devoted to conserving natural and historic areas, protecting endangered or important species, and increasing public awareness. If you wish to send a tax deductible donation, make the check payable to ECNAMP and address it to National Parks Trust, Ministry of Natural Resources, Box 860, Road Town, Tortola, British Virgin Islands. Individual membership is $20, and family membership is $30. Ex-Exxon tanker captains, Dow Chemical CEOs, and others may partially atone for their environmental sins by donating $1,000 or more and becoming a benefactor.

Sports

diving and snorkeling: This is detailed in the sections on individual locations. Diving and snorkeling's environmental impact has been limited here by the smaller numbers of visitors. Expect to pay around $45 for a one-tank dive and $65 for a night dive. Unlike the waters surrounding the Caymans, these islands lack steep dropoffs or sheer walls. Most range in depth from 30-50 ft. (9-15 m) and many are only 10-30 ft. (3-9 m). The sites lack physical drama, but they have an exceeding abundance of natural beauty, with a wide variety of sponges, soft corals, fish, and other phantasmagorical marine life. The best visibility is found between Norman and Ginger islands, which can easily be reached on a daytrip. Ginger Island has mushroom coral offshore which grows up to 35 ft., underwater canyons, and garden eels. The deepest and most famous dive is the wreck of *The Rhone*. Other sites include Carrot Rock off of Cooper island, the Indians, Blond Rock, and the wreck of *The Fearless* off Peter Island. While Anegada offers spectacular diving, it is difficult to get there.

deep-sea fishing: The BVI are some of the world's richest sport fishing grounds. Spearfishing is prohibited. Charters operate on Tortola, Virgin Gorda, and Anegada. Wahoo, dolphin (the fish), tuna, and kingfish abound. The world's record Atlantic blue marlin, weighing in at nearly 1,300 lbs., was caught here. Great deep-sea fishing spots include the **Sea Mount**, a volcanic island that rises 2,000 ft. from the seabed and is 20 mi. E of Virgin Gorda; the **Saddle**, an area NE of Jost Van Dyke which drops off to 1,000 ft.; and the section beyond Anegada's Horseshoe Reef. The BVI Yacht Club sponsors a number of annual tournaments including the Game Fish Tournament, which coincides with the August Festival, and the Charity, Easter, and Ladies' tournaments. Permits are required: contact the Fisheries Division (tel. 494-3429) for information.

surfing: The best surfing is found at Cane Garden Bay and at Apple and Carrot beaches on Tortola.

windsurfing: Known as "boardsailing" here. Many resorts provide or rent equipment. **Boardsailing BVI** (tel. 495-2447, Box 537, Long Look), at Beef Island's Trellis Bay, provides lessons. The *Catariba* is a 70-ft. catamaran designed for windsurfing charters of up to 20.

British Virgin Islands Tourist Board Offices

BVI
The British Virgin Islands Tourist Board
P.O. Box 134, Road Town, British Virgin Islands
(809) 49-43134

USA
B.V.I. Tourist Board
370 Lexington Avenue
New York, N.Y. 10017
(212) 696-0400
(800) 835-8538
(Nationwide except New York)

BVI Information Office
1686 Union St.
San Francisco, CA 94123
(415) 775-0344
(800) 922-4876
(Nationwide except California)
(800) 922-4873
California state only)

CANADA
801 York Mills Road, Ste. 201
Don Mills, Ontario, Canada M3B 1X7
(416) 443-1859

UNITED KINGDOM
BVI Information Office
FCB Travel/Marketing
110 St. Martin's Lane
London, WC2N 4DV
44-71-240-4259
fax: 44-71-240-4270

EUROPE
BVI Information Office
Sophienstrasse 4
D-6200 Wiesbaden, Germany
49-611-300262
fax: 49-611-300766

Windsurfing cruising, a new type of windsurfing, is being popularized here. Owing to technological advances, long boards and sails have been lightened making it feasible to windsurf from island to island. In one day you can windsurf from Tortola across the Sir Francis Drake Channel, go to Anegada (15 mi.), or to North Sound (10 mi.).

horseback riding: Shadow's Stables (494-2262) on Tortola takes you on trips to Cane Garden Bay or up Mt. Sage.

Tortola

Ferries from St. John to St. Thomas ply along beautiful coasts and past romantic, deserted islets to reach this very attractive island. Although development has made an impact here (most of the British Virgin Islands' 10,000 population resides on Tortola), there is none of the sprawling concrete architecture that has spoiled the majesty of St. Thomas. Protected from heavy traffic by a bypass, the administrative capital Road Town (pop. about 1,500) still retains its small-town flavor. The rest of the island has only been touched by a well-disguised and harmoniously built hotel here and there. Split lengthwise by a ridge of sharply ascending hills, the island is studded with islets, coves, sandy beaches, and bays. Sugarcane cultivation having ceased long ago, much of the land has been reclaimed by nature. If you look carefully, however, you can still see the outlines of what once were fields. In addition to sugar, the island supplied Britain with Sea Island cotton–more than a million pounds of it by 1750. It declined as cheaper green seed cotton from the American South became available, and Sea Island cotton was supplanted by sugar, which declined in its turn.

Travel here is steep but sweet. The paved concrete roads are embossed with the criss-cross impressions of rake heads. These roads shoot sharply up hills giving way to majestic panoramas before descending in curves to the bold blue bays below. Sky World, a restaurant above Road Town, offers a 360-degree panorama.

Practicalities

beaches: The finest beaches are all on the N side of the island. Set at the westernmost end, **Smugglers Cove** offers good snorkeling. Secluded, difficult to reach, and calm, it's reached by an unpaved but passable road. **Long Bay** is a mile-long white sand beach; its W end is skirted by seagrapes and palms. Just over the hill from Long Bay is **Apple Bay**, popular with surfers, where the Bomba Shack is

located as well as the Apple and Sebastian's. The beautifully curved **Cane Garden Bay** is popular with yachtspeople, and any water sport you can name is available at the hotels here. Named after the refineries which once flourished there, **Brewers Bay** is the home of the campground of the same name and offers some of the island's best snorkeling or (when the water is turgid) body surfing. Only made accessible by car in recent years, **Elizabeth Bay** is past **Josiahs Bay** to the E (home of the resort of the same name), which offers good surfing. Other beaches of note include **Little Apple Bay** and **Carrot Bay**.

dive sites near Tortola: As noted above, the best visibility is generally found between Ginger and Norman Islands. Premier dive destination is the wreck of the *HMS Rhone*. Located six miles to the N of Beef Island, at a depth of 75 feet, *The Chikuzen*, a 246-ft. refrigerated vessel, sank in 1981. Numerous species of fish find it a pleasant place to live. A cultivated pearl among the natural varieties, *The Fearless*, a 97-ft. 300-ton ship, is the BVI's newest dive site. A former mine sweeper which never saw naval action, the ship served as Triton's machine shop at Nanny Cay. When it began to sink at the dock, it was donated to the BVI Dive Operators Association who then anchored and sank the boat off Peter Island. Although the boat was apparently already sinking, she refused to go down when she arrived at her intended gravesite and tons of water had to be pumped into her hold before she sank. **Blond Rock**, resembling a natural amphitheater, lies submerged in 12 ft. of water and covered with fire coral. Accessible only in calm water, it lies between Dead Chest and Salt Island. Lobsters, crabs, fan

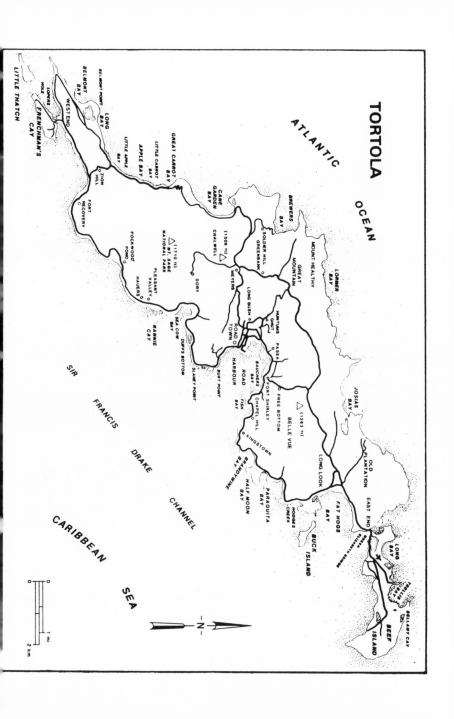

corals, and fish live here and love it. Its name comes from its yellowish dunce cap of fire coral. Lying about a mile from Norman Island in the direction of St. Croix, **Santa Monica Rock** is another underwater pinnacle. Its location makes it an ideal site to see spotted eagle rays, nurse sharks, and barracudas. Less than 100 yards from Ginger I., SE of Tortola, is **Alice in Wonderland**, with its profuse cornucopia of corals. The name comes from its mushroom shaped corals. Partially protected, it is best approached in calm weather. **Brenner's Bay**, accessible by dinghy from Norman Island, is a good dive spot for beginners. Located 200 yards from the W of the Bay, **Brewers Bay Pinnacle** houses stingrays and tarpon. A small cave lies on the E side of the bay. The tips of **The Indians** protrude near Pelican Rock. Soft and hard corals prosper in the canyons and grottoes of these formations. Exceptionally calm, this site is suitable for both scuba and snorkeling. Other sites around the BVI include the Rhone's anchor (with its coral-encrusted chamber pot and the anchor itself); the parallel reef lying off the coast of the S side of Great Dog and "The Chimneys"–a series of submarine arches and canyons–lying nearby; "Painted Walls" (off the SW point of Dead Chest I.); the decaying wreck of the *Rocus* off Anegada; and the back side of Green Cay.

transport, tours, and car rentals: For shared taxi rates see the Introduction. You can walk (the hills are steep and the sun hot), and you can hitch. At Wickham's Cay I., the **BVI Taxi Association** (tel. 494-2875/2322, 495-2378) offers tours and transport. **Scato's Bus Service** (tel. 494-2365) provides some public transportation, special tours, and airport and boat pickups. On the Waterfront Plaza, **Travel Plan Tours** (tel. 494-2872) features every manner of car rentals, water sports rentals, diving, and tours. Linked to the Brewers Bay Campground, **Style's Tour Operator** (tel. 494-2260, day; 494-3341, eve.) operates out of Wickhams Cay. They'll arrange tours, park trips, and diving. **Fly BVI** (tel. 495-1747) will take you over the water and give you great photo opportunities.

car rentals: Expect to spend from $24 pd on up, and you must pay $10 for a temporary permit. For current rates check with the operators or see *The Welcome*. Agencies include **Airways Car Rentals** (tel. 494-4502) in the Inner Harbour Marina, **Alphonso Car Rentals** (tel. 494-3137) at Fish Bay, **Avis** (tel. 494-3322,494-2193) near the Botanic Gardens, **Budget** (tel. 494-2639) at Wickhams Cay I., **Caribbean Car Rental** (tel. 494-2595) at Maria's on the waterfront, **Interna-**

Tortola Taxi Fares

Charter rates are for maximum of 3 persons. Rates in parentheses are for each additional person in excess of 3. Tours (2 1/2 hours max.) $45 for 1 to 3 persons; additional persons $12 each.

From Beef Island Airport to:	Per Person	Taxi Charters
East End/Long Look	2.00	
Maya Cove/Paraquita Bay	3.00	7.00 (3.00)
Brandywine Bay/Hope/Josiah's Bay	3.00	8.00 (3.00)
Kingstown/Fish Bay/Jean Hill/Baugher's		
Bay/Port Purcell/Free Bottom	4.00	10.00 (4.00)
Wickham's Cay I./Road Town/Prospect Reef/		
Huntum's Gut/Lower Estate	5.00	15.00 (5.00)
Sea Cow's Bay/Nanny Cay/Palestina	7.00	21.00 (7.00)
West End/Little Apple Bay/Long Bay/		
Carrot Bay/Can Garden Bay/Brewer's Bay/		
Doty/Harrigan's	8.00	24.00 (8.00)
Smuggler's Cove	10.00	30.00 (10.00)

From Road Town to:		
Prospect Reef/MacNamara/Port Purcell		
Roundabout/Lower Estate/Treasure Isle/		
Wickham's Cay I.	2.00	
Upper Huntum's Ghut/CSY/Fort Hill/		
Baugher's Bay/Purcell/Free Bottom	3.00	
Pieces of Eight/Duff's Bottom/Sea Cow's Bay		
Fish Bay/Kingstown	3.00	8.00 (3.00)
Harrigan's	3.00	8.00 (3.00)
Meyer's/Belle Vue/Brandywine/Colonial		
Manor/Chalwell/Fahie Hill/Long Trench/		
Sky World	3.00	9.00 (3.00)
Nanny Cay/Pleasant Valley/Palestina	4.00	8.00 (4.00)
Havers/Coxheath/Pockwood Pond/Doty/		
Soldiers Hill/Hodge's Creek/Lower Hope	4.00	10.00 (4.00)
East End/Long Look	4.00	12.00 (4.00)
Brewer's Bay/Cane Garden Bay/West End/		
Little Apple Bay/Beef Island Airport/		
Trellis Bay/Frenchman's Cay/Long Bay		
Hotel/Carrot Bay/Ballast Bay/Windy Hill	5.00	15.00 (5.00)
Smuggler's Cove	7.00	21.00 (7.00)

From West End Jetty to:		
Frenchman's Cay/Fort Recovery/Zion Hill/		
Lower Romney Park	2.00	
Cappoon's Bay/Little Carrot Bay/Sugar Mill		
Long Bay Hotel/Upper Romney Park	3.00	
Ballast Bay/Windy Hill/Great Carrot Bay/		
Pockwood Pond	3.00	9.00 (3.00)
Cane Garden Bay/Smuggler's Cove/		
Nanny Cay/Palestina/Sea Cow's Bay/		
Duff's Bottom	4.00	10.00 (4.00)

Fort Burt/Prospect Reef/Huntum's Ghut/Road Town/Joe's Hill/Treasure Isle/Wickham's Cay I./Baugher's Bay/ Purcell/ Free Bottom	5.00	15.00 (5.00)
Harrigan's/Great Mountain/Kingstown/ Meyers/Belle Vue/Fahie Hill/Hope Estate	6.00	18.00 (6.00)
Brewer's Bay/Long Look/East End	7.00	21.00 (7.00)
Beef Island	8.00	24.00 (8.00)

tional Car Rentals (tel. 494-2516/2517), **Rancal Rent-A-Car** at Prospect Reef Resort (tel. 494-4534) and at Long Bay Beach Resort (tel. 495-4330), **Denzil Clyne Car Rentals** (tel. 495-4900) at West End, **Hertz** (tel. 495-4405) at West End, and **National** (tel. 494-3197) at Duff's Bottom. At Cane Garden Bay, **Del's Scooter Rental** (tel. 495-9356) rents out scooters by the hour, day, or week.

Road Town

Road Town was originally known as Road Harbour. Small but charming, this is the administrative capital of the B.V.I. and the only settlement truly worthy of the description "town." It lies sandwiched between the island's foothills and the sea. The Wickham's Cay developments and the main road through town have been constructed on reclaimed land. Despite the opening of a disco or two, not much happens here except a bake sale on Saturdays. Roosters and hens, a goat or two, and an occasional herd of cattle still supplement the pedestrian population. **getting around:** It's easy and comfortable to walk everywhere in town. The reclaimed land along the waterfront has changed the town's face dramatically. Once, it could take an hour to drive along Main St. through the town. These days, Main Street has been preserved as a bastion of tranquility: the picture postcard West Indies as it once was. Unfortunately, however, the Concrete Box school of architecture has taken over the better part of town and is threatening to consume Main Street as well. Enjoy it while you can.

Road Town Sights

The old part of town is all along Main St. which, believe it or not, backed directly onto the harbor until 1968. The town's area has been expanded through landfill. Best place to begin a walking tour is Road Town's small **museum** on Main Street. Unfortunately, it has moved to a smaller structure and is no longer as engaging as it

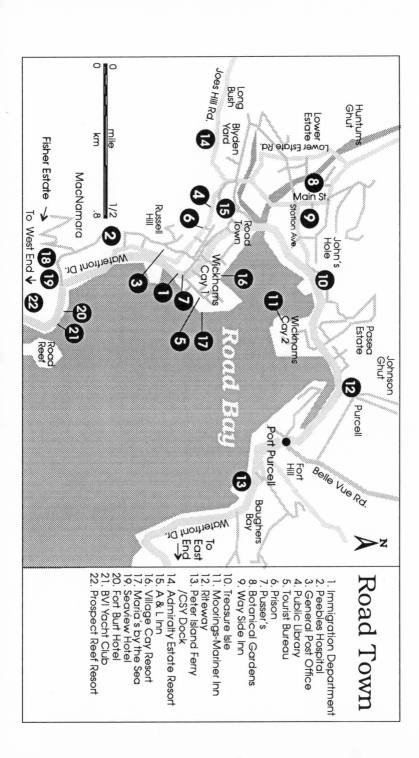

Road Town

1. Immigration Department
2. Peebles Hospital
3. General Post Office
4. Public Library
5. Tourist Bureau
6. Prison
7. Pusser's
8. Botanical Gardens
9. Way Side Inn
10. Treasure Isle
11. Moorings-Mariner Inn
12. Riteway
13. Peter Island Ferry /CSY Dock
14. Admiralty Estate Resort
15. A & L Inn
16. Village Cay Resort
17. Maria's by the Sea
18. Seaview Hotel
19. Fort Burt Hotel
20. BVI Yacht Club
21. Prospect Reef Resort

once was. Because influences from outside the islands are so pervasive, many old structures have been pulled down in a misguided attempt to modernize the islands. (Open Tues. to Fri., 10-4, Sat. 10-1). The **Administration Building,** facing Sir Olva Georges Plaza, was constructed in 1866 from local stone. The century-old **De Castro Building** is a bit farther on; it contains an unusual brick circular staircase. The wooden columns and stone walls inside **Cell 5 Restaurant,** once a private residence, are also of note. Down the street to the L stands **Britannic Hall,** built by a surgeon in 1910. A bit farther and also on the L is the early 19th C **St. Georges School Room.** The Anglican and Methodist churches are nearby. The **prison** (still in use) is the oldest building in town. Just past the corner of Fleming St. and Joe's Hill Rd. lies the **Sunday Morning Well,** where the Emancipation Act was reportedly read on 1 Aug. 1834. The Legislative Council sits in session and court hearings are held in the **Courthouse** or Legislative Council Chamber nearby. The **Survey and Planning Building,** near the Police Headquarters, was originally a cotton factory. At the other end of town near Peeble's Hospital stands **Government House,** the governor's residence and the most representative example of colonial architecture in Road Town. Four forts surround Road Town: George, Shirley, Charlotte, and Burt. Although the latter three are in ruins, **Fort Burt** has been converted into a hotel. The **Old Methodist Church** is probably Road Town's finest timber-framed building. Other landmarks include **H.R. Penn's shop, Niles rum shop,** and the unique **Grocery and Meat Market.** The pickup truck parked out in front is the oldest vehicle on the island. The so-called **Purple Palace** is the most unusual and conspicuous architectural landmark on the island. Atop Harrigan's Hill in the MacNamara section of town, **Fort Charlotte** was once one of the island's largest fortifications, built by the Royal Engineers in 1794. Now all that remains are a few walls, a cistern, and an underground magazine.

parks: Established in 1987, the five-acre **J. R. O'Neal Botanic Gardens** provide a peaceful refuge and an introduction to the islands' flora. They are maintained by the National Parks Trust and the BVI Botanical Society. Open Mon. to Fri., 8-4; Sun., noon-5. A small community park bordered with white cedars–the territorial tree–**Queen Elizabeth Park** stands near Government House.

Road Town Accommodations

low budget: The best deal in town is **Way Side Inn Guest House** (tel. 494-3606; Box 258, Road Town), which has all-year rates of $20 s or d and caters to down-islanders. Vanita Parsons has slightly cheaper rooms but is not recommended. Next up on the price scale is the **Sea View Hotel** (tel. 494-2483; Box 59, Road Town), with 28 rooms for $35 s or d plus 10% service charge. More expensive studios and efficiencies are available. It's just out of the town's center to the S by the turnoff for Hotel Castle Maria.

centrally-located hotels: Providing 14 a/c rooms with phone and television, **A & L Inn,** (tel. 494-6343/6344/6345, fax 494-6656; Box 403, Road Town), Flemming St., is two blocks in from the sea. Rates run from $60 s or d. Weekly and monthly rates are available. On Wickham's Cay and in the vicinity of the marina, motel-style 20-unit **Maria's By The Sea** (tel. 494-2595; Box 206, Road Town) has a bar/restaurant and a pool. Some units have kitchenettes with refrigerator, hotplate, and toaster. Rooms start at $70. Offering elegant suites, **Village Cay Resort Marina** (tel. 494-2771, fax 494-2773, Box 145, Road Town) is set amidst a complex of shops. Facilities include a restaurant, secretarial services, cable TV, a/c, in-room refrigerators, and *New York Times* fax at breakfast. Its standard rooms rent for $69 and range up to $125 for the best rooms during the high season; waterfront rooms and suites are the most expensive. Some have balconies. Also here, the **Village Cay Marina Apartment** (tel. 494-2020; Box 3017, Road Town) has a luxurious a/c one-bedroom with kitchen and cable TV. **Village Cay Gardens** (tel. 494-5353; Box 306, Road Town) has one-bed-room and two-bedroom/two-bath apartments with centralized a/c, kitchen, lounge, and dining room. Rates for are $100 s or d ($130 winter), with weekly rates available.

heading N out of town: On a hillside overlooking the harbor at Road Town, **Treasure Isle Hotel** (tel. 494-2501, fax 334-2435, telex 7922; Box 68, Road Town) offers an assortment ranging from 25 motel-style rooms to 15 suites. There's a pool, and dining is offered on the covered terrace in its Veranda Restaurant. There is a pool, tennis courts, bar, and marina. It is now operated in conjunction with the Moorings-Mariner Inn and they are billed together as "Club Mariner." Rates start at $80 d and range up to $215 d. In the US or Canada call 800-334-2435, 813-538-8760, fax 813-530-9497, or telex 4949716. Located on the outskirts of town, the **Moorings-Mariner Inn** itself (tel. 494-2332; Box 139, Road Town) has no beach. It has 39 rooms plus two suites in two blocks of two-storey buildings. Nearly all guests stay here for the boating. The Moorings Charter Boat operation here encompasses Treasure Isle Hotel. Diving and sailing package holidays are offered. Winter rates run from $130-$180 with summer rates available.

heading S out of town: Overlooking Road Town, peaceful and private **Hotel Castle Maria** (tel 49-42553/2515 fax 494-2111; Box 206, Road Town) is run by Alfred Christopher, a delightful and unforgettable host. The advantage of staying here is that, while close to town, it is far enough out of the way to be quiet. The hotel offers 30 units with a/c or fan, some with kitchenettes and sea views, a bar, and a large pool. Lush and carefully tended gardens border the entrance. The chief minister and the governor live near here. Rates start at $55 s (garden view), $70 d and rise to $90 d (harbor view) during the winter. Triples ($85-$105, depending upon room and season) and quads ($95-$130) are also available. Weekly rates are obtainable on request. To find this hotel, turn R when you reach the Sea View and head on to the R. Set on a small hill at the SW edge of Road Town, **Fort Burt Hotel** (tel. 494-2587, fax 494-2002; Box 3225, Road Town) has seven rooms and a suite in a 300-yr.-old Dutch-English fort. The a/c rooms have TVs, and balconies. There's a pool and a view of the harbor. Rates start at $55 s, $75 d, and a 10% service charge is added. Set on the W edge of Road Town, **Prospect Reef Resort** (tel. 494-3311, 800-356-8937; Box 104 Road Town) first opened in the 1970s. Plans were to sell the apartments here, a plan that never materialized. The 131 rooms are close-set and offer a/c (in some units), kitchen, and phone. On the premises are charter boats, snorkel and scuba, deep-sea fishing, pools, seven tennis courts, shops, hairdressing salon, health spa, and two restaurants. Rates begin at $80 and range up to $390 during the winter. A 10% service charge is added.

villas, condos, and other accommodations: In Road Town near the Botanical Gardens and featuring fully equipped kitchens and private patios overlooking a garden, each of **Jennie's Housekeeping Units** (tel. 494-3300; Box 150, Road Town) is available for weekly rental. There are one-bedrooms which accommodate two, one-bedrooms which accommodate four, and two-bedroom units. A rental TV is available. Prices range from $325-$470 during the summer to $395-$600 in season. A more expensive ($450 and up) group are at Todman's Estate above Brewer's Bay. The **New Happy Lion Apts.** (tel. 494-2574/4088; Box 402, Road Town) offers two housekeeping units with kitchen and TV; it has a restaurant. With an efficiency and a two-bedroom, six-person house plus pool, TV/VCR, and phone, **Casa Bella** (tel. 494-3772; Box 629, Road Town) rents out its houses for $1,500 pw in the summer and $2,000 in the winter; the efficiency rents for $500 pw.

up in the hills: Set on the hills above Road Town, **Admiralty Estate Resort** (tel. 494-0014, fax 494-0015, 800-223-9815, Box 158, Road Town) offers a set of luxurious condominium villas grouped around a pool. The one- and two-bedroom suites come with balcony, kitchen, living room, and dining room. Superior units have color TV/VCR and skylight roof. The Admiral's Grill serves meals. Rates include continental breakfast and taxi service to beach. A pink-roofed one- and two-bedroom apartment complex overlooking the sea and Drake's Channel on Slaney Hill at the W end of Road Town, **Sea Breeze Living** (tel. 494-2629; Box 191, Road Town) has kitchens, living-dining areas, and terraces. Rates run from $100 pd summer to $150 pd winter. Offering nine one-bedroom units on two floors, **Mountain Valley Apartments** (tel. 494-3357, Box 402, Road Town) provides dinette-kitchen, living room with TV, porch; there's a sofa bed in each living room. The Castaway Bar is here, and it's a 15-min. walk to town. Set on Ridge Rd. between Fahie Hill and Great Mountain with a view of Guana Island off in the distance, **Lloyd Hill Villas** (tel. 494-2481, Box 163, Road Town) provides two- , three- or four-bedroom units with maid service, living and dining rooms with TV, gardens, and a pool shared between two houses. Rates start at $1,000/pw for a two-bedroom and rise to a high of $2,310/pw for a four-bedroom villa during the winter. A 10% service charge is added. Overlooking Sir Francis Drake Channel, **The Perch** (tel. 494-3138; Box 190, Road Town) offers kitchen, living room, TV/VCR, stereo, and a phone. A restaurant and other facilities are nearby.

towards West End from Road Town: At Sea Cow's Bay to the W of Road Town, **Villa Manatee** (tel. 966-6115, 212-966-6115; 142 Greene St., NY, NY 10012) has a two- bedroom apartment and one guest cottage with TV. Rates are available upon request. Set at a marina on the W coast S of Road Town, **Nanny Cay Resort and Marina** offers week-long rentals, although many are rented out long-term.

All studios are a/c and feature private balcony/patio, kitchenette, mini-bar, cable TV/VCR, and phones. A restaurant, pool, boutique, car rental, a complete range of water sports including a windsurfing school, and other facilities are on the premises. Call 914-833-3300, 800-786-4753, fax 914-833-3318, or write Box 284, Larchmont, NY 10538. Set at Hannah's Estate between Sea Cow Bay and the West End near Nanny Cay, **Sir Francis Drake Vacation Homes** (tel. 494-0290; Box 942, Road Town) has three "super deluxe" two-bedroom apartments with kitchen, living room, and dining room from $205 summer up to $240 high season. Farther on towards the West End and near Havers Estate, **Hall's House** (tel. 494-3946) offers a fully equipped main house and a guest house. Call (902) 742-8828 or write Box 642, Yarmouth, Nova Scotia, Canada B5A 4B6.

Road Town Dining and Food

In town, there are a large variety of small restaurants, a bakery, and some supermarkets.

local food: You shouldn't leave the BVI without at least sampling the local food. Breakfast, at the **Midtown Restaurant** near the center of Main Street, costs $6; sandwiches are $2.50 and up; and fish and chips are around $6. They also serve local cuisine like conch fritters ($4 for a very small portion). **The Palms**, located in Sir Olva Georges Plaza, on Main Street serves local food including conch in butter sauce and fish dishes. Overlooking the harbor, **Maria's By the Sea** is centrally located and offers upscale dining. In Palm Grove Shopping Centre, a/c **Mario's** serves gourmet-style local food. Upstairs from Sylvia's Laundromat on Flemming St., **Scato's Snack Bar** is open daily and serves local dishes, sandwiches, and beverages. Near the round-about on Wickhams Cay I., **Popeye's Inn** serves three daily meals. **Scatcliffe's Tavern**, near the high school, serves local dishes along with pies, cakes, and drinks. Located on Russel Hill just below the Purple Palace, the **Roti Palace** offers a variety of rotis (chapati-wrapped curries) along with other Indian delicacies. In Purcell Estate the **C & F Bar & Restaurant**, one of the best local restaurants, serves dinner including BBQ and curried dishes. At Baugher's Bay, the **Aries Club** presents daily fish and West Indian specialties. In the Baugher's Bay Beach Club here, the **Beach Club Terrace** serves traditional local food daily. Also here and opposite ZBVI, **Pick 'O Pick** offers three meals except on weekends.

snacks, bakeries, and light dining: If you're on a budget or a diet, try a conch patty or other quick snack at one of these places. Across from Road Reef Marina, **Crandall's Pastry Plus** serves cakes, tarts, lobster and conch patties, and other light food. Behind Aviks in town, the **New Happy Lion** offers breakfast and lunch; dinner is by request. In The Cutlass Bldg. in the town center near the water, **M & S Pastry Plus** offers cafeteria-style food (spinach, rice, quiches) at very reasonable prices as well as pastries and pizza. With an a/c dining room, **Marlene's Delicious Designs** has baked goods, salads, sandwiches, patties, rotis, pastries, and desserts. **Delicious Designs II** on the waterfront has patties (salt fish for $2), quiche (crab for $4.50), pizza, sandwiches, and a wide variety of pastries. The **Happy Heart Snack Bar & Barber**, Wickhams Cay I., combines these unlikely of enterprises. On the waterfront road, **Chad's** serves ice cream and sells phone cards. **pizza: Paradise Pizza** has two branches–one at Port Purcell and another at the foot of Fort Burt Hill.

other dining: At the Rufus L. De Castro Center and facing the water, **Cell 5** serves three meals daily and offers local specials. Seafood including lobster is available for dinner; breakfast is quite reasonably priced. On the water overlooking the harbor, the **Paradise Pub** (tel. 494-2608) has a range of international delicacies ranging from vegetarian to sausage or pizza; a buffet is offered on Wed., Fri., and Sat. Serving international dishes, **Santa Maria (Dinghy's)** is a casual dockside restaurant with steaks and seafood and located in Village Cay Marina. Near the waterfront, **Spaghetti Junction** serves homemade pasta dishes as well as daily specials. Its $14 entrees include fettucini and lasagna. Specializing in English pub-style fare, the **Tavern in the Town** serves burgers, salads, mixed grills, and fish and chips. In addition to nightly specials, it features fisherman's pie and "poor man's surf and turf" (prawns and a hamburger). **The Virgin Queen** offers dining amidst antique and Tiffany lamp decor. An open air restaurant in the Columbus Centre, **The Fish Trap** has local lobster, burritos, teriyaki chicken, and conch fritters on its menu. Listing French and continental cuisine on the menu, the **Captains Table** is at Inner Harbour Marina; dishes include fresh fish, live lobster from the tank, and escargot in puff pastry. Lunch (exc. weekends) and dinner are offered. **The Hungry Sailor Garden Cafe** has less expensive dishes. For Chinese Szechuan food cooked with a West Indian touch, try **Chopsticks** near Wickhams Cay. It's rather expensive: fried rice is $10. Near the Village Cay marina, Pusser's Country Store and Pub has dishes for as low as $9.99 (as well as a special Sunday brunch from 11-3) at its **Pusser's Outpost** (tel. 494-4199) upstairs; the downstairs pub features sandwiches and pizza as well as their line of drinks. Near the Moorings Marina, the **Mariner Inn** serves basic American fare including a "Yachtsman's Special." Dinner is by candlelight and includes jumbo gulf shrimp. To the E of town, **Brandywine Bay** (tel. 495-2301) offers Italian fare in a former private hilltop home. Expect to pay $80/couple at a minimum. Serving international and Caribbean fare, **Treasure Isle Restaurant** offers three meals daily. Set at MacNamara about 10 min, on foot to the S of town, the **Sea View Hotel** (tel. 494-2483; reservations requested) serves seafood and steaks. Overlooking the lagoon at Prospect Reef, the **Upstairs Restaurant** (tel. 494-3311/2228; reservations requested) serves steak and seafood for lunch and dinner. Offering W Indian and continental dishes, pizza, and beer on tap, the **Cloud Room** (tel. 494-2821) overlooks the town and will bring you to and from your hotel as part of the meal cost. Serving good food, it has a moveable roof which retracts at night. Atop Ridge Rd., **Skyworld** (tel. 494-3567) serves lunch and dinner fare ranging from onion rings to conch fritters or pasta. You can also dine at Peter's Island. Elegant and open air, the **Fort Burt Restaurant** serves specialties such as lobster and shrimp with wild mushroom in puff pastry. Offering seafood, burgers, and salads in a casual atmosphere, the **Harbour Cafe** is next to the lagoon at Prospect Reef and offers three meals.

Sea Cows Bay/Nanny Cay dining: At the Sea Cow's Bay race track, **Chuck's Drive In** offers West Indian dishes and seafood. Also featuring local dishes, the colorfully named **Struggling Man's Place** serves everything from rotis to curried mutton to fish & chips. In the plaza at Nanny Cay Marina, the canopied **Marina Plaza Cafe** serves a variety of Caribbean and international dishes for its three daily meals. Set above the water's edge here, **Peg Leg Landing** also serves international dishes including seafood, soups, and salads.

fast food: Bobby's Supermarket near Wickham's Cay I. contains three fast food establishments: **Bobby's Burger, Bobby's Chicken,**

and **Bobbino's Pizza**. Visit it at night when the complex is all aglow: the Las Vegas of Road Town. Popeye's Service Station has even gotten into the act with **Popeye's Fried Chicken and Chips**.

market shopping: There is a public market in Road Town, but there never seems to be a hell of a lot in it. At the Mill Mall, small and expensive **Nature's Way** (tel. 494-6393) carries a complete line of health food and beauty aids. One of the main supermarkets in town is **Bobby's**. Sample prices: Country Hearth whole wheat bread $1.97/loaf, kingfish filets $3.17/lb., bananas 75¢/lb., tomatoes $1.16/lb, green peppers $1.09/lb., eggs $1.58/dozen, Peter Pan Peanut Butter $3.16/18 oz., milk $2.61/half gallon, Mott's Apple Juice $2.87/64 oz., Johnny Walker Red Label $8.43/fifth, J&B Scotch $8.90/fifth, and Cruzan Rum $2.72/fifth. **SupaValu** is a wholesale outlet near the roundabout at Wickhams Cay I., and **Riteway Super Market** is on Main Street, at Pasea Estate, and at The Pub at Fort Burt Marina. The Port Purcell shopping area near the deepwater dock boasts **K-Marks Super Market** and the **Port Purcell Market**. **Franklin's General Market** is at Wickhams Cay I. **Dorothy's Superette** is on Main Street. **Sunrise Bakery**, also on Main Street, has delicious baked goods. **The Ample Hamper**, located inside Village Cay Marina, has every kind of imported delicacy for the gourmet-minded. Also try the **Gourmet Gallery**. **Bon Apetit**, Wickhams Cay I., sells cheese and prepared food. A final such specialty shop is **Little Circle** at Prospect Reef.

booze: Alcohol is available at all the supermarkets, and at **The Bubblin Barrel** on Main St., **The Ample Hamper** at Wickhams Cay I., **TICO** at Wickhams Cay I., the **Discount Liquor Store & Mini Mart** at Village Cay Marina, **Esme's Shoppe** at Sir Olvia Georges Plaza, the **Fort Wines & Spirits Store** at Port Purcell, and **A. H. Riise** in the O'Neal Complex at Port Purcell. Aside from the brew sold by the Callwood Distillery in Cane Garden Bay, the BVI's only indigenous brew is the Tortola Spiced Rum Pirates' Blend which is available around Road Town for a pricey $13 a bottle.

events: See the list of events in the Introduction.

entertainment: Not exactly downtown Manhattan, to say the least. Much of the entertainment happens out of town at Cane Garden Bay or other locales. Check the *Limin' Times*, which has a calendar. **The Pub**, at Fort Burt Marina, often has live bands (reggae, calypso, rock) on weekend evenings. **Treasure Isle Hotel** (tel. 494-2501) features music on Wed. and Sat. including a fungi band. Fungi and steel bands alternate Thursdays at **The Moorings** on Wickham's Cay I. The **Downstairs Restaurant** at Village Cay Marina features live music on Mondays. **Bobby's Disco** stands above Bobby's supermarket near Wickhams Cay I. Just nearby, **After Dark**, a bar and nightclub, has a disco and sometimes has live music. **The Paradise Pub** (tel. 494-2608) has a disco on Thurs., Fri., and Sat. nights. **Pusser's Landing** has a BBQ and band on Sundays. They also have a "dinner with movie night" for $15. If nothing is going on there you can always deposit a quarter and have your future analyzed by a fortune teller in a glass box. **The Drop Inn Bar**, at Prospect Reef on the way to West End, has a nightly happy hour. **Peter Island Resort** also features live music including steel-bands. **outlying:** If you have dinner, **Mrs. Scatliffe** and her family will frequently entertain you with their scratch band afterwards at Carrot Bay. Garfield George rules the roost with his calypso riffs during **Sebastian's** Thursday night West Indian buffet. **The Sugar Mill** at Little Apple Bay presents local music from 8 on Sat. The fish fry here is a local event you can participate in. At **Tamarind Country Club**, in East End off of Ridge Road, Big Al and Del play Motown, rock, and country ballads. At Cane Garden Bay, balladeer Quito Rhymer holds forth at **Quito's Gazebo** (tel. 495-4837) on Thurs., Fri., and Sat., and a band plays on Sat. **Myett's** has live music on Fri. **The Wedding** (tel. 495-4022) has reggae on weekends in season. In Apple Bay, **Sebastian's** (tel. 495-2412) has movies on Wed. and Sat., a fungi band on Sat. and Sun. Singer Reuben Chinnery performs at **The Apple** on Sun. night. And **The Bomba Shack** (tel. 495-4148) has a band on Sun. at 4 and Wed. at 8 as well as a monthly "Full Moon Party." **Long Bay Beach Resort** (tel. 495-4252) has a steel band on Tues. and a fungi band on Thurs. **Bing's Drop in Bar and Restaurant** (tel. 495-2627) has after hours dancing and a late night menu. Much more happens at these places–in the way of barbecues and live bands–during the height of the winter season.

other entertainment: **Bobby's Cinemax** (tel. 494-2098), the sole cinema in town, is up the road from the market. It plays films like Sniper, The Vanishing, and The Crying Game. For a uniquely BVI experience catch a dance rehearsal by the Heritage Dancers at **Briercliffe Hall** in Road Town, Mondays from 9:30. Groups to watch out for include The Shooting Stars, a steel band, local calypsonians such as Benji V, and bands such as Caribbean Ecstasy.

shopping: A variety of goods (many of them from the "down islands"–located to the S) are available along with tee shirts ("Get Hooked on a Virgin," etc.) and other such touristic items. The best tee shirts to pick up are the polos with the National Park logo or the "Give Turtles A Chance" logo, both of which are sold at the **National Parks Trust headquarters** (tel. 494-3904) in town on Fishlock Rd. near the Fire Station. The majority of stores are on Main Street and in Wickhams Cay. These days, the two are running together into one large shopping area. **Esme's Shop** sells magazines, books, imported newspapers, and alcoholic beverages. **The Bubbling Barrel** sells alcohol, tee shirts, cigars, and handmade dolls. Set in the O'Neal Courtyard on Waterfront Drive and opposite the ferry dock, **Antiquities Unlimited** sells books, antiques, and crafts. **Samarkand** sells gold and silver jewelry. In the Rufus L. de Castro Centre are **Carol's Gift Shop**–with resort wear, tee shirts, jewelry and other items—as well as **Creative Craft and Things** with dolls, crochet items, etc. Set next to the bakery, **Bonkers Gallery** sells a variety of casual clothing and bathing suits. In the Abbot Bldg., **Sea Urchin** sells beachwear and other accessories, **Kids in De Sun** sells children's clothing, and **Kaunda's Kysy Tropix** has jewelry, TVs and other such equipment. A silk-screen studio and shop, **Caribbean Handprints** sells clothing and fabric desighs. **Oooh La La** features tee shirts, postcards, and other items designed by owner Sophie. Set in an old house, **Mumbo Jumbo** offers crafts including Rasta-style caps and bags. The **Pusser's Company Store**, one of the largest shops around, sells the famed local rum and other memorabilia. Offering gold and silver jewelry, **Felix Silver and Gold** also has items which use coral and shell. Set in a traditional house and one of the most attractive shops found anywhere in the Caribbean, **The Sunny Caribee Herb and Spice Company** offers attractively packaged selections of spices from all over the Caribbean; they also sell a wide range of unusual and high quality Caribbean arts and crafts. Pick up their catalog or write for one (Box 286, Main St., Tortola or Box 3237 VDA, St. Thomas 00803-3237), fax them at 494-4039, or call 494-2178. **Flamboyance** specializes in duty-free perfume. **The Carifta Store** sells women's clothes, gold chains, perfumes, china and crystal. **Little Denmark** sells a selection of gold and silver jewelry, watches, snorkeling and fishing gear, and other items. One of the most distinctive stores,

Serendipity sells hand-painted tee shirts, hand-dyed sarongs, and other exotic brightly colored clothing. Also in a traditional house, **Domino** sells imported European clothes and Caribbean handicrafts. Filled with Caribbean and BVI handicrafts, **H & B Handicrafts** offers a wide assortment. Set across from the Methodist Church, **J. R. O'Neal Ltd. Decorative and Home Accessories Store** sells everything from Mexican glassware to bold ceramics. At the end of Main St., **Creque's Department Store** sells leather shoes as well as clothing. Near Bobby's Supermarket on Main St. is **Growing Things** which sells flowers and plants. Next to Tico near the roundabout, **Turtle Dove** has perfumes, fashions, and home accessories. In an old house across from Wickhams Cay, the **Shirt Shack** sells casual clothing. Across the way, **P & M Sports** sells hand-painted tee shirts. Just past Chopsticks, **Pacesetter** sells shoes, accessories, and clothing. At the Prospect Reef Hotel, **The Pink Pineapple** carries a variety of unusual gifts; **On the Beach** here sells beachwear, clothing, and hats.

Wickhams Cay shopping: Bolo's Record and Leather Shop has a wide selection of music as well as shoe repairs. In an old house in the Crafts Alive Market, the **House of Crafts** carries a wide variety of crafts. In addition to sewing accessories and fabrics, **Clovers** sells shoes. At the Mill Mall is another branch of the **Sea Urchin**. At Columbus Centre, **Collector's Corner** sells larimar, gold, and silver jewelry, and **Castaways** sells casual clothing as well as snorkeling equipment. In Village Cay Marina, **Personal Touch** offers embroidered cotton polos and other items. In the Tropic Isle Bldg., **Violet's** sells sleepwear, lingerie, and accessories. **The Carousel Gift Shop** sells crystal, crafts, ceramics, and embroidered tablecloths. **La Gregg's** sells books as well as snacks and refreshments. **The Globe** has everything from cosmetics to souvenirs to swimware. **Dawn's Shoe Shop** sells shoes from Italy, Spain, and Brazil as well as handbags and hosiery. **The Learn & Fun Shop** has toys, games, and books. In the Palm Grove Shopping Centre, **Jehmary's** sells local handicrafts. In Wickhams Cay I., **Naucraft Galleries** has art from the BVI and the Caribbean as well as antique items.

other items: Stamps are available from the new **philatelic bureau** located in the Mill Mall behind Barclay's Bank on Wickhams Cay, while authentic coins (80 cents' worth for $1) are sold at a window to the left outside the G.P.O. on Main Street. **Omega Caribbean Limited**, at Wickhams Cay I., has woodworked souvenirs.

outlying area stores: At Nanny Cay, **Castaways** sells casual clothes and swimwear. At Skyworld, **Sunny Caribbee** sells Haitian and other Caribbean artwork. Other stores are found at Trellis Bay in Beef Island, at Soper's Hole in the West End, and at hotel shops throughout the island.

services and information: Next to Immigration on the bypass, the **BVI Tourism Board** is open Mon. to Fri. 9-4:30. The **General Post Office**, Main Street, is open Mon. to Fri. 8-4, Sat. 9-1:30. Faxes can be sent here. Banks include **Barclays International**, **Chase Manhattan**, **The Bank of Nova Scotia**, and **First Pennsylvania**. The local **library** is on Main Street up from the prison. The BVI Community College also has a small library on Main St. At Prospect Reef Resort, **Golden Palms Health Spa** (tel. 494-0138 or 494-3311, ext. 245) has a massage service, workout equipment, and daily spa packages.

other services: Bolo's, at Wickhams Cay I, has one-hour film processing. **Sylvia's Laundromat** (tel. 494-2230) is on Fleming St. **Travel Plan Tours** (tel. 494-2347/5720) is a competent travel agent which also offers island tours. **Tortola Travel Services** (tel. 494-2215/2216/2672) is another alternative. The **Kis 1-Hour Photo** at Columbus Centre will take care of all of your photo needs. **Video Big Leo** (tel. 494-3983, in Mill Mall and at Long Swamp in East End) rents movies as well as equipment, and you can pick up and drop off at either store. For underwater camera rental and instruction, **Rainbow Visions Photography** (tel. 494-2749, fax 494-6390, VHF Ch. 16; Box 680, Road Town), Prospect Reef, rents eqipment and offers instruction and processing.

pay telephones: The only ones in the center of Road Town are in front of the Cable and Wireless office. International calls may be made and telegrams may be sent from inside the main office. Office hours are Mon. to Fri., 7-7, Sat 7-4, and Sun. 9-noon. Pay phones are at the Recreation Ground (near the police station); Village Cay Marina, The Moorings, Peebles Hospital, Nanny Cay Marina, Port Purcell, West End Jetty, and Beef Island Airport. The new pay phones have digital readouts and take either quarters (call everywhere) or phone cards which come in denominations of $5, $10, and $20. Cards can be purchased at any phone card agency.

drugstores: Next to the PO on Main St., **J. R. O'Neal** sells drugs, gifts, film, and other items. **The Lagoon Plaza** is on upper Main St. nearby. **Medicure** is in the Hodge Bldg. near the roundabout. Both **Vanterpool Enterprises** and **OMA Drugs** are on Wickhams Cay; the former is near the roundabout and the latter is in the Palm Grove Shopping Centre.

car rentals: See the list at the beginning of this chapter.

day sails: Lunch and drinks are generally included, and rates vary but run around $30-50 for a half-day sail and $60-$80 for a full-day sail. *Ppalu* (tel. 496-7258, 495-7500; Box 896, Road Town), a large and fast 75-ft. catamaran, sails daily to locations such as Anegada ($90), The Baths ($70), Cooper Island, and Norman Island's caves. Built in 1978, it's named after the title of the traditional Micronesian navigator who was always sure of his location on the seas. Very comfortable, this impressive sailing vessel has a large lounge and dining area and lots of deck space above for you to lounge about. Arriving at The Baths you get an optional tour and can snorkel for about an hour. Then it's back on the boat for a 1 PM departure to Norman Island. Lunch (spinach quiche, chicken, and dinner rolls) is served on the boat along the way. Anchoring at Norman, you spend about 45 min. snorkeling before heading back. The motor may be used for part of the trip, depending upon the winds. Everything is included in the rates–from lunch and drinks to snorkeling and instruction; special group rates are available. **Carriacou Day Sails** (tel. 494-3003; Box 176, Road Town) operates a 34-ft. Morgan sloop. At the Village Cay Marina, **Kings Charters, Ltd.** (tel. 494-5820; Box 145, Road Town) has day charters and "super snorkelers." Running charters and day trips to the Baths (Virgin Gorda) as well as to The Caves (Norman Island), the *White Squall II* (tel. 494-2564), an 80-ft. schooner, is berthed at "A" dock at the Village Cay Marina. Operating out of Prospect Reef, the *Island Hopper* (tel. 495-4870; Box 104, Road Town) is a 23-ft. Zodiac. A 50-ft. luxury catamaran, the *Kuralu* (tel. 495-4381; Box 609, West End), sails from West End to Jost Van Dyke, Sandy Cay, and other locations for $70 pp with a four-person minimum; children are half-price. A 48-ft. catamaran running out of Village Cay Marina, the *Patouche II* (tel. 494-6300; Box 987, Road Town) offers snorkeling at Norman Island as well as a full-day trip which stops at Peter Island Resort. At Nanny Cay, **Sea Escape Daysails** (tel. 494-0119, 496-0044; Box 281, Road Town) runs excursions in its

Sunday Morning, a 53-ft. schooner. At Prospect Reef Resort, **Take Two Charters** (tel. 494-5208/3311; Box 104, Road Town) has a 35-ft. Niagra sloop which offers half- and full-day sails (plus overnights and cruises by request). Out at Trellis Bay, *The Last Resort* (tel. 495-2520; Box 530, Long Look), a 50-ft. cruising catamaran, operates half- and full-day charters. At Village Cay Marina, **Radical Rider** (tel. 496-7258/7500; Box 896, Road Town) conducts snorkeling and sightseeing tours in a 35-ft. high speed inflatable.

diving: Baskin in the Sun (tel. 494-2858, fax 494-2507, 800-494-2507; Box 108, Road Town) has branches at Long Bay, Sugar Mill, and at Prospect Reef. Operating a PADI 5-star dive center, they have a tremendous number of dive packages including a "land and sea" version which enables you to combine yachting with diving. Offering personalized service, they also have three specialty courses including an intriguing "PADI Caribbean Reef Ecology" course. A second PADI five-star center, **DIVE BVI LTD.** (tel. 495-5513, 800-848-7078; Box 1040, Virgin Gorda) operates out of Virgin Gorda Yacht Harbour, Leverick Bay, and Peter Island, and has a variety of boats. **Underwater Safaris** (tel. 494-3235/3965, 800-537-7032; Box 4447 Veterans Drive Station, St. Thomas 00803; Box 139, Road Town) offers packages (from $747 pp for seven days), instruction, rentals, dive/sail packages, and other tours including rendezvous with yachts. Underwater photography is offered through collaboration with Rainbow Visions. They operate out of The Moorings and have an additional full service dive shop at Cooper Island. **Island Diver** (tel. 494-3878; Box 3023, Road Town) is based at the Village Cay Marina. **Blue Water Divers** (tel. 494-2847, fax 494-0198, VHF CH. 16; Box 846, Road Town) have operated out at Nanny Cay Marine Center since 1980. They offer introductory and certification courses as well as guided tours; packages and rentals are available. **Rainbow Visions Photography** (tel. 494-2749, fax 494-6390, VHF Ch. 16; Box 680, Road Town) is a dive operator based at Prospect Reef. They also rent video and other cameras and offer instruction and processing. **Yacht Promenade** (tel. 494-3853, 494-5577; Box 3100, Road Town) has a 65-ft. crewed trimaran, and the **Trimarine Boat Co., Ltd.** (tel. 494-2490, fax 494-5774; Box 362, Road Town) operates two trimarans.

Tortola marinas: These generally have a full range of facilities. Check a current issue of *The Welcome* or contact the marina concerned for specifics. At Wickhams Cay I., the **Moorings-Mariner**

Inn (tel. 494-2332; Box 139, Road Town) permits dockage for up to 90 boats. The **Fort Burt Marina** (tel. 494-4200; Box 243, Road Town) offers overnight and permanent berths. At the same marina, **Tortola Yacht Services** (tel. 494-2124; Box 74, Road Town) operates a repair and maintenance service. The **Village Cay Resort Marina** (tel. 494-2771; Box 145, Tortola) provides dockage for 106 boats up to 150 ft. **Prospect Reef Resort** (tel. 494-3311; Box 104, Road Town) offers dockage for yachts of up to 45 ft. At the West End are **Sunsail Yachts** (tel. 495-4740; Box 609, West End) and **Soper's Hole Marina** (tel. 495-4553; Box 601, West End) provides 36 slips and moorings. Offlying **Peter Island Resort** and **Marina Cay** also have marinas.

sportfishing: Operating out of the Prospect Reef Hotel, **Miss Robbie Charter Fishing** (tel. 494-3311/4870) has fishing trips from $400/half-day on up.

From Roadtown To The East

St. Phillip's Church, or the "African Church," is at Kingstown. This church was built in 1833 for the use of 600 Africans who had been removed from the bowels of a slave ship around 1815 (after the abolition of the slave trade, but before emancipation on the island). Known as the Kingstown Experiment, these slaves were placed in a freed reservation after serving an apprenticeship with the planters. While the roof is gone, its walls, sporting faded scriptural excerpts painted by an Anglican priest, still stand. Hub of Quaker activities and seat of government for a while after it had been transferred from Spanish Town on Virgin Gorda, **Fat Hogs Bay** still contains a ruined Quaker cemetery. The Long Look-Look East area is second in size in terms of population. From just before Long Look a road heads up to Josiahs Bay on the N coast. **Josiahs Bay accommodations:** At Josiahs Bay, **Serendipity House** (tel./fax 495-1488) has a deluxe two bedroom, two bath with pool, TV, and complimentary bar and coffee. Rates start at $400 pw. For more information fax (705) 534-4557 or write General Delivery, Victoria Harbour, Canada LOK 2AO. Offering nine units–a mix of cottages, suites, bungalows, and efficiencies, **Josiahs Bay Cottages** (tel. 494-6186, fax 494-2000, 800-842-6260, Box 306, Road Town) offers nine attractive units on landscaped grounds with pool. All units are one-bedrooms with kitchens and living room area. There are efficiency suites, traditional cottages, and deluxe bungalows. The beach is a five min. walk away. Rates start at $180 for three nights in a suite and range up to $875 for seven nights in a bungalow during the high season. **The Tamarind Country Club Hotel** (tel. 495-2477; Box 509, East End) here has 120 rooms with kitchen, two three-bedroom villas, and pool, restaurant, and bar. Rates start at $50 d and range up to $70 during the high season. Weekly rates are available. Near the beach at Josiah's Bay, **Stout's Vacation Apts.** (tel. 495-2628; Box 661, Road Town) has a kitchen, restaurant, babysitting service and other facilities. Rates start at $65 summer, $100 winter; weekly and monthly rentals are available. Under the same ownership, **Stout's Villa** has a kitchen, restaurant, and TV. Rates run from $475-$625 pw with a 40% off-season discount.

Elizabeth Beach: With two- and three-bedroom villas, the **Elizabeth Beach Resort** (tel. 495-5871, 800-225-4255; Box 534, East End) has kitchens, large patios, and use of a jeep. Rates range from $170 to a high season rate of $410. A 10% service charge is added. Also here, the **Elizabeth Beach Villa** (tel. 495-9458; Box 46, Virgin Gorda) has a/c three-bedrooms with tel., TV/VCR, stereo, kitchen, and washer/dryer. Rates are $1,500 pw summer and $2,200 pw winter.

East End: The Seabreeze Marina Hotel (tel. 495-1560, fax 495-1561; Box 59, Road Town) has seven rooms and includes the Sea Breeze Bar and Restaurant (an informal establishment which serves three meals), a bar, gift shop, pool, and boat charters. **Bing's Drop in Bar and Restaurant** provides the local fare which made it popular originally. Reservations are advised. At Tropic Island Yachts overlooking Maya Cove, **The Pelican Roost** serves three meals daily; dishes include BBQ chicken, fresh fish, and conch fritters. **The Tamarind Club** (tel. 495-2477, reservations suggested) is set by a pool. While sandwiches and Mexican dishes are served for lunch, dinner features cordon bleu cuisine.

Beef Island: Some maintain that this island's name stems from the period when it provided beef for buccaneers; others claim it comes from the cows a solitary old lady used to bring to pasture here. Yet another explanation maintains that Quakers raised indigo and cattle here during the 18th C. The island remained virtually uninhabited up until 1939 when a Polish sailor arrived in Trellis Bay. Returning after the war, he erected the Trellis Bay Club, a set of stone buildings. This must be one of the smallest islands ever to boast an international airport. A 300-ft. channel, which separates the island from Tortola, is spanned by the **Queen Elizabeth Bridge** which her Imperial Majesty herself dedicated in 1966. (Although a tollkeeper collects a 50¢ toll during the day, it's Scot-free at night.). Crossing the bridge, the road to the L leads to the remains of a cattle estate house. At the small airport, the **Airport Restaurant** (tel. 494-2323, dinner reservations required) serves breakfast, West Indian-style lunches, dinners, and snacks. Near the 3,600-ft. runway is **Long Beach**—suitable for a dip before departure or after arrival. Leave nesting terns in peace by entering the beach from behind rather than through the salt pond. **practicalities:** Marina Cay, a small, six-acre island nearby, was once the home of Rob White, author of *Our Virgin Isle*. Moorings are available here for $10. (For more information see listing below). Three luxurious villas with pool and Jacuzzi, **Rama Villas** (tel. 494-5972, fax 494-3782) are near beaches. The three-bedroom units offer kitchen, living-dining area and master bedroom with private Jacuzzi. A set of one- and two-bedroom houses, **Little Mountain Estate** (tel. 495-2538, 800-528-7750; Box 478, East End) has kitchens with microwaves, a pool, and a beach. Rates run from $500-$1,850 summer to $700-$2,200 winter. **Trellis Bay:** A well protected anchorage and one of the best windsurfing spots, Trellis Bay houses a number of restaurants and facilities. Here, **Beef Island Guest House** (tel. 495-2303, fax 495-1611, VHF Ch. 16; Box 2, West End) has four rooms priced at $65 summer and $100 winter; weekly rates are available, and a 10% service charge is added. Its **De Loose Mongoose Restaurant & Bar** serves sandwiches, salads, dolphin burgers, and like fare. **The Conch Shell Point Restaurant** (tel. 495-2285, VHF Ch. 16, reservations) serves prime ribs, seafood, and steak. **The Last Resort** (tel. 495-2520) is an English-style restaurant on the nearby islet of **Bellamy Cay** (named for the pirate Black Sam Bellamy); it's run by local one-man cabaret entertainer Tony Snell. Following a roast beef and fish dinner at 7:30 PM, Tony performs. Lunch is served from 12:30-2, and the gift shop is open all day. In Trellis Bay, a hotline can be used to call the ferry. If you visit the hill above the bay, you can see the remains of a house. This belonged to the Widow George, a devout 18th C Quaker, who—in retaliation for pirate raids on her cattle—is said to have invited them up to the house and poisoned them with punch. After she confessed her crime to Gov. Pickering, he made her head of the first Quaker meeting house, the remains of which can also be seen here. **shopping:** At Trellis Bay, **Flukes** sells maps, prints and hand-painted tee shirts. **The Pit Stop**, also here, sells batiks, ethnic jewelry, and other gifts. At Bellamy Cay, **The Last Resort** has a boutique. **The Trellis Bay Market** sells food items.

Great Camanoe: Near Bellamy Cay, this island has the ruins of a great house on it. It is also the home of **Porthole**, a fully equipped three-bedroom, three-bath hilltop villa at Privateers' Bay, which rents for $1,000 pw for six in summer and $1,400 pw in winter; add'l persons are $55 pp pw. Use of a jeep is included. For more information call (617) 484-0988 or write 35 Elizabeth Road, Belmont MA 02178.

Marina Cay: Located to the N of Beef Island (five min. by launch from Trellis Bay) and sandwiched between Great Camanoe and Scrub Island, this six-acre resort features two restaurants (beach BBQ on Fri.), boutique, and rooms with private balconies. Watersports (including scuba) abound here. It is notable as the setting for the book *Our Virgin Island* by Rob White; the film version starred Sidney Poitier and John Cassavetes. Rates (MAP) range from $140 on up to $250 d during the high season. Contact: Marina Cay, PO Box 76, Road Town; tel. (809) 494-2174, VHF Ch. 16.

From Road Town To West End

Bordering the Caribbean, the road was built only in the 1960s. The sea wall was wiped out by Hurricane Hugo and has been replaced by boulders. A red-and-white sign to the R a few miles out of town marks the site of **Pockwood Pond Fort**. Built by the Dutch in 1648, it was later rebuilt by the English Royal Engineers. Its nickname "The Dungeon" stems from the underground cell (with antique graffiti carved into its walls) which may have held prisoners. It was designed to protect island shipping. **Fort Recovery**, erected by the Dutch in 1660, is a small circular fort which now faces the seaside in the middle of a private resort complex. At Soper's Hole, a deep anchorage sheltered on the SW by Frenchman's Cay, stands the small village of **West End** with its houses painted in pastel shades, along with immigration and customs offices. Boats leave here regularly for St. John (See "From Tortola"). See the small mahogany framed sailboats under construction at The Woodworks.

West End Accommodation and Dining

If you're arriving or leaving here by boat, you can eat at the **Jolly Roger** or at informal **Zelma's Courtesy**, one of the two small restaurants across from the ferry. It sells sweet cakes, johnny cakes, fried fish, patés, lottery tickets, and newspapers (including *The New York Times*). The casual six-room **Jolly Roger Inn & Restaurant** (tel. 495-4559, fax 495-4184; Box 437, Road Town) charges from $40 on up; weekly rates are available. A set of cabins with a total of 12 beds, **Turtle Dove Lodge** (tel. 495-4430, fax 495-4070; Box 11, West End) is on Long Bay Hill. Rates are from $40 d winter; a 20% off-season discount is applied. No credit cards are accepted. A few minutes on foot from the pier at the West End, the **BVI Aquatic Hotel** (tel. 494-4541/2114; Box 605, West End) is a two-storey set of 14 units with kitchenettes. Prices start at $25 s, 40 d; weekly rates available. Its restaurant specializes in West Indian dishes, curries, and seafood. Across the harbor from West End, the 12-acre attractively landscaped **Frenchman's Cay Resort** (tel. 495-4844, fax 495-4056, 800-235-4077 in the US, 800-463-0199 in Canada; Box 1054, West End) offers one- and two-bedroom condos grouped in semi-circular fashion around a small beach. Each has a shaded terrace, kitchen, and living room; the two-bedrooms have two baths. Guests max out at 46, and there's daily maid service. A restaurant (**The Clubhouse** which serves West Indian and continental dishes and has Sun. beach BBQs) and tennis courts are available, as are a full range of watersports, horseback riding, and other activities and services. Rates start from $96 for a one-bedroom villa, up to $290 for a high season two-bedroom villa holding six. A 10% service charge is added. It's reached by a L turn as you approach from Road Town. **Soper's Hole Marina** (tel. 495-4553, fax 495-4560. Box 601, West End) here is a full service marina with a five-star dive center, charter yacht company, restaurant, and boutiques including **Island Treasures** (a fine art gallery and shop at Frenchman's Cay), **Zenaida's** (which features jewelry, bags, straw hats, sarongs, and artifacts), **Pusser's Company Store** (which is similar to the one in Road Town), **Sea Urchin** (beach ware), and the **Ample Hamper** (food, alcohol, and deli items). **Pusser's Landing** inside the store here serves fish and lobster as well as other dishes. **other nearby accommodation:** At West End, **The Towers** (tel. 495-4725, 775-6647; West End) has two bedrooms and a kitchen. Rates start at $45 summer and $65 winter; weekly rates are available. Also here, **Towers Villa** (tel. 494-3566; Box 99, Road Town) offers three-bedrooms with kitchen, TV, and stereo. Rates run $1,500 pw summer and $2,500 pw winter. At Frenchmans Cay, **Smith's Villa** (tel. 495-4312; Box 215, Road Town) has both efficiencies and luxury apartments. Rates run from $25 summer and $35 winter. **Villa Del Mar** (tel. 494-2726; Box 307, West End) has two bedrooms with kitchen for $80 pd; summer is 40% less. Near West End, **Rockview Holiday Homes** (tel. 494-2550, fax 494-5866; Box 263, Road Town) offers villas (with maid service) which hold from two to eight. Rates start at $840/pw for a two bedroom "standard" up to a high season high of $4,200/pw for a four-bedroom "luxury." A 10% service charge is added. At West End Point, **Pebble Beach Cottage** (tel. 494-6197, fax 494-5127; Box 188, Road Town)–a two-bedroom unit with one bath, dock, kitchen with microwave, and phone– rents for $200 pd or $1,400 pw. Near the junction of the roads heading to the N Coast and to Road Town, and built around a 17th-C. Dutch fort, **Fort Recovery Estate Beachfront Villa Resorts** (tel. 495-4467, 800-367-8455, fax 495-4036; Box 239, Road Town or Box 11156, St. Thomas 00801) offers a variety of villas which include maid service and a pricey commissary. Yoga and meditation classes, massages, babysitting service, water sports, and other services are available. A car is advised if staying here. Rates start at around $108 d for a two-person villa and range up to $572 d for a four-bedroom luxury house; continental breakfast is included. A 10% service charge is added, and each additional person is $20. At Pockwood Pond to the E of Fort Recovery, **Te-Hana Villa** (tel. 494-2446; Smiths Gore, Box 135, Road Town) is a two-bed-room/two-bath and one-bedroom/one bath house with a pool. Rates start at $1,700 pw summer and climb to $2,800-3,000 pw winter.

Sage Mountain

Take a left turn at Meyers, then drive a few miles on down the road, following the base of a hill containing communications towers, to reach the trailhead leading to the top of Mt. Sage (1,780 ft.). It's an attractive area, with the remains of old houses and orchids peeking out from the primeval forest. The highest mountain in the Virgin Islands, it has been declared a protected area covering 92 acres under the administration of the National Park Trust. From visiting the park, you can get an idea of how the island must have looked when the Europeans first arrived.

flora and fauna: The 15-20-ft.-tall fern trees are "living fossils," virtually unchanged since the Coal Age. The bulletwood trees can be identified by their straight trunk and thick brown cracked bark. West Indian mahogany, silk cotton, white cedar (the colony's national tree), and broadleaf mahogany trees are found here. Cocoplums (related to the rose), mountain guavas (small white blossoms and green edible fruit), and red palicoureas (small red flowers blooming on a red stalk with black fruit) are among the flowering plants found here. There are also a number of species of anthurium on the ground. Among the birds are Antillean crested hummingbirds, pearly-eyed thrashers, American kestrels, mockingbirds, and Caribbean martins.

touring the park: A beautiful view of Jost Van Dyke can be had from the parking lot. To enter, take the path straight ahead, unhook the gate, and follow the gravel path until you come to an immense strangler fig. On your return, take the loop trail, which branches off to your left and then returns to the main trail. Exit through the gate again and then unlatch and enter another gate to your right. This takes you through stands of mahogany to a fork in the path. One path marked "view" leads to a place where there would be a view if you were eight feet tall! The other path leads to the summit of Mt. Sage, which has no view at all. Take the "exit," along a grassy slope punctuated by tree ferns, back to your point of origin. Allow at least an hour for this part of your visit. You may also wish to explore the newer trails. There are now two loop trails, a second trail to the peak, and two additional trails from the gate to the fig tree.

accommodation: Mount Sage Villas (tel. 495-9567; Box 821, Road Town) has two-bedroom/two-bath villas with kitchen, living room, TV, phone, and laundry. Horseback riding is available. At Chalwell to the E of the junction of Sage Mountain Rd. with Ridge Road, **Shannon House** is a luxurious six-bedroom, seven-bath villa with pool and gardener. Rates are available on request. Write c/o Imago Recording Company, 152 W 57th St., NY, NY 10019 or call (212) 554-7918.

Brewers Bay

A steep and winding road from Road Town leads over the hills and down to this secluded campground. From the top of the road

Sugar mill ruins, northwest St. Croix

Anegada

The Baths, Virgin Gorda

leading down, there's a majestic view of Jost Van Dyke with Little Jost and Sandy Cay in the background. Dark reefs shine through the crystal-clear water. The road leads down to a rustic campsite after passing by the ruins of an old sugar oven. Above the bay along the way up to Ridge Rd. are the remains of an old sugar mill, the only extant example on the island, which lies within Mt. Healthy National Park, a beautiful picnic area.

accommodations: Run by Noel Callwood, **Brewers Bay Campground** only starts to fill around mid-Dec.; between April and then you'll have the place virtually to yourself. It's as close to the life of Robinson Crusoe as you can imagine. Good snorkeling out on the reefs, and a good place to base yourself for island walks. Bare sites below the coconut trees rent out for $7 per night. Already erected tents rent out for $20 for two (extra persons $2.50.) Showers are available; a terrace near the office has chairs and tables. Two two-bedroom cottages next to the beach at Brewers Bay, **Ronneville Cottages** (tel. 494-2260/3337) offer kitchens, living/dining areas, terraces, TV, and maid services. Rates run from $400-450 pw summer to $650-700 pw winter for two to four persons. Overlooking Brewers Bay, **Diamond Apartment** (tel. 494-2593, eve. 494-3164)–a one-bedroom with living room, dining room, and kitchen as well as TV–rents for $350 d pw during the summer and $500 d pw during the winter. At Luck Hill off Brewers Bay Rd. West, **Hawks View** (tel. 494-2550, fax 494-5866; Box 263, Road Town) is a deluxe fully equipped one-bedroom with TV/VCR, phone, and stereo. It rents for $1,050 pw during the winter with a 30% discount during the summer. Set at Little Bay near Mt. Healthy on the North Shore, **Over the Hill** (tel. 496-0253) is a set of secluded beachside guest houses. Rates are $60 for a room, $800-$1,000 pw for a house, and the off-season discount is 40%. For more information write the Bakewell Family,12 Magnolia, St. Louis, MO 63124 or call (800) 952-9338. **food:** Expensive food is sold at the commissary. Bring your own from town or St. Thomas. There's a sandwich and refreshment bar, but it's closed off-season. Coconuts drop at your feet; bring along your own machete to hack them open.

Cane Garden Bay

Home to one of the island's most beautiful beaches, Cane Garden– a palm-tree-lined white crescent–should by all rights be renamed Rhymer's Bay because James E. Rhymer and family have so strik-

ingly transformed the Bay's landscape. At the rear of his Cane Garden Bay Hotel is Rhymer's Beauty Salon and Laundromat. Pink **Rhymer's Beach Bar and Restaurant**, in front of the hotel, has beach chairs and public showers ($2). It's open for three meals daily. The local store is next to the restaurant and under the hotel. Nephew Quito has built his **Gazebo** to the far right. Meals here are varied and range from burgers and rotis for lunch to a fish fry on Fri. The newest entry is Myett's a restaurant and boutique run by Kareem "Jabbar" Rhymer and his brother, Leon "Sandman" Rhymer. Kareem–who lived, studied, and worked for 14 years in San Francisco–has fulfilled a long-held dream in opening this facility. Lying across a dingy moat with a tuckered out old horse that sleeps standing up, **Callwood's Distillery**, run by the Callwood sons, has some of the most potent rum in the Caribbean. Fifths, quarts, and half gallons are available. This is one of the three functioning distilleries left on the island. (The others are at Baughers Bay and at Meyers.) For the sunset, ascend to Soldier's Hill above. Between Cane Garden Bay and Carrot Bay to the SW, the overgrown ruins of St. Michael's Church lie atop Windy Hill. The main road leads on to Great Carrot Bay and beyond. Set on Windy Hill above Carrot Bay along the N coast, **Heritage Villas** (tel. 800-642-6260, fax 494-5842; Box 2019, Road Town) offers three two-bedroom and six one-bedroom units with maid service, bar, and complimentary coffee and tea. The management prides itself on catering to guests. Rates run from $65 during the summer with a winter high of $160 or $1,120 pw. At Carrot Bay, the **North Shore**

Shell Museum shows shells, shell crafted work, and also shows other examples of island culture.

accommodations: The 27-rm. **Cane Garden Bay Beach Hotel** (tel. 495-4639, fax 495-4820) has clean and comfortable rooms with daily maid service and private balconies. Some rooms have a/c, tel., and TV. Attractive murals by Jerome Brown grace the hallways. Rates start at $35-45 off-season. Complete water sports are available on the premises. Located on the beach, **Clyne's Beach Suites** (tel. 442-2888, 445-4543) provides five deluxe one-bedrooms with kitchenettes; some have a/c. Winter rates are $100-$110 with weekly rates available. Summer rates are 40% lower. Set in a converted 300-yr.-old sugar factory above Cane Garden Bay, **Ole Works Inn** (tel. 495-4837) offers eight a/c rooms with bath, refrigerator, TV, patios, and set in the midst of coconut groves. Rates start at $60 and range up to $125 during the winter season; weekly rates are available. A luxury house set right on the beach, the **Cane Garden "On the Beach" House** has three bedrooms with TV, phone, and other amenities. It rents for $1,800-$2,400 pw with a 40% reduction during the summer season. For more information call (212) 777-9127, fax (212) 995-5989, or write 465 W. Broadway, NY, NY. **Harbour View Guest House** (tel. 495-4549; Box 547, Cane Garden Bay) offers 15 rooms with kitchen and babysitting available. Rates from $100-$240 pw during the summer and $120-$420 pw during the winter. A set of one-bedrooms, **Mongoose Apartments** (tel. 495-4421; Box 581, Cane Garden Bay) rent for $420 pw summer and $560 pw winter; a 10% discount is accorded seniors. **Arundel Villa** (tel. 494-2375) offers three elegant four-bedroom homes which can hold up to six. Rooms have a phone and kitchen, and there's a pool and an ocean view. Rates are available upon request. Call 800-862-7863 or write 3826 Van Ness St., NW, Washington, DC 20016. Another set of housekeeping cottages, **Cane Garden Bay Cottages**, have TV, kitchen, and babysitting service. Rates are from $700-800 with a 40% off-season discount applied. For more information call (516) 567-5204 or write Box 362, Sayville, NY 11782. Overlooking Cane Garden Bay, **The Generation Villa** is deluxe and fully equipped. An efficiency is also available from the owners. Call (914) 624-0531 or write Donald Martin, 2 Erin Lane, Chestnut Ridge, NY 10977. Rates run from $350-$600 pw during the summer to $450-$850 during the winter. **Sunset Vacation Apartments** (tel. 495-4315; Cane Garden Bay PO) offers four one-bedroom apartments with kitchens. Rates run from $50 d summer and $60 d winter; weekly rates are available. The **Indigo Beach House** has a phone and rents from $1,800-$2,000 pw during the winter with a 30% reduction during the summer. Call (505) 982-5014 or write James Havard, Box 2945, Santa Fe, NM 87504. **The Elm** (tel./fax 494-6455; Box 96, Road Town) offers five a/c units which sleep four. Kitchenettes and maid service are provided. Each unit has a porch or balcony. They rent for $135 and $150 winter with a 40% discount during the summer.

food: Rhymer's Beach Bar & Restaurant has breakfast specials, hamburgers, steak, chicken, and seafood specialties. **Quito's** has comparable fare and prices. The newest entry is **Thee Wedding**. Further down the road are **Columbus Sunset Bar & Variety Store** which has meals (local food) for around $6. **Callwood's Superette**, just a little farther on, has prices and stock similar to Rhymer's Store. **Cline's Bakery**, across the main drag from the hotel, sells a limited variety of baked goods. **entertainment:** Local youths delight in parking in front of the gas station and jacking up the volume on their car stereos to as high a level as possible. At his **Gazebo** on the beach, Quito Rhymer sings his island folk tunes most evenings with selections by the likes of Bob Marley, Jimmy Cliff, and Jimmy Buffet. Quito, who traveled widely in the US before settling down back home in the BVI, has also penned his own tunes like "All God's Children Got Soul" and "My Daddy's Calloused Hands." **events:** Sponsored by the Cedar School, a big **Mother's Day Music Festival** is held at Thee Wedding (tel. 495-4022) every Mother's Day in Cane Garden Bay. A **Bacardi Rum Beach Party** is held here (tel. 495-4639 for info) in conjunction with Territory Day on July 1.

Heading West From Cane Garden Bay

A rough road leads on to Ballast Bay and then the Great and Little Carrot Bays. Across from the Isabella Morris Primary School and E of Sugar Mill is the home of **Mrs. Scatliffe** (tel. 495-4556) who serves dinner ($15-22; reservations essential) made with garden grown vegetables from 7 PM nightly. After dinner, she and her family will sometimes entertain guests with fungi music. Down the road are **Clem's By the Pier** which has cassava cakes, local confections, and sandwiches. Then you reach the Seventh Day Adventist Church; Dawson's Variety Store; Tripple "A" Bar; and Jule's Place. The latter is a former BVI Festival booth. It's then another climb and descent to Little Apple Bay. **The Cliff Houses** (tel. 495-4727, fax 495-4958; Box 3103, Road Town) offer house-keeping cottages with kitchenettes which run from $700-$3,000 d pw with a summer discount of 40%. Accommodation under the same management in other locations (mostly situated on the beach)—ranging from Soper's Hole to overlooking Long Bay–range in price from $350/wk up to $1,900 pw for six during the winter. Also here is **Daiquiri House** (tel. 495-4315) which offers a two-bedrooms with great views, phone, and babysitting service at rates ranging from $475 pw to a winter season high of $995 pw. For more information call (609) 624-0052 or write 8 Dana Ave., Ocean City, NJ 08230. **The Apple**, a small restaurant here, specializes in seafood dishes. Coconut chips and conch fritters are served during happy hour. Its sports bar has a cable TV. Reservations (tel. 495-4437) are essential. Certainly the most unusual structure on the entire island (and perhaps in the entire Caribbean), **The Bomba Shack** is the closest thing Tortola has to a modern art museum. With its graffiti, hanging painting of a psychedelic mushroom, suspended life jacket, deteriorated Canon camera body, rusted blender base, and more, Bomba is one pretty explosive little bar! **Cetta's Bar & Restaurant**, down the road, has plates of local food for $5. **Cameron's Place** has a Bar-B-Q and a live steel band on Thursdays from 7 PM; a fish fry is held here on Saturday nights from 8.

Set on the NW coast E of Sebastian's and Long Bay at Little Apple Bay, the intimate **Sugar Mill Hotel** (tel. 495-4355, 800-462-8834, fax 495-4696; Box 425, Road Town) is one of the island's most attractive resorts, and is centered around the ruins of a ruined sugar mill. It has 18 bedrooms with kitchenettes and balconies, one deluxe villa with private garden, a/c in bedrooms, cable TV, and a complete kitchen; and two standard twin accommodations with balcony and wet bar. Its boutique sells Haitian paintings, *The New York Times* ($3), stuffed bears ($65 for a large one), and Janet Rutnik-designed tee shirts ($18 each). Facilities include a pool and a highly-rated restaurant. Lunch and an a la carte dinner is served at the "Islands" beach bar. "Honeymoon" and "Adventure" pack-ages are available. Rates start at $110 s, $120 d and range up to $475 for a two-bedroom villa during the winter. A 10% service charge is added. In Britain contact BVI Holidays (Wingjet) at 0279-506747 or fax 0279-506616. At Little Apple Bay, **Bananas on the Beach** (tel. 495-4318, fax 495-4299; Box 2, West End) has house-keeping villas along with a beach bar and babysitting service.

Rates are $420 pw summer and $700 pw winter. At Little Apple Bay, **Casa Caribe** (tel. 494-3186; c/o Island Real Estate, Box 677, Road Town) rents two deluxe fully-equipped waterfront villas. Rates are $800 pw summer and $1,125 pw winter for two to four persons.

Long Bay has an absolutely gorgeous beach panorama. A small resort set on 50 acres, the **Long Bay Beach Resort** (tel. 495-4242; Box 433, Road Town) offers 62 hillside rooms and studios plus cabanas along the beach. Rooms include a/c, tel., refrigerator, and TV. The facility centers around a "club" which has a pool and two restaurants: The **Beach Restaurant** is built on the ruins of a two-century-old rum distillery; the other is the more formal **Garden Restaurant**. Vegetarian food is available, and dietary preferences can be catered to. One of the best beaches is here, as is the world's smallest non-miniature golf course. No-see-ums proliferate at dusk. Road Town is a half-hour drive and the airport about an hour. Rates run from $85 s, $170 d for oceanview rooms up to $340 d for beachfront deluxe rooms during the winter season. Packages run from $399 pp for three nights to $1,909 pp for 14 nights on land and sea or $1,999 for seven nights for a family of four. All packages differ but may include frills such as meals, diving, sailing, and car rentals. Call 800-729-9599, or write Island Destinations, Box 284, Larchmont, NY 10538; call 0800 898379 in the UK. A 15-min. drive from town in Apple Bay, **Sebastian's On the Beach** (tel. 495-4212, fax 495-4466, 800-336-4870; Box 441, Road Town) is at the junction of a steep road leading up and down to the West End side of the island. In order of increasing quality, rooms are tropical yard units (set 150 ft. from the beach), four rear units or two inn units, and eight beachfront rooms with balcony or porch. Rooms have fans and refrigerators. Watersports and a restaurant (seafood and West Indian) are available. Rates start at $55 s, $65 d and head up to $170 s, $180 d for beachfront rooms during the winter. MAP is $35 additional, and a 10% service charge (15% if on MAP) is included. A variety of packages are available. Beyond Sebastian's the main road deteriorates and leads past Long Bay to Belmont and then on to secluded Smuggler's Cove. A set of deluxe and fully equipped one- and two-bedroom apartments at with kitchen, living and dining area, and patio, **Grape Tree Vacation Rentals** (tel. 495-4229; Box 435, Road Town) also have cable TV. Rates run from $460 pw during the summer to a winter high of $1,200 pw for the best units. It's right on Long Bay Beach. At Long Bay, deluxe and fully equipped **Sun-**

set View Vacation Rental (tel. 494-4315; 494-3142; Box 612, Tortola) rents for $400 pw summer and $675 pw winter. It has cable TV. At Long Bay, **Amberjack House** offers a luxurious four-bedroom villa which holds up to six. It has a kitchen equipped with a microwave, a phone, TV, and a pool. It rents for $1,750 pw during the low season and $3,500 pw during the high. For more information call (617) 868-5340, fax (617) 661-4580, or write 17 Berkeley St., Cambridge, MA 02138. **nearby accommodation:** Featuring two one-bedroom units, **Ocean View Delight Apts.** (tel. 495-4731; Box 203, Road Town) are set in the hills above Long Bay, about 15 min. from West End and a half hour from Road Town. Units have kitchen and fan with maid, cook, and babysitting service available along with special packages. Winter rates are $100 s or d with reductions for weekly and monthly rentals and a 30% off-season discount. Overlooking Long Bay, the five-bedroom **Sunset House** (tel. 494-2550, fax 494-5866, Box 263, Road Town) is a Spanish-Mediterranean style villa with five baths, and Jacuzzi. Summer rates are from $3,675 pw. Right along the coast, **Sunset Villa** is under the same management. It can hold up to four comfortably. Right by the sea, it has two floors, each with bedroom, bath and veranda. There are two kitchens, fan, and daily maid service. Rates for Sunset Villa (without meals) start at $2,975/wk. for two to four. At Belmont Estates to the N of the West End, **Equinox House** (tel. 494-2550) offers luxurious three-bedrooms with a pool which rent for $1,750 pw during the summer and $2,730 pw during the winter. A service charge is applied. For more information call (212) 242-8413 or write Charles Baily, 42 King St., NY, NY 10014. In the cove of the same name, **Smugglers Cove Beach Resort** (tel. 495-2434; Box 4, West End) has four rooms with solar-powered hot water, ceiling fans, kitchens and a beach with offshore snorkeling. Much of the action for the NBC TV movie *The Old Man and the Sea* was filmed here in 1989. Rates start at $63 s, $68 d.

From Tortola

There is a $5 international departure tax (air) or $4 (sea). Times listed here are current at the time of publication; consult the latest issue of *The Welcome* for current departure times.

for Peter Island: A ferry leaves Caribbean Sailing Yachts (CSY) Dock–named after the now-bankrupt chartering company–at 7,

8:30, 10, 2, 3:30, 5:30, 6:30, and 11. It returns at 8, 9, noon, 2:30, 4:30, 6, 10, and 11:30.

for Virgin Gorda: *Speedy's Fantasy/Speedy's Delight* (tel. 495-5240/5235) departs from Road Town at 9, 1:30, and 4:30 on Mon. to Fri., on Tues. and Thurs. at 10:10 and 6:15, and on Sun. at 9 and 5:15. Smith's Ferry Services (tel. 494-4430/2355, 495-4495) leaves from Road Town on Mon. to Sat. at 7, 9, and 12:30; and on Sun. at 8:30 and 12:30. **from Beef Island:** The *North Sound Express* (NSX, tel. 495-2271, 494-2746) runs from Beef Island to the North Sound daily at 6:30, 10:30, 3:30, and 5:30 (with an add'l 7:15 PM run for connecting airline passengers only) for $18 OW. Bus service runs between Pusser's Store (except for the 6:30 AM and 7:15 PM departures). Virgin Gorda Ferry Service (tel. 495-5240/5542) runs from Beef Island to The Valley daily at 12:15 , 3:15, 5:15, and 7 PM. **by air:** Atlantic Air BVI (tel. 495-2000) flies to Virgin Gorda daily. Four Star Aviation also flies daily.

for Jost Van Dyke: The Jost Van Dyke Ferry Service (tel. 494-2997) leaves West End at 7:30, 9:45, 1:30, and 4 on Mon to Sat. and at 9:30, 1:30 and 4 on Sun. Reel World (tel. 494-9277) leaves West End at 9:30, 1, and 4:15.

for Anegada: Gorda Aero Services (tel. 495-2271) flies on Mon., Wed. and Fri. (lv. 8:20, return 5:20) for approximately $54 RT.

for St. Thomas: Four Star Aviation flies daily. Smith's Ferry Services (tel. 495-4617) departs Road Town from Mon. to Fri. at 6:15 AM, on Sat. at 6:15 and 8:45, and on Sun. at 3:30; it runs from the West End on Mon. to Fri. at 7 and 10 with an add'l trip at 3 on Wed.; on Sat at 7, 10, and 2:30; and on Sun. at 9:15 and 4. *Native Son* (tel. 495-4617) leaves Road Town from Mon. to Fri. at 6:15 AM with an add'l trip on Wed. at 2:15; and on Mon. to Fri. from the West End at 7 and 10 with an add'l trip at 3 on Wed.; on Sat at 7, 10, 2:30, and 5:45; and on Sun. at 9:30 and 4. An add'l trip runs daily from the West End (via Cruz Bay and Red Hook) at 8:30, 12:30, and 4.

for St. John and Red Hook, St. Thomas: From the West End, Smith's Ferry Services (tel. 495-4617; $16 OW, $28 RT, 30 min.) heads out for Cruz Bay and on to Red Hook, St. Thomas. Ferries leave daily at 8:20, 12:20, and 4. Inter-Island Boat Services (tel. 495-4166) runs from West End to Cruz Bay from Mon. to Sat. at

9:15, 12:15, and 4:15, with an add'l trip on Fri. at 5:30; and on Sun. at 9:15, 12:15, and 5:15.

for St. Croix: Sunaire (tel. 495-2480) flies to St. Thomas where you can connect for St. Croix.

for San Juan, Puerto Rico: Sunaire Express (tel. 495-2480) flies daily as do American Eagle and Atlantic Air BVI (tel. 495-2000; around $70 RT).

for the southern Caribbean: LIAT (an acronym some maintain stands for "Leave At Any Time") flies daily to Antigua, St. Kitts, St. Lucia, St. Maarten and Dominica.

Jost Van Dyke

Less than four miles N of St. John, Jost Van Dyke seems to be more American than British in character. Named after a Dutch pirate, this long, narrow island has hills running like a camel's humps from head to tail. The main town is **Great Harbour** (pop. 150) where customs, facilities, school, and a church are located. There are few vehicles, and no paved roads or airports. There are just two phones. You must get around by foot or water taxi. To the W of Great Harbour is **White Bay**, which contains a long white sand beach. Unlike Great and Little Harbour, which are well protected and calm anchorages, White Bay may be subject to winter swells. **getting there:** Jost Van Dyke can only be reached by private boat (many yachts run day trips here) or by the *Mona Queen* (tel. 776-6597/6282 in the USVI), which runs from Red Hook, St. Thomas ($28 RT) and St. John ($31 RT) on Fri., Sat., and Sun. at 8 and 2 (8:30 and 2:20 from Cruz Bay) and also on Fri. and Sun. only at 5:15 PM (5:40 from Cruz Bay).

Practicalities

Good snorkeling here. On the beach at Great Harbour, **Foxy's** (tel. 495-9258; dinner reservations by 5 PM) is run by calypsonian Filiciano "Foxy" Callwood and is the island's oldest and most famous watering hole. Dinner features "Calypso Caribbean Lob-

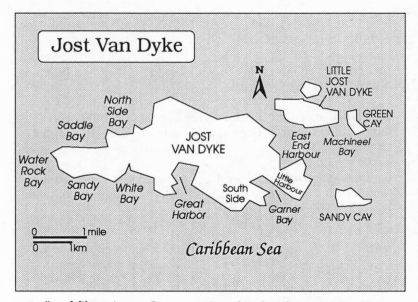

Jost Van Dyke

ster" and filet mignon. Large parties take place here on New Year's Eve, St. Patrick's Day, April Fool's Day, Memorial Day, during Labour Day's Wooden Boat Race, and at Halloween. Foxy is also a talented guitarist and a conservationist who is working to preserve the island as it is. Set at the other end of the harbor, **Rudy's Bar and Restaurant** is owned by Rudy George (see above) who puts on a barbecue pig roast every Tues. and Sat. night in season. Prices in the restaurant are in the $10-$20 range. A reggae/calypso band plays. The proximate **Rudy's Mariner Inn** (tel. 495-9282, 775-3558, VHF Ch. 16) has three rooms with ocean views, terraces, and kitchenettes. Rates range from $55 to a winter high of $220. Between the two are a number of places including **Ali Baba's** (casual with three meals and happy hour), and **Happy Laury's** (a restaurant serving three meals including West Indian dinners; there's a pig roast and BBQ Fri. night in season). **The Paradise Club** (tel. 495-9267) offers sandwiches and burgers for lunch and specials including a pig roast on Wed. night; you can pick your own lobster from the holding tank. Dishes vary from Barbados flying fish sandwiches to grilled mahi mahi to sherried shrimp. **Little Harbour:** A path leads from the hill above Great Harbour and down eastward to Little Harbour, where you'll find a set of eateries and accommodations. **Sidney's Peace and Love** (tel. 495-9271) offers three meals and features seafood. **Harris' Place** is open for three meals and happy hour daily. **Abe's By the Sea Vacation Apart-**

ment (tel. 495-9329, fax 495-9529) offers a three-bedroom unit with kitchen for $75. Supplemented by a grocery store, Abe's restaurant offers seafood chicken, and spare ribs. During the tourist season, a pig is roasted on Wed. eve. Run by Harris Jones's daughter Cynthia, **Tula's N & N Campground**, Little Harbour, has both bare and tent sites available. Bare sites go for $15 for three people during the high season. Tents are $25-35 per couple during the winter and reduced to $10/tent and $4 pp during the off-season. For more information write General Delivery, West End PO, Tortola; tel. (809) 495-9566. Set on the island's E end farther on, **Sandy Ground** (tel. 494-3391, fax 495-9379) offers eight villas with terra-cotta floors as well as an 800-ft. beach. Prices start at $780/wk. Write Box 594, West End, Tortola. From Sandy Ground it's possible to hike along the island's E edge, skirting mangroves and ruins facing Jost Van Dyke. Offshore are Green Cay (popularly known as "Snake Island") and other cays. It's possible to swim or wade across to reach these. Continuing, the trail narrows and passes above steep bluffs, from which it's possible to spot sea turtles. It's dangerous to climb down to the beaches along this stretch. It's possible to return to Great Harbour by hiking through thick brush and over several ridges. **White Bay practicalities:** Set to the W, this bay can be reached on foot or by boat. Opened in 1993, **White Bay Campground** has both equipped tents and bare sites, a bar and restaurant, and tours. Call Ivan Chinnery or Gertrude Coakley at 495-9312. On a hill overlooking White Bay, **The Sandcastle** (tel. 771-1611, fax 775-3590) has four beach villas ranging in price from $175 FAP to $295 FAP during the high season. There's a restaurant, beach bar, and windsurfing rentals. Write 6501 Red Hook Plaza, Ste. 201, USVI 00802-1306. Its informal restaurant (reservations required) serves dishes such as stuffed grouper and Duck a l'Orange. The Soggy Bottom Bar is also here. **entertainment:** Check out Foxy Tamarind's calypso ballads. Rudy's has live entertainment on Tuesday evenings. **events:** Vintage wooden vessels from throughout the Virgins gather each and every Labor Day for Foxy's Wooden Boat Race.

from Jost Van Dyke: The Jost Van Dyke Ferry Service (tel. 494-2997) leaves for the West End at 8:30, 11, 3, and 5 on Mon. to Sat. and at 11, 3 and 5 on Sun. Reel World (tel. 494-9277) leaves for the West End at 7:15, 12, and 3 daily. (Tours and charters are available). **for the USVI:** St. John Transportation services has a ferry to Cruz

Bay, St. John and Red Hook, St. Thomas at 9:15, 3:15, and 9:15 on Fri. and Sun. and on Sat. at 9:15 and 3:15.

Virgin Gorda

The third largest but second most important of the BVI is Virgin Gorda It was named the "fat virgin" by the Spanish because its mountainous profile, when approached by boat from the S, is reminiscent of a woman lying on her back. Eight square miles in area, its 10-mile length naturally divides itself into two parts. While the NE is mountainous, the SE is flat. All lands above 1,000 ft. are part of the National Park; the highest point, Gorda Peak, is 1,370 ft. At the top, accessible by road, is an observation tower. The trail head is off the main road on the way from Gun Creek to Spanish Town. The island is bordered by splendid beaches, strewn with large boulders, and characterized by the ubiquitous bleating goat. **Spanish Town**, more a settlement than a town, is a pretty but otherwise totally unremarkable place. Modern amenities (roads, phones, electricity) have come here only recently. One of the island's peculiarities is a rare lizard, the Virgin Gorda gecko, which measures only 1/2 to 3/4 of an inch and resides in the boulders. The common or tree iguana is found only at Biras Creek here and on Peter Island.

history: During the late 1600s, while ownership of Tortola was disputed between the English and Dutch, Puerto Rican Spaniards occasionally raided settlements here. The original seat of the colonial government was located at Spanish Town around 1710. Although population exceeded 7,500 in the early 17th C, currently only 1,443 people live on Virgin Gorda. Population declined after the introduction of the sugar beet to Europe and the emancipation of slaves in 1834. In modern times, the island has grown because of Laurance Rockefeller's personal interest in it. In the early 1950s, the island had no electricity, telephones, sewers, doctor, paved road, or adequate educational facilities. Only when construction at Little Dix Bay began in the 1960s did the island begin to enter modern times. Because the resort required a massive influx of capital in order to create the needed infrastructure, the project was dubbed "the British Virgin Islands' Red Cross." In 1989, Fanta spared no expense in shooting a 30-second spot underwater near Devils Bay. Virgin Gorda has come a long way!

getting there: Ferries run from St. Thomas, St. John, and Tortola. For specifics check the "from" sections under the particular islands concerned. **by air:** Sunaire flies daily from St. Croix and St. Thomas via Beef Island.

beaches: There are 16 of them–enough for a week's exploring. Although Little Dix and Biras Creek have been developed, Savana and Pond are excellent for shell hunting. Other beaches include Spring Bay Beach near The Baths, Berchers Bay Beach, St. Thomas Bay Beach, Pond Bay Beach, Mahoe Bay Beach, Devil's Bay Beach, Leverick Bay Beach, and North Sound's Deep Bay Beach.

The Baths and vicinity: The premier tourist site in the British Virgin Islands, this magnificent beach area is located at the S tip of the island. The Baths are truly the island's calling card. Here, huge granite boulders the size of houses topple over one another above underlying grottos of clear turquoise water. Enter the dim caverns to bathe. Light enters between the cracks, giving each grotto a different atmosphere, which changes continually as the tide pounds in and out. You have to navigate a series of stairwalks and a ropewalk through the grottos to get from one side to another. These granite boulders probably were born during the Tertiary Period some 70 million years ago. Magma (molten rock) formed huge sections of granite which contained large quantities of feld-spar and quartz. Some 15-25 million years ago, the granite was exposed through faulting and uplifiting of the sea floor and squared boulders were exposed. Over the course of millions of years, they eroded, broke and fell on top of each other, and became rounded. One important source of erosion was rainfall, which reacts with carbon dioxide as it falls to form a weak carbonic acid. This reacts with the feldspar and granite but not the quartz. The rough spots on the flaking area are caused by the quartz particles, which are exposed yet still held in place by the surrounding rock. The hollows in the boulders were formed by easterly and south-erly winds which accelerate the erosion on these rock faces. For more information see Dr. Charles A. Ratte's booklet *The Story of the Boulders*. **orientation: The Poor Man's Bar** here sells drinks, bur-gers, and tee shirts. As its entrepreneurial owner charges $1.25 for water and the other prices are comparable, he certainly won't

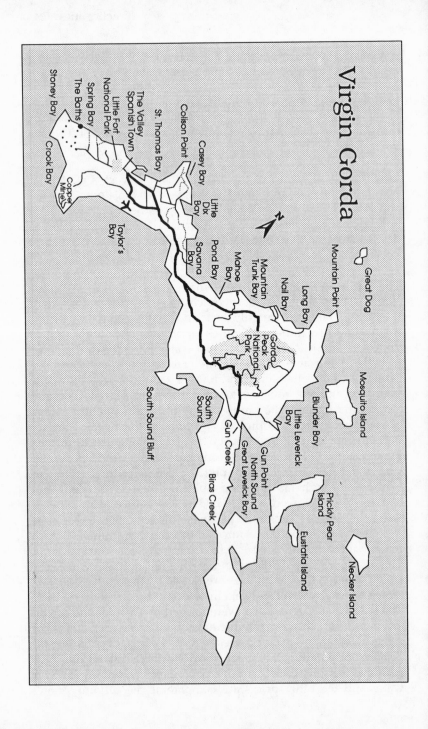

Virgin Gorda

remain impoverished for long. The area offshore to the L has fine snorkeling. Crouch and waddle to enter the Baths. Some of the boulders resemble animals such as a lion and a whale. In the area surrounding the Baths, you can find pitch apple, frangipani, white cedar and turpentine trees as well as different species of cactus, wild tamarind, box briar, and wild sage. A 15-min. walk from The Baths to the S brings you to 58-acre **Devil's Bay National Park**, set around a secluded coral sand beach; the trail through the boulders from The Baths terminates here. The 36 acres of **Little Fort National Park**, just S of the Yacht Harbour, comprise boulder-strewn forest and are a wildlife sanctuary. Once the site of a Spanish fortress, some masonry walls (including the remains of the "Powder House") still stand on the hillside. Set between Little Fort and The Baths, **Spring Bay** and **The Crawl** is a recreational beach area comprising 5.5 acres. There's good snorkeling off of its small but beautiful boulder-covered beach, and it's the place to go when the cruise ships are in port and hordes of taxis are parked at The Baths. It's possible (albeit difficult) to clamber over the rocks back and forth between the two. There's no water here so–as is true throughout the area–bring your own!

other sights: Nearby at **Copper Mine Point** are the rather undistinguished ruins of a copper mine which was first mined by Spaniards from Puerto Rico during the 16th century. Its last spate of operation, under the control of Cornish miners, was from 1838-67. The ruins of the chimney, boiler house, a large cistern, and mine shaft entrances can still be found here. **Nail Bay**, on the E coast, contains an 18th C ruined stone, coral, and brick sugar mill. The 265-acre area surrounding **Virgin Gorda Peak** has become a National Park with a self-guiding nature trail leading to a lookout point which joins with a paved road leading to Little Dix Bay. It has been extensively reforested with mahogany. Under the auspices of the North Sound Heritage Project, hiking trails are also under development at North Sound. These trails will follow the originals which ran up hills and to distant flatlands during the sugar era.

dive sites near Virgin Gorda: Nearest and most accessible is "The Blinders." Located near The Baths, it is a mirror image of them–30 ft. underwater. Virgin Gorda shares some of the same dive sites as Tortola, such as "Alice in Wonderland" and *The Rhone*. Other Virgin Gorda sites include "Wall to Wall", "the Chimney", "Oil Nut Bay", "Van Ryan's Rock," "Two Ray Bay," "Tiger Mountain," and

"Tow Rock." The last is a pinnacle which rises from 70 ft. to 15 ft. below the water's surface.

yacht marinas: The **Virgin Gorda Yacht Harbour** (tel. 555-5555, fax 495-5706; Box 1805, Virgin Gorda), St. Thomas Bay, operated by the Little Dix Bay Hotel Corporation, gives the first hour of moorings for free and charges $3 ph thereafter with a 60¢ per foot daily charge ($18 minimum). Dockage is available for 100 yachts of up to 120 ft. Complete facilities including showers are available. The **Bitter End Yacht Club & Resort** (tel. 494-2746; Box 46, Virgin Gorda) can hold 18 yachts of up to 100 ft. There are also 100 moorings and complete facilities. **Biras Creek Estate** (tel. 495-3555; Box 54, Virgin Gorda), North Sound, has a marine railway for do-it-yourself repairs. It can hold ten yachts of up to 60 ft.

yacht charters and sailing schools: At North Sound, the Bitter End Yacht Club & Resort (tel. 494-2746; Box 46, Virgin Gorda) has a wide range of boats as well as instruction in sailing and windsurfing at the **Nick Trotter Sailing School** (tel. 494-2745) here. Operating out of the Yacht Harbour, the **Misty Isle Yacht Charters** (tel. 495-5643, fax 495-5300; Box 1118, Virgin Gorda) and **Euphoric Cruises** (tel. 495-5542; Box 55, Virgin Gorda) offer charters; day and other trips are available. At Biras Creek Marina in North Sound, **Virgin Gorda Villa Rentals Watersports** (tel. 495-7376; Box 63, Virgin Gorda) offers instruction in water skiing and other sports as well as dinghy rental by the day or week.

Spanish Town/The Valley accommodation: Olde Yarde Inn (tel. 495-5544; Box 26, Virgin Gorda) is near the yacht harbor. It has a large library with a TV/VCR and piano. Rates run from $85 to $170 (breakfast included) with a winter season high of $220 and a discount for a stay of 14 days or more. In The Valley and near the Yacht Harbour, 20-room **Fischers Cove Beach Hotel** (tel. 495-5252/5253, fax 495-5820; Box 60, Virgin Gorda) is a small beachfront cottage colony-style resort. Offering a menu written on sea grape leaves, its restaurant **The Water's Edge** is well known. Also here is the **Rum Barrel Bar**. Rooms are studio cottages (standard and beachfront), efficiency cottages (family-sized with kitchenette and refrigerator, coffee maker, and microwave), and hotel rooms (equipped with refrigerator and coffee maker). Rates start at $90 for hotel rooms and range to $265 for an efficiency cottage during the high season. MAP is $40 pp add'l. There's also a 10% service

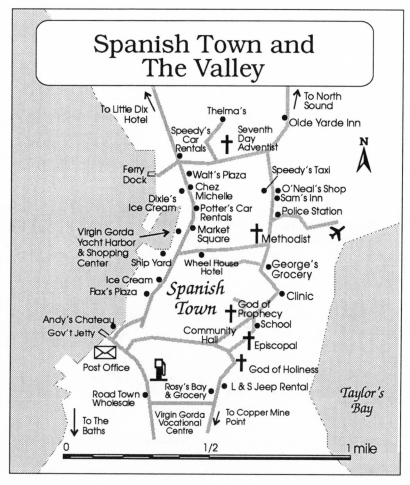

Spanish Town and The Valley

To Little Dix Hotel
Thelma's
To North Sound
Olde Yarde Inn
Speedy's Car Rentals
Seventh Day Adventist
N
Speedy's Taxi
Ferry Dock
Walt's Plaza
Chez Michelle
Dixie's Ice Cream
Potter's Car Rentals
O'Neal's Shop
Sam's Inn
Police Station
Virgin Gorda Yacht Harbor & Shopping Center
Ship Yard
Market Square
Methodist
Wheel House Hotel
George's Grocery
Ice Cream
Flax's Plaza
Spanish Town
Clinic
Andy's Chateau
Gov't Jetty
God of Prophecy
School
Community Hall
Episcopal
Post Office
God of Holiness
Rosy's Bay & Grocery
L & S Jeep Rental
Taylor's Bay
Road Town Wholesale
Virgin Gorda Vocational Centre
To Copper Mine Point
To The Baths
0   1/2   1 mile

charge, and weekly rates are available. Formerly the Ocean View, the 12-room a/c **Wheel House Hotel** (tel. 495-5230, 800-621-1270; Box 66, Virgin Gorda) is conveniently located in town. Rooms have phone and TV. Rates are $50 s, $60 d, with $70 s and $80 d charged during the winter; there's one free night with a weekly stay, and breakfast is included. A 14% service charge is added. Virgin Gorda's most famous hotel is the 105-room Rockresort **Little Dix Bay Hotel** (tel. 495-5555, fax 495-5661; Box 70, Virgin Gorda). Constructed in 1964 at a cost of $9 million, this resort–at $136,000 per room–is the most expensive of its size ever built. The employee-to-guest ratio is three-to-one, and it includes 500 acres of land. There are five tennis courts here and a restaurant as well as sports and excursions. Rates start at $190 and range to a winter season high of $520. MAP is available on request. Located near the phone company, **Sam's Inn** (tel. 495-5644/7421) has one- and two-bedroom furnished apartments with kitchens, a/c, cable TV, and maid service for $65 s or d in the one-bedroom and $100 s or d in the two-bedroom (holds four; $12 pp add'l). Rates include taxes. A set of three two-bedroom apartments with living and dining rooms and TV, 2 1/2 baths, and kitchens, **Bayview Vacation Apts** (tel. 495-5329; Box 1018, Virgin Gorda) is just off of Main St. in The Valley. A spiral staircase leads to the roof for private sunbathing. Rates run from $65-95 s to $95 and up winter.

outlying accommodation: The following are near Spanish Town. In The Valley, **Taddy Bay** (tel. 495-5618; Box 1032, Virgin Gorda) is a two-bedroom/two-bath home with kitchen, TV, and phone. It rents for $750 pw summer and $850 pw winter. At Little Trunk Bay, **Rockmere** (tel. 415-929-7705; 1824 Green St., SF, CA 94123) is a two-bedroom villa holding a maximum of four. There's a phone and babysitting service, and it rents for $1,200 pw summer and $1,600 pw winter. Daily rates are available. Also at Little Trunk Bay, **Island Time** (tel. 495-5227, 914-834-8637) is a five-bedroom/bath house with kitchen, tennis, TV/VCR, babysitting service, and phone. For more information write 55 Woodbine Ave., Larchmont, NY 10538. At Little Trunk Bay, **Vistas** (tel. 495-5201; 613-829-5933) is a two-bedroom villa with babysitting service and phone. It rents for $1,200 pw summer and $1.600 pw winter, accommodating a maximum of four. For more information write 44 Parkland Crescent, Nepean, Ontario K2H 7W5. At Little Trunk Bay, **Southern Gables** (tel. 495-5201, 804-277-8669; Box 160, Roseland, VA) is a three-bedroom with babysitting service. Rooms are $45 pp pd. **near Spring Bay:** At Spring Bay, **Tamarind Hope** (tel. 495-5644, fax 495-5820) is a two-bedroom/bath villa with phone and babysitting service. The **Casa Rocalta** (tel. 495-5227), a luxury three-bedroom house with phone, is managed by Guavaberry-Spring Bay Vacation Homes Property Management and charges $2,800 pw summer and $3,500 pw winter, plus a 12% service charge. A 20% discount is available for a rental by four or fewer persons, and a fourth bedroom is also available. **Beach Villa at Spring Bay** (tel. 495-5268, fax 495-5466; Box 52, Virgin Gorda) is a two-bedroom villa with kitchen, phone, and shaded terrace which is near a beach. Rates for up to six run from $800-$2,800 pw during the summer up to $1,200-$3,600 pw in winter. At Spring Bay, the **Pink House** (tel.

595-5368; Box 1020, Virgin Gorda) is a two-bedroom/bath with living/dining room, deck, TV, phone, and babysitting service. Rates run $1,200 pw summer and $1,600 pw winter; there's a three-day minimum, and a 10% discount for stays of two weeks or more. Near the Baths, 21-room **Guavaberry Spring Bay Vacation Homes** (tel. 495-5227, fax 495-5283; Box 20, Virgin Gorda) has a group of 14 modern fully-equipped a/c one- and two-bedroom homes It has living, dining and cooking facilities, and patios with views are available. It's a five-minute drive to town. There's a commissary, beach, and a babysitting service is available. Rates run from $96 to a high of $225 during the winter season. A 12-14% service charge is applied.

accommodation N of The Valley: The **Mango Bay Resort** (tel. 495-5672; Box 1062, Virgin Gorda) is a set of recently constructed luxury one- to four-bedroom villas and studios with kitchens (including dishwasher) and patio. A private jetty is provided at Mahoe Bay. Cooks are available, and you can snorkel at the beach. Rates range from $95 to a winter season high of $735. Also at Mahoe Bay, **Paradise Beach Resort** (tel. 495-5871, 800-225-4255; Box 1105, Virgin Gorda) offers one- to three-bedroom private villas with kitchens, patios, babysitting and maid service, and a beach. Use of a jeep is included. Rates run from $110 to a winter season high of $500. A 10% service charge is applied. **Turtle Bay:** Set on the N coast at Turtle Bay, 14-room **Diamond Beach Club** (tel. 495-5452, 908-233-8353; Box 69, Virgin Gorda) has a small house and a few villas. Rates run from $98 to a winter high of $230. A service charge is applied. **Calypso House** (tel. 495-7367) offers four efficiencies with kitchen, BBQ, good views, and snorkeling. Rates are $50 pd summer and $70 pd winter with weekly rates available. Write Ben & Terri Herrington, The Valley.

North Sound: One of the most popular places with yachtspeople, this area offers a wide variety of food and accommodation. Found on the island's E tip, N Sound is shielded by surrounding Mosquito, Prickly Pear (lovely Vixen Point here is a white sand beach with beach bar; VHF CH. 16; overnight moorings available), Eustatia, and other islands. Boats over five ft. in draft should enter from the NE at Calquhoun Reef. Otherwise, in calm weather, you can use the Anguilla Point entrance. **Leverick Bay Hotel and Marina** (tel. 495-7421,7365, 800-848-7081, fax 495-7367; Box 63, Virgin Gorda) is at North Sound. It's divided into a/c resort rooms, resort one-bedroom apartments, and two-bedroom resort condominiums. Facilities include restaurant, beach, tennis, marina, shops, and laundry. Rates run from a low of $96 s or d for a resort room to a high of $255 for a two-bedroom condo (holds 1-6) during the high season. The associated **Virgin Gorda Villa Rentals** has efficiencies, one-, two-, and three-bedrooms which range in price for $670/wk. for the Sea Breeze efficiency to a high season peak of $2,975 for the Double Sunrise and Euphoria three-bedrooms, which have pools. All prices listed include tax and maid service. They also have a tie-in with Dive BVI, and it is the home of North South Charters. The 150-acre **Biras Creek Estate** (tel. 494-3555/3556; Box 54, Virgin Gorda) at North Sound was originally the creation of a Norwegian fishing magnate. There are 34 rooms including 15 two-suite units running along the shore here, and a main building which has dining room, commissary, and bar. There's a pool, and a beach at Deep Bay is a short walk away. There's a bird sanctuary (with a series of well marked trails), a marina, tennis, scuba, snorkeling, and sailing, as well as special packages. High season rates run from $350-$495 MAP. Also at North Sound, the 100-room **Bitter End Yacht Club & Resort** (tel. 494-2746; Box 46, Virgin Gorda) may be reached by boat from the Gun Point Dock on the North Sound. They also run charter flights each Sat. AM to Tortola, which meet the North Sound Express, at a cost of $50 pp RT. This means that you can fly to St. Thomas, meet the flight, and be at the resort at 4 PM that same day. The best (and quieter) rooms here–which include villas and chalets–are a bit removed from the resort center. There are also eight live-aboard yachts. Facilities include two restaurants, pool, sailing school, a full range of watersports including scuba, and a fitness trail. There's also a deli and store. Their "Fast Tack Sailing Festival" runs from late Oct. to mid-Dec. and includes regattas, beach picnics, lectures, sailing clinics and the chance to join up with the greatest stars in sailing. Rates run from $270 FAP to a winter high of $495 FAP for the best rooms. A new development here is **The Commodore Club**, a "Premium Resort" consisting of 20 secluded hillside bungalows. They rent in daily and eight-day/seven-night all-inclusive packages; rates run $425 pd and up. A day excursion here includes pickup at the dock, use of watersports equipment, and lunch for around $50. To get here you take the North Sound Express from Beef Island or the Potter's Taxi over the mountain to Gun Creek where you meet the Club Launch. If you have time, be sure to explore the hiking trails, bird sanctuary, and lookout point. For more information on the resort call (800) 872-2392 or write 875 N Michigan Ave., Chicago, IL 60611. In the UK call toll free 0800 591 897, fax (0) 737 769565, or write 28 Shrewsbury Rd., Redhill, Surrey, RH1 6BH. In the rest of Europe, call 44 (0) 737 769565. Set on tiny 125-acre Mosquito (Moskito) Island, **Drake's Anchorage Resort Inn** (tel./fax 494-2254; Box 2510, North Sound) offers two Italian-stone villas with tile floors and eight rooms and two suites. The electricity is provided by a windmill and solar panels heat the water. Windsurfing and other water sports, as well as bicycles, are available, and there's a restaurant. It is closed from mid-August to mid-September. Rates run from $175 to $360, with higher winter rates available upon request. It takes ten min. by water taxi to get here. If hiking around the **Lime Tree Gulch Trail**, be sure to note the tyre palms.

The Valley/Spanish Town food: The casual mariner-oriented **Bath & Turtle** (tel. 495-5239, VHF Ch. 16) at the Yacht Harbor serves pub-style dishes for lunch and dinner as well as pizza, daily specials, and a Sunday brunch. It also has a library and an attached liquor store. In the South Valley, **The Crab Hole** (tel. 495-5307) serves local dishes including callalou, fish, and conch in an informal, homelike atmosphere. Set in The Valley near the Virgin Gorda Yacht Harbour, **Chez Michelle Restaurant** (tel. 495-5510, reservations requested) serves French dishes and other international cuisine for dinner. One of the best (but very expensive) seafood places is **Fischer's Cove** (tel. 495-5252), which is on the beach near the harbor. Three meals are served daily. In season, a dinner buffet is served from 7-10. The **Little Dix Bay Hotel** (tel. 495-5555, ext. 174) offers gourmet international dining including a buffet lunch. **Anything Goes** (tel. 495-5062, VHF Ch. 16) is a simple but expensive local restaurant (curries and seafood) which is on the way into town. **The Wheel House** has an attached informal restaurant which offers inexpensive lunches. With West Indian dishes and a selection of international dishes every Wed., **The Valley Inn** (tel. 495-5639) serves lunch and dinner. **Friendly Andy's Ice Cream Parlour** serves local snacks such as johnny cakes and fried fish. A small unnamed boat made into a bar stands next door. Set by the sea (great views) and across from the PO, **Andy's Chateau de Pirate** serves lunch and dinner and offers specials. **The Olde Yarde Inn** (tel. 495-5544, reservations requested) serves gourmet international dishes. At Princess Quarters, **Teacher Ilma's** (tel. 495-5355, reservations needed) serves hearty West Indian dinners at moderate prices. The **LSL Bake Shop** has a small selection of treats for $1 each; a hamburger-cheeseburger stand is next door. Out at The Baths, the **Mad Dog** serves sandwiches and drinks. **food shopping: The Wine Cellar** sells a wide variety of alcohol, cheese, bread and pastries. **Buck's Food Market** sells groceries ranging from fresh fish to vegetables. On the road to the Baths, **RTW Wholesale & Cash & Carry** sells everything from bulk peanuts to alcohol to orange juice. In addition to gas for around $2 a gallon, Delta has a minimart with snacks and cold beers ($1.50). You can sit at the counter and watch the 700 Club on TV. Grocery items can also be found at the Commissary and Ship Store run by the Little Dix Bay Hotel. The **De Goose Snack Bar** features saltfish patties, local drinks, and other delicacies; it plays reggae in the evenings. **Ocean Delight** sells ice cream and other treats. **other shopping: Paradise Gifts & Herbs** is a combination health food and religious shop. It shares a building with **South Sound Records** which has local recordings, such as those of the Sensations band, and other Caribbean music. **Pussers Company Store** is at Leverick Bay.

North Sound dining: Overlooking North Sound, **Biras Creek** (tel. 494-3555) provides gourmet dining for nautical types. Three meals are served; dinner is a five-course fixed-price menu and has a dress code. At the Bitter End Yacht Club & Resort which overlooks Gorda Sound, **The Clubhouse** (tel. 494-2746) serves three meals daily. Dinner includes steak, seafood, and local specialties. Set at Leverick Bay on the North Sound, **Pusser's Pub** (tel. 495-7369) will pick you up around the yacht harbor for their evening meals. They serve seafood, English pies, steaks, and offer specials. **Pirate's Pub** (tel. 495-9537) is also out here on outlying Saba Rock across from the Bitter End. A Virgin Gorda scratch band plays here twice a week, and there are near-nightly jam sessions; bring your own instruments or use theirs. It offers a low key atmosphere replete with West Indian snack food and special drinks made with melon liqueur. You can even "build-your-own" sub sandwiches here. Many of the guests swim in. On Mosquito Island, **Drake's Anchorage Resort Inn** (tel./fax 494-2254) serves full-course French-style dinners as well as breakfast and lunch. Needless to say, anchorage is available.

transport, tours, and rentals: The **Mahogany Taxi Service** (tel. 495-5469, fax 495-5072) operates guided tours and offers packages for day trippers. **Andy's Jeep and Taxi Rental** (tel. 495-5252/5353) rents out everything from jeeps to Daihatsus to Wranglers for around $50 pd plus other expenses; they also offer guided tours. **Hertz** (tel. 495-5803) rents jeeps and cars. In South Valley, **L & S Jeep Rental** (tel. 495-5297) has 4-, 6-, and 10-passenger jeeps. Back up in The Valley, **Honda Scooter Rental** (tel. 495-5212) rents scooters from by the hour to by the week. **Anything Goes** (tel. 495-5811) also rents scooters.

Virgin Gorda Taxi Fares

From Valley to:	Per Person	Per Person Over 2
Baths/Devil's Bay/Spring Bay	3.00	2.00
Savanna/Trunk Bay/Pond Bay	5.00	2.50
Mango Bay/Copper Mine	5.00	5.00
Gun Creek/Leverick Bay/Galleon Beach/ Turtle Bay		5.00
From Dock to:		
Fischer's Cove/Olde Yard Inn/Little Dix Bay Airport/Church in Village	3.00	2.00

Waiting charges: first 10 minutes free. Thereafter, every 15 minutes, $3. Grand Tours (1 1/2-2 hours: Valley, Coppermine, Baths, Gorda Peak) $10 per person.

services: A branch of **Barclay's Bank** is located next to the Wine Cellar and Bakery in the shopping complex at the Yacht Harbour. **Rush It Courier Service** has photocopies (25¢/sheet) and expensive mail forwarding. For travel arrangements contact **Travel Plan Tours** (tel. 495-5568). Post offices are at The Valley and North Sound. Pay telephones are found at the airport and Yacht Harbour. **Virgin Gorda Tours** is another local tour agent. **O'Neal and Grandson** offers guided horseback riding as well as underwater camera rentals. **Beauty Therapy Services** (tel. 495-5437/7375) has a range of services–from massage therapy to electrolysis to waxing. Providing everything found in the average US drugstore, the **Island Drug Centre** can be found at the Yacht Harbour and also next to the police station.

entertainment: It can be quiet here. There's a weekend disco at **Andy's Chateau** across from the PO. You can find live music at **The Bath and Turtle** and at **Little Dix Bay**. In the S part of The Valley, **The Crab Hole** features a DJ every Sat. evening. At the **Pirate's Pub** and **Bitter End**, there's live music and/or DJs.

events: The Bitter End Yacht Club (tel. 800-872-2392) sponsors the **Fast Track Sailing Festival** and the **Pro-Am Regatta** in October and the **Women's Sailing Week** in December. For current information on major yachting, angling, and rugby events in the BVI, write to the BVI Yacht Club (tel. 49-43286), PO Box 200, Road Town, Tortola, BVI.

shopping: This is best near the yacht harbour in town. **Pelican's Pouch Boutique** offers casual clothes and swimwear. **Scoops** sells a variety of Caribbean crafts. **Dive BVI Ltd.** sells jewelry, sundry items, and sportswear. **Thee Artistic Gallery** in the Yacht Harbour sells crafts and books. The **Virgin Gorda Craft Shop** sells local crafts. **Kaunda's Kysy Tropix** sells electronic goods as well as jewelry. **Flamboyance** specializes in perfumes. **Margo's Jewelry Boutique** offers an international selection of jewelry as well as batiks and handicrafts. **Misty Isle** offers tee shirts, maps, charts, and has phone service. There's also a small shop in the Bath and the Turtle Pub which sells tee shirts, post cards, and the like. Featuring works by island artists, **Island Silhouette** is in Flax Plaza near Fischer's Cove. At the Olde Yard Inn, **Boutique** has a small store featuring handicrafts. At Little Dix Bay Hotel, the **Pavilion Gift Shop** sells sportswear and other accessories. At North Sound, Bitter End's **Emporium** sells jewelry, sportswear, and gift items.
food: Buck's Food Market has branches at the Yacht Harbor and at Leverick Bay. Sample prices: Frozen corn on the cob 4 ears/$4.05; frozen muffins $3.09/six; tomatoes $1.59/lb.; cabbage 50¢/lb.; fish fillet $4.25/lb.; Coke Classic $2.99/two liters; Puerto Rican ground coffee $2.69/lb. **The North Sound Superette** is here as well.

diving and water sports: DIVE BVI, Ltd. (tel. 495-5513, fax 495-5347, 800-848-7078; Box 1040, Virgin Gorda) offers a variety of services ranging from PADI and NAUI certifications to dives, a first aid course, and will meet you out sailing with a dive boat. It operates out of the Yacht Harbour and Leverick Bay. **Leverick Bay Water Sports** (tel. 495-7376) has water skiing, boat rentals of all sorts, sailing excursions, and other activities. With a 10% discount if you bring your own gear, **Kilbride's Underwater Tour** (tel./fax 495-9638; Box 46, Virgin Gorda) is at North Sound.

sportfishing: At Biras Creek in North Sound, **Classic** (tel. 494-3555; Box 14, Virgin Gorda) has a 38-ft. fully equipped Bertram; rates run from $450/half-day.

From Virgin Gorda

Departure schedules may change so be sure to check with your hotel or the ferry company to reconfirm well before departure.

for Road Town: Speedy's Fantasy/Speedy's Delight (tel. 495-5240/5235) departs from Virgin Gorda for Road Town Mon. to Sat. at 8, 11:30, and 3:30; and on Sun. at 8 and 4:30. Smith's Ferry Services (tel. 494-4430/2355, 495-4495) leaves for Road Town Mon. to Fri. at 7:50, 10:15, and 4; and on Sat. at 10 and 5.

for Beef Island: The North Sound Express (tel. 495-2271, 494-2746) operates between the North Sound and Beef Island ($18 OW) daily at 7:10, noon, and 4:15. The Virgin Gorda Ferry Service (tel. 495-5240/5542) plys the same route daily at 10:25, 1:45, 3:45, and 6:30.

for St. Thomas: Speedy's Fantasy/Speedy's Delight (tel. 495-5240/5235) departs from Virgin Gorda for St. Thomas on Tues. and Thurs. at 6:30 and 2:45; and on Sat. at 8:30.

for St. John: Transportation Services of St. John (tel. 776-6282/6597 on St. John) operates a ferry on Thurs. and Sun. at 3 PM.

by air: Sunaire flies to Tortola and on to St. Thomas and St. Croix.

Anegada

Most atypical and northernmost of all the Virgin Islands, Anegada ("drowned land") received its name because the surf pounding its reefs rises so high that it threatens to engulf the entire island. Every rule that applies to other Virgin Islands is contradicted here: it's neither steep nor craggy; there are no mongooses, Anglican churches, or water shortages. **The Settlement**, a collection of unremarkable frame buildings along with a few rusting pickup trucks and garage-sized churches, is home for most of the island's 150-strong population. Besides fishing, most people make a living by working on other islands. Several major tourist development schemes have been proposed but, happily for the sake of the natural environment, have never materialized. Of the many beau-

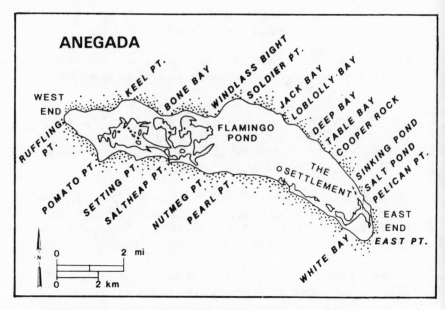

tiful beaches, **Loblolly Bay Beach** is the most well known. Set at the island's southern extension, **Horseshoe Reef** is one of the Caribbean's largest reef systems and is a protected area.

the land: Only 28 ft. (8.5 m) above sea level at its highest point, the 15-sq-mi. (39-sq-km) island is nine miles long and one to four mi. wide and easily affected by rising and falling tides. Consisting of limestone grating, it is completely flat in the S, and central portions have scattered lagoons, salt ponds, and marshes, as well as glorious beaches. A Pacific atoll in the Caribbean similar to islands found in the Bahamas to the N, its surrounding reefs are its most spectacular feature. It is the only British Virgin Island with freshwater springs of any size.

flora and fauna: A great variety of animal and plant life thrives here, some of which cannot be found elsewhere in this island group. The monotony of the bracken and mangrove vegetation is punctuated by spreads of lilac-colored wild orchids (*petramicra elegans*) which grow in profusion along Red Pond's salt flats. There are plenty of century plants as well as epiphytes (air plants) and lots of loathesome machineel trees. Other trees include tamarind, turpentine fir, and the ubiquitous coconut. Birds include roseate spoonbills, snowy and reddish egrets, nesting willets, great blue herons, ospreys, little blue, tricolor and green-backed herons, northern water thrushes, Antillean nighthawks, and the more commonplace frigates, plovers, and pelicans. Sandwich, roseate, and gull-billed terns come to visit during the summer months. A lesser creature, but no less significant, is the Anegada Rock Iguana (*iguana pinguis*) of which about 400 remain. This endangered lizard may reach five feet in length and weigh 20 lbs. A local delicacy, they have been hunted to near-extinction. They are most commonly seen on the island's N coast where certain trees have been banded with orange paint to denote where they live. Flamingos have been caught and roasted to the extent that Flamingo Pond–once a habitat for great flocks of the birds–had been entirely depopulated of them until a small flock, donated from a zoo, was re-introduced in 1992. In former times, huge swarms of enormous mosquitos, known as "gallon nippers," roamed the island, appearing and disappearing at 10-year intervals. Their bites, in large concentration, have proved fatal to sheep and sent wild goats fleeing into villages for human protection. These goats, as well as small wild horses, donkeys, and a special Spanish strain of cattle, still roam freely and greatly outnumber bipeds.

history: Used first by the Indians who left heaps of conch shells behind them on the E end, the island's maze of reefs afforded protection for pirates like Kirke, Bone, and the French pirate Normand (now known as "Norman"). Although the first settlers did grow some food and cotton, they came here expecting to profit from the spoils of the frequent shipwrecks. No sooner was the cry of "vessel on the reef!" heard than the residents, sidearms in hand, would be off and running, competing to be first aboard. The shipwrecks, which occurred with alarming frequency, were occasionally helped along by unscrupulous residents who would set out lamps to lure unsuspecting ships onto the treacherous reef. Even though the reefs were well marked on charts, shipwrecks still occurred because of a powerful and unknown NW current which prevails from March to June. More than 300 ships met their doom here. Today 138 wrecks are charted. These include the *Paramatta*, a British steamship which hit Horseshoe Reef in 1853 in the dead of night; the *HMS Astrea*, a 32-gun British frigate which sank in 1808; and the *Rocus*, a Greek freighter carrying the unusual cargo of animal bones, which went down off the E coast.

getting there: The only choice is to fly here from Tortola's Beef Island with Gorda Aero Services (tel. 495-2271) on Mon., Wed., and Fri. Don't plan on sailing here unless you're very experienced; more than 13 miles of barely penetrable reef surround this island. The catamaran *Ppalu* offers excursions here from Tortola.

getting around: You can rent bicycles from the Anegada Reef. It may be slow going, however, as the roads are frequently sand covered. **D.W. Jeep Rentals** (tel. 495-8018) rents jeeps of course.

accommodations and food: The oldest hotel, the **Anegada Reef Hotel** (tel. 495-8002), has a 12% service charge and does not accept credit cards for its 12 AP rooms. It has a restaurant (freshly caught seafood), fishing, a tackle shop, snorkeling, and scuba tank fills. Rates run from $150 on up to a winter high of $215. Contact: Anegada Reef Hotel, Setting Point, Anegada; tel. (in St. Thomas) 809-776-8002. Owned by the Soares family, of Portuguese origins, who came to the BVI from the Azores via Bermuda, **Neptune's Treasure Seaside Restaurant** (VHF Ch. 16 or 68, Radio 494-3111) serves fresh seafood as well as inexpensive fare and offers taxi service. The least expensive way to visit the island is to stay at their **Anegada Beach Campground** (tel. 495-9466; Box 2710, Anegada) which rents 8 x 10 ft. and 10 x 12 ft. tents. Rates are $20-30 summer and $26-$36 winter. Service is 10% add'l. A band plays here Thursday nights. Amidst a garden setting, **Pomato Point Inn** (tel. 495-8038) has owner Wilfred Creque's display of artifacts–ranging from Arawak pottery shards to 17th C cannonballs–on display. It also has a campground. **The Pomato Point Beach Restaurant** (tel. 495-9466, VHF Ch. 16) serves seafood and other dishes for lunch and dinner; it also has a champagne breakfast. Also at Pomato Point, the **Beach Cottage** (tel. 495-9236; Box 2711, Anegada) is a modern one-bedroom on the beach, with kitchen, living room, dining room, and patio. It rents for $250/weekend, $550 pw, $1,600/mo. At the Settlement and serving three meals daily, **Banana Well Bar & Restaurant** (tel. 495-9461) offers local food, fish, fast food sandwiches, and cold drinks. Also here, **Del's Restaurant and Bar** (tel. 495-8014, reservations recommended) serves West Indian lunches and dinners. Owned by Aubrey Levins, the **Big Bamboo** restaurant serves conch and lobster. At Loblolly Bay East, **Flash Of Beauty** (tel. 495-8014, VHF Ch. 16) serves sandwiches and seafood dishes. You can shop for Anegada-made souvenirs at **Pat's Pottery & Art** (495-8031).

dive sites around Anegada: With an estimated 17 wrecks per sq mile–some lying atop one another–the area should be a diver's paradise. However, many are disintegrated and lie buried in silt–thus limiting their visibility. Settled 35 ft. down, the *Parmatta* lies broken into two parts and overgrown with elkhorn coral. Animal bones litter the deck of the *Rocus*, which lies 40 ft. down. There's also a noose which marks the spot where her captain, unable to face Greek authorities, hung himself. Although nothing is left of the *Astrea* itself, stocks of cannonballs, cannons, iron ballast, and anchors remain. Humpback whales migrating from S. America to Greenland are commonly sighted in the Anegada Passage between mid-Feb. and mid-April.

Rhone National Marine Park

Extending over an 800-acre area, this marine park's most famous feature is *The Rhone*, a British mail packet ship which went down in the hurricane of 1867 and was smashed in two on the sharp rocks at Black Rock Point. The remains of the 310-ft. two-masted steamer now lie at depths of 20-80 ft. Viewed in the crystal-clear water, it's a veritable underwater museum and one of the most famous dive sites in the entire Caribbean.

history: The pride of the Royal Mail Steam Packet Company, *The Rhone* was at anchor outside of Peter Island's Great Harbour and planning to return to England when the storm commenced. The captain planned on moving to a safer spot during a lull, but the anchor chain split off. He then gunned the motors and headed for open seas with the intention of riding the storm out. Instead, the storm forced her onto the rocks at Salt Island. Almost the entire crew (some 125 people) perished. Weighing 2,738 tons, the boat was 310 ft. long and 40 ft. wide. The wreck achieved a measure of fame after being used as a location in some scenes from the film adaptation of Peter Benchley's novel, *The Deep*.

visiting the park: Anchor at moorings provided at Lee Bay or at Salt Pond Bay; the moorings directly above the wreck are reserved for commercial dive boats which have permits. Anchors have damaged the marine life as well as the park itself. Usually visited in two dives, bow and stern sections are located near Salt Island. Thickly covered with coral, the bow section lies 80 ft. down, while the stern–containing the remains of engine and propellor–lies at 30 feet. Both host brilliantly colored coral and myriad varieties of fish. You can locate the bow section, condenser, engines, prop shaft, and propeller. The anchor is outside Great Harbour off Peter Island at a depth of 55 ft. (It can be hard to find; a guided tour is recommended). As the stern is in shallower water, it's more suitable for snorkelers, as is the Rhone Reef. This is a fringing reef located to the S of the wreck, which has two coral caves at a depth of 25 ft., as well as colorful marine life. "Blond Rock," resembling a natural amphitheater, lies submerged in 12 ft. of water. Accessible only in calm water, it lies between Dead Chest and Salt Island. Lobsters, crabs, fan corals, and fish live here and love it. Its name comes from its yellowish dunce cap of fire coral. As there is heavy swell and strong current, it is best suited to the experienced. Included in the park boundaries, the 34-acre **Dead Chest Island** is to the W. It is reputed to be the island where Blackbeard abandoned his crew: "Fifteen men on a Dead Man's Chest–Yo Ho Ho and a bottle of rum." Rising to 214 ft., seabirds (including bridled terns and noddies) nest on the cliffs facing its SW side. While the island's N slopes are covered with dry forest, there are salt ponds fringed with machineel and mangroves in a flat expanse in the N. Cactus scrub–including organ pipe and red-topped barrel cactus grow along the steep slopes on its S side. To its SE are the Painted Walls, a series of submerged rocks which form 20-50 ft. canyons. Their name comes from the colorful sponges, algae, and corals that cover their surfaces. **regulations:** You may not remove any marine or terrestrial plant, animal or historical artifact. Fishing without a license is prohibited. Dispose of garbage only at correct garbage disposal points. Building fires and waterskiing are prohibited activities within park waters.

Smaller Islands

Besides the larger and better-known islands, there are numerous small islands and cays. Many are imaginatively named: Cockroach, Asbestos Point, Great Dog, The Indians, King Rock, Lizard Point, The Invisibles. Some of the more interesting are described below.

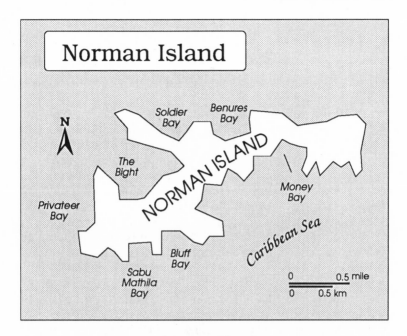

Norman Island

Some claim this is Stevenson's Treasure Island. Reportedly, treasure from the *Nuestra Señora* was recovered here in 1750. It is said to have been named after a French buccaneer named Normand who settled here along with his booty. Adventurous mariners can anchor S of Treasure Point, where there are four caves with excellent snorkeling. (Many boats run excursions here). Row into the southernmost cave with a dinghy and see where Stevenson's Mr. Fleming supposedly took his treasure–eerie and dark, except for phosphorescent patches on the ceilings. Bats fly overhead and the only sound is the whoosh of the sea being sucked in and out. Watch out for tides and the wild cattle (temperamental at times) which roam the land above. There's a small salt pond here where birds congregate. Climb the half-hour path to the top of Spyglass Hill, a viewpoint once used by pirates searching for Spanish galleons. Popular dive sites Pelican Island and the Indians lie nearby. **food and entertainment:** Reuben plays 12 string guitar on Thurs. and Sat. nights aboard the *William Thornton,* a Baltic trader converted into a floating restaurant. A launch runs out here from Fort Burt Marina daily at 5:15 PM and returns later in the evening. For information call 494-2564 or reach them via VHF Ch. 16 or Tortola Radio.

Peter Island

Accessible by sailboat or by private ferry from Tortola, the island is dominated by **Peter Island Hotel and Yacht Harbour**. Amway Corporation, which administers the resort, owns the entire island save the 16 acres owned by fisherwoman Estelle La Fontaine. She has steadfastly refused to sell out despite substantial pressure. The beach at Deadman's Bay, just five min. downhill from the units on the island's E tip, has been acclaimed the best in the British Virgins. According to local lore, the shining pink shells on the graves in the nearby cemetery serve to stave off evil spirits. It's a popular anchorage. Yachtspeople are requested to anchor in the extreme SW corner and to be wary of swells, particularly during the winter months. While the beach at Little Deadman's is near its parent, Spring Bay is a stiff half hour hike away. While on the island be sure to keep your eyes peeled for the common or tree iguana which is only found here and at Biras Creek on Virgin Gorda. The anchor of *The Rhone* can be found outside Great Harbour off Peter Island at a depth of 55 ft. (A guided tour there is recommended). **getting there:** The Peter Island Boat (tel. 494-2561) connects the CSY dock in Road Town with the Island. Trips are daily at 8, 9, noon, 2:30, 4:30, 6, 10, and 11:30. **accommodation:** The resort offers A-frame Scandanavian-built houses which are supplemented by beachfront rooms. These have a/c, fans, and phones. A three-bedroom, two-bath private villa—with its own boat, two maids, gardener, and minimoke vehicle—is for rent (around $10,000 for six nights; it holds eight). Another rental is Sprat Bay, a smaller cottage which houses six. Tennis courts, a pool, darts, billards, ping pong, and other games are offered. There are several beaches, a pool, and windsurfing, scuba and snorkeling are offered. It's tied in with an Ashore/Afloat plan. Room rates (FAP) range from $400 to a winter high of $520. Contact: Brian Webb, PO Box 211, Road Town; tel. 494-2561/2562; fax 494-2313. **dining: The Deadman's Bay Bar & Grill** serves lunch. The rotating menu at the elegant **Tradewinds Restaurant** offers continental and West Indian dishes for lunch and dinner (evening dress code). **entertainment:** Steel band or fungi music can be found in the Yacht Club lounge every evening.

Salt Island

Off the NW point of this island is a small settlement where the entire population (of nine) resides. Islanders collect salt from the three salt ponds as they have been doing for the past 150 years. The gathering season is in April and May. Formerly, these ponds supplied salt for the Royal Navy. They're still owned by the illustrious British queen whose representative comes over once a year to collect a bag of salt for the rent! Moorings are provided at Lee Bay which is just N of the *Rhone* wreck. Yachtspeople can also anchor at Salt Pond Bay off the settlement. Both of these anchorages can be rough and are recommended for day use only. Salt Island is the number-one diving destination in the BVI. owing to the wreck of the *Rhone*.

Cooper Island

This island (pop. nine) is the home of the intimate **Cooper Island Beach Club** (tel. 494-3721) at Machioneel Bay on the NW; the 20 moorings in the marina are free to beach club patrons ($10 for overnight). It's a good lunch stop for those sailing upwind to Virgin Gorda. Food offerings in the casual ocean-front restaurant (open daily for lunch and dinner) include grilled mahi-mahi, lobster, and mixed salad. A BBQ/disco is held on Thurs. night, and there's good swimming and snorkeling on the beach. Follow a trail to the top of the hill for a panoramic view of the surroundings. In operation for over a decade, this is hardly your typical resort. Each villa has two rooms which are equipped with kitchenette, shower, rattan furniture, and a selection of books and games. Water comes from cisterns underneath the buildings, and lighting and ceiling fans are powered by 12 V DC. Rates start at $55 s and $75 d. A 10% service charge is added. Write Box 859, Road Town or Box 175, Millers Falls, MA 01349; call 800-542-4624, 413-659-2602, or fax 413-659-2514. A variety of packages (including diving) are also available. Offering three one- to three-bedroom cottages along the beach, **Cooper Island Hideaways** has kitchens and other facilities; they rent from $630-$700 pw summer and $700-$805 pw winter. For more information call (513) 232-4126 or write 1920 Barg Lane, Cincinnati, OH 45230-1702. **Underwater Safaris** offer diving, and Carrot Rock, a dive site fronted by large pillar corals, lies offshore.

Guana Island

Another privately owned island run by the Guana Island Club. This 850-acre island has nature trails, white sand bathing beaches, and water sports. Its white-walled cottages were constructed as a private club in the 1930s on the foundations of a Quaker home abandoned by its owners after they found sugar cane slavery to be morally unconscionable. The main building is set on a hilltop. There are two tennis courts. The remainder of the island, including its seven beaches, remains undeveloped. Although most beaches can be reached on foot, two are accessible only by boat. As yachties are unwelcome, an atmosphere of serenity and privacy prevails. Introduced from a zoo, four friendly flamingos now live here. If arranged in advance, a boat will meet guests at Beef Island's airport from 9-5. Rates (AP) for the 15 rooms are divided into three time periods and range from $345 s, $395 d on up. "Rent The Island" rates ($5,400/night and up) upon request. Contact: PO Box 32, Road Town; tel. (800) 544-8262, (809) 494-2354, (914) 967-6050, or fax 914-967-8048.

Fallen Jerusalem National Park

When viewed from the sea, this 12-acre island resembles the ruins of an ancient city owing to its gigantic granite boulders. It excites the imagination of all who see it. Now a National Park, the island's goats have been removed in order to protect the vegetation, and birds such as the pearly-eyed thrasher, common ground-dove, scaly-naped pigeon, and the Zenaida dove are found here. Nesting seabirds here (and on neighboring Round Rock and Broken Jerusalem) include brown boobies, laughing gulls, terns, brown pelicans, noddies, and red-billed and white-billed tropicbirds. Its stretch of beach may be visited on calm days.

Sandy Cay

Located to the E of Little Jost Van Dyke, this uninhabited islet, owned by Laurence Rockefeller, sports a white sand beach and hiking trails. The water is deep until you are very near the shore, and the area is subject to swells, so it does not make a good anchorage year-round.

The Dogs

This miniature archipelago covers 165.5 acres of land and 4,435 acres of sea. Occupying 24 acres, **West Dog** is a refuge for laughing gulls and nesting doves. Popular with divers and yacht people alike, the best anchorages here are at **George Dog** to the W of Kitchen Point and on the S side of **Great Dog**. The area is a good place to stop when sailing from North Sound to Jost Van Dyke.

Great Tobago

Some 210 acres on this, the most westerly of the BVI, is a sanctuary for the magnificent frigatebird.

Necker Island

Owned by Richard Branson–whose other properties include Virgin Air–the Balinese-style house (sleeps 20) on this 74-acre island can be rented for around $9,900 pd on up. All water sports are provided. Guests here have included Princess Di and her family. Contact Ruth Kemp (tel. 071-938 3618) in London for reservations and information.

Virgin Islands Glossary

bareboat–a charter boat which comes without crew.

calabash (calabaza)–small tree native to the Caribbean whose fruit, a gourd, has multiple uses when dried.

callaloo–Caribbean soup made with callaloo greens.

Caribs–original people who colonized the islands of the Caribbean, giving the region its name.

cassava– staple crop indigenous to the Americas. Bitter and sweet are the two varieties. Bitter must be washed, grated, and baked in order to remove the poisonous prussic acid. A spongy cake is made from the bitter variety as is cassareep, a preservative which is the foundation of West Indian pepperpot stew.

cays–Indian name which refers to islets in the Caribbean.

century plant–also known as karato, coratoe, and maypole. Flowers only once in its lifetime before it dies.

conch–large edible mollusk usually pounded into salads or chowders.

cutlass–the Caribbean equivalent of the machete. Originally used by buccaneers and pirates.

duppy–ghost or spirit of the dead which is feared throughout the Caribbean. Derives from the African religious belief that a man has two souls. One ascends to heaven while the other stays around for a while or permanently. May be harnessed for good or evil through obeah. Some plants and birds are also associated with duppies.

escabeche–Spanish and Portuguese method of preparing seafood.

Johnkonnu–festivities dating from the plantation era in which bands of masqueraders, dressed with horse or cow heads or as kings, queens or as devils. Now a dying practice throughout the Caribbean, it is preserved largely as a tourist attraction.

love bush–orange colored parasitic vine, found on Jamaica, St. John, and other islands. Resembles nothing so much as the contents of a can of spaghetti.

machineel–small toxic tree native to the Caribbean. Its fruit, which resembles an apple, and its milky sap are lethal. See clearly marked specimens near the Annenberg ruins on St. John.

obeah–Caribbean black magic imported from Africa.

poinciana–beautiful tropical tree which blooms with clusters of red blossoms during the summer months. Originates in Madagascar.

sea grape–West Indian tree, commonly found along beaches, which produces green, fleshy, edible grapes.

sensitive plant–also known as mimosa, shame lady, and other names. It will snap shut at the slightest touch.

star apple–large tree producing segmented pods, brown in color and sour in taste, which are a popular fresh fruit.

woman's tongue–Asian plant whose name comes from its long seed pods, dry when brown, which flutter and rattle in the breeze, constantly making noise.

Virgin Islands Dive Operators

St. Thomas

Aqua Action Dive Center
PO Box 15, St. Thomas
USVI 00802; (809) 775-6285
(809) 775-1501; fax (800)
524-2250

Arnoldo Dive Center
PO Box 10894, St. Thomas USVI
00802; c/o Grand Palazza Resort
(809) 775-3333

Caribbean Divers
56 Frydenhoj, St. Thomas USVI
00802; (809) 775-6384; fax (809)
776-9873

Chris Sawyer Diving Center
Compass Point Marina, 41-6-1
Estate Frydenhoj, St. Thomas USVI
00902; (809) 775-7320; (809) 779-2008;
fax (800) 882-2965

Coki Beach Dive Club
PO Box 5279, St. Thomas USVI
00803; (809) 775-4220

Dive In
PO Box 8088, St. Thomas USVI
00801; (809) 775-6100, fax (809)
775-4024

Hi-Tech Watersports, Inc.
PO Box 2180, St. Thomas USVI
00803; (809) 774-5650

Joe Vogel Diving Company
PO Box 6577, St. Thomas USVI
00801; (809) 775-7610

Ocean Fantasies
PO Box 6030, St. Thomas USVI
00803; (809) 774-5223, fax (809)
779-6376, (800) 842-3483

Ocean Quest Divers
PO Box 3184, St. Thomas USVI
00803; (809) 776-5176

Sea Horse Dive Boats
PO Box 306994, St. Thomas USVI
00803; (809) 774-2001, fax (809)
774-2001

St. Thomas Diving Club
PO Box 7337, St. Thomas USVI
00801; (809) 776-2381, fax (809)
775-3208, (800) 524-4746

Sugar Bay Plantation Resort
6500 Estate Smith Bay, St. Thomas
USVI 00802; (809) 777-7200, fax
(800) HOLIDAY, (800) 927-7100

Underwater Safaris
PO Box 8469, St. Thomas USVI
00801; (809) 774-1350

VI Diving Schools
PO Box 9707, St. Thomas USVI
00801; (809) 774-8687

St. John

Cinnamon Bay Watersports
PO Box 720, Cruz Bay, St. John
USVI 00831; (809) 776-6330; (809)
776-6462; fax (809) 776-6458

Coral Bay Watersports
10-19 Estate Carolina, St. John, USVI
00830; (809) 776-6850

Cruz Bay Watersports
PO Box 252, St. John, USVI 00831
(809) 776-6234; (809) 776-8303; fax
(800) 835-7730

Low Key Watersports
PO Box 431, St. John USVI 00831;
(809) 776-7048, fax (809) 776-6042,
(800) 835-7718

Paradise Watersports
PO Box 54, St. John USVI 00831;
(809) 776-7618, (809) 776-6111

St. Croix

Anchor Dive Center
Salt River Marina, Box 5588, St.
Croix USVI 00823; (809) 778-1522,
fax (809) 772-3059, (800) 532-DIVE

Blue Dolphin Divers
Box 5261, St. Croix USVI 00823; (809)
773-8634

Cane Bay Dive Shop
PO Box 4510, Kingshill, St. Croix
USVI; 00851; (809) 773-9913, fax
(809) 778-5442

Cruzan Divers, Inc.
12 Strand St., Frederiksted, St.
Croix USVI 00840; (809) 772-3701,
fax (809) 772-1852, (800) 352-0107

Dive Experience, Inc.
PO Box 4254, Christiansted, St.
Croix USVI 00822; phone/fax
(809) 773-3307, (800) 235-9047

Dive St. Croix
59 Kings Wharf, Christiansted, St.
Croix USVI 00820; (809) 773-3434,
fax (809) 773-9411, (800) 523-DIVE

The Waves at Cane Bay
PO Box 1749, Kingshill, St. Croix,
USVI 00851; (809) 778-1805, (800)
545-0603

V.I. Divers, Ltd
Pan Am Pavilion, Christiansted,
St. Croix USVI 00820; (809) 773-
6045, fax (809) 778-7004, (800) 544-
5911

Booklist

Travel and Description

Arciniegas, German. *Caribbean: Sea of the New World*. New York: Alfred A. Knopf, 1946.

Blume, Helmut. (trans. Johannes Maczewski and Ann Norton) *The Caribbean Islands*. London: Longman, 1976.

Bonsal, Stephen. *The American Mediterranean*. New York: Moffat, Yard and Co., 1912.

Caimite. *Don't Get Hit by a Coconut*. Hicksville, NY: Exposition Press, 1979. The memoirs of an Ohio painter who escaped to the Caribbean.

Carter, Dorene E. *Portraits of Historic St. Croix: Beofre and After Hurricane Hugo*. Frederiksted, St. Croix: Caribbean Digest Publishing, 1991.

Creque, Darwin D. *The U.S. Virgins and the Eastern Caribbean*. Philadelphia: Whitmore Publishing Co., 1968.

Dammann, Arthur E. and David W. Nellis. *A Natural History Atlas to the Cays of the United States Virgin Islands*. Sarasota, FL: Pineapple Press.

Doucet, Louis. *The Caribbean Today*. Paris: editions j.a., 1977.

Eggleston, George T. *Virgin Islands*. Melbourne, Florida: Krieger, 1973. A somewhat dated (1959) travelogue of special interest to the cruise set.

Fillingham, Paul. *Pilot's Guide to the Lesser Antilles*. New York: McGraw-Hill, 1979. Invaluable for pilots.

Hansen, Knud. *From Denmark to the Virgin Islands*. New York: Dorrance and Co., 1947.

Hart, Jeremy C. and William T. Stone. *A Cruising Guide to the Caribbean and the Bahamas*. New York: Dodd, Mead and Company, 1982. Description of planning and plying for yachties. Includes nautical maps.

Hartman, Jeanne Perkins. *The Virgins: Magic Islands*. New York: Appleton-Century, 1961.

Hayward, Du Bose. *Star Spangled Virgin*. New York: Farrar and Rhinehart, 1939.

Holbrook, Sabra. *The American West Indies, Puerto Rico and the Virgin Islands*. New York: Meredith Press, 1969.

Kurlansky, Mark. *A Continent of Islands*. New York: Addison-Wesley, 1992. One of the best books about the Caribbean ever written, a must for understanding the area and its culture. Although the Virgin Islands are only touched upon, it provides an excellent backdrop to understanding.

Morrison, Samuel E. *The Caribbean as Columbus Saw It*. Boston: Little and Co.: 1964. Photographs and text by a leading American historian.

Naipaul, V.S. *The Middle Passage: The Caribbean Revisited*. New York: MacMillan, 1963. Another view of the West Indies by a Trinidad native.

Radcliffe, Virginia. *The Caribbean Heritage*. New York: Walker & Co., l976.

Robertson, Alan H. and Fritz Henle. *Virgin Islands National Park: The Story Behind the Scenery*. Las Vegas: KC Publications, 1974.

Rodman, Selden. *The Caribbean*. New York: Hawthorn, 1968. Traveler's description of the Caribbean by a leading art critic.

Van Ost, John R. and Harry Kline. *Yachtsman's Guide to the Virgin Islands and Puerto Rico*. North Miami, Florida: Tropic Isle Publishers, Inc., 1984. Where to anchor in the area.

Ward, Fred. *Golden Islands of the Caribbean*. New York: Crown Publishers, 1967. A picture book for your coffee table. Beautiful historical plates.

Wood, Peter. *Caribbean Isles*. New York: Time Life Books, 1975.

Wouk, Herman. *Don't Stop the Carnival*. Glasgow: Fontana Books, 1979. The classic novel of expatriate life in the Virgin Islands.

Zucker, Eric. *The Virgins: Places and People*. St. Thomas: FLICKS Productions, 1992.

Flora and Fauna

Humann, Paul. *Reef Fish Identification*. Jacksonville: New World Publications, 1989. This superb guide is filled with beautiful color photos of 268 fish. Information is included on identifying details, habitat and behavior, and the reaction of various species to divers.

Humann, Paul. *Reef Creature Identification*. Jacksonville: New World Publications, 1992. The second in the series, this guide covers 320 denizens of the deep. Information is given on relative abundance and distribution, habitat and behavior, and identifying characteristics.

Humann, Paul. *Reef Coral Identification*. Jacksonville: New World Publications, 1993. Last in this indispensable series (now available as a boxed set entitled "The Reef Set"), this book identifies 240 varieties of coral and marine plants. The different groups are described in detail.

Jadan, Doris. *A Guide to the Natural History of Saint John*. St. John: Environmental Studies Program, 1979.

Kaplan, Eugene. *A Field Guide to the Coral Reefs of the Caribbean and Florida*. Princeton, N.J.: Peterson's Guides, 1984.

Little, E. L., Jr., F. J. Wadsworth, and J. Marrero *Arboles Comunes De Puerto Rico y las Islas Virgenes*. Rio Piedras: University of Puerto Rico Press, 1967.

MacLean, Dr. William P. *Reptiles and Amphibians of the Virgin Islands*. London: 1982.

Raffaele, Herbert A. *A Guide to the Birds of Puerto Rico and the Virgin Islands*. Princeton, NJ: 1989, Princeton University Press.

de Oviedo, G. Fernandez. (trans./ed. S.A. Stroudemire. *Natural History of the West Indies*. Chapel Hill: University of North Carolina Press, 1959.

History

Boyer, William W. *America's Virgin Islands*. Durham, North Carolina: Carolina Academic Press, 1983. A superb overview of the political and social history of the islands.

Deer, Noel. *The History of Sugar*. London: Chapman, 1950.

Dookhan, Issac. *A History of the Virgin Islands of the United States*. St. Thomas: College of the Virgin Islands, Caribbean Universities Press, 1974.

Hill, Valdemar A., Sr. *Rise to Recognition, An Account of Virgin Islanders from Slavery to Self-Government*. St. Thomas: St Thomas Graphics, 1971.

Hovey, Graham and Gene Brown, eds. *Central America and the Caribbean*. New York: Arno Press, 1980. This volume of clippings from *The New York Times*, one of a series in its Great Contemporary Issues books, graphically displays Amnerican activities and attitudes toward the area. A goldmine of information.

Hunte, George. *The West Indian Islands*. New York: The Viking Press, 1972. Historical overview from the Western viewpoint with information added for tourists.

Jarvis, J. Antonio. *The Virgin Islands and Their People*. Philadelphia: Dorrance & Co., 1944. Fascinating account of the USVI during the 40s.

Knight, Franklin W. *The Caribbean*. Oxford: Oxford University Press, 1978. Thematic, anti-imperialist view of Caribbean history.

Lewisohn, Florence. *St. Croix under Seven Flags*. Hollywood, Fla: Inernational Graphics, Inc., 1966. An absorbing account of the history of the British Virgin Islands.

Lewisohn, Florence. *"What So Proudly We Hail," The Danish West Indies and the American Revolution*. St. Croix: Prestige Press, 1976.

Lewisohn, Florence. *The Romantic History of St. Croix*. St. Croix: St. Croix Landmarks Society, 1964.

Low, Ruth Hull and Rafael Valls. *St. John Backtime*. St. John: Eden Hill Press, 1985.

Mackie, Cristine. *Life and Food in the Caribbean*. New York: Amsterdam Press, 1990. More than just a recipe book (although it is that as well), this is a brilliant history of the interactions between the peoples of the Caribbean with their environment. Native American, African, British, and Chinese influences are detailed.

Mannix, Daniel P. and Malcolm Cooley. *Black Cargoes*. New York: Viking Press, 1982. Details the saga of the slave trade.

Olwig, Karen Fog *Cultural Adaptation and Resistance on St. John*. Gainesville, FL: University of Florida Press, 1985.

Williams, Eric. *From Columbus to Castro: The History of the Caribbean*. New York: Random House, 1983. Definitive history of the Caribbean by the late Prime Minister of Trinidad and Tobago.

Politics and Economics

Barry, Tom, Beth Wood, and Deb Freusch. *The Other Side of Paradise: Foreign Control in the Caribbean*. New York: Grove Press, 1984. A brilliantly and thoughtfully written analysis of Caribbean economics.

Blanshard, Paul. *Democracy and Empire in the Caribbean*. New York: The Macmillan Co., 1947.

Gooding, Bailey W. and Justine Whitfield. *The West Indies at the Crossroads.* Cambridge, Ma.: Schenkmann Pulblishing Co., Inc., 1981. A political history of the British Caribbean during the 1970s.

Mitchell, Sir Harold. *Caribbean Patterns.* New York: John Wiley and Sons, 1972. Dated but still a masterpiece. The best reference guide for gaining an understanding of the history and current political status of nearly every island group in the Caribbean.

O'Neill, Edward A. *Rape of the American Virgins.* New York: Praeger, 1972. Scathing history and revealing account of trouble in American Paradise.

Sociology and Anthropology

Abrahams, Roger D. *After Africa.* New Haven: Yale University Press, 1983. Fascinating accounts of slaves and slave life in the West Indies.

Horowitz, Michael H. (ed) *People and Cultures of the Caribbean.* Garden City, New York: Natural History Press for the Museum of Natural History, 1971. Sweeping compilation of social anthropological essays.

Art, Architecture, and Archaeology

Buissert, David. *Historic Architecture of the Caribbean.* London: Heinemann Educational Books, 1980.

de Jongh Woods, Edith. *The Royal 3 Quarters of the Town of Charlotte Amalie.* St. Thomas: MAPes MONDE Editore, 1992.

Gosner, Pamela. *Historic Architecture of the USVI.* Durham, NC: Moore Publishing Company, 1971.

Gosner, P. *Caribbean Georgian.* Washington D.C.: Three Continents, 1982. Well illustrated guide to "Great and Small Houses of the West Indies."

Lewisohm, F. *The Living Arts & Crafts of the West Indies.* Christiansted, St. Croix:Virgin Islands Council on the Arts, 1973. Local crafts illustrated.

Willey, Gordon R. *An Introduction to American Archeaology, Vol. 2, South America.* Englewood Cliffs, New Jersey: Prentice-Hall, Inc., 1971.

Music

La Motta, Bill and Joyce. *Virgin Islands Folk Songs.* St. Thomas: Joyce La Motta's Tuskimaro V. I. Tunes by the late composer and his wife.

Bergman, Billy. *Hot Sauces: Latin and Caribbean Pop.* New York: Quill, 1984.

Language

Highfield, A. R. *The French Dialect of St. Thomas, Virgin Islands: A Descriptive Grammar with Text and Glossary.* Ann Arbor: Karoma Publishers, Inc., 1979.

Literature

Anderson, John L. *Night of the Silent Drums.* New York: Scribner, 1976. Fictional narrative of a Virgin Islands slave rebellion.

Whitney, Phyllis A. *Columbella.* New York: Doubleday, 1966. Mystery-romance set in St. Thomas.

Index